Jozina Vander Klok, Núbia Ferreira Rech and Simone Guesser
Modality in Underdescribed Languages

Trends in Linguistics
Studies and Monographs

Editors
Chiara Gianollo
Daniël Van Olmen

Editorial Board
Walter Bisang
Tine Breban
Volker Gast
Hans Henrich Hock
Karen Lahousse
Natalia Levshina
Caterina Mauri
Heiko Narrog
Salvador Pons
Niina Ning Zhang
Amir Zeldes

Editor responsible for this volume
Daniël Van Olmen

Volume 357

Modality in Underdescribed Languages

―

Methods and Insights

Edited by
Jozina Vander Klok,
Núbia Ferreira Rech and Simone Guesser

DE GRUYTER
MOUTON

ISBN 978-3-11-163169-1
e-ISBN (PDF) 978-3-11-072147-8
e-ISBN (EPUB) 978-3-11-072156-0
ISSN 1861-4302

Library of Congress Control Number: 2022940349

Bibliographic information published by the Deutsche Nationalbibliothek
The Deutsche Nationalbibliothek lists this publication in the Deutsche Nationalbibliografie;
detailed bibliographic data are available on the internet at http://dnb.dnb.de.

© 2024 Walter de Gruyter GmbH, Berlin/Boston
This volume is text- and page-identical with the hardback published in 2023.
Typesetting: Integra Software Services Pvt. Ltd.

www.degruyter.com

Contents

Jozina Vander Klok, Núbia Ferreira Rech & Simone Guesser
Introduction to *Modality in underdescribed languages: Methods and insights* —— 1

Part I: Contributions of different methods for studying modality

Luiz Fernando Ferreira & Ana Müller
1   Fieldwork techniques in semantics —— 15

Zahra Kolagar & Jozina Vander Klok
2   Studying modality through targeted construction storyboards —— 47

Jozina Vander Klok
3   Discourse contexts targeting modality in fieldwork: A revised modal questionnaire —— 95

Daniel Reisinger, Lisa Matthewson & Hotze Rullmann
4   Using corpora to investigate modal-temporal interactions —— 141

Ailís Cournane & Valentine Hacquard
5   Adapting acquisition methodologies to study modality in underdescribed languages —— 191

Part II: Lessons from case studies on underdescribed languages

Isabella Coutinho Costa & Ana Lúcia Pessotto
6   On applying semantic fieldwork elicitation techniques to describe modality in Ye'kwana —— 237

Sihwei Chen
7   Modality in elicited data and spontaneous texts: A case study of Atayal —— 257

Ana Lívia Agostinho & Núbia Ferreira Rech
8   Lessons from the field: Irrealis mood in Lung'Ie —— 295

Marianne Huijsmans
9 Analyzing ʔayʔaju̇θəm evidentials: Evidence for epistemic modality —— 337

Pablo Fuentes
10 Parameters for the production of discourse contexts: Eliciting the semantics of obligations and desires in Mapudungun —— 391

Subject index —— 421

Jozina Vander Klok, Núbia Ferreira Rech & Simone Guesser
Introduction to *Modality in underdescribed languages: Methods and insights*

1 The study of modality cross-linguistically

The study of modality – that is, how speakers express possible or necessary states-of-affairs, such as with the use of *may, must* or *should* in English – has recently grown to include more in-depth studies from a diverse set of languages. These include, for example, St'át'imcets; Salishan, Canada (Davis et al. 2009), Gitksan; Tsimshianic, Canada (Peterson 2010; Matthewson 2013), Badiaranke; Niger-Congo, Senegal, Guinea, Guinea-Bissau (Cover 2010), Japanese; Japonic, Japan, and Chinese; Sino-Tibetan, China (Narrog 2012), Javanese; Austronesian, Indonesia (Vander Klok 2013; Vander Klok and Hohaus 2020), Paresi; Arawakan, Brazil (Brandão 2014; Rech and Brandão 2018), Washo; Isolate, USA (Bochnak 2015), Luganda; Bantu, Uganda (Kawala et al. 2018), Daakaka; Austronesian, Vanuatu; and Saliba-Logea, Austronesian, Papua New Guinea (von Prince and Margetts 2019), Hebrew; Afro-Asiatic, Israel (Herberger and Rubinstein 2019), and Logoori; Bantu, Kenya (Gluckman and Bowler 2020), among many others. These studies have shown the need to further develop a grammatical typology of modality pertaining to the expression of at least three factors: (i) modal force (e.g., possibility vs. necessity), (ii) modal strength (e.g., weak necessity), and (iii) modal flavour

---

Acknowledgments: We would like to thank the Brazilian National Council for Scientific and Technological Development (CNPq; processes 424025/2016–7) and the Graduate Program in Linguistics from Universidade Federal de Santa Catarina for their partial financial support. We would also like to thank Ana Lívia Agostinho, Ryan Bochnak, Margit Bowler, Strang Burton, Ailís Cournane, Isabella Coutinho, Francesca Dell'Oro, Luiz Fernando Ferreira, Pablo Fuentes, John Gluckman, Vera Hohaus, Marianne Huijsmans, Zahra Kolagar, Nala H. Lee, Marcus Lunguinho, Ana Müller, Sarah Zobel, and five anonymous reviewers for their time and work.

Jozina Vander Klok, Humboldt-Universität zu Berlin, Unter den Linden 6, Berlin, 10099, Germany, e-mail: jozina.vander.klok@hu-berlin.de
Núbia Ferreira Rech, Universidade Federal de Santa Catarina, R. Eng. Agronômico Andrei Cristian Ferreira, s/n – Trindade, 88040-900, Florianópolis-SC, Brazil,
e-mail: nubiarech1971@gmail.com
Simone Guesser, Federal University of Roraima, Avenida Capitão Ene Garcez, 2413 – Aeroporto, 69310-000, Boa Vista-RR, Brazil, e-mail: simoneguesser@yahoo.com.br

https://doi.org/10.1515/9783110721478-001

(e.g., epistemic, based on someone's beliefs or knowledge; or deontic, based on a body of rules or regulations).

For example, it is known that various modal flavours can be expressed by distinct grammatical strategies, or by the same strategy. Languages such as English, Spanish or Portuguese express multiple modal flavours with the same lexical item; we understand these modals to be referentially ambiguous across the different modal flavours. In Brazilian Portuguese, for instance, the modal auxiliary verb *dever* 'must' can be used to express deontic modality as well as epistemic modality, as shown in the following examples:[1]

(1) *Conforme   o   código   de   trânsito   brasileiro,*
    according.to   DET   code   PREP   traffic   Brazilian
    *o   motociclista **deve** usar   capacete.*
    DET   motorcyclist MODAL   wear   helmet
    'According to the Brazilian traffic code, the motorcyclist must wear a helmet.'

(2) *Esse   cão   está   com   coleira.   Ele   **deve**   ter   dono.*
    DEM   dog   COP   PREP   collar   3SG   MODAL   have   owner
    'This dog has a collar. It must have an owner.'

Example (1) expresses an obligation given certain circumstances (the (non-)use of a helmet by a motorcyclist) and a set of laws (Brazilian Traffic Code), illustrating deontic modal flavour. Epistemic modality, on the other hand, involves a state of information, which may be based on someone's knowledge, beliefs or understanding. In (2), the modal refers to the speaker's world knowledge, which includes the fact that dogs that wear a collar have an owner.

Other languages have distinct grammatical strategies, such as different lexical items, to express different types of modal flavour. This is the case for Paresi (Brandão 2014; Rech and Brandão 2018; Rech, Brandão and Wit 2018), St'át'imcets (Matthewson 2016), Gitksan (Matthewson 2013), Javanese (Vander Klok 2013), and Atayal (Chen 2018), among others. Examples (3) and (4) show distinct epistemic and deontic markers, respectively, in Paresi:

---

[1] The following abbreviations are used in the glosses: 1,2,3 first, second and third person; AV actor voice; BEN benefactive; CIRC circumstantial modality; DEF definite; DEO deontic modality; DEM demonstrative; DET determiner; EPIS epistemic modality; INF infinitive; NEC necessity; NEG negation; POS possibility; POSS possessive; PREP preposition; PRT particle; ROOT root modality; SG singular; VM verbal marker.

(3) Maitsa **ala** maiha æ=tyo-ita   kalini.
     NEG   EPIS   NEG   3SG=come-INF today
     'He must not come today.' (Rech and Brandão 2018: 2822)

(4) **Maika** eze   cracha ha=moka   hi=hiye   ha=wena-ne   kitxiya
     DEO   DEM   badge   2SG=for   2SG=BEN   2SG=life-POSS until
     'You must wear this badge during your visit.' (Rech, Brandão and Wit 2018: 232)

In (3), the particle *ala* is used, which corresponds to a marker of epistemic modality in Paresi (Brandão 2014). In (4), a marker of deontic modality is used: the *maika* particle (Rech and Brandão 2018). Paresi is a language that marks the type of modal flavour in the lexicon, showing different vocabulary items for epistemic and deontic modal flavours. In contrast, these markers are both compatible with different modal force (necessity and possibility), as suggested by the discourse contexts in (5) and (6), and illustrated with the particle *maika*:

(5) Context: Diana likes to eat chocolate all the time when she is on vacation. So, Marina, Diana's mother, before going to work, gives the following instruction to the nanny:
     Maika makani   weta   taita chocolate Diana ana h=itsa.
     DEO   tomorrow early only   chocolate Diana BEN 2SG=give
     'You must give chocolate to Diana only early in the morning. / Give chocolate to Diana only early in the morning.' (Rech and Brandão 2018: 2823)

(6) Paula, **maika** h=ehokoty-ao.
     Paula DEO   2SG=liedown-VM
     'Paula, you can lay down.' (Brandão 2014: 229)

Example (5) shows the *maika* particle in a context of obligation (deontic necessity). The same particle appears in (6), which describes a permission context (deontic possibility). These examples show that in Paresi the same lexical item is used to express necessity and possibility for deontic modality. And for Brazilian Portuguese *deve*, which can express multiple modal flavours and necessity modal force, as in (1) and (2), it can express a wider range of modal strength, as stronger than possibility and weaker than necessity, argued to be the result of a modal without a dual (Pessotto 2015). That modals allow for variable force has expanded the cross-linguistic typology of modality and how to formally account for variation in the expression of modal force, and in connection, modal strength (see, e.g., Rullmann, Matthewson and Davis 2008; Deal 2011; Narrog 2012; Bochnak 2015; Pessotto 2015, among others).

Other recent studies on expressions of modal strength, such as weak necessity, has demonstrated the need for more in-depth cross-linguistic semantic fieldwork in this area. For example, Vander Klok and Hohaus (2020) show that the suffix *-ne* in Javanese derives weak necessity modals from strong necessity modals, as shown in (7) with *kudu* 'have.to', but this same suffix cannot attach to possibility modals to derive weak possibility.

(7) *Wong wong jawa* **kudu-ne** *iso ngomong kromo,*
person person java ROOT.NEC-NE CIRC.POS AV.talk high.speech
terus anak-e rojo yo **kudu** *iso.*
then child-DEF king PRT.YES ROOT.NEC CIRC.POS
'Javanese people ought to be able to speak Krama, and the Sultan's son has to be able to.' (Vander Klok and Hohaus 2020: 2)

Javanese illustrates a different strategy to derive weak necessity than many Indo-European languages, which might lexicalize modal strength distinctions or use counterfactual morphology. This study reinforces that "...weak modal strength is not a uniform phenomenon across languages, neither lexico-morphologically nor semantically" (Vander Klok and Hohaus 2020: 42). At the same time, Javanese brings up the question of what might be a cross-linguistic paradigm of modal strength; for instance, whether languages prioritize grammaticalizing weak necessity over weak possibility.

Overall, these studies have shown the need to expand the theoretical analyses of modality based on new empirical observations. The present state of research into modality in underdescribed languages is limited to several in-depth studies, including the aforementioned ones, that consider modal flavour, force, and strength in developing a cross-linguistic typology of modal expressions, and how this typology integrates into the wider grammatical system of language. Other work on diverse languages has also advanced the interaction of modality expressions in other areas of research, such as on semantic and pragmatic change (e.g., Bybee et al. 1994; Narrog 2012), or with other grammatical components, such as on the split between epistemic and root modality and its interaction with syntax (e.g., Nauze 2008), as well as on the interaction of modality with temporality (e.g., Chen et al. 2017; Rullmann and Matthewson 2018).

However, in many past and present scholarly works, the study of modality in poorly investigated languages still tends to be based on translation. In semantic fieldwork, translations are at best clues to pinpoint the contribution of meaning of a morpheme, and cannot be used as a conclusive result (e.g., Matthewson 2004). At the same time, modality can be difficult to elicit and subsequently describe in field research because these expressions are often intertwined with tense, aspect, or mood, or the contexts necessary to elicit modality are too cumbersome. As a result, often a full description of how the semantic and/or morphosyntactic dimensions of modality are expressed in a given language is either lacking or translation-based in reference grammars, and inclusive, in-depth studies are left for future research.

Expanding the study of modality to a wider set of underdescribed languages will undoubtedly bring added value for the general enterprise of understanding modality and towards a cross-linguistic typology of modal expressions. As Matthewson (2016: 28) aptly puts, "Assuming that our ultimate goal is a theory of universals and variation in human language, one important task for the field is to gather information about modality in unfamiliar and understudied languages. Formal research on such languages will allow us to develop a formal typology of modality, which in turn will facilitate greater theoretical understanding."

2 About this volume

In order to facilitate describing and analyzing aspects of modality across the world's languages, *Modality in underdescribed languages: Methods and insights* brings together key methods for how linguistic researchers can approach the study of modality, especially from the perspective of working together with speakers of underdescribed languages. This volume arose out of the 2019 "Intermediate meeting of the grammar theory working group" (National association for research and graduate studies in Letters and Linguistics – ANPOLL), organized by Simone Guesser (Federal University of Roraima, Federal University of Rio de Janeiro) and Núbia Ferreira Rech (Universidade Federal de Santa Catarina), with Jozina Vander Klok (Humboldt-Universität zu Berlin) as one of the invited speakers. At the time, Núbia Ferreira Rech led the project 'Modals, a study on the syntax-semantics interface: Brazilian Portuguese and Wapichana' (CNPq, process 424025/2016–2017) in collaboration with Simone Guesser. Through discussion on the challenges and insights of using different methodologies to study modality, we partnered to solicit and bring together demonstrations of various methodologies and specific case studies on underdescribed languages within one volume.

This volume aims to facilitate the study of modality in more diverse languages by explicitly discussing and illustrating a nuanced set of methods beginning with practical semantic fieldwork techniques, and also including storyboards, questionnaires, corpora research, and experimental tasks stemming from studies used in language acquisition. As such, this book also aims to bring the study of modality to a wider participant base, such as in language acquisition. The methodological protocols tested and employed by the authors can be applied as cross-linguistic tools, with special reference for how this can be applied to underdescribed languages, ranging from in an oral setting or as based on a transcribed corpus. This forms Part I on *Methodologies for studying modality*, where the focus is on how linguists can use one particular method or the combination of different approaches to study modality in underdescribed languages.

Part I of the book begins with the chapter *Fieldwork techniques in semantics,* by Luiz Fernando Ferreira (Federal University of Roraima) and Ana Müller (University of São Paulo). The authors present and illustrate a mix of fieldwork techniques that can be used to enhance the quality of the data collection on modality. Based on their experience conducting research on Karitiana, an Amazonian language of the Tupi family, the authors discuss the following techniques: (i) training sessions and control conditions; (ii) the use of storyboards with the goal of tracking and improving the consultant's attention level; and (iii) the use of online forms in data elicitation.

The second chapter, *Studying modality through targeted storyboard constructions* by Zahra Kolagar (Fraunhofer Institute for Integrated Circuits IIS) and Jozina Vander Klok (Humboldt-Universität zu Berlin), shows how modality can be studied using storyboards, both within a language as well as a cross-linguistic tool. The authors present the insights and the challenges of using storyboards in fieldwork. Through discussion of the results on modality in Tabari, a Caspian language of the Indo-European family, their findings reinforce the view that targeted construction storyboards are an important, adaptive, and fun tool in semantic fieldwork.

The third chapter, *Discourse contexts targeting modality in fieldwork: Lessons from conducting the modal questionnaire* by Jozina Vander Klok (Humboldt-Universität zu Berlin), evaluates and expands on the discourse contents in a revised questionnaire from Vander Klok (2014) created to target and identify different expressions of modality within a language. Based on results from a variety of independent studies on diverse languages and further fieldwork on Javanese, an Austronesian language spoken in Indonesia, the author considers the successes and failures of a number of the discourse contents in the original questionnaire, building new ones to overcome the current failures, and widening the coverage of the modal questionnaire to target a further range of modal expressions connected to modal strength. This chapter also presents a short overview of different applications of how this revised questionnaire can be conducted within and across languages, ranging from various types of elicitation to experimental implementation.

The fourth chapter of Part I, *Using corpora to investigate modal-temporal interactions* by Daniel Reisinger, Lisa Matthewson, and Hotze Rullmann (University of British Columbia), describes two corpus studies that focus on the temporal interpretation of modals: a larger case study using English data from COCA, and a pilot study on an underdescribed language, St'át'imcets (Salish), with data drawn from a story collection (Alexander 2016). The two parameters of temporal perspective and temporal orientation (Condoravdi 2002) are investigated, testing hypotheses developed in an earlier theoretical study (Rullmann and Matthewson 2018). The authors discuss the advantages and shortcomings of the corpus methodology to investigate modality, and for this study, they ultimately emphasize the importance of consulting with native speakers to interpret corpus data, showing the relevance of methodological pluralism.

The fifth and final chapter of Part I, *Methods for studying modality in language acquisition* by Ailís Cournane (New York University) and Valentine Hacquard (University of Maryland), focuses on approaches used to test modality in child language acquisition. Emphasizing some methodological paradigms of modal development, the authors consider the advantages and challenges associated with adapting these methods to study underdescribed languages. They also approach how fieldworkers might be able to make the best use of these methods in a way that complements existing methods, again showing the importance of bringing the results of mutiple methods together.

In Part I, the chapters focus on how different research methods can be implemented to conduct more in-depth research on modality, with the intention of inspiring more research on underdescribed languages, starting with practical (semantic) fieldwork guidelines. As each methodological approach has its own inherent advantages and disadvantages, these chapters offer ideas and illustrations of which method or which combination of methods may be the most fruitful to research modality on the language under study.

A further objective of this volume is to present descriptions and analyses of languages from different families in order to better understand how the variation between languages occurs in relation to modality marking, while at the same time, showing the challenges and successes of different methodological contributions. This objective forms Part II of this book, *Lessons from case studies from underdescribed languages*, where the primary focus is on data results with a secondary focus on the successes and challenges as based on the type of method or combination of methods used.

The underdescribed languages represented in Part II include Atayal (Formosan; Austronesian), Ye'kwana (Cariban), Mapudungun (Araucanian), ʔayʔaǰuθəm (Salishan), and Lung'Ie (Portuguese-based creole). This diverse set of languages adds to the focus of Part I on methodology, which were also illustrated by different, mostly under-studied languages, including Karitiana (Tupi), Javanese (Malayo-Polynesian; Austronesian), Tabari/Mazandarani (Indo-Iranian; Indo-European), St'át'imcets (Salishan), and English (Germanic; Indo-European). Overall, the languages represented in this volume span six different language families.

The first chapter of Part II, *On applying semantic fieldwork elicitation techniques to describe modality in Ye'kwana* by Isabella Coutinho (State University of Roraima) and Ana Pessotto (Federal University of Rio de Janeiro), shows how modality is expressed in Ye'kwana, a language spoken on the Brazilian and Venezuelan border (Costa 2018). The authors claim that the morpheme *-jhai* is used to convey an inference from evidence of the speaker's context interpretations, and may express possibility in epistemic or deontic contexts, while the morpheme *-ne* contributes to the interpretation of modal force. The authors describe how they achieve this result, testing the deontic possibility vs. necessity interpretations and epistemic possibility vs. necessity from the theoretical model proposed by Kratzer (1981, 1991) and the methodology for conducting semantic fieldwork from Mathewson (2004) and Vander Klok (2014). This chapter provides a detailed illustration of how they conducted the elicitation tasks and how the consultants responded, giving food for thought for linguists preparing for semantic fieldwork.

The second chapter, *Modality in elicited data and spontaneous texts: A case study of Atayal* by Sihwei Chen (Academia Sinica), addresses the advantages and disadvantages of employing two types of methods in studying modality: conducting direct elicitation with designed, controlled contexts and observing modal utterances in naturally produced stories which had been transcribed. The focus is on Atayal, an Austronesian language that has a typologically unique modal system in which all different types of modal flavour are grammaticalized except the expression of epistemic necessity. Through investigating Atayal modality, the author discusses to what extent the result that is reached based on elicitation can be validly concluded from textual observation.

The third chapter, *Lessons from the field: Irrealis mood in Lung'Ie* by Ana Lívia Agostinho and Núbia Ferreira Rech (Universidade Federal de Santa Catarina), presents and discusses the benefits and the drawbacks of using two methods, storyboards and traditional stories, for studying modality of underdescribed and endangered languages, focusing on Lung'Ie, a Portuguese-lexifier creole language spoken in São Tomé and Príncipe, located in the Gulf of Guinea. Based on the results from these two methods, they propose that *ka* is an irrealis mood marker in Lung'Ie.

The fourth chapter, *Analyzing ʔayʔaǰuθəm evidentials: Evidence for epistemic modality* by Marianne Huijsmans (University of British Columbia), focuses on two evidential clitics, the inferential clitic $\check{c}\varepsilon$ and the reportative clitic $\overset{.}{k}{}^wa$, in ʔayʔaǰuθəm, a Central Salish language. She shows that these clitics are epistemic modals that contribute a strong modal claim to the at-issue content of the clause and an evidential presupposition. As the author points out, the behaviour of these evidentials provides counterevidence to the claim that evidentiality and epistemic modality are non-overlapping categories (De Haan 1999; Aikhenvald

2004); instead, these evidentials provide additional evidence that at least some evidentials are epistemic modals (e.g., Matthewson et al. 2007). Considering that the current and commonly used diagnostics for distinguishing between modal and non-modal evidentials have all been previously criticized, the author has as her main goal to identify which diagnostics can be used to argue for a modal (or non-modal) analysis and how they can be implemented in a fieldwork situation.

The fifth and final chapter of Part II, *Parameters for the production of discourse contexts: Eliciting the semantics of obligations and desires in Mapudungun* by Pablo Fuentes (Universidad Católica de la Santísima Concepción), focuses on overcoming methodological challenges when eliciting primary data related to the expression of obligation and desire. Through a case study on the combination of the frustrative suffix (-*fu*-) with modals in Mapudungun, an endangered Araucanian language, the author shows that Mapudungun behaves like so-called transparent ought/wish languages (cf. von Fintel and Iatridou 2008). In addition to discussing methodological challenges related to the study of these phenomena, Fuentes provides a guideline for producing controlled scenarios that can be used as the basic content of appropriate discourse contexts.

Each of the chapters in Part II demonstrates the results of using various methods, and in some cases, comparing different methods. These methods included storyboards, traditional stories, theory-driven elicitation, textual observation from a corpus, and questionnaires, complementing a number of the methods discussed in Part I. The first three chapters in Part II (Costa and Pessotto, Chen, and Agostinho and Rech) provide in-depth illustrations of the methodologies used for studying modality (and mood) through case studies on individual languages. Through the case studies on modality in last two chapters in Part II, Huijsmans and Fuentes provide tools, one for diagnosing evidentials, and one for building discourse contexts for cross-linguistic use, which can then be applied in the way a researcher sees fit, such as elicitation, experimental, or questionnaire tasks.

Overall, the themes of Part I and II indicate the intertwined values of linguistic theory and data collection: linguistic theory informs our fieldwork, while at the same time, data collected using a variety of methodologies allows us to refine and update our linguistic theory, thereby broadening the empirical base of our understanding of a grammar of language.

We hope that *Modality in underdescribed languages: Methods and insights* will be an important and useful resource for researchers to consult on designing and implementing methodological protocols to investigate modality in underdescribed languages, and will set the stage towards expanding the diversity of languages under study in this domain.

References

Aikhenvald, Alexandra Y. 2004. *Evidentiality*. Oxford: Oxford University Press.
Alexander, Carl. 2016. *Sqwéqwel' múta7 sptakwlh: St'át'imcets narratives by Qwa7yan'ak (Carl Alexander)*, transcribed, translated and edited by Elliot Callahan, Henry Davis, John Lyon & Lisa Matthewson. Vancouver & Lillooet: UBCOPL & USLCES.
Bochnak, M. Ryan. 2015. Variable force modality in Washo. In Thuy Bui and Deniz Özyıldız (eds.), *Proceedings of the Annual Meeting of the North Eastern Linguistic Society (NELS) 45* (1), 105–114. Amherst: GLSA.
Bochnak, M. Ryan & Lisa Matthewson (eds.). 2015. *Methodologies in semantic fieldwork*. New York & Oxford: Oxford University Press.
Brandão, Ana Paula. 2014. *A reference grammar of Paresi-Haliti (Arawak)*. Austin, TX: University of Texas at Austin dissertation.
Bybee, Joan, Revere Perkins & William Pagliuca. 1994. *The evolution of grammar: Tense, aspect, and modality in the languages of the world*. Chicago: University of Chicago Press.
Chen, Sihwei. 2018. *Finding semantic building blocks: Temporal and modal interpretation in Atayal*. Vancouver, BC: University of British Columbia dissertation.
Chen, Sihweh, Vera Hohaus, Rebecca Laturnus, Meagan Louie, Lisa Matthewson, Hotze Rullmann, Ori Simchen, Claire K. Turner & Jozina Vander Klok. 2017. Past possibility cross-linguistically: Evidence from 12 languages. In Ana Arregui, María Luisa Rivero & Andrés Salanova (eds.), *Modality across syntactic categories*, 235–287. Oxford: Oxford University Press.
Condoravdi, Cleo. 2002. Temporal interpretation of modals: Modals for the present and the past. In David Beaver, Luis Casillas Martinez, Brady Clark & Stefan Kaufmann (eds.), *The construction of meaning*, 59–88. Stanford, CA: CSLI Publications.
Costa, Isabella. 2018. *A quantificação em Ye'kwana: a distinção contável-massivo* [Quantification in Ye'kwana: The count/mass distinction]. Rio de Janeiro: Universidade Federal do Rio de Janeiro dissertation.
Cover, Rebecca. 2010. *Aspect, modality, and tense in Badiaranke*. Berkeley, CA: University of California Berkeley dissertation.
Davis, Henry, Lisa Matthewson & Hotze Rullmann. 2009. A unified modal semantics for out-of-control in St'át'imcets. In Lotte Hogeweg, Helen de Hoop & Andrey Malchukov (eds.), *Cross-linguistics semantics of tense, aspect and modality*, 205–244. Oxford: John Benjamins.
Deal, Amy Rose. 2011. Modals without scales. *Language* 87. 559–585.
De Haan, Ferdinand. 1999. Evidentiality and epistemic modality: Setting boundaries. *Southwest Journal of Linguistics* 18 (1). 83–101.
von Fintel, Kai & Sabine Iatridou. 2008. How to say 'ought' in foreign: The composition of weak necessity modals. In Jacqueline Guéron & Jacqueline Lecarme (eds.), *Time and modality*, 115–141. Dordrecht: Springer.
Gluckman, John & Margit Bowler. 2020. The expression of modality in Logoori. *Journal of African Languages and Linguistics* 41 (2). https://doi.org/10.1515/jall-2020-2010.
Herburger, Elena & Aynat Rubinstein. 2019. Gradable possibility and epistemic comparison. *Journal of Semantics* 36 (1). 165–191.

Kawalya, Deo, Gilles-Maurice de Schryver & Koen Bostoen. 2018. Reconstructing the origins of the Luganda (JE15) modal auxiliaries *-sóból-* and *-yînz-*: A historical-comparative study across the West Nyanza Bantu cluster. *South African Journal of African Languages* 38 (1). 13–25.

Kratzer, Angelika. 1981. The notional category of modality. In Hans-Jurgen Eikmeyer & Hannes Rieser (eds.), *Words, worlds, and contexts: New approaches in word semantics*, 38–74. Berlin: Mouton de Gruyter.

Kratzer, Angelika. 1991. Modality. In Armin von Stechow & Dieter Wunderlich (eds.), *Semantics: An international handbook of contemporary research*, 639–650. Berlin: Mouton de Gruyter.

Matthewson, Lisa. 2004. On the methodology of semantic fieldwork. *International Journal of American Linguistics* 70. 369–415.

Matthewson, Lisa 2013. Gitksan modals. *International Journal of American Linguistics* 79. 349–394.

Matthewson, Lisa. 2016. Modality. In Maria Aloni & Paul Dekker (eds.), *Cambridge handbook of formal semantics*, 525–559. Cambridge: Cambridge University Press.

Matthewson, Lisa, Hotze Rullmann & Henry Davis. 2007. Evidentials as epistemic modals: Evidence from St'át'imcets. In Jeroen Van Craenenbroeck (ed.), *Linguistic variation yearbook*, Volume 7, 201–254. Amsterdam: John Benjamins.

Narrog, Heiko. 2012. *Modality, subjectivity, and semantic change: A cross-linguistic perspective*. Oxford: Oxford University Press.

Nauze, Fabrice. 2008. *Modality in typological perspective*. Amsterdam: Universiteit van Amsterdam dissertation.

Pessotto, Ana Lucia. 2015. Força e evidência: uma análise teórico-experimental da semântica de 'pode', 'deve' e 'tem que' [Force and evidence: An experimental-theoretical analysis of the semantics of pode, deve and tem que]. Florianópolis: Universidade Federal de Santa Catarina dissertation.

Peterson, Tyler. 2010. *Epistemic modality and evidentiality in Gitksan at the semantics-pragmatics interface*. Vancouver: University of British Columbia dissertation.

von Prince, Kilu & Anna Margetts. 2019. Expressing possibility in two Oceanic languages. *Studies in Language* 43 (3). 628–667.

Rech, Núbia F. & Ana Paula Brandão. 2018. A marcação de modalidade deôntica no Paresi [Deontic modality marking in Paresi]. *Fórum Linguístico* 15 (1). 2816–2827.

Rech, Núbia F., Ana Paula Brandão & Marina de Wit. 2018. The relationship between irrealis mood and deontic modality in Paresi (Arawak). *LIAMES: Línguas Indígenas Americanas*, 18 (2). 229–252.

Rullmann, Hotze & Lisa Matthewson 2018. Towards a theory of modal-temporal interaction. *Language* 94 (2). 281–331.

Rullmann, Hotze, Lisa Matthewson & Henry Davis 2008. Modals as distributive indefinites. *Natural Language Semantics* 16. 317–357.

Vander Klok, Jozina. 2013. Pure possibility and pure necessity modals in Paciran Javanese. *Oceanic Linguistics* 52 (2). 346–378.

Vander Klok, Jozina. 2014. *Questionnaire on modality for cross-linguistic use*. Retrieved from http://www.eva.mpg.de/lingua/tools-at-lingboard/questionnaires.php and on TulQuest http://tulquest.huma-num.fr/fr/node/70 (Accessed 9 March 2022).

Vander Klok, Jozina & Vera Hohaus. 2020. Weak necessity without weak possibility: The composition of modal strength distinctions in Javanese. *Semantics & Pragmatics* 13 (12). https://doi.org/10.3765/sp.13.12.

Part I: **Contributions of different methods for studying modality**

Luiz Fernando Ferreira & Ana Müller
1 Fieldwork techniques in semantics

Abstract: This chapter focuses on techniques to be used in semantics fieldwork. More specifically, we discuss complementary techniques, such as the use of storyboards to contextualize elicitations, the implementation of training sessions and control sentences, and the use of Google Forms. These techniques are to be implemented alongside traditional methods, such as questionnaires, contextualized translations, truth judgment tasks, and storyboards. Good linguistic analysis heavily depends on the quality of the data collected during fieldwork. There are two kinds of factors that may impair the quality of the data. The first includes factors inherent to the methodology, such as the use of contexts in order to determine the exact truth conditions of a sentence. The great number and variety of contexts tends to make consultants feel fatigued or bored during elicitation sessions. The second kind of factors that may lead to poor quality data relates to external conditions. Examples of these are consultants having a bad day or failing to understand instructions because they are not fluent speakers of the contact language. Being prepared for these kinds of problems increases the chances of successful fieldwork. This chapter argues that the combination of different methods yields more reliable fieldwork results. We contextualize our argument by presenting data we have collected during fieldwork that turned out to be unreliable. We also argue that the implementation of the suggested complementary techniques has a positive impact on fieldwork sessions. It increases consultants' attention level and furnishes important feedback on how much we can rely on data from each particular consultant.

Acknowledgments: The authors would like to thank the National Council of Scientific and Technological Development – CNPq (grants #142209/2017-1 to Luiz Fernando Ferreira and #312816/2017-0 to Ana Müller). We also thank the Coordination for the Improvement of Higher Educational Personnel – CAPES (grant #88887.370125/2019-00 to Luiz Fernando Ferreira) and the São Paulo Research Foundation – FAPESP (grant #2018/17029-5 to Ana Müller). We want to thank the editors of this volume for their support since the first draft of this chapter. We are greatly indebted to two anonymous reviewers whose contributions, we believe, helped improve the chapter. We also want to thank all Karitiana consultants who participated in our elicitation sessions. Without them, this chapter would not have been possible. Of course, all mistakes here are exclusively our own.

Luiz Fernando Ferreira, Federal University of Roraima, Av. Nova Iorque, Bloco I, 69310-010 Boa Vista, Brazil, e-mail: fernando.ferreira@ufrr.br
Ana Müller, University of São Paulo, Av. Prof. Luciano Gualberto 403, 05508-010 São Paulo, Brazil, e-mail: anamuler@usp.br

https://doi.org/10.1515/9783110721478-002

1 Introduction

This chapter presents and illustrates a mix of fieldwork techniques – storyboards for contextualizing elicitations; the use of training sessions; the use of control sentences; and the implementation of elicitation sessions through online forms. It describes how they can be used to enhance fieldwork practices and improve the quality of the collected data when working with indigenous languages. We claim that adopting a variety of techniques provides the linguist with more reliable data. These techniques have been tested by one of the authors in the elicitation of data on tense and on bouletic modality in Karitiana, an Amazonian language of the Tupi family. Thus, we will be able to demonstrate their positive impact on the elicitation sessions.

Our main motivation for adopting the fieldwork methods that we describe in this paper was two problems we faced: fatigued consultants and their misunderstanding of the context or the task. These kinds of problems are not uncommon (see Louie 2015) and linguists should pay special attention to them, since fieldwork that is carried out under such conditions may yield unreliable data, which, in turn, may lead to linguistic analyses that are not consistent with the facts of the language.

The causes of fieldwork problems may be inherent to the applied methods or external to them. Semantic fieldwork tends to rely on many pairs of contexts and sentences. Depending on the phenomenon under investigation, those contexts become rather long. Thus, it is not unexpected that the consultant will feel fatigued during an elicitation session. This illustrates a problem that is inherent to the method, as argued by Louie (2015). In order to solve it, we suggest replacing verbal contextualization by the use of storyboards in our truth judgment tasks. The inclusion of technological tools such as online forms also helps since they add novelty and make the elicitation more appealing to the consultants.

The cause for the lack of attention and misunderstandings may also be due to external factors. External causes for fatigued/bored consultants may include not getting enough sleep the previous night or not being fluent in the contact language. Linguists do not have control over these factors.[1] We illustrate how training sessions and control conditions may be used in fieldwork in order to detect whether consultants are paying attention to the given context when providing their judgments. These complementary techniques can be implemented within

---

[1] The literature on semantic fieldwork (see Vander Klok and Conners 2019; Bochnak and Matthewson 2020) usually distinguishes the contact language from the target language. The contact language is the language the linguist uses to communicate with the consultant and present the contexts/storyboards whereas the target language is the language under investigation.

the most common methods in semantics fieldwork: questionnaires, contextualized translations, truth judgment tasks, and storyboards (see Matthewson 2004; Sanchez-Mendes 2014; Bochnak and Matthewson 2015, 2020; Vander Klok 2019; Vander Klok and Conners 2019). We show how the metadata they provide may help us decide how much we can rely on certain data.

Lastly, we discuss the beneficial impacts that technological tools may have on fieldwork. We illustrate this by showing how online forms such as Google Forms have helped us to improve the way we collect and analyze data, since they can: (i) add a novel element, making consultants more excited about the elicitation session; (ii) save data automatically in the cloud, reducing the risk of losing it; (iii) automatically tabulate data by exporting the results of questionnaires to Excel tables; (iv) automatically generate graphs; and (v) monitor incorrect options in control conditions and give us real-time feedback on consultants' attention level.

This chapter is divided into five sections. Section 2 discusses the impacts of internal and external conditions on fieldwork, using our own experience with the Karitiana community as an illustration. Section 3 presents the methods for data elicitation. In 3.1 we focus on the most common methods used in semantics fieldwork; in 3.2, we discuss one of the methods we have implemented in our fieldwork (i.e., the contextualization of data elicitation through storyboards). Section 4 discusses some complementary methods, such as the use of training sessions and control conditions. Section 5 discusses the positive impact of technological tools. It shows how elicitations can be implemented using online forms, which make storage and feedback on the quality of the data even easier. The last section presents our final remarks.

2 Internal and external conditions of fieldwork

Before discussing elicitation methods, we will discuss internal and external conditions of fieldwork based on the dynamics of our own fieldwork with Karitiana speakers. This discussion is relevant to the understanding of what motivates the implementation of the methods we discuss in sections 3 and 4.

Bochnak and Matthewson (2015: 3) pointed out that "each field situation is unique and presents its own set of challenges, and so the fieldworker must adapt methodological tools to meet the challenges encountered in the field." This means that linguists should always take the conditions of the field into account before preparing for fieldwork. There are two types of conditions that should be taken into account: (i) those inherent to the methodology itself; and (ii) those external to it. Ignoring one or the other will have a negative impact on the success of fieldwork.

Internal/inherent conditions have to do with the fact that we conduct fieldwork on the semantics of a language. The advantages and disadvantages of each technique must be weighed against this fact. For instance, an investigation of some aspects of the semantics of a language will yield better results with the use of contextualized elicitation than with the use of translations without the introduction of any context (Matthewson 2004; Sanchez-Mendes 2014). Thus, when choosing one methodology or another, linguists should be aware of the pros and cons of each method.

Taking into account external conditions is equally important when planning data elicitation. Linguists should devote some time to considering external facts. The answers to the following questions provide important information for linguists to guide their elicitation:
- Does the linguist travel to the speech community or do the speakers come to the linguist?
- How easy is access to the community and to the consultants?
- How many days can the linguist stay with the community or the consultants stay with the linguist? How long do these visits last? How frequent are they?
- What will the contact language be? How fluent is the linguist in it? How fluent are the consultants in it?
- Does the target language have a writing system? Do the consultants use it?

The success of field trips depends heavily on how adequate the methods are to those conditions. We will illustrate the importance of taking internal and external conditions into account by using the case of Karitiana, which is a language of the Tupi branch and of the Arikém family.

2.1 Internal conditions of fieldwork

Semanticists usually depend on a number of methods of data elicitation: translations; contextualized data elicitation, which can be contextualized translations or truth judgments (Matthewson 2004; Sanchez-Mendes 2014); questionnaires (Vander Klok and Conners 2019; Bochnak and Matthewson 2020); and storyboards (Burton and Matthewson 2015; Vander Klok 2019; Bochnak and Matthewson 2020). There are specific advantages to each of these methods. Contextualized data elicitation, for instance, demands less preparation time than storyboards. On the other hand, data from storyboards are more natural than data from contextualized elicitations. We go over the advantages and disadvantages of each of these methods in more detail in section 3.1.

In this section, we focus on the inherent conditions of our methods that had the strongest impact on our fieldwork with the Karitiana; specifically, the consultants struggled to pay attention to the given contexts. Louie (2015) points out that, because we tend to organize our elicitation in paradigms, our tasks become extremely boring for consultants. This is a big problem inherent to the method. Context is of primary importance in semantic fieldwork (Bochnak and Matthewson 2015) and the fieldwork that is carried out under these conditions may yield unreliable data, which, in turn, may lead to linguistic analyses that are not consistent with the facts of the language. Thus, linguists should invest in techniques that make the sessions more appealing and in techniques that help detect when consultants stop paying attention to the given contexts.

Paying close attention to the consultants' mood is a good way of spotting when they are fatigued or bored. In our case, the consultants: (i) show signs of exasperation/impatience; (ii) take a long time to answer the questions; (iii) try to change the topic; (iv) constantly ask for breaks for coffee/cigarettes, etc. Most of these signs have also been reported by Louie (2015).

Louie (2015: 64) comments on some cases of bored consultants. One of the indicators is when they start complaining that the contexts/sentences sound the same to them. We have heard similar complaints from Karitiana speakers, who usually say, "You just said that"; "This is the same sentence as the last one"; and "It's the same".

The second way to spot fatigued/bored consultants is within the data. Depending on the linguists' proficiency level in the target language, they will be able to spot some inconsistencies in the data. Example (1) illustrates this kind of inconsistency.[2] It comes from an elicitation session with a truth judgment task that targeted non-future tense in Karitiana, using Brazilian Portuguese as the contact language.

(1) Fieldworker: *Uma criança vê Inácio matando a cobra e começa a chorar. Você poderia dizer "Ombaky Inácio oky tykiri, nakahyryp õwã." para descrever essa situação?*
'A child sees Inácio killing a snake and starts crying. Could you say "Ombaky Inácio oky tykiri, nakahyryp õwã." to describe this situation?'
Consultant: *Sim*
'Yes'

---

2 This sentence belonged to the training session. The mismatch between context and sentence was there on purpose so we could verify if the consultants were considering the details of the presented context when evaluating the sentence. We talk more about training sessions in section 4.

The presented sentence is glossed and translated in (2):[3]

(2) Ombaky Inácio oky   tykiri, Ø-naka-hyryp-Ø   ōwã.
    jaguar Inácio kill when   3-DECL-cry-NFUT   kid
    'When Inácio killed the jaguar, the kid cried.'

The judgment that the consultant gave us in (1) is not consistent because the sentence meaning is incompatible with the context. In the context, Inácio kills a snake, and the consultant's sentence states that he killed a jaguar. It is not uncommon for consultants to ignore the contexts in a truth judgment task. Let's see another example:

(3) Fieldworker: *Elivar disse que quer tomar sopa e que ele vai tomar sopa amanhã. Você usaria "Elivar naka'yt sopa" para descrever esta situação?*
'Elivar said that he wants to have some soup and that he is going to have it tomorrow. Would you use "Elivar naka'yt sopa" to describe this situation?'
    Consultant: *Sim*
                 'Yes'

The presented sentence is glossed and translated in (4):

(4) Elivar Ø-naka-'y-t   sopa.
    Elivar 3-DECL-ingest-NFUT   soup
    'Elivar ate/eats soup.'

The judgment that the consultant gave us in (3) is not consistent. Elivar wants to have soup in the future, and the sentence presented by the consultant is stated in the non-future tense.

We suspect that these inconsistencies in the data result from fatigued/bored consultants since they also showed signs of boredom during the elicitation session. However, this may not be the only cause. Another inherent problem to this method is *yes-biased* answers. Experimental studies with children have observed that some participants show the bias of accepting all experimental

---

[3] We follow the Leipzig glossing rules (Comrie, Haspelmath, and Bickel 2015). The following abbreviations will be used here: 3 third person; ADV adverbializer; COP copula; DECL declarative; FUT future; IPFV imperfective; N non-; NOM nominalizer; OBL oblique.

items as "true" (Schmitt and Miller 2010). Vander Klok and Conners (2019) also discuss the possibility of *yes-bias* in their fieldwork.

One last possibility is that the consultant did not understand the task and was providing us with grammaticality judgments instead of truth condition judgments. This may occur due to the internal conditions we have already mentioned. Since it is exhausting to pay close attention to the contexts and keep track of the changes from one context to the other, the consultants stop paying attention to them and start providing us with grammaticality judgments. However, misunderstandings may also be due to external factors, as discussed in the next subsection.

2.2 External conditions of fieldwork

External factors should also be considered when preparing for fieldwork. This subsection discusses external factors in light of our experience with the Karitiana community. Karitiana currently has about 400 hundred native speakers (Storto and Rocha 2018). The Karitiana people live mainly in five tribes inside their indigenous reservation, located in the northwest Amazonian rainforest. The red square in Figure 1 shows the reservation, which is located in the state of Rondônia, about 100 kilometers from the city of Porto Velho (the capital of the state).

Figure 1: Karitiana reservation.[4]

---

4 Available at https://terrasindigenas.org.br/pt-br/terras-indigenas/3725. Accessed on March 31, 2020.

We usually do fieldwork once a year, either traveling to the Karitiana community or paying for the speakers to come to São Paulo. Until 2019, the community did not have Internet or phone signals. Therefore, access to the community and to the consultants was not very easy. Our grants allowed us to bring consultants to us or to stay in the community for one to two weeks. These are important conditions external to the fieldwork methods. If something went wrong in an elicitation session and we did not find it in time, we would only have another opportunity to check it in the subsequent year.

The small number of speakers makes Karitiana an endangered language. An important external condition to take into account is the fact that the Karitiana people mostly speak Karitiana among themselves. They only use Portuguese to talk to non-Karitiana speakers. Children learn Karitiana as their first language, and only start learning Portuguese when they go to school. Since Portuguese is a second language for them, the Karitiana people speak it with various degrees of fluency. This makes a very good example of an external condition one has to take into account when preparing for fieldwork. We chose Brazilian Portuguese as our contact language, since our informants are more proficient in Brazilian Portuguese than we are in Karitiana. Nevertheless, our consultants are not native speakers of Brazilian Portuguese. Thus, depending on the consultant we work with, the degree of fluency in the contact language can be a problem and the consultant may have trouble following the linguist's instructions. This may lead to inconsistencies such as those illustrated in (1) and (3). We exemplify this with one kind of noise that occurred in the elicitation section targeting bouletic modality.

The consultant was presented with a storyboard in which a couple, Maria (the wife) and José (the husband), go to a restaurant that cooks a whole fish that serves two people. They take a look at the menu in order to decide what to eat. Maria and José do not want to eat the same fish. Maria wants to eat Tucunaré and José wants to eat Tambaqui.[5] They leave the restaurant without ordering anything because José does not want to eat the fish that Maria wants to eat and Maria does not want to eat the fish that José wants to eat.

After hearing the story, the consultant was given a pen and a paper with many sentences in Portuguese that should be translated to Karitiana. All sentences were tied to the storyboard, which served as context for them. After each sentence in Portuguese, there was a space for Karitiana consultants to write their answers.[6]

---

[5] Tucunaré and Tambaqui are Amazonian fish.
[6] Karitiana has a writing system that many consultants know how to use. This is another important condition because when we know an informant can write, we record the sentences, but we also ask them to write them down.

Fieldworker instruction: *Com base na história que eu acabei de te contar, como você falaria "Hoje José quer comer Tucunaré" em Karitiana?*[7]
'Based on the story I have just told you, how would you say "Today, José wants to eat Tucunaré" in Karitiana?'

Consultant's answer:

(5) *Kiri   Ø-na-siki'y-j   José syryho-ty   em Karitiana*
    today 3-DECL-want.eat-FUT   José Tucunaré-OBL   in Karitiana
    'Today José wants to eat Tucunaré in Karitiana'

When we went through the consultant's answer, we realized the consultant thought "in Karitiana" was a part of the sentence. Actually, all sentences in this elicitation ended with "em Karitiana".[8] Consultants may even be aware that they do not understand the task. Nevertheless, there is a good chance that they will not acknowledge this either because they feel ashamed or because they do not want the linguist to think they are unfit for the task and not invite them for further sessions.

Another example of an external problem is that the chosen date may not be felicitous. In 2018, Luiz Fernando Ferreira scheduled his fieldwork trip for the first two weeks in February. It was Carnival time in Brazil and Porto Velho, the city close to the Karitiana reservation, holds a big traditional street party that lasts for days. For this reason, consultants were eager for the elicitation sessions to finish as soon as possible so they could attend the party. Thus, knowing the community and their main festivities is also relevant because it can affect consultants' performance in elicitation sessions.

Still another external factor that must be taken into account is that not every consultant is good at every task. The linguist will only learn about consultants' distinct potentials after working with the community a few times. For instance,

---

[7] A reviewer pointed out that the linguist may be asking the wrong question, since the question seemed to be ambiguous. We agree that the oral instruction was ambiguous. Nevertheless, since consultants also had a written version of the sentence they should translate, it did not cross our minds that they would interpret the "in Karitiana" as part of the sentence they should translate because it was not in the sentences on the paper.
[8] Although not ideal, this insertion did not cause much harm since, if we ignore "em Karitiana," the sentence provided by the speaker seems compatible with the context.

Karitiana elders usually perform badly on elicitations about the semantics of the language. They are illiterate, so the linguist can only rely on oral presentations of the relevant contexts. Moreover, many times their memories are not apt to keep track of the small changes from one context to the other. In addition, they tend to misunderstand their role as consultants and assume that they are there to teach us to speak the language. One case in point is the community's *pajé* – the traditional religious leader. He has been working with linguists for more than 20 years and has participated in many elicitation sessions. Even so, he gets upset when presented with ungrammatical sentences or when presented with several context/sentence pairs that he judges to be wrong. For him, it looks as though the linguist is insisting on the mistake and failing to learn.[9] However, he performs very well when asked for spontaneous data, such as traditional narratives and stories.[10]

Young speakers may also perform badly on the tasks assigned to them.[11] We have experienced many kinds of misunderstandings during fieldwork with such speakers. For example, the consultant in (5) was a young girl in her late teens participating in an elicitation session for the first time. Thus, the consultant's lack of experience was another external factor that played a role in the misunderstanding illustrated in this example. A linguist who has worked with a community for some time learns which members of this community are the best fit for certain tasks. Louie (2015: 49), in her work on Blackfoot (Algonquian), an Indigenous Canadian language, was able to identify a speaker as the ideal consultant. This was so because this speaker had already participated in previous fieldwork and was interested in/inclined toward analyzing his/her own language. This speaker tended to spontaneously provide extra facts about the data and to correct infelicitous contexts, replacing them with felicitous ones.

Our fieldwork experience has taught us that our best Karitiana consultants are the teachers at the village schools. They attended a college for indigenous people in order to obtain their certification as teachers, in addition to receiving some formal education in Portuguese. Therefore, they are also the most fluent in Portuguese, and are able to read and write in both Portuguese and Karitiana. Because of this formal education, if the linguist does not understand an answer,

---

9 Louie (2015: 64) reports the same problem in a footnote.
10 Since storyboards are argued to be a more spontaneous way of eliciting data (see Burton and Matthewson 2015), we predict that those consultants could perform better in semantic elicitation using the storyboard method. However, we have not tested this.
11 By young, we mean those 20 years old or younger.

the consultants are able to write it down.[12] On top of that, a number of teachers have already participated in several fieldwork projects. This gives them some expertise, which leads to better performance. Moreover, they generally show more interest in working with their language than other consultants.[13]

Given that we already know which consultants perform better at each task, the logical decision, from the fieldworker's perspective, would be to only work with the consultants that perform better in the methodology one intends to use. However, this is not so simple. Choosing only certain consultants can actually do more harm, because the community may see it as the linguist playing favorites. In our work with the Karitiana community, selecting particular consultants has created attrition in the past, which lead to problems when negotiating for the next research projects. Thus, creating and maintaining a good relationship with the community is a fundamental part of the fieldworker's task. Louie (2015: 57) mentions how the elicitation may get interrupted by consultants who wants to tell a story; meanwhile, interrupting the consultant cannot be done easily without risking the cordiality of the relationship between the consultant and the linguist.

Since it is not always possible to work with experienced consultants, our recommendation is to always adopt a training session and control conditions for the elicitation, as will be discussed in section 4.

3 Fieldwork techniques

This section discusses the most relevant fieldwork techniques for semanticists and illustrates them by describing how we have implemented them in our fieldwork with the Karitiana. It is divided in two subsections. The first section briefly discusses the most usual techniques when eliciting data in semantics fieldwork

---

[12] One reviewer asked what we would recommend for linguists working in a community for the first time. Since experience seems to lead to better performance at fieldwork tasks, trying to work with consultants who have worked with linguists before can make the fieldwork easier. In case the community has never worked with a linguist, our personal advice would be to try to work with consultants who have received some formal education. We are aware that it is not always the case that one can choose the consultant. In such cases, investing some time to develop a good training session minimizes inconsistent data and using control sentences helps to assess consultants' performance in a given task, as demonstrated in section 4.
[13] Their interest in analysing the language might be an advantage, but it might also become a problem. Burton and Matthewson (2015) argue that, when presenting storyboards, it is important for the speaker not to know which structure the linguist is targeting, since they might then let prescriptivism guide their judgments.

(i.e., translations, contextualized data elicitation, and storyboards) and their pros and cons. The second section describes how we complemented them with some other, more sophisticated techniques and how that impacted our fieldwork.

3.1 Usual techniques in semantic fieldwork

As discussed by Bochnak and Matthewson (2015), fieldwork in semantics has very specific needs. Other linguistics subfields (e.g., phonetics, phonology, morphology, and syntax) deal with more tangible entities, such as phonemes, morphemes, and phrases. In these fields, the data itself provides information about grammatical and well-pronounced expressions. The same is not true for semantics. The main task of semanticists is to find out which meanings a given structure/word/morpheme has, as well as which meanings it does not have. The problem is that a semantically well-formed utterance provides the linguist with very incomplete cues about what that utterance means (Bochnak and Matthewson 2015).

Because of this, fieldwork techniques in semantics are construed to make the meaning under investigation as salient as possible. This is why simple translation is often condemned as an elicitation practice. Translation is considered a less efficient method in semantics fieldwork because it introduces high interference by the communication language in the target language. Another problem with translation is that ambiguities in sentences in the communication language may lead to inaccurate translations in the target language. For these reasons, data from translations are least reliable (see Matthewson 2004; Bochnak and Matthewson 2020). Another problem with using translations as a method is that they do not provide negative data.[14]

The contextualized elicitation method involves two steps: Contextualized translations and truth judgment tasks. Contextualized translation is more reliable since the presentation of contexts avoids ambiguities and minimizes the chances of getting inaccurate translations. Judgment tasks, on the other hand, are able to provide semanticists with the negative data they need for their analysis (Matthewson 2004; Sanchez-Mendes 2014). Contextualized translation tasks and truth judgment tasks are organized in a paradigmatic way (i.e., the contexts or the sentences differ minimally from one another) in order to allow for fine-grained semantic analysis. These elicitation methods are based on the following dynamics:

---

14 Negative data here refers to the meanings a sentence cannot have.

Example of a truth judgment task:
- Fieldworker: Think about this context (presents a context).
- Fieldworker: Would you use sentence *p* in such a context?
- Fieldworker: Now think about this other context (presents another context that differs minimally from the previous one).
- Fieldworker: Would you use sentence *p* in such a context?

Three problems persist in the use of these methods: the interference of the communication language; the lack of naturalness of the data produced under these circumstances (Burton and Matthewson 2015); and the use of paradigms, which becomes mentally exhausting for consultants since it is hard for them to keep track of the minimal changes in the presented contexts and/or sentences (Louie 2015). Louie (2015) suggests that, to mitigate these problems, instead of presenting a context for each sentence in a paradigmatic way, we could use story arcs to create a context that includes several sentences at a time.

Story arcs are a way of making the elicitation more interesting for the consultant. Nevertheless, they do not solve problems related to the lack of naturalness, since the consultants still have to translate sentences. One elicitation method which avoids both problems are storyboards. In this method, the linguist presents a narrative in the communication language using a series of pictures. Then, the consultant has to retell this story in the target language using only the pictures. According to Burton and Matthewson (2015), the use of storyboards avoids the interference of the communication language since the consultants rely on pictures when retelling the story. Burton and Matthewson compared the perception of stories collected with storyboards to spontaneous stories told to a linguist by Japanese native speakers. They found that the stories elicited with storyboards were perceived as being as natural as spontaneously told stories. The application of storyboards to fieldwork in a variety of languages has confirmed its effectiveness for semantic fieldwork (Vander Klok 2019).

Despite their advantages, storyboards may not be sufficient to elicit some aspects of the meaning of a targeted linguistic structure. Thus, Burton and Matthewson (2015) suggest to combine storyboards with other methods, such as contextualized data elicitation (contextualized translation and truth judgment tasks). A story arc is basically a storyboard with no illustrations. So, if the story arc technique is complemented with illustrations, we get to the contextualization of our translations and judgments tasks by the use of storyboards. Bochnak and Matthewson (2020: 14) mention that storyboards may also be used as visual representations of contexts.

One of the disadvantages of using storyboards and story arcs is that creating a story arc or a storyboard for data elicitation requires much more planning than the more traditional methods. A specific disadvantage of the storyboard method is that, since consultants speak freely and are guided only by the pictures, the data may be more difficult to gloss and analyze. Moreover, one may not get the targeted structure or meaning (see Vander Klok 2019).

3.2 Complementary methods for semantic fieldwork

So far, we have discussed inherent and external conditions that influence fieldwork based on our own experience with Karitiana. We have also discussed the usual methods for semantic fieldwork and their pros and cons. Considering what we have discussed so far, we now describe and illustrate some complementary methods that can be used in semantic fieldwork. We show how they have helped us to improve and guarantee the quality of the data elicited in our fieldwork with Karitiana consultants.

The techniques we describe have been tested by one of the authors in the elicitation of data on tense and on bouletic modality in Karitiana. Note that Karitiana has a future vs. non-future temporal system. The goal of our investigation of tense was to discover whether the non-future inflection conveyed <u>either</u> present or past or <u>both</u> present and past (See Matthewson 2006; Jóhannsdottir and Mathhewson 2008). We assume that an expression conveys bouletic modality when it expresses desires (Von Fintel 2006; Von Fintel and Iatridou 2017). Our investigations on the expression of bouletic modality in Karitiana aimed to discover which linguistic structures were used to convey desires in the language. The results of this research are described in detail in Müller and Ferreira (2020) and in Ferreira (2020; 2022). We briefly refer to the results here as well, but this chapter will focus more on the elicitation methods.

In order to avoid boredom due to the use of a multiplicity of context/sentence pairs, we presented a single story that encompassed the context of the totality of sentences to be elicited (Louie 2015). Our story arcs were illustrated with pictures to make them more interesting and easier for our consultants to follow. Since an illustrated story arc is in essence a storyboard, we refer to this practice as a contextualization of many sentences with a storyboard. The reason we argue in favor of implementing storyboards as a part of translation and truth judgment tasks is to make the elicitation less boring and tiresome. The stories were presented to the consultants in a slideshow fashion. After the presentation, they were asked to perform one of two tasks: translate sentences from the contact language to the target language based on the story that was presented to them; or judge sentences in the target language as true or false according to the story.

In order to collect data on bouletic modality in Karitiana, we created five story arcs and illustrated them with pictures. The main characters in the stories were a couple, José and Maria. The stories were presented to consultants in the communication language with slides.¹⁵ One story arc we used is illustrated below:¹⁶

Figure 2: Example of illustrated story arc.¹⁷

After being introduced to the story, we presented our consultants with two types of activities. The first was a contextualized translation of Portuguese sentences into Karitiana. We asked them to consider the story they had just heard when translating these sentences. This is illustrated below:

---

15 We were not the first researchers to use illustrations as a facilitating method in Karitiana fieldwork. Vivanco (2014, 2018) created a short-illustrated story to collect data on syntax. One difference is that, because semantic analysis requires an enriched context, our stories are relatively longer than those prepared by her.
16 We would like to remind the reader that these are smaller, translated versions. The story arcs were originally in Portuguese and had about 8 slides. We reduced them to four in our example for the sake of space.
17 The drawing from this storyboard was replicated to one used in the field. The pictures from this storyboard were drawn by Luiz Fernando Ferreira.

(6) Fieldworker: *Considering the story you have just heard; how would you say the sentence below in Karitiana?*[18]
'Maria does not want José to buy Antônio's motorcycle.'
Consultant: Maria   Ø-na-aka-t   i-py'eep-Ø   Antônio
Maria   3-DECL-COP-NFUT   3-not.want-ADV   Antônio
moto-ty   José   ami-ty
motorcycle-OBL   José   buy-OBL
'Maria does not want José to buy Antônio's motorcycle.'

Why not just ask our consultants to retell the story? The problem with storyboards is that, since consultants can retell the story freely, they can omit a certain structure that was relevant for the linguist. In the case of the storyboard illustrated above, consultants may say "He wanted [$_{DP}$ the motorcycle]" instead of "He$_1$ wanted [$_{TP}$ t$_1$ to buy the motorcycle from Antônio", which was the structure we were aiming at. This kind of result may also occur with contextualized translations; however, in that case it is easier for the linguist to spot. One illustrative example of not getting the targeted data is reported in Vander Klok (2019). The author developed the storyboard *Bill vs. the weather* targeting the use of modal expressions that did not come out when the consultant narrated the story freely. Ideally, if time and budget permit, the linguist should use both methods.

In the case of our fieldwork on bouletic modality, we used the data collected in this first stage to formulate hypotheses about the phenomenon. Our second step was to test those hypotheses by using a truth judgment task.

Note that there is no overt negation in sentence (6) produced by the consultant. Based on this fact, we concluded that the verb *py'eep* conveys a negative desire, which is a combination of bouletic modality and negation. In formal semantics, negation is analyzed as an operator over the sentence under its scope. Modality, on the other hand, is analyzed as quantification over possible worlds. Our hypothesis was that the verb *py'eep* both quantifies over all possible worlds compatible with the subject's desires and introduces a negation. The question this hypothesis poses is about the relative scope between the two operators introduced by the modal. We know that differences in scope give rise to different interpretations.[19] If negation is under the scope of the universal quantifier ($\forall w: \neg\ p(w) = 1$), sentence (6) should mean that Maria has the desire that José does not buy a motorcycle. If the quantification over possible worlds is under the scope of negation

---
18 This instruction was given orally by the fieldworker. The sentence was written on a piece of paper that was given to the consultant.
19 We thank Professor Marcelo Ferreira for pointing that out to us.

($\neg \forall w: p(w) = 1$), sentence (6) should mean that Maria is indifferent towards José's buying of the motorcycle. The story arc supported the first analysis.

The truth condition judgment tests were applied to validate these conclusions. In this second step, we presented the context in the contact language and the sentence in Karitiana. We illustrate the task using English.[20]

(7) Fieldworker: Suppose José is planning to buy a motorcycle. Then, somebody in the tribe says the following: "Maria naakat ipy'eep Antônio mototy José amyty." If José buys the motorcycle, do you think Maria will be mad?
    Consultant: She will be so mad she may even cut his penis off.

As can be seen above, the truth judgment task confirmed our initial hypothesis about the meaning of *py'eep*. If the verb expressed Maria's indifference, there would be no reason for her to be so mad. Therefore, the use of storyboards to contextualize translations and truth judgments provided the kind of data we needed for our semantic analysis. One result of using storyboards was that we could work longer than usual. As mentioned in section 2, it was common for speakers to ask for coffee or time to smoke a cigarette, or grab their cell phones when they started getting bored with a task. This distraction would happen every 15 minutes to every hour, depending on the consultant. The storyboard kept their attention for longer periods and there were fewer interruptions. It took consultants about one hour to translate all sentences related to a storyboard. Most speakers remained focused for the entire session.

So far, we have discussed some complementary methods that can make elicitation more interesting and less tiring for consultants. One drawback of these methods is the time it takes to prepare elicitations that include their use (Louie 2015). They require a lot of creativity on the part of linguists to come up with stories that provide the data they need.

Using a methodology that is more interesting and less tiring for consultants is a good beginning. Nevertheless, it does not fully guarantee that consultants will pay attention to contexts. As we mentioned in section 2, there are many external factors that influence fieldwork such as bad timing, aptitude of consultants, or

---

20 This task was elicited with another consultant who had not heard the original story of storyboard. The story makes it clear that Maria does not want José to buy the motorcycle. The consultant who hears the story could favor the first reading, since this is the one it appears in the storyboard. Thus, in some cases, linguists cannot use the same storyboards for subsequent truth judgment tasks.

linguists not being one hundred percent fluent in the contact language, etc. Linguists should be prepared for such factors; this is where complementary methods enter the scene.

4 Training sessions and control sentences as complementary methods

Making elicitation more interesting for consultants is a step in the right direction, but it does not guarantee that the consultants' level of attention will always be high. The predisposition of consultants on a given day depends on many external factors that are outside fieldworkers' control. Therefore, we propose that linguists should employ a variety of complementary techniques. These techniques will give linguists metadata on consultants' attention when they perform certain tasks. As a result, fieldworkers will be able to evaluate the reliability of their data. In this section, we argue for the benefits of adopting training sessions and control conditions in semantic fieldwork. These methods are commonly used in psycholinguistic experiments involving children. Schmitt and Miller (2010: 38–39) mention that:

> Experiments need both target and control conditions [...] Experimental sentences in the target conditions(s) assess the linguist structure(s) that are of interest to the researcher. Experimental sentences in the control condition(s) ensure that any result in the experimental condition is due to the linguistic variable under study rather than some issue to the task procedure.
>
> In order to ensure that subjects, especially young children, understand the task procedure, it is important to have an initial training phase or a set of practice items at the beginning of the experiment. The number of training items will depend on the difficulty of the task procedure.

The problems faced by fieldworkers are similar to those faced by linguists who are working with children. Depending on their age and how complex the task is, the data from the experiment may be unreliable because the children did not understand what they were supposed to do. Studies on psycholinguistics use techniques to provide feedback on children's degree of attention and their understanding of the tasks: training sessions and control conditions (Crain and Thornton 1998; Schmitt and Miller 2010). Training sessions, as the name suggests, are sessions that involve tasks similar to those that consultants will be asked to complete. Control conditions in a linguistic experiment are situations for which researchers know the answers. They are there to provide feedback on speakers' understanding of the task and of their attention level. We argue that, since working with indigenous consultants poses problems that are similar problems to those faced by psycholinguists, we should implement psycholinguistics methods in our fieldwork.[21]

The relevance of training consultants for a certain task has already been brought up in publications discussing semantics fieldwork. Burton and Matthewson (2015) point out that it is important for a consultant to repeat the storyboard and be trained in telling the story before doing it for real. Vander Klok and Conners (2019) also argue for the use of training sessions when eliciting data through questionnaires.

Training sessions should precede the elicitation. After the relevant instructions, the consultants go through a session in which the task is the same as the one in the elicitation session but involves only control sentences/contexts. This way, the fieldworker can verify whether the consultants understand the task.

We here illustrate how to go about a training session by describing our fieldwork on tense in Karitiana. The language has a future vs. non-future tense system (Storto 2002). An important question concerning this kind of system is whether the non-future tense is an ambiguous marker (meaning either present or past) or an underspecified marker (meaning both present and past at the same time). Matthewson (2006) and Jóhannsdóttir and Matthewson (2008) investigated two native Canadian languages – St'át'imcets (Lillooet Salish) and Gitxsan (Tsimshianic). These two languages also encode non-futurity in their tense systems. Thus, the authors faced the same question about the non-future tense that we faced for Karitiana. In order to answer that question, these authors used a truth judgment task. The consultants had to judge whether the sentences uttered after the presented context were true. The context and its correspondent sentence are illustrated below.

(8) Context: "Last year, John didn't go fishing, so he had no dried salmon last winter. Then summer came, and he went fishing. He got a lot of dried salmon. Fred didn't go fishing then, so Fred has no dried salmon now."[22]
(wa7) zúqw-cen s-John múta7 s-Fred
(IPFV) die-foot NOM-John and NOM-Fred
'John and Fred were/are starving.' (not at the same time)
(Matthewson 2006: 22)

---

[21] The cause of the problems may be different. In a psycholinguistic experiment, a child may not understand a task due to lack of maturity, whereas for fieldwork with indigenous consultants, the misunderstandings may be due to the consultants or the linguist not being 100% fluent in the contact language.
[22] The contexts were presented in St'át'imcets (Lillooet Salish). We have used their English translations to save space.

The fact that a sentence such as in (8) comes out as true in a context in which the described eventuality occurs both in the past and in the present shows that the non-future tense in the language under investigation is underspecified. We decided to investigate the semantics of the non-future tense in Karitiana using the same kind of truth judgment tests, as illustrated below.

(9) Context: "A professora Luciana estava em Porto Velho mês passado, mas ela já foi embora. Depois da Luciana ir embora, a Ana chegou e está na cidade neste momento." Nesta situação, você poderia dizer "Luciana Ana naakat iakat Porto Velho pip?"
'Professor Luciana was in town (Porto Velho) last month, but she has already left. After Luciana left, Ana arrived and she is in the city right now." In this situation, can you say "Luciana Ana naakat iakat Porto Velho pip?"'
Luciana Ana Ø-naakat   i-aka-t   Porto Velho pip
Luciana Ana 3-DEC-COP-NFUT   3-COP-ADV   Porto Velho in
#"Luciana and Ana were/are in Porto Velho." (not at the same time)
(Müller and Ferreira 2020: 14)

In order to avoid the problems described in section 2, we developed a training session with 10 context/sentence pairs. Some of the sentences were true in the context, as illustrated by context/sentence pair (10) below. They represented half of the training session (five pairs of context/sentences). We also included five sentences that could be judged true, but were not grammatical, as illustrated by sentence (11). Sentence (11) is ungrammatical because the word "kytopo" should be marked for oblique case, as in "kytopoty", since the verb "iengyt" is intransitive in the language.

(10) Context: Uma cobra aparece na casa. Inácio mata essa cobra. Você usaria "Inácio naokyt boroja"[23] para descrever essa situação?
'A snake appears in the house. Inácio kills this snake. Would you use "Inácio naokyt boroja" to describe this situation?'
( ) Sim ( ) Não
 'Yes'   'No'

---

23 Inácio Ø-na-oky-t   boroja.
   Inácio 3-DECL-kill-NFUT snake
   'Inácio killed the snake'

(11) Context: Mauro bebeu muita chicha ontem na festa e vomitou.
Você usaria "Mauro naakat iengyt kytopo" nessa situação?²⁴
'Mauro drank a lot of chicha (A drink prepared for celebrations and rituals using fermentation) yesterday at the party and vomited. Would you use "Mauro naakat iengyt kytopo" in this situation?'
( ) Sim ( ) Não
    Yes   No

There were also pairs in which the sentences were grammatical but not true, as illustrated in examples (1) and (2) in section 2. In these cases, the context states that Inácio killed a snake, and the sentence in the target language says that he killed a jaguar. Another example of mismatch is illustrated in examples (3) and (4) in section 2, in which the context describes a future event, but the sentence in the target language is marked for the non-future.

Since the linguist knows the appropriate answers to all the context/sentence pairs presented in a training session, he/she is able to find out whether consultants understood their task. In case of poor performance, they may also be able to find out what the problem was. For example, in our training session for the investigation of the meaning of the non-future in Karitiana, the perfect scenario was the one in which a consultant answered YES to the sentences that were both grammatical and true, such as in (8), and rejected all the others. If the consultant rejected only the ungrammatical sentences, we would be able to conclude that they were giving grammatical judgments instead of truth condition judgments. If they consistently accepted sentences (3), (5), and (9), we would know that they were not paying enough attention.

A total of five consultants participated in in individual one-on-one training sessions.²⁵ Both the linguist and the consultant sat in front of the computer. Contexts were then presented through Google Forms. We read the context out aloud to the consultants. The consultants answered the question orally and the linguist marked 'yes' or 'no' according to their answers. Table 1 presents the percentage of correct answers for each consultant.

---

24 *Mauro Ø-na-aka-t   i-engy-t   kytopo.
Mauro   3- DECL-cop-NFUT   3-vomit-ADV   chicha
'Mauro has vomited chicha.'

25 For this research, we have worked with 11 consultants, but not all of them answered the questionnaire about tense. The complete training session is available in Ferreira (2022).

Table 1: Consultant correct answer rates.[26]

	Context 1	Context 2	Context 3	Context 4	Context 5	
Consultant 3	yes	no	no	yes	no	
Consultant 5	yes	yes	yes	yes	yes	
Consultant 9	yes	yes	no	yes	no	
Consultant 10	yes	no	no	yes	yes	
Consultant 11	yes	no	no	yes	no	
	Context 6	Context 7	Context 8	Context 9	Context 10	Rate
Consultant 3	yes	no	no	yes	no	100%
Consultant 5	yes	no	yes	yes	no	60%
Consultant 9	no	no	no	yes	no	80%
Consultant 10	yes	no	no	yes	no	90%
Consultant 11	yes	no	yes	yes	no	90%

Experimental psycholinguists recommend creating a small training session of around five items. In our case, short training sessions with only five items would not be enough to train our consultants. Our training session had ten items and, by the end of the session, there were still consultants who had problems to understand the task such as consultant 5 in the table above. For experiments with children, short training sessions might not be a problem because children are often dismissed (Crain and Thornton 1998) if they do not do well in those short training sessions. Thus, these short sessions are used more as a filter than as a training method *per se*. Proper training would involve explaining the task one more time to the consultants who performed badly and running another training session.

What do we do when a consultant does not do well on the training session, as was the case for Consultant 5? When this happens with children, they are often dismissed from the study (Crain and Thornton 1998). However, dismissing a consultant after just a few questions could lead to a political problem with the tribe, depending on who the consultant is. We decided to go through all the context/sentence pairs with all the consultants and used the control conditions to monitor their performance.[27]

---

26 The wrong answers are marked in red.
27 One option might be to have a backup training session so the linguist can explain the instructions again and apply the backup training session only for those cases. Unfortunately, we did not anticipate the need for a backup training session. So, we do not know how effective it is to repeat the instructions one more time and reapply another training session.

The control conditions were context/sentence pairs similar to those used in the training session. They presented true grammatical sentences, false and grammatical sentences, and true and ungrammatical sentences. They were spread throughout the task (for every 10 context/sentence pairs, three were control pairs). Having control sentences throughout the entire elicitation session was important. The fact that a consultant did well on the training session does not guarantee that he/she would not get bored or fatigued in the middle of the session. Here is the overall rate for the consultants using the control sentences:

Table 2: Consultant correct answer rates.

	Context 1	Context 2	Context 3	Context 4	Context 5
Consultant 3	yes	no	no	yes	no
Consultant 5	yes	yes	no	yes	no
Consultant 9	yes	no	no	yes	no
Consultant 10	yes	yes	no	no	no
Consultant 11	yes	no	no	no	no
	Context 6	Context 7	Context 8	Context 9	Rate
Consultant 3	no	yes	no	no	100%
Consultant 5	no	yes	yes	yes	66%
Consultant 9	no	yes	no	no	100%
Consultant 10	no	yes	no	no	77%
Consultant 11	no	yes	no	no	88%

The training session seemed to have a positive impact on consultant 9, who started hesitantly but, by the time the training session was over, was comfortable with the task. Her answers to the control sentences showed her improvement. Nevertheless, overall the training sessions did not seem to improve the consultants' rate of correct answers. Consultant 5 performed poorly in both the training session and the control sentences; Consultant 3 had outstanding performance in both the training session and the control sentences.

So far, we have discussed the implementation of control methods for traditional context/sentence pair elicitations. For the story arc method, we used a different control method, which was a true or false test to be applied immediately after the presentation of the story. As mentioned in section 2, not all Karitiana speakers have the same fluency in Portuguese. Therefore, we developed this true or false test in the communication language as a way to verify how much of the context the consultant had absorbed. For instance, after presenting the storyboard in Figure 2, the speaker had to complete the following test:[28]

According to the story you just heard, mark (T) if the sentence is true or (F) if the sentence is false.	
Antônio wants to sell his car.	( )
Antônio wants to sell his motorcycle.	( )
José wants the motorcycle.	( )
José wants the car.	( )
Maria does not want José to buy the car.	( )
Maria does not want José to buy the motorcycle.	( )

Two consultants heard seven storyboards and answered true or false questions, which was our control method. The control was carried out after the consultants had finished the contextualized translations or the truth judgment tasks described in section 2. Table 3 shows a comparison of the results of these two consultants on these tests. We then determined their attention level based on how many correct answers they gave on the tests. The true or false questionnaire had six sentences. If the consultant answered three of them correctly, we would conclude that they were probably guessing, since they did achieve a rate of attention of 50%. The results for each consultant are presented in the table below.

Table 3: Consultants' rate control 2.

Storyboard	Consultant 4	Consultant 5
1	61%	88%
2	54%	67%
3	38%	84%
4	70%	75%
5	–	90%
6	46%	74%
7	58%	91%
TOTAL	54%	81%

As can be observed, the control test was able to provide information about how much the consultants had grasped from the story. What the table above shows is

---

28 The test was, of course, presented in the contact language – Portuguese.

that Consultant 5 had a good understanding of the context that was presented to him, whereas Consultant 4 did not. This indicates that Consultant 4 either did not understand the stories or did not pay attention to them. Independent of what was causing it, what is important is that the data from contextualized translations from this consultant should count as mere translations, and the data from the truth judgment task should not be considered at all.

We also believe that the true or false questions we used as a control method can be used, not only as a control method, but as motivators, contributing to increasing speaker attention levels. Some consultants started to pay much more attention after completing the first round of tests. Some even asked to go back to the slides to reread the story independently one more time before we proceeded to the questions. Based on his/her poor performance, we decided not to consider data provided by Consultant 5 (Tables 2 and 3) in our analysis of tense in Karitiana. Moreover, when consultants disagreed on a judgment, we checked the metadata before opting for an analysis. If Consultant 5 and Consultant 10 answered 'yes', and Consultant 3 and Consultant 9 answered 'no' to the same question, the fact that the latter paid more attention than the former is something that we took into account. How much weight should be given to such results is a question each linguist has to answer based on their fieldwork experience. These methods proved very fruitful in letting us know how confident we could be about the data we elicited.

5 Technology and fieldwork

This section describes how certain virtual tools can be used to help semanticists in preparing for fieldwork and in facilitating linguistic analyses. We report our experience with online forms that have gained popularity as tools for collecting data. These forms allow linguists to create questionnaires and store them on the Internet, so that anyone with a computer available and access to the Internet will be able to answer the questions from the elicitation. We argue that there are advantages in the use of these forms, even in face-to-face, one-on-one fieldwork settings. There are websites that enable the creation of forms. We present examples of some of the tools offered by these websites using Google Forms, which is the form builder from Google.[29]

Before presenting some of the tools a form can offer, we start by pointing out that online forms, as the name suggests, stay online. Thus, they can only be implemented as an elicitation method if linguists have access to the Internet in the field.

---

[29] One may access it through <https://www.google.com/forms/about/>.

In our case, it is only possible to make use of online forms when we work with the Karitiana people at the University of São Paulo, or when we work with them in Porto Velho city. Even though there is access to the Internet in their village, their electricity comes from generators that are only turned on at night. For this reason, there is no stable Internet connection and, therefore, it is not feasible to use online forms.

One of the useful tools that Google Forms provides is that it automatically saves the data on Google Drive. Therefore, the data is very safely stored; if something happens to a researcher's computer, the data can be easily retrieved by another computer.[30] Let us illustrate the use of online forms with the truth judgment task concerning tense in Karitiana. This task was entirely created using Google Forms. We start it with an identification section, as illustrated in Figure 3 below.

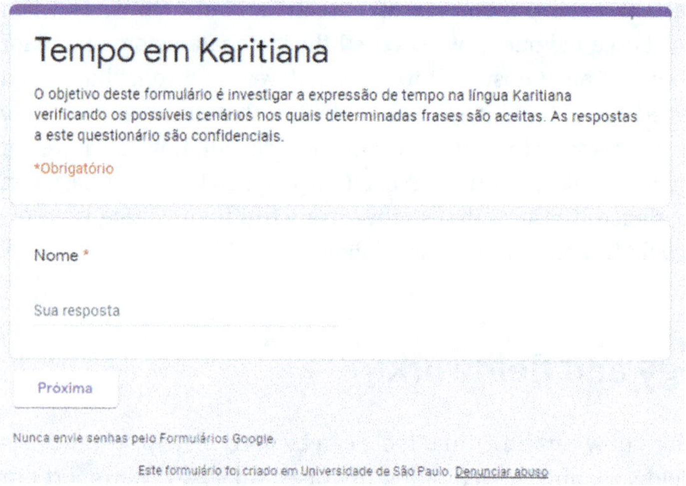

Tempo em Karitiana

O objetivo deste formulário é investigar a expressão de tempo na língua Karitiana verificando os possíveis cenários nos quais determinadas frases são aceitas. As respostas a este questionário são confidenciais.

*Obrigatório

Nome *

Sua resposta

Próxima

Nunca envie senhas pelo Formulários Google.

Este formulário foi criado em Universidade de São Paulo. Denunciar abuso

Figure 3: Online form identification section.[31]

---

[30] This was one important point that made us choose Google Forms. The University of São Paulo has an agreement with Google to provide its professors and students with unlimited space on Google Drive. When using Google Forms, we do not have to worry about space. We recommend that linguists do research on form builders and choose those that are the most adequate according to their fieldwork conditions.

[31] Translation: Tense in Karitiana
This form's purpose is to investigate tense expression in Karitiana's language verifying the possible scenarios in which some sentences are accepted. The answers to this questionnaire are confidential.
*Compulsory
Name*: Your answer
Next

This introductory section provides information about the elicitation to consultants and, at the same time, is used to obtain some metadata, such as the consultant's name and the date of their registration. Linguists can ask more questions (e.g., age, gender, etc.) if relevant for the research they are conducting. Including an introductory section to collect metadata is relevant, since "such information makes it possible to interpret the data with a finer-grained approach than perhaps anticipated" (Vander Klok and Conners 2020: 90). For instance, Storto (2002) argues that the Karitiana verbal prefix *pyn-* has a deontic use. Ferreira (2017) investigated deontic modality in the language. Contrary to expectations, the *pyn-* prefix did not appear spontaneously in his data. Instead, consultants used a modal verb *pydn*. Ferreira's (2017) hypothesis was that, since Storto's data came from narratives and her consultants were much older, the deontic prefix *pyn-* was becoming archaic and was only used by elders in traditional narratives. This conclusion was made possible because the metadata on consultants' ages was available.

Another relevant tool is a test mode that Google Forms allow us to create. This test is illustrated in Figure 4 below. Once the test mode is activated, linguists can go to their control conditions and mark the appropriate answers, as illustrated in Figures 5 and 6.

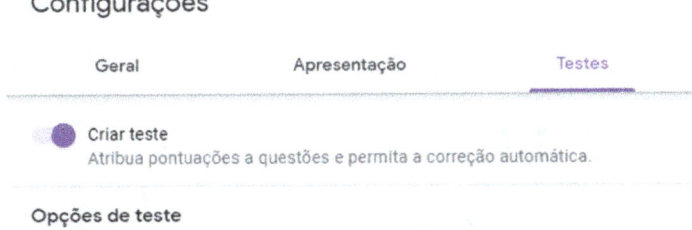

Figure 4: Test mode activation.[32]

---

32 Translation:
Settings
General Presentation Tests
Create test
Attribute scores to the questions and allow automatic correction.

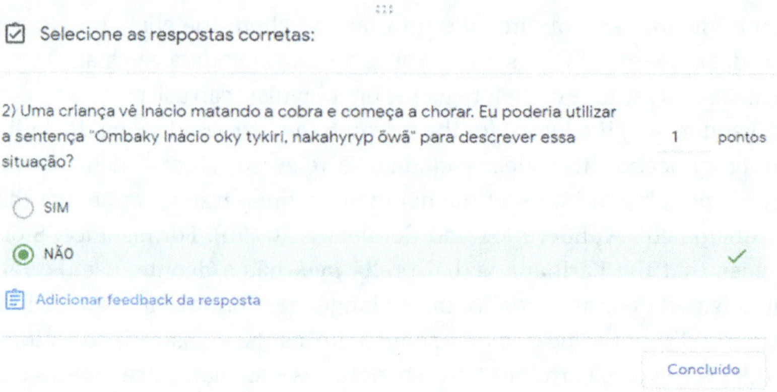

☑ Selecione as respostas corretas:

2) Uma criança vê Inácio matando a cobra e começa a chorar. Eu poderia utilizar a sentença "Ombaky Inácio oky tykiri, nakahyryp õwã" para descrever essa situação?   1   pontos

○ SIM

◉ NÃO   ✓

📋 Adicionar feedback da resposta

Concluído

Figure 5: Selecting the appropriate answer.[33]

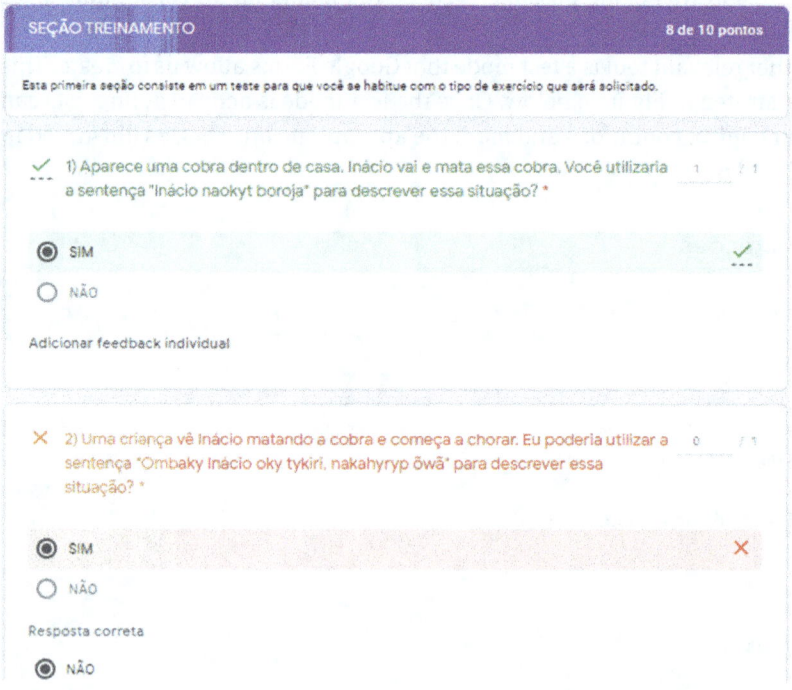

Figure 6: Control score.[34]

---

33 We presented the translation for this question when we discussed example (1).
34 The translations of (1) and (2) in Figure 6 were presented in examples (10) and (1), respectively.

5) As professoras Luciana e Ana estão na cidade de Porto Velho agora. Então você consegue uma carona para a cidade e começa a se arrumar. Quando sua mãe te pergunta quem está na cidade, você usaria a sentença "Luciana Ana naakat iakat Porto Velho pip" para falar que Luciana e Ana estão na cidade?

5 respostas

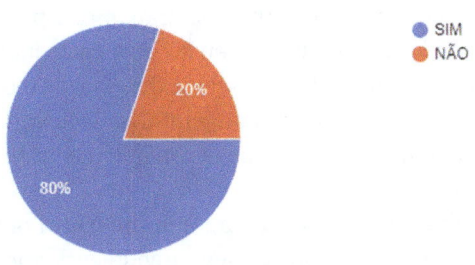

6) A professora Luciana estava na cidade mês passado, mas já foi embora. Depois que a Luciana foi embora, a Ana chegou e está na cidade agora. Nessa situação você usaria a sentença "Luciana Ana naakat iakat Porto Velho pip" ?

5 respostas

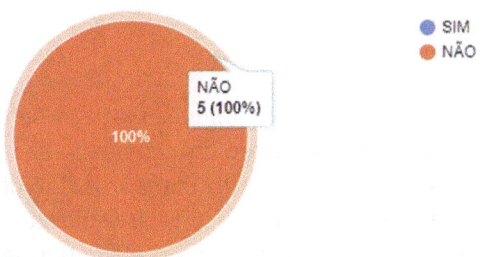

Figure 7: Graphs generated by Google Forms.

Once the test is created, a score is available immediately after each elicitation session. It shows the consultant's total score for a given questionnaire, and their score for each section. Thus, combining the control procedures described in the previous subsection with the tools described in this subsection provides fieldworkers with an easy and fast way of assessing consultants' performance in the training session and control conditions that the linguist has developed.[35]

---

35 The score of the training sessions and control conditions from the elicitation sessions on tense were not communicated or discussed with the consultants.

One last aspect of Google Forms that can facilitate linguists' work is the ability of the forms to automatically generate statistical graphs from consultants' answers, as illustrated in Figure 7 below. We do not claim that it necessarily makes sense to analyze fieldwork data statistically. A quantitative analysis is not feasible for many communities due to the low number of speakers (see Bochnak and Matthewson (2015) for relevant discussion). Nevertheless, graphs can provide linguists with visual representations of consultants' consensus on a given judgment.

Linguists tend to use online forms only if they have to collect data from a large group in a virtual setting. We recommend that fieldwork linguists become familiar with tools such as Google Forms and make use of them in a variety of fieldwork environments.

We have argued that there are advantages in the use of online forms even in face-to-face/one-on-one settings, since they provide easy and fast access to the data and metadata. Having fast feedback may be vital for linguists who stay in the community for a short period of time. They need to decide whether consultants are adequate for their corresponding tasks. Moreover, Google Forms tend to make elicitations more interesting for the consultants, since working with a computer adds novelty to the fieldwork.

6 Final remarks

This chapter presented a number of techniques that can be used to elicit data during semantics fieldwork. We discussed how contextualizing many sentences in a single-story arc, as we have done with the use of storyboards, tends to be more effective than creating one context for each sentence of a questionnaire (Louie 2015). We argued that this approach makes elicitation sessions more interesting and less tiring for consultants. We also showed that training sessions and control conditions are interesting tools to assess whether consultants are good at certain tasks. These methods are also able to give feedback on consultants' attention levels/understanding of the tasks. We illustrated how true/false tests can be used with storyboards as a control technique. Lastly, we discussed the use of technologies during fieldwork. We argued that online forms, such as Google Forms, provide tools that help linguists control the quality of their data.

All the techniques suggested in this chapter can be used at the same time. Storyboards, for instance, can be used to make contextualized translations and truth judgment tasks more interesting. They can be combined with tests in to control consultants' levels of attention. Online form tools, on the other hand, can be combined with control methods to make control conditions easier to track.

They provide us with a way to check the reliability of our data and facilitate linguistic analysis, with more transparent results for linguists.

References

Bochnak, Ryan & Lisa Matthewson. 2015. Introduction. In Ryan Bochnak & Lisa Matthewson (eds.), *Methodologies in semantic fieldwork,* 1–10. Oxford: Oxford University Press.

Bochnak, Ryan & Lisa Matthewson. 2020. Techniques in complex semantic fieldwork. *Annual review of linguistics* 6 (1). 261–283.

Burton, Strang & Lisa Matthewson. 2015. Targeted construction storyboards in semantic fieldwork. In Ryan Bochnak & Lisa Matthewson (eds.), *Methodologies in semantic fieldwork,* 135–156. Oxford: Oxford University Press.

Comrie, Bernard, Martin Haspelmath & Balthasar Bickel. 2015. The Leipzig glossing rules: Conventions for interlinear morpheme-by-morpheme glosses. *Department of Linguistics of the Max Planck Institute for Evolutionary Anthropology and the Department Linguistics of the University of Leipzig.* https://www.eva.mpg.de/lingua/resources/glossing-rules.php (accessed 08 August 2020).

Crain, Stephen & Rosalind Thornton. 1998. *Investigations in universal grammar – A guide to experiments on the acquisition of syntax and semantics.* Cambridge: The MIT Press.

Ferreira, Luiz Fernando. 2022. *Tempo e aspecto na expressão de contrafactualidade: Uma análise a partir de línguas de sistemas temporais distintos* [Tense and aspect in counterfactuality expression: An analysis with languages with distinct temporal systems]. São Paulo: University of São Paulo dissertation.

Ferreira, Luiz Fernando. 2020. Modalidade bulética em Karitiana [Bouletic modality in Karitiana]. *Cadernos de Linguística* 1 (2). 1–19.

Ferreira, Luiz Fernando. 2017. *Modo em Karitiana* [Mood in Karitiana]. São Paulo: University of São Paulo MA thesis.

Von Fintel, Kai. 2006. Modality and language. In, Donald M. Borchert (ed.). *Encyclopedia of Philosophy,* 2 edn., 1–16. Detroit: MacMillan Reference USA.

Von Fintel, Kai & Irene Heim. 2020. Intensional semantics. *Unpublished lecture notes.*

Von Fintel, Kai & Sabine Iatridou. 2017. The linguistics of desire. First handout for the seminar 'The linguistics of desire'.

Jóhannsdóttir, Kristin M. & Lisa Matthewson. 2008. Zero-marked tense: The case of Gitxsan. In Željko Bošković, Suzi Lima, Kevin Mullin & Brian Smith (eds.), *NELS 37: Proceedings of the 37th annual meeting of the North East Linguistic Society,* 299–310. Urbana-Champaign: University of Illinois.

Louie, Meagan. 2015. The problem with nononsense elicitation plans for semantic fieldwork. In Ryan Bochnak & Lisa Matthewson (eds.), *Methodologies in semantic fieldwork,* 47–71. Oxford: Oxford University Press.

Matthewson, Lisa. 2004. On the methodology of semantic fieldwork. *International Journal of American linguistics* 70. 369–415.

Matthewson, Lisa. 2006. Temporal semantics in a superficially tenseless language. *Linguistics and Philosophy* 29. 673–713.

Müller, Ana & Luiz Fernando Ferreira. 2020. O sistema aspecto-temporal da língua Karitiana [Karitiana's temporal and aspectual system]. *Cadernos de Estudos Linguísticos* 62. https://periodicos.sbu.unicamp.br/ojs/index.php/cel/article/view/8658731 (accessed 08 August 2020).

Sanchez-Mendes, Luciana. 2014. Trabalho de campo para análise linguística em semântica formal [Fieldwork for linguistic analysis in formal semantics]. *Revista Letras* 90. http://dx.doi.org/10.5380/rel.v90i2.36278 (accessed 08 August 2020).

Schmitt, Cristina & Karen Miller. 2010. Using comprehension methods in language acquisition research. In Elma Blom & Sharon Unsworth (eds.), *Experimental methods in language acquisition research*, 35–56. Amsterdam & Philadelphia: John Benjamins.

Storto, Luciana Raccanello. 2002. Algumas categorias funcionais em Karitiana [Some functional categories in Karitiana]. In Ana Suelly Arruda Câmara Cabral & Aryon Dall'Igna Rodrigues (eds.), *Atas do Encontro internacional de grupos de trabalho sobre línguas indígenas. Línguas indígenas brasileiras: Fonologia, gramática e história*, 151–164. Belém: Editora Universitária.

Storto, Luciana Raccanello & Ivan Rocha. 2018. Inventário sociolinguístico da língua Karitiana [Sociolinguistic inventory of Karitiana language]. *INDL (Inventário Nacional da Diversidade Linguística)*, IPHAN-MPEG.

Vander Klok, Jozina. 2019. Exploring modality and temporality interactions through the storyboard Bill vs. the weather. *Semantic Fieldwork Methods* 1. 1–29.

Vander Klok, Jozina & Thomas J. Conners. 2019. Using questionnaires as a tool for comparative linguistic field research: Two case studies on Javanese. In Aimée Lahaussois & Marine Vuillermet (eds.), *Methodological tools for linguistic description and typology*, 62–96. (Language Documentation & Conservation Special Publication 16.) Honolulu: University of Hawai'i Press. http://hdl.handle.net/10125/24858.

Vivanco, Karin Camolese. 2014. *Orações relativas em Karitiana: Um estudo experimental* [Relative clauses in Karitiana: An experimental study]. São Paulo: University of São Paulo MA thesis.

Vivanco, Karin Camolese. 2018. *Perguntas qu-, orações subordinadas e ordem de palavras em Karitiana* [Wh- questions, embedded clauses, and word order in Karitiana]. São Paulo: University of São Paulo dissertation.

Zahra Kolagar & Jozina Vander Klok
2 Studying modality through targeted construction storyboards

Abstract: This chapter details how modality can be studied using targeted construction storyboards, both within a language as well as a cross-linguistic tool. We discuss the insights as well as challenges of using storyboards in general in fieldwork, and underline its usefulness to investigate the semantics of modal expressions. We illustrate this method by introducing two storyboards, *The delicious lunch* and *The poetry contest*, designed to elicit specific modality types and modal force, and through its application to Tabari (Caspian, Indo-Iranian; Iran). Through discussion of the results on modality in Tabari, our findings reinforce the view that targeted construction storyboards are an important tool in semantic fieldwork, and we advocate for its use in research on modality in particular.

1 Introduction

Since the introduction of targeted construction storyboards by Burton and Matthewson (2015), this method has been a valuable tool within the field linguistics toolkit, especially for semantic fieldwork. This chapter advocates for the use of this method in research on modality; that is, the study of possibility or necessity claims in natural language, such as with *may* or *must* in English. Towards this goal, we introduce two new storyboards, *The delicious lunch* (Kolagar 2018a) and *The poetry contest* (Kolagar 2018b), designed to target potential distinctions

---

Acknowledgments: We would like to thank the Tabari language consultants for their time, and having fun doing the storyboards with the first author! We also thank two reviewers for their insightful comments. The research presented in this chapter was conducted while Zahra Kolagar was studying at Eberhard Karls University of Tübingen, Germany, and is part of her MA thesis presented to the Department of English Linguistics. We thank the Athene grant (#4041002837, awarded to Vera Hohaus) for partial funding support of the MA thesis. Jozina Vander Klok conducted this research while at the University of Oslo, Norway.

Zahra Kolagar, Fraunhofer Institute of Integrated Circuits IIS, Am Wolfsmantel 33, 91058 Erlangen, e-mail: zahra.kolagar@iis.fraunhofer.de
Jozina Vander Klok, Humboldt-Universität zu Berlin, Unter den Linden 6, 10117 Berlin, e-mail: jozina.vander.klok@hu-berlin.de

across modal flavours and modal force in modal expressions in a given language. We illustrate the usefulness of this method through the results of these two storyboards as applied to Tabari (Indo-Iranian, Indo-European), an underdescribed Caspian language spoken in Iran, as well as more generally, in how this method and these storyboards can be applied cross-linguistically. From a methodological perspective, this chapter also takes into account the challenges and solutions of using storyboards discussed in the literature as well as encountered and addressed in our own fieldwork experience. We believe that these discussions are necessary as a way for future researchers to be prepared in their own field linguistic research.

This chapter is organized as follows. In section 2, we first outline what are targeted construction storyboards following Burton and Matthewson (2015), and describe the benefits and challenges of this methodology. In section 3, we address how they can be a useful tool in field research on modality in particular. We then introduce the storyboards *The delicious lunch* and *The poetry contest* in section 4, showing which types of modal expressions these storyboards are designed to elicit. Section 5 is a case study of these storyboards based on the results from Tabari, including background information on the Tabari language and its modal system, the procedure employed with speakers, and how the data results compared to our hypotheses based on the storyboard design. Section 6 concludes.

To illustrate how the full storyboards were narrated in Tabari, we have also included transcribed versions of both storyboards as appendices: Appendix A is a version of *The delicious lunch*, and Appendix B is a version of *The poetry contest* as told by one Tabari speaker.

2 Targeted construction storyboards for research on modality

2.1 What are targeted construction storyboards?

Targeted construction storyboards were first developed by researchers at the University of British Columbia as part of the Totem Field Storyboards project, lead by Strang Burton and Lisa Matthewson. As defined by Burton and Matthewson (2015), a targeted construction storyboard is a narrative illustrated by a set of pictures that is designed to elicit some linguistic phenomena as based on a specific hypothesis. They combine the elicitation of a picture-based narrative (hence, they are *storyboards*) with a hypothesis-based inquiry about the relation between linguistic forms and a specific context (hence, they have a *targeted construction*). In the following, we will refer to targeted construction storyboards as "storyboards" for short.

The methodological procedure that Burton and Matthewson (2015: 146–147) propose for storyboards embodies the combination of the spontaneous speech of a narrative with hypothesis-based research. They propose that the linguist first tells the storyboard to the speaker in a contact language (a language shared by both the linguist and the speaker). The speaker can optionally practice telling the story in the target language, and once they are comfortable, the narration of the storyboard by the speaker is then recorded by the linguist. After the story-telling, the linguist can follow-up with additional questions, eliciting positive or negative data as based on the hypotheses of the storyboard and the results of the narration. We follow this procedure in implementing the storyboards *The delicious lunch* and *The poetry contest* with Tabari speakers, as described in section 5.

2.2 What makes targeted construction storyboards useful?

The linguistic benefits of using of storyboards in collecting semantic data are tremendous, as storyboards provide an opportunity to gather spontaneous utterances without potential contact language or translation-based influences (Burton and Matthewson 2015: 138–139). In this way, they have the same advantage of elicited narrative tools based on visual cues in that they produce spontaneous speech, such as with *The pear story* as based on a six-minute film by Chafe (1980) or *The frog story* as based on the picture book *Frog, where are you?* by Mayer (1969) (see examples in Berman and Slobin (2013)). In addition to avoiding possible linguistic interference of a contact language, storyboards also share the advantages of narratives like *The frog story* in eliciting connected speech and enabling potential cross-linguistic comparison (Klamer and Moro 2020: 239).

But unlike the latter elicited narratives, storyboards are specifically designed to test how a given language expresses some linguistic phenomena in a specific discourse context (Burton and Matthewson 2015: 136). This is useful in collecting many kinds of linguistic data, including data that is sensitive to information structure or data requiring a linguistic antecedent across clauses. Furthermore, in their proposed structure for storyboards, Burton and Matthewson (2015: 145) argue that there should be iterations of the targeted linguistic construction in case of unintentional ungrammaticality due to lexical idiosyncrasies. The narrative pattern builds in the opportunity for the linguist to obtain multiple instances of the targeted construction, and thus rigorous results. We outline the overall narrative pattern of storyboards in section 4, in connection with *The delicious lunch* and *The poetry contest*.

As part of confirming or disproving the hypotheses concerning the targeted constructions within the storyboard, the narration of a storyboard can also be followed by elicitation tasks. As described by Burton and Matthewson (2015: 137), these tasks following the storyboard narration allow for the collection of negative data, which are an important part of semantic fieldwork in that it allows the linguist to understand the constraints of what sentences can mean and in which discourse contexts they are felicitous. We also add that these follow-up tasks can also reveal ungrammatical sentences due to the syntactic structure of the language; thus, the responses of the speakers to the negative data should be carefully analyzed. We refer the reader to Matthewson (2004) and Davis, Gillon, and Matthewson (2015), among others, on the importance of negative data, as well as the use of different elicitation tasks including acceptability judgment tasks or truth-value judgment tasks.

Storyboards thus are designed for producing replicable, reliable, and rigorous linguistic data; identified to be three essential components of linguistic data (e.g., Featherston 2007). The data are not "uncheckable": they can be replicated within the storyboard or in follow-up elicitation, and across speakers within one language, as well as across languages; see e.g., Chen et al. (2017) for an example across languages with the storyboard *Feeding Fluffy* (TFS Working Group 2012). The data are reliable in the sense that there is less chance of "translationese" and that the linguist and the speaker both have converged on the discourse context. In this way, there is less chance that there are additional silent imagined contexts (Bochnak and Matthewson 2020). Lastly, the data are rigorous in that multiple target constructions across different lexical items are produced and tested within one storyboard.

In tandem with its linguistic benefits, storyboards are useful in fieldwork for a number of practical reasons. Storyboards are arguably more efficient when it comes to describing and establishing the discourse context because of its visual and narrative presentation (Burton and Matthewson 2015: 137–138). Relatedly, Louie (2015) also finds that creating a narrative arc — a crucial aspect of a storyboard — is helpful and efficient in elicitation tasks. Establishing a discourse context that is shared by the linguist and speaker is an essential aspect of fieldwork, and particularly for semantic and pragmatic fieldwork in which the meaning of a sentence can change depending on the discourse context. This aspect (and its challenges!) has been expounded on by many; see, among others, Matthewson (2004); Krifka (2011); Bohnemeyer (2015); Deal (2015); Bochnak and Matthewson (2020); as well as Ferreira and Müller (this volume) for discussion. We discuss this aspect in the context of studying modality in section 3.

Storyboards are also practical in their implementation. Since storyboards do not require a written version for use with speakers, they are particularly helpful for studying languages that do not have a written form or are primarily oral, or have only a scarce set of written text available for linguistic analysis. We will show in section 5 that this aspect was important in conducting fieldwork on Tabari, which is primarily an oral language. Finally, storyboards often amuse the speakers as pointed out by Burton and Matthewson (2015: 155). This aspect is further corroborated by the authors' own individual fieldwork experiences in using storyboards — it is a fun task for both the speaker and the fieldworker (Kolagar 2019; Vander Klok 2019). The use of storyboards in collecting linguistic data can provide both the speaker and the linguist with a relaxed atmosphere where the speaker does not feel pressure, for instance, as might be the case with (semi-) forced choice tasks in elicitation.

2.3 What are the challenges of targeted construction storyboards?

The preparation of a storyboard matters greatly. The linguist may be preparing a storyboard with a particular language in mind, but they should at the same time consider its usefulness as a cross-linguistic tool with an aim for replicability of data. At the same time, storyboards are often created to conform to the social rules and norms of the targeted society. In this vein, we show how *The delicious lunch* and *The poetry contest* storyboards were both designed with the socio-cultural norms in Iran in mind. If the storyboard does not conform to the social rules or norms of the targeted society, this might be a challenge for some speakers or linguists. This cross-cultural challenge has also been documented for using *The frog story* narratives (e.g., Strömqvist and Verhoeven 2004). In some cases, such issues can be circumvented by asking speakers to imagine that the context of the story takes place in another country or another world that has different cultural or social expectations. In other cases, the speakers can rename the characters in the story or imagine certain animals to be another species to conform to their own world-view. However, this may not always be possible, and care must be taken by the linguist to make sure the storyboard is respectable and does not make the speaker feel uncomfortable. After all, storyboards aim to have a fun factor!

In preparation of a storyboard, the linguist might also consider its length. On the one hand, visual stimuli aid with conveying and understanding the discourse context. On the other hand, Nouri-Hosseini (2018) maintains that storyboards could pose a heavy cognitive burden on the speaker's memory, and longer storyboards may not be as successful as shorter ones in obtaining the relevant linguistic phenomena. While a longer length may be taxing by itself, the guidelines proposed by Burton and Matthewson (2015) include iterations of the targeted construction, and such iterations would likely lessen the cognitive burden. For instance, Vander Klok (2019) reports that despite the longer length of the storyboard *Bill vs. the weather*, which has a total of 23 figures, the participants (three Javanese speakers) were all able to stay on task in retelling the narrative. Only one speaker required a prompt at one of the initial figures, and no speakers required prompts for the figures that included the targeted linguistic phenomenon. It is hard to say anything more concrete at this point, since there is no formal study thus far explicitly studying the cognitive burden of longer vs. shorter storyboards.

Another challenge concerns the practical implementation of storyboards, which can also feed into the type of data obtained. First, for the procedure outlined by Burton and Matthewson (2015) (see section 2.1), the speaker needs to have a very good grasp of the contact language. The second author faced some challenges in eliciting a storyboard with English as a contact language in an East Java village, where it turned out that one of the speakers was not able to follow the narrative in English. In that case, the second author was able to switch to a different contact language, Indonesian, but which presented a drawback in potential priming, in that some of the modal expressions that were targeted had cognates of the same form in Javanese.[1] Another way of mitigating this challenge is to allow the speaker to practice several times before recording in one session, or for the speaker to take the storyboard visuals home to go over the narrative, and then recording the storyboard in a later session. This latter method was used by Klamer and Moro (2020) in recording *The frog story* with one speaker of Teiwa (Papuan; Indonesia), and resulted in data with a higher degree of naturalness (as measured based on lexical density, tail-head linkage, and speech rate) in comparison with elicited narratives of the same story from two other Teiwa speakers who did not study the story beforehand. The approach of allowing the speaker to become familiar with the story could also be advantageous in cultures where storytelling based on books or picture stimuli is not a cultural norm (for discussion, see e.g., Klamer and Moro 2020 and Agostinho and Rech, this volume).[2] Of course, the timeline of this approach has to be considered with the available time of the linguists and speakers.

Second, a general challenge for all fieldwork tools that involve the linguist, is the challenge of the so-called "Observer's paradox" (Labov 1972), or the possible influence of the linguist on the data obtained. Within the methodological procedure of storyboards as conducted by a linguist who is an outsider of the community (and specifically one who is not a native speaker of the target language),

---

[1] See also AnderBois and Henderson (2015) for discussion of linguistic reasons why to avoid a certain language in establishing a discourse context for semantic fieldwork.

[2] A reviewer notes that a related challenge is explaining thought or speech bubbles where this is not familiar or known. We suggest that the approaches outlined here as well as in Klamer and Moro (2020) could help with this challenge.

the presence of the linguist cannot be avoided. In order to minimize the possible influence of the linguist, we suggest that the same principles used in elicitation must be mentioned in the context of storyboards. That is, explicitly telling the speakers to narrate the storyboard as if they are narrating it to a friend or family member is essential. The second author believes that this was an essential aspect in the instructions for storyboards on Javanese (Austronesian; Indonesia). Klamer and Moro (2020: 246) also find this to be an important aspect of eliciting *The frog story*, and additionally mention that the presence of other speakers of the language also have prevented speakers from using "foreigner talk". We discuss this potential challenge in the context of when the linguist herself is a native speaker of the target language in section 5.

Relatedly, it is well known that elicited narratives are considered less natural than free narratives although both produce spontaneous speech (e.g., Himmelmann 2002). Depending on what the linguist is aiming for with respect to the results and the purpose of using storyboards, the issue of "naturalness" may or may not be a challenge. While storyboards easily elicit spontaneous utterances, the question arises as to how natural the storyboard results are. Burton and Matthewson (2015: 153–154) address this question with a pilot study comparing the naturalness of an elicited storyboard vs. a free narrative. Five reviewers (all linguists) evaluated the two stories as based on measuring vocabulary choice, intonation pattern, narrative transitions, discourse sensitive items, and freedom from apparent translation interference. The pilot study results suggest that storyboard narratives were at a "...high intermediate level of naturalness, not quite as natural as speech with no prompt, but also not highly degraded from it"(Burton and Matthewson 2015: 154).

The pilot study by Burton and Matthewson (2015) left open how storyboards would compare with picture-based translation tasks in terms of naturalness. Nouri-Hosseini (2018) investigates one aspect of this using the storyboards *What matters*, (Bogal-Allbritten, Coppock, and Nouri-Hosseini 2018) and *Bake-off* (TFS Working Group 2011a). Two versions of narrating the storybords were conducted, one as following the guidelines in Burton and Matthewson (2015) without any text, and one version as a picture-aided translation task with text. In annotation of the results for faithfulness to the narrative, Nouri-Hosseini (2018) found that the picture-aided translation task rated 20% higher with the *What matters* storyboard, and 10% higher with the *Bake-off* storyboard as compared to the narration of the storyboard with no translation. Faithfulness was defined as meeting the same general truth conditional meaning as the original narrative; thus cases of unfaithful translation included misinterpretation, forgotten text, or only rough ideas (Nouri-Hosseini 2018: 19). Nouri-Hosseini (2018: 35–36) suggests that the *Bake-off* storyboard has only a 10% increase in faithfulness as a picture-aided translation task because it is already short and simple, as compared to *What matters*. Nouri-Hosseini (2018) suggests that, depending on the goals of the linguist and the target construction, if faithfulness is important, picture-aided translation tasks may be a more efficient way to conduct the storyboard.

In terms of comparison with the "naturalness" of the translation task as compared to storyboards, this aspect was not explicitly measured in Nouri-Hosseini (2018) (only qualitatively by the author who is, however, inherently biased). Thus this study cannot be directly compared to the pilot study of Burton and Matthewson (2015), and it remains an open question as to how the data of translation-based storyboards compare in naturalness to storyboards as implemented as elicited narratives (without translation).

Klamer and Moro (2020) specifically address the question of naturalness from the perspective of comparing oral free narratives with elicited narration of *The frog story*, the latter which shares a number of properties as a tool with storyboards. Based on quantitative measures on lexical density (defined as noun-pronoun ratio), the frequency of direct speech reports, tail-head linkage, and speech rate, they clearly show that elicited narratives come at a cost of less naturalness compared to free narratives. Thus, if one is creating a storyboard in which the targeted construction under study relies on any of these measures, storyboards may not be the best method. However, storyboards still have the advantage over elicited narratives like *The frog story* in that they specifically target a linguistic phenomenon. At least from the qualitative pilot study by Burton and Matthewson (2015), it seems that naturalness of storyboards is not at issue, at least plausibly in contrast to data results from elicitation. Overall, the linguist must weigh the individual advantages and disadvantages of each method in the context of their research goals before design and implementation.

3 Why use storyboards to research modality?

Modal expressions are sensitive to a number of different linguistic parameters relevant to syntax, semantics, and pragmatics, and some of these aspects may or may not be lexicalized or have a grammaticalized strategy in the language under study. Research on modal expressions therefore must be in tandem with establishing a discourse context. Storyboards are a natural choice as one of the tools in linguistic fieldwork for studying modality because storyboards lend themselves easily to creating a salient discourse context that is shared between the researcher and the speaker, with presumably less cognitive load than a written context with no images.

Descriptively speaking, modal expressions often have a specific grammatical strategy or lexicalize across two main semantic dimensions: (i) *modal force*, which includes possibility vs. necessity, and (ii) *modal flavour*, which divides into two broad semantic categories: epistemic and root modal flavours. Epistemic modality concerns claims based on someone's knowledge or deduced information. Evidentiality, which grammatically encodes the source of the information, such as direct perceptual evidence, or different types of indirect evidence (e.g., inferential, hearsay, reported) may also be included within epistemic modality according to the analysis of the evidential marker (e.g., Izvorski 1997; Matthewson, Davis, and Rullmann 2007; Huijsmans, this volume). Root modality is a broader category that subsumes deontic modality (based on a body of rules or regulations, such as "permission" or "obligation"); circumstantial modality (based on the facts of the actual world, such as "ability"); or teleological modality (based on someone's goals or aims). Bouletic modality (based on someone's desires or needs) is also often included as a type of root modality. There are many different terms on modality in use within the literature; see Portner (2009) and Narrog (2012) for an overview and comparison. See also Matthewson (2016) for an overview of different theoretical analyses of modality.

Concerning modal force, the two polar strengths correspond to possibility and necessity. Under the view that modals are quantifiers over possible worlds, a necessity modal is a universal quantifier, and a possibility modal is an existential quantifier (Kratzer 1981, 1991). In addition to these two quantificational modal forces, languages have ways of expressing different *modal strengths*, such as weak necessity or strong possibility (Kratzer 1981). The linguistic phenomena of modal strength, and the crosslinguistic ways of how languages may grammaticalize these distinctions is currently understudied.

Another aspect of modality that is important to keep in mind is its interaction with *temporality*. In Condoravdi's (2002) seminal paper on English *might have*, she shows that it is necessary to distinguish between *temporal perspective* and *temporal orientation*, where the temporal perspective is the time at which the modal claim holds, and temporal orientation is the relation between the time of the event and the temporal perspective. Building on Condoravdi (2002), one recent architecture put forward in Rullmann and Matthewson (2018) is that modals are themselves tenseless, and the temporal perspective is supplied by tense (syntactically located above modals), while the temporal perspective is supplied by aspect (syntactically located below modals) in the given language. These interactions are, again, understudied from a cross-linguistic perspective (see Reisinger, Matthewson and Rullmann, this volume, for a corpus study on this topic). Studying modality should ideally control for these different parameters.

Without storyboards, it may be taxing for both the researcher and speaker to convey the discourse context for the relevant modal and obtain judgments of sentences without the speaker or linguist silently adding to the discourse context, the speaker disregarding the discourse context, or resorting to pictures (see also, Louie 2015, and Ferreira and Müller, this volume).

A wide set of storyboards have been developed specifically for modality, indirectly supporting their usefulness. At the *Totem Field storyboards for language documentation* website, there are currently ten storyboards tagged for modality.[3] *Tübingen-Manchester elicitation materials for linguistic fieldwork*[4] also has a number of storyboards designed for studying aspects of modality, including the two under discussion in this chapter developed by the first author. In addition, the *MelaTAMP storyboards*[5] are designed for collecting data on tense, aspect, modality and polarity in Melanesia. Here we point to some examples in how storyboards have been useful in research on modality.

Burton and Matthewson (2015) have already indicated the usefulness of storyboards for research on the semantics of modality, in their illustration of this method. They draw from examples of *Chore Girl* (TFS Working Group 2011b) and *Sick Girl* (TFS Working Group 2011d), which both target the distinction in modality between circumstantial possibility ("ability"), deontic possibility ("permission") and deontic necessity ("obligation") as well as interactions with negation. One result was that in all the languages investigated except for ASL, negation scopes over the possibility modal to express "not possible (not permitted/able)" and cannot be interpreted as "possibly not" (Burton and Matthewson 2015: 150).

Chen et al. (2017) show the advantages of storyboards in studying temporal-modal interactions through eliciting past possibility epistemic claims with *Feeding Fluffy* (TFS Working Group 2012). In particular, this storyboard focuses on how a epistemic possibility claim with past temporal perspective and a present temporal orientation is expressed in a given language, responding to the claim that past temporal perspective is not possible with epistemic modals (e.g., Cinque 1999; Hacquard 2006). Chen et al. (2017) take a comparative linguistic approach, using this storyboard across twelve different languages, including English, Dutch, and German (Germanic); Mandarin (Sino-Tibetan); St'át'imcets (Northern Interior Salish); Northern Straits Salish and Halkomelem (Central Salish); Gitksan (Tsimshianic); Blackfoot (Algonquian); Javanese and Atayal (Austronesian); and Ktunaxa (Isolate). Vander Klok (2019) additionally highlights the use of story-

---

3 See <http://www.totemfieldstoryboards.org/tags/modality/>
4 See <https://fieldworkhub.wordpress.com/>
5 See <https://wikis.hu-berlin.de/melatamp/Elicitation_materials>

boards in eliciting modal-temporal interactions, and shows how language-internal evidence can help in disambiguating modal claims (in this case, between a epistemic possibility claim with a past temporal perspective and future temporal orientation, and a past counterfactual claim, which differs minimally in having a circumstantial modal base instead of an epistemic one).

Storyboards have been in use for research on modality since their development, and have been gaining in use, but may not yet be a standard tool for cross-linguistic use. This chapter further supports the benefits of the storyboard methodology to research modality (and especially for underdescribed languages) by illustrating the application of two new storyboards.

4 Two storyboards for studying modality

This section introduces the storyboards *The delicious lunch* (Kolagar 2018a) and *The poetry contest* (Kolagar 2018b), wherein the handdrawn images and narrative text were designed and created by the first author. *The delicious lunch* targets the modal force distinction between the expression of epistemic possibility and epistemic necessity, while *The poetry contest* targets the distinction between deontic possibility and deontic weak necessity among other root modal distinctions.

Both follow the narrative structure guidelines for a targeted construction storyboard proposed by Burton and Matthewson (2015: 143–146) (as also outlined in section 2.1). Each storyboard first opens by introducing the characters involved. Second, a series of events leads up to the targeted linguistic phenomenon, and this targeted construction is reiterated to potentially avoid pitfalls due to lexical idiosyncrasies. The storyboard then ends with an engaging conclusion, adding to the fun factor.

These storyboards were initially designed for use with eliciting modality expressions in Tabari (Caspian, Indo-Iranian) as spoken in Iran. Thus, the setting is Iranian, and the details in the pictures follow the local social norms, such as school girls wearing a hijab and the school uniform according to social regulations as illustrated in *The poetry contest*.

4.1 The delicious lunch

The storyboard *The delicious lunch* revolves around a boy named Ali, who is going home from school, and is wondering what might be for lunch. Upon arriving home, he checks the kitchen and sees three pots of different colours on the stove, and makes assumptions on which pot contains food. After seeing that the first two pots were empty, he is certain that food must be in the remaining pot.

This storyboard is designed to elicit epistemic modal expressions, and more specifically, targeting the distinction between possibility and necessity. As indicated below, the figures corresponding to lines (3) and (4) as well as (7) and (8) target epistemic possibility modal expressions, while the figure in line (9) targets an epistemic necessity modal expression. Henceforth, we will refer to these as "figure (1)", etc..

(1)  This is Ali.

(2)  Ali is on his way home from school.

(3)  He thinks to himself: "Maybe there will be something delicious for lunch today."
[Target: Epistemic possibility]

(4)  He thinks: "Maybe, there's even Ghorme Sabzi[a] for lunch today."
[Target: Epistemic possibility]
[a] Ghorme Sabzi is a traditional Iranian herb stew.

(5)  Ali can already smell the food coming from the kitchen.

(6)  There are three pots in the kitchen; blue, yellow, and green.

(7)  Ali thinks: "Maybe, the food is in the yellow pot."
But, the yellow pot is empty.
[Target: Epistemic possibility]

(8)  Ali thinks: "Maybe, the food is in the blue pot."
But, the blue pot is empty.
[Target: Epistemic possibility]

(9)  Ali thinks: "Well, then the food must be in the green pot."
[Target: Epistemic necessity]

(10)  Yes! There is food in the green pot.
...and it is Ghorme Sabzi.

4.2 The poetry contest

The storyboard *The poetry contest* depicts a school girl Maryam who is wondering whether she can participate in a poetry contest held in her school, despite being weak in literature. Therefore, when she asks her mother if she can do it, her mom decides to consult Maryam's teacher first. The teacher then advises that Maryam should accomplish certain tasks, and Maryam's mother tells the literature teacher that Maryam can do so. The story ends with Maryam having won the contest because of her efforts.

This storyboard targets root modal expressions, and in particular, strength distinctions between possibility and weak necessity. Figures corresponding to lines (5) (the second question) and (6) target circumstantial possibility modal expressions as based on Maryam's capabilities, and the first question in line (5) targets deontic possibility modality as based on the permission of her mother. Then, figures in (7)–(9) target deontic weak necessity modality, as based on the teacher's requests. Lastly, the figures in (10)–(12) target a circumstantial possibility ("ability") interpretation, as based on what her Mom thinks Maryam is capable of doing. Another possible interpretation of these contexts is teleological (goal-oriented) possibility modality, as based on the goals for Maryam in order to meet the goal of winning the poetry contest. Lastly, the figure in (3) targets bouletic necessity modality, in English expressed as 'want'. These targets are indicated alongside the text.

(1)  This is Maryam. She is a junior high school student and she is very ambitious.

(2)  This is Maryam's Persian literature teacher, Mrs. Rahimi.

(3)  Maryam wants to participate in the poetry contest (and she really wants to win).
[Target: Bouletic necessity]

(4)  However, she is weak in Persian literature.[a]
[a] the divisions shown in the speech bubble represent school's grading system.

(5)  Maryam asks: "Mom, can I sign up for The poetry contest?
[Target: Deontic possibility]
Do you think I can win?"
[Target: Circumstantial possibility]

(6)  Her mom goes to school and asks Maryam's literature teacher: "Do you think that Maryam can take part in the poetry contest?"
[Target: Circumstantial possibility]

(7)  The teacher says: "First, Maryam should improve her grades in literature."
[Target: Deontic weak necessity]

(8) Then the teacher says: "Also, Maryam should read up on famous poets."
[Target: Deontic weak necessity]

(9) At last, the teacher says: "Maryam should also practice and recite a lot of poems."
[Target: Deontic weak necessity]

(10)  The mother says: "So, Maryam can get better grades."
[Target: Teleological/circumstantial possibility]

(11)  She adds: "Sure, Maryam can read more on famous poets."
[Target: Teleological/circumstantial possibility]

(12)  "Okay, and Maryam can also practice and recite a lot of poems."
[Target: Teleological/circumstantial possibility]

(13)  Maryam does all that, and then next year, she wins at the poetry contest.

5 A case study on *The delicious lunch* and *The poetry contest* with Tabari

5.1 Language background

Figure 1: Map of the Tabari language.[6]

Along with closely-related Gilaki and other south Caucasian languages, Tabari (also known as Mazanderani or Mazani) is an Iranian language of the Northwestern branch of Indo-Iranian languages. Tabari is mainly spoken in Mazandaran province in Iran located along the southern coast of Caspian Sea, as shown in Figure 1. Speakers of Tabari are also found outside of Mazandaran province, extending to the east in Golestan and Semnan provinces as well as extending to the west and south in Tehran and Alborz provinces.

According to Ethnologue, there are around three million native speakers of Tabari residing in the aforementioned provinces. Most speakers of Tabari are bilin-

---

[6] Mazandarani Language Map. Created on 16 July 2007 by Siamax. License: CC BY-SA 3.0. Retrieved from Wikipedia on 10 October 2018. Edited to add place names.

gual with Persian, although there remain some monolinguals, primarily among those who live in rural areas (see Eberhard, Simons, and Fennig 2020).

The Tabari language includes various dialects such as Saravi, Amoli, Baboli, Ghaemshahri, Chaloosi, Nuri, Shahsavari, Ghasrani, Shahmirzadi, Damavandi, Firoozkoohi, Gorgani, Astarabadi and Katouli. The Saravi dialect is spoken mainly in the city of Sari and adjacent villages. It is considered the ideological standard because of its prestige as spoken in the capital of Mazandaran province and the most important cultural center since the 1998 separation of Golestan and Mazandaran provinces (see Borjian 2005; Borjian and Borjian 2008; Yoshie 1996). For the purposes of this research, the first author was able to consult 3 speakers of the Saravi dialect, 3 speakers of the Baboli dialect, 2 speakers of the Gorgani dialect, 1 speaker of the Amoli dialect, and 1 speaker of the Katouli dialect.

Tabari has been considerably influenced by Persian (Farsi), the official language of Iran. For historical and political reasons, Tabari had made use of Persio-Arabic alphabet for writing purposes. The specifics of the Persian writing system underspecify the phonological differences across the Tabari dialects, because they are not very well reflected in the writing system. However, as Tabari is not being taught at schools, there is very little written text available in this language, and the speakers prefer writing in Persian for better employment opportunities. Due to this reason, the literacy rate in Tabari is very poor and there are few Tabari texts (Eberhard, Simons, and Fennig 2020). Tabari is thus primarily an oral language.

5.2 Background on the modal system in Tabari

In this section, we provide the basic background on the modal system on Tabari. Kolagar (2019) presents the first research on modal expressions in Tabari, previously not described or analyzed. In Table 1, we summarize Kolagar's results in order to provide the relevant background data for the storyboards. All modals are adverbs, except for *betonesten* 'can', which is a modal verb. These results are based on personal introspection of the first author as a native speaker of Tabari as well as on elicitation data collected from other native Tabari speakers by the first author, and will be further tested as based on the storyboard results.

As shown in Table 1, modal expressions in Tabari typically lexically encode distinctions of quantificational force, but leave the distinction in the root modal flavours to be determined by the discourse (Kolagar 2019). The modal compound *hatmen-vene* in (1a), for instance, unambiguously expresses necessity while the modal *betonde* in (1b) unambiguously expresses possibility. However, both

Table 1: Tabari modal system (Kolagar 2019).

Modal Flavour	Modal Force			
	Possibility	Necessity		
		Weak Necessity	Necessity (weak & strong)	Strong Necessity
	betonesten	shayed	vene / vese	hatmen	hatmen-vene / hatmen-vese
Epistemic		✓		✓	
Bouletic	✓		✓		✓
Deontic	✓		✓		✓
Circumstantial	✓		✓		✓
Teleological	✓		✓		✓

modals allow for bouletic, circumstantial, deontic or teleological interpretations depending on the context.[7]

(1) a. *Ve* **hatmen-vene** *sere davashe.*
   3SG ROOT.NEC house be.3SG.PRS.SBJV
   'He must be home.'

 b. *Ve* **betonde** *sere davashe.*
   3SG ROOT.POS.3SG.PRS house be.3SG.PRS.SBJV
   'He can be home.'

As for expressing epistemic necessity modality, only *hatmen* expresses epistemic modality. Using *hatmen*, a loan adverb from Persian, the Tabari modal system has compensated for the epistemic reading which was not available using *vene* or *vese* as illustrated in (2). *Hatmen* in Tabari is compatible with both strong and weak necessity modal force. In contrast, *vene* or *vese* is only compatible with root weak necessity modality, as illustrated in (3) for *vene*.

---

[7] The following abbreviations are used according to the Leipzig Glossing Rules (https://www.eva.mpg.de/lingua/resources/glossing-rules.php): 1,2,3 first, second and third person; DUR durative, SG singular; PL plural; PRS present; PST past; SBJV subjunctive; IND indicative; REFL reflexive. Additional abbreviations used are EPIS epistemic modality; LK linker; NEC necessity; OBJMAR object marker (a preposition that indicates the preceding word as object); POS possibility; QP quantifier phrase; ROOT root modality. We represent the modal compound as *hatmen-vene/hatmen-vese* in our data, but it is written as two words in Tabari.

(2) Context in Persian: *Maryam dar otagh-e kar-e khod nesheste va mashghul be kar ast. otaghe u panjere nadarad va ba khod fekr mikonad otaghash u ra ghamgin mikonad.Nagahan, do ta az hamkaranash dar hali ke lebase barani pushide va chatre khis dar dast darand vared mishavand. Maryam fekr mikonad,...*.('Maryam is sitting in her office working. Her room does not have a window and she thinks it is a bit gloomy. Suddenly, two of her co-workers come in wearing wet rain coats and holding wet umbrellas. Maryam thinks,....')

   a. # **Vene** varesh biyare.
       ROOT.NEC.NON-PST rain come.3SG.PRS.SBJV
       'It should rain.'

   b. **Hatmen** dare varesh ene.
       EPIS.NEC DUR rain come.3SG.NON-PST.IND
       'It must be raining.'

(3) Context in Persian: *Moallem daneshamuz-an-ra ghabl-e emtehan nasihat mi-konad.* ('The teacher is advising the students before the exam.')
Adem **vene** khub dars bekhonde.
human ROOT.NEC.NON-PST good lesson study.3SG.PRS.SBJV
'One should study well.'

Vene is used in Tabari exclusively in present tense with present and future orientation, while *vese* is used with past tense with past orientation. We can say that the language differentiates between non-past and past weak necessity. Moreover, both *vene* and *vese* like all modals in Tabari except *hatmen* trigger subjunctive mood, which is discussed in more detail below.

Morpho-syntactically, *shayed* 'maybe, may, might' (a loan word from Persian *shayad*), *hatmen* 'must, should (epistemic)', and *vene/vese* 'ought to' are all adverbs because they do not inflect for person and tense, and appear either sentence-initially or predicate-initially, as shown in (4).[8]

(4) a. (**Shayed**) veshan (**shayed**) khastene ame-hamrah
      EPIS.POS they EPIS.POS want.3PL.PST with-us
     biyaren
     come.3PL.PST.SBJV
     'They might have wanted to come with us.'

---

8 The brackets around the modal expression indicate their different positions, but they cannot both be present nor can they be both absent to produce the modal meaning.

b. (**Hatmen**) te (**hatmen**) she piyer mar-re sar
EPIS.NEC you EPIS.NEC REFL father mother-OBJMAR head
bazen.
hit.2SG.PST.IND
'You should/must visit your father and mother.'

c. (**Vese**) te (**vese**) she dars-re
ROOT.NEC.PST you ROOT.NEC.PST REFL lesson-OBJMAR
bekhonestbibui.
study.2SG.PST.SBJV
'You should have studied your lesson.'

Betonesten is the only modal auxiliary verb in Tabari, owing to the fact that not only does it take a full agreement inflection, it also inflects for tense, as illustrated in (5a-b).[9]

(5) a. Sara **betonde** emtehan-e-dele movaffegh
Sara ROOT.POS.3SG.PRS exam-LK-in.LOC successful
bavashe.
become.3SG.SBJV
'Sara can be successful in the exam'

b. Ali **betoneste** tamir-gah kar hekane.
Ali ROOT.POS.3SG.PST garage-LOC work do.3SG.SBJV
'Ali could work in the garage.'

Lastly, similar to many other Indo-European languages, in Tabari the sentence mood in the presence of modals (except for *hatmen*, discussed below) changes from indicative to subjunctive mood. This aspect shows that Tabari, like Persian, possesses both modals (lexical items which quantify over possible worlds) and subjunctive moods (agreement paradigms which usually require a licensing modal element). Like Italian and Spanish, subjunctive mood in Tabari is also licensed by attitude verbs.

Concerning the modal *hatmen* in Tabari, two points need to be put forward here regarding its status as a loan word from Persian. First, the adverb *hatmen* does not have the same semantics in Tabari as in Persian. While it indicates a great certainty on the part of the speaker in Persian, in Tabari, it can be interpreted as less certain as illustrated in (6). In other words, *hatmen* in Tabari allows for

---

[9] See Kolagar (2019) for details, including on how Tabari modals interact with negation.

both weak and strong necessity readings, while *hatman* in Persian only allows for strong necessity readings (and in both languages this modal lexically specifies for epistemic modality).

(6) a. Tabari:
Na-dombe, **hatmen** *ghabul vumbe.*
NEG-know.1SG.PRS.IND EPIS.NEC accept become.1.SG.PRS.IND
'I do not know, I should pass.' (There is a good chance I will pass.)

b. Persian:
Ne-midanam, **hatman** *ghabul mishavam.*
NEG-know.1SG.PRS.IND, EPIS.NEC accept become.1SG.PRS.IND
'I do not know, surely I will pass.'

Second, while the semantics of the adverb *hatmen* has changed in Tabari, its syntactic features have been preserved. Hence, it is still accompanied by the indicative mood in the sentence rather than the subjunctive mood. This is not unusual, as languages are known to preserve the syntactic features of loanwords, but alter their meaning (see Hock and Joseph 2019).

To summarize the main points here, modal expressions in Tabari are adverbs, except for *betonesten*, which is a modal verb. Moreover, the modal system in this language is categorized according to existential (possibility) vs. universal (necessity) modal force, as well as epistemic vs. root modal flavour, as shown in Table 1. Thus epistemic modality is expressed with *shayed*, lexicalized for possibility, and *hatmen*, which allows both weak and strong necessity. The root modals allow for any type of modality in this domain, but lexicalise for modal force: *betonesten* as a root possibility modal, *vene/vese* as a root weak necessity modal, and the combination of *hatmen-vene/vese* as a root strong necessity modal. These findings are further corroborated with the storyboard results, as we show in the following sections.

5.3 Methodological procedure and challenges addressed

5.3.1 Method

The fieldwork on Tabari was conducted by Zahra Kolagar, the first author. The storyboard technique was used for two main purposes. The first purpose was to collect spontaneous utterances of modal expressions with little influence from the language of wider communication (Persian). The second was to avoid misunderstandings that might occur from a written discourse context, as most native speakers the first author consulted had almost no literacy rate in Tabari, and there is scarcely any written text in this language.

Kolagar ran each storyboard with 10 native speakers of Tabari, following the general guidelines proposed by Burton and Matthewson (2015). Each language consultant was first presented with the pictures (and no text), and Kolagar walked them through the stories by telling the story in Persian (the contact language) before asking them to re-tell the stories in Tabari (the target language). (See also the appendix for a full example of each storyboard.) In most cases, language consultants asked for a practice round before they were recorded. In very few cases, they asked questions regarding what was said for a particular picture in order to make sure they were still following along the line of what was presented. The consultants were later on asked some follow-up questions to elicit further positive and negative evidence, particularly at those pictures where the target sentences were used. Except for two cases, the follow-up sessions followed immediately after the recordings were done.

The reason to run each story with 10 different speakers was to capture possible dialectal differences of Tabari language, as the first author is only proficient in Gorgani dialect. As mentioned, Kolagar was able to consult speakers across 5 different dialects (3 Saravi, 3 Baboli, 2 Gorgani, 1 Amoli, and 1 Katouli). In the end, there were no lexical differences in the modal expressions across these dialects, and only some phonological differences between the Katouli and Saravi dialects.

In general, while both storyboards were found to be enjoyable by all Tabari speakers, *The delicious lunch* was favoured. They found the twists and turns of the story to be amusing and as the story was short — 10 figures in total — they did not complain of boredom. On the contrary, speakers were so involved in the process of re-telling the story, that in most cases, they even added more descriptions than was intended. Although in most cases, they only added a few more sentences to each presented image, in some Kolagar was obliged to interrupt the speakers and remind them that they needed to move on to the next figure. *The poetry contest* was also found engaging by all the Tabari speakers, and was also found to be a good length (with 13 figures total). In particular, most consultants expressed their sympathy with the protagonist of the story (Maryam) who was able to overcome the challenges to win the contest.

5.3.2 Encountering and addressing challenges in our implementation

One challenge in implementing the storyboards was that two of the consultants also had the feeling that they should re-tell the stories using the exact same words, as if it was a translation task from Persian to Tabari. However, they were assured early on and went back to re-telling the story according to what they were presented with in each figure using their own words. Kolagar also experienced some challenges in thinking about the ways to narrate the storyboard in the contact language, Persian, as compared to English, the language the storyboard is presented in (as the academic language) for cross-linguistic use. For instance, the word 'ambitious' which appeared in the English version of the figure (1) of *The poetry contest* story is literally translated to Persian as *jah-talab*, meaning 'greedy'. Since the word 'ambition' carries a negative connotation when translated literally, it was replaced by the adjective phrase *ba telash* meaning 'hard working'. This experience suggests that the linguist also needs to be aware of the differences between English and the contact language in which the stories are presented. When presenting the storyboards, not only do we need to be cautious about the social appropriateness of the picture contexts, but also word connotation.

A different challenge that may arise in regard to the use of a contact language to present the storyboards is possible priming effects. Although there is some evidence that the use of contact language does not affect the experiment (Matthewson 2004; Krifka 2011), there is also evidence that this claim is only accurate to a certain extent (AnderBois and Henderson 2015). Since Persian, as the official language of Iran, has influenced the Tabari language greatly throughout years, it is possible that loanwords prime the consultants into producing the same constructions in the target language. This could be the case for the modals *shayed* and *hatmen* in Tabari, both loanwords from Persian *shayad* and *hatman* respectively, as the Persian modals were used in the first author's narration of *The delicious lunch* storyboard (see Appendix; see also 5.2 for a discussion of these modals). While Kolagar did experience that these loanwords were produced in some of the Tabari narrations of the storyboards, other modal constructions (such as *ve geman kande* 'he guesses') were produced as well by other speakers, suggesting that this (possible) priming was not always the case. Another way that Kolagar ensured that these modals were not simply the result of priming was to elicit *The delicious lunch* with a monolingual speaker of Tabari, through simply presenting the pictures, and then asking for a narration. In this case, the Tabari speaker used the loanword modals, without any influence of the use of Persian by Kolagar. Lastly, the use of other methods is helpful. That is, this priming effect may be more inevitable in other types of semantic fieldwork methodologies that involve written text such as translation tasks and the use of questionnaires, and can be avoided considerably through follow-up elicitation sessions, such as eliciting other modal constructions.

It is also worth mentioning that while both the consultants and the first author were native speakers of Persian and Tabari which facilitated their communication in the follow-up elicitation sessions, there is a possibility that Kolagar being a native speaker might have presented a bias, or primed the consultants into producing a certain constructions — this is in spite of her attempt to avoid unnecessary intonation patterns or emphasis on the targeted constructions. Such disadvantages, however, could be partially avoided by involving a variety of elicitation methods while conducting semantic fieldwork to bring confidence in the obtained results. As such, Kolagar (2019) uses the results from storyboards as well as elicitation and personal introspection to analyze modal expressions in Tabari. In short, we advocate for the use of multiple methods to simultaneously avoid possible priming effects and allow for replication.

One last issue related to the creation of storyboards that we address here is the appearance of two target constructions for the description of one figure, found in figure (5) of *The poetry contest*. Since two (or more) target constructions for one figure might add to the complexity and length of the context description, Nouri-Hosseini (2018) proposes that it is ideal to only have one target construction per figure.

Figure 2: Figure (5) in *The poetry contest* (Kolagar 2018b).

(7) Context (Figure 2): Maryam asks her mother:
    a. *Mar, man **betombe** moshaere-e*
        Mother, I ROOT.POS.3SG.PRS.PROG poetry-LK
        mosabeghe-e dele sherkat hakenem?
        contest-LK in participate do.1SG.PRS.SBJV?
        'Mom, can I sign up for the poetry contest?'

b. *Fekr kandi man **betombe** barande bavasham?*
think do.2SG.PRS.PROG I ROOT.POS.1SG.PRS.PROG win
be.1SG.PRS.SBJV
'Do you think I can win?'

As illustrated in example (7), the modal verb *betonesten* can express two different modal flavours, namely deontic (in the first question) and circumstantial (in the second question). All 10 Tabari speakers produced both target constructions (both questions by Maryam to her mother), showing that while one target construction may be ideal as per Nouri-Hosseini (2018), it is not a major issue to have multiple target constructions per figure. In the next two subsections, we look at each storyboard in turn, presenting the hypotheses and results as applied to Tabari.

5.4 Hypotheses and results for Tabari modal expressions in *The delicious lunch*

5.4.1 Hypotheses

As outlined in section 4, *The delicious lunch* storyboard is designed to investigate epistemic modal expressions, and more specifically, target the distinction between the expression of possibility and necessity modal force. As based first on personal introspection by the first author, in Tabari, epistemic possibility modality is expressed by the adverb *shayed*, while epistemic (strong and weak) necessity is expressed by the adverb *hatmen*. In re-telling the stories, Kolagar thus expected the consultants to make use of *shayed* to express the events in figures (3), (4), (7), and (8), as these set up a context to elicit the expression of epistemic possibility. In figures (3) and (4), Ali, the protagonist of *The delicious lunch* story, is expressing some guesses as he is on his way home, while in figures (7) and (8), Ali is making some assumptions, as he is faced with three possibilities. But in figure (9), Ali has ruled out other possibilities and is therefore certain that there is only one possible answer to his original assumption, hence the use of the modal adverb *hatmen* was expected here.

5.4.2 Results

The storyboard *The delicious lunch* clearly showed the distinction between epistemic possibility and necessity in Tabari, where only *shayed* is used in epistemic possibility cases. As expected for figures (3), (4), (7), and (8), *shayed* was spontaneously produced by all the speakers who were consulted. This is illustrated in the following examples for figures (3), (7), and (8) respectively. In the elicitation session, consultants were asked if they find the sentences containing *hatmen* to be felicitous in these contexts. Their opinion on the matter was unanimous; they all rejected *hatmen* as a possible candidate. Consultants mentioned that the fact that Ali "is just making a guess", makes *hatmen* a wrong choice for the context in figures (7) and (8).

Figure 3: Figures (3) and (7) in *The delicious lunch* (Kolagar 2018a).

(8) Context (Figure 3): On his way home, Ali wonders…
   a.   **Shayed** emruz khashmazze gheza dashte bibuim.
         EPIS.POS today delicious food have.PTCP be.1PL.PFV.PROG.SBJV
         'Maybe we'll have a delicious lunch today.'

   b. # **Hatmen** emruz khashmazze gheza darim.
         EPIS.NEC today delicious food have.1PL.PRS.IND
         'We must be having a delicious lunch today.'

(9) Context (Figure 7): Upon observing three different coloured pots on the stove, Ali guesses that it is possible that the food is in any of the pots. As he first lifts the lid of the yellow pot, Ali says…
   a.   **Shayed** gheza zard-e lave-e dele davashe.
         EPIS.POS food yellow-LK pot-LK inside.LOC be.3SG.PRS.SBJV
         'The food might be in the yellow pot.'

   b. # **Hatmen** gheza zard-e lave-e dele dare.
         EPIS.NEC food yellow-LK pot-LK inside.LOC be.3SG.PRS.IND
         'The food must be in the yellow pot.'

One can also clearly see that *shayed* allows for the expression of epistemic reading. The other possibility modal, *betonestan*, is not felicitous in this context, as it conveys an ability.

(10) Context (Figure 8): In the second instance of checking the pots, and as he lifts the lid of the blue pot, Ali says...

a. **Shayed** gheza abi lave-e dele davashe.
   EPIS.POS food blue pot-LK inside.LOC be.3SG.PRS.SBJV
   'The food might be in the blue pot.'

b. # Gheza **betonde** abi lave-e dele
   food ROOT.POS.3SG.PRS.IND blue pot-LK inside.LOC
   davashe.
   be.3SG.PRS.SBJV
   'The food is capable of being in the blue pot.'

As Ali takes the lid of the blue pot, he realizes that the blue pot is also empty. Being left with no other option, he is now certain that the food is in the green pot. In this context, *shayed* is not produced, but *hatmen*, as illustrated in (11). In follow-up elicitation, *shayed* was judged to be unacceptable in this context, as the possibility modal adverb *shayed* is used in Tabari to express the speaker's lack of confidence in the stated proposition.

Further, regarding whether figure (9) could be expressed using *vene*, all consultants mentioned that using *vene*, although grammatically correct, does not make much sense since there is no indication of obligation or giving advice, and that Ali is only drawing a conclusion based on what he can see in the kitchen. This suggests that *vene* is incompatible with epistemic modality as in (11c).

(11) Context (Figure 9): In the third instance, as he lifts the lid of the final pot, the green one, Ali says...

a. Gheza **hatmen** sabz-e lave-e dele dare.
   food EPIS.NEC green-LK pot-LK inside.LOC be.3SG.PRS.IND
   'The food must be in the green pot.'

b. # Gheza **shayed** sabz-e lave-e dele davashe.
   food EPIS.POS green-LK pot-LK inside.LOC be.3SG.PRS.SBJV
   'The food might be in the green pot.'

c. # *Gheza* **vene** *sabz-e lave-e dele*
food   ROOT.NEC.NON-PST   green-LK   pot-LK   inside.LOC
davashe.
be.3SG.PRS.SBJV
'The food ought to be in the green pot.'

5.4.3 Summary

The delicious lunch aimed at drawing a distinction between epistemic possibility expressed by the modal adverb *shayed* in figures (3)-(4) and (7)-(8), and the epistemic necessity modal adverb *hatmen* corresponding to figure (9) of the story. In follow-up elicitation, it was shown that neither the modal adverb *hatmen* 'must, should (epistemic)' nor the modal verb *betonesten* 'can' are felicitous in the epistemic possibility contexts elicited from *The delicious lunch* storyboard.

5.5 Hypotheses and results for Tabari modal expressions in *The poetry contest*

5.5.1 Hypotheses

While *The delicious lunch* story only targeted epistemic modality, *The poetry contest* story targets root modal expressions. Recalling from section 4, figure (5) (the second question) and (6) target circumstantial possibility modal expressions, as based on Maryam's capabilities; and the first question in figure (5) targets deontic possibility modality, as based on the permission of her mother. Then, based on the advice from Maryam's teacher, figures (7)–(9) target deontic weak necessity modality. Finally, figures (10)–(12) target a teleological (goal-oriented) or circumstantial (ability) possibility modal expression, as based on Maryam's goals or abilities towards participating in the poetry contest.

    In the re-telling of this story in Tabari, Kolagar expected the consultants to make use of the modal verb *betonestan* to express circumstantial, teleological, and deontic possibility claims, and thus occur in figures (5)–(6) and (10)–(12). And in figures (7)–(9), Kolagar hypothesized that the consultants would produce utterances in Tabari containing the modal adverb *vene*, as in these contexts, Maryam's literature teacher is providing Maryam's mother with information on certain tasks Maryam should accomplish in order to prepare herself to participate in the poetry contest. The consultants are not expected to produce sentences containing the modal adverb *vese*, as this modal expresses a past root (weak) necessity, nor the modal adverb compound *hatmen-vene*, as it expresses strong necessity, which is uncalled for in these contexts.

5.5.2 Results

We first look at which modal expressions Tabari speakers used for the contexts targeting root possibility. The first question corresponding to figure (5) intended to be representative of some schools in Iran which require parents' permission for their children to be able to take part in a poetry contest, thus creating a discourse context for deontic possibility modality. Consultants produced the modal verb *betonestan*, as shown in (12), indicating that *bestonestan* is compatible with deontic modality and possibility force.

(12) Context (Figure 5, Question 1):
Mar,   men   **betombe**   mosabeghe-ye   dele
Mom,   I   ROOT.POS.1SG.PRS   contest-LK   in.LOC
sherkat   hakenem?
participation   do.1SG.SBJV
'Mom, can I sign up for the poetry contest?'

Thus, this question can be constructed using *betonesten*. Further, as based first on Kolagar's intuition, it is also possible to form this question using the attitude verb *ejaze dashten* 'to be allowed to', which also takes the subjunctive mood, as illustrated in (13).

(13) Context (Figure 5, Question 1): Maryam asks her mother:
Mar,   man   **ejaze**   **darme**   moshaere-e   mosabeghe-e
Mother, I   permission   have.3SG.PRS   poetry-LK   contest-LK
dele   sherkat   hakenem?
in   participate   do.1SG.PRS.SBJV?
'"Mom, am I allowed to sign up for the poetry contest?"'

Despite the fact that the application of the attitude verb *ejaze dashten* 'be allowed to' is plausible, none of the consultants produced such construction. We put forward two explanations here. First, it is possible that the use of the attitude verb *ejaze dashten* 'be allowed to' is not as common as the use of the modal verb *betonesten* 'can' in daily conversations; although this explanation has to be verified. Second, this could be due to the priming effect of the contact language

Persian. The use of the Persian modal verb *tavanestan* 'can' might have primed the consultants to use the Tabari modal verb *betonesten* 'can' while re-telling the stories.

We now turn to the teleological/circumstantial possibility modality targets in figures (10), (11), and (12).[10] After the teacher expresses the necessary steps Maryam should take in order to be able to participate in the poetry contest, Maryam's mother mentions that Maryam can accomplish these tasks. In Tabari, consultants also used the modal verb *bestonestan*, as shown in (14) and (15) for figures (10) and (11) respectively, replicated in Figure 4.

Figure 4: Figures 10 and 11 in *The poetry contest* (Kolagar 2018b).

(14)   Context (Figure 4-left): After the teacher gives some advice, Maryam's mother says:
"*Kha,   Maryem   **betonde**   she*
well,   Maryam   ROOT.POS.3SG.PRS.PROG.IND   REFL
nomre-ha-re   beh-tar   hakene."
grade-PL-OBJMAR   good-COMP   do.3SG.PRS.SBJV
"'So, Maryam can get better grades.'"

---

10 Note that in the original storyboard of *The poetry contest*, Kolagar intended to target a weak necessity modal in figure (12), where Maryam's mother advises that her daughter recite lots of poems, following the advice of the teacher. As such, consultants offered the weak necessity modal *vene*, as shown in the Appendix. We have changed the original target to have the same modal force across Figures (10)–(12) as possibility, in order for ease of presentation and replicability of the results.

(15) Context (Figure 4-right): After the teacher gives some advice, Maryam's mother adds:
"*Metmaen bash, Maryem*
sure be.3SG.PRS.IND, Maryam
betonde *bish-tar shenas-e*
ROOT.POS.3SG.PRS.PROG.IND more-COMP famous-LK
shaer-a-e mored motale'e hakene."
poet-PL-LK about study do.3SG.PRS.SBJV
'"Sure, Maryam can read more on famous poets."'

In the follow-up sessions, speakers were asked if it is alright to replace the root possibility modal *betonesten*, with the root weak necessity modal *vene* in examples (14) and (15). Although grammatically correct, all participants except for one participant were hesitant to do so. Among the reasons mentioned by the consultants to rule out the use of the weak necessity modal *vene* in these contexts were that Maryam's mother "does not seem to be repeating the advice the teacher gave, but is assuring the teacher that Maryam will do as she is told", and "she is only saying that it is possible for Maryam to accomplish these tasks".

Second, we look at which modal expressions were used by Tabari speakers in figures (7)–(9) of *The poetry contest*, which were hypothesized to target root (deontic) weak necessity modality. As illustrated in section 4, we saw that Maryam's literature teacher provides Maryam's mother with some recommendations, so that Maryam would be able to prepare herself and meet the standards for participating in the poetry contest, as illustrated in (16) based on figure (7). In this example, the modal *vene* is used.

(16) Context (Figure 7): After asking for advice on what Maryam should do to be able to participate in the poetry contest, Maryam's teacher tells her mother that,...
*avel, Maryem **vene** she nomre-e adebiyat-re*
first, Maryam ROOT.NEC.NON-PST REFL grade-LK literature-LK
beh-tar hakene.
good-COMP do.3SG.PRES.SBJV
'First, Maryam should improve her grades in literature.'

In fact, *vene* was used across figures (7)–(9) in *The poetry contest*. In the follow-up question session, the consultants were asked if they could replace *vene* with *hatmen-vene* in the context of figure (8), demonstrated below in (17). Although from a grammatical point of view, the use of both modals is structurally acceptable and both necessitate a subjunctive mood, all consultants — except for one — were

Figure 5: Figures 7 and 8 in *The poetry contest*.

wary of the use of *hatmen-vene*. As nine out of ten speakers believed, it indicated "a great obligation" on what the teacher was advising Maryam to do. One participant even mentioned jokingly that the first author "should have drawn a frowning teacher" if she wanted the speakers to produce a sentence containing the modal adverb *hatmen-vene*. In regards to *vene* (and *vese*), speakers commented that these two modals do not express a hard line rule, instead they seem softer, and are more appropriate for suggestions and advice, while *hatmen-vene/hatmen-vese* are better off expressing laws and regulations. This is an interesting observation, as it clearly suggests that Tabari grammatically distinguishes the strength in root necessity modal expressions. The speakers' comments, although used as a *clue*, have been very helpful in distinguishing the strength of the root necessity modals into weak and strong necessity.

(17) Context (Figure 8): Maryam's teacher also says to her mother:
  a. *Maryam*   **vene**   *darmored-e* *shaer-a* *bishtar*
      Maryam   ROOT.NEC.NON-PST   about-LK   poet.PL   more
      motalee *hakene.*
      study   do.3SG.PRS.SBJV
      'Maryam should read up more on poets.'

  b. # *Maryam*   **hatmen-vene** *darmored-e* *shaer-a* *bishtar* *motalee*
       Maryam   ROOT.NEC   about-LK   poet-PL   more   study
       hakene.
       do.3SG.PRS.SBJV
       'Maryam must read up more on poets.'

Consultants were also asked if they could replace any of the targeted constructions in (17a) or (17b) with the phrase *beyter haste* 'it is better'. All of them mentioned that they would only replace the modal adverb *vene* in (17a) with the above mentioned phrase, since the modal adverb *hatmen-vene* in (17b) imparts much more constraint on the requirement mentioned in this context. For more examples on weak and strong necessity in Tabari, see Kolagar (2019).

5.5.3 Summary

The poetry contest storyboard elicited different types of root possibility modality (including circumstantial, deontic, or teleological modal flavours) in figures (5), (6), and (10)–(12) making use of the modal auxiliary verb *betonesten*, while figures (7)–(9) targeted the weak necessity root modal *vene*. We observed that the modal adverb *hatmen-vene* denotes a strong necessity, and therefore could not replace *vene* in figures (7) through (9) in this storyboard.

5.6 Outlook of the results

The delicious lunch targets epistemic possibility vs. necessity modality. It is similar with the storyboard *On the lam* (TFS Working Group 2011c) in that both have the same target constructions, but different cultural contexts. *The delicious lunch* and *On the lam* also differ in the way that they target epistemic necessity. In the storyboard *On the lam*, there are two protagonists who are running away from the police, and the police are checking inside a cabin as to where they might be hiding. There are three possibilities according to the police officers: they might be hiding in a box, under the bed, or behind the curtain. The first two possibilities are ruled out because inside the box is too small, and under the bed is too short. The final possible hiding spot is intended according to the script to target an epistemic necessity modal (e.g., *must* in English). However, the target construction with the necessity modal *They must be behind that curtain* is only felicitous if the narrator considers this to be the last option. In the story, the two protagonists are not actually behind the curtain, but have jumped out the window! If the narrator chooses to be omniscient in taking into account a further possibilities that they are outside the cabin, then a possibility modal is possible. The second author, Jozina Vander Klok, has experienced in eliciting the storyboard *On the lam* that Javanese speakers produced either a possibility or a necessity modal in this context, and this was confirmed in follow-up elicitation (cf. Vander Klok 2013). Discovering the distinction between epistemic possibility and necessity with *On the lam* may prove to be difficult because of this potential ambiguity in the narrator perspective (see also the results from Atayal in Chen, this volume). *The delicious lunch* storyboard solves this problem: in this storyboard, there is no other option for where the food could be, except for the last pot, targeting only an epistemic necessity interpretation. This aspect is useful for cross-linguistic use in understanding the precise distinction between epistemic possibility and necessity.

The poetry contest storyboard targets the distinction between root possibility modals (of different flavours), but also targets different modal strengths beyond pure possibility and necessity modal forces; namely, weak necessity. This storyboard will be useful for cross-linguistic research on modal strength, since to the best of our knowledge, only one storyboard targets the distinction between weak and strong necessity modals: *A Wug's journey* (Meunier and Zen 2020).

Lastly, one also needs to keep in mind that drawing a conclusion based on only a few examples might not be appropriate, and further investigation is required to confirm the results. These storyboards were originally part of Kolagar (2019) and were followed by two questionnaires as based on Vander Klok (2014, this volume) including various examples to illustrate the distinctions more accurately. This means that although the use of storyboards in data collection is undeniable, it was useful to also apply a combination of methods to confirm the results of how modal expressions are grammatically expressed in Tabari.

6 Conclusion

Since their creation, storyboards are increasingly used in field research. This aspect is indicated by their development by a wider set of researchers, and across different cultural settings and geographical locations. Storyboards — as with any linguistic tool — have both advantages and disadvantages, which we have detailed in this chapter as based on the current literature as well as the authors' own experience conducting storyboards. Our main aim in this chapter was to further advocate for the use of storyboards in research on modality because of the advantages in establishing a salient discourse context while, at the same time, controlling for different linguistic properties that modal expressions are sensitive to. In this endeavour, we have presented two new storyboards *The delicious lunch* and *The poetry contest*, and demonstrated their application to the underdescribed Tabari language. Our second main aim was to equip future researchers with the knowledge of past research and our own fieldwork experiences in order to address and overcome potential challenges that have previously been encountered creating and using this tool. In this way, we have built on the literature to provide future researchers with suggestions on how to use storyboards successfully. Overall, we encourage linguists to make storyboards a standard tool in the linguists' toolkit, especially for describing and analyzing modal expressions across the world's languages.

References

AnderBois, Scott & Robert Henderson. 2015. Linguistically establishing discourse context: Two case studies from Mayan languages. In M. Ryan Bochnak & Lisa Matthewson (eds.), *Methodologies in semantic fieldwork*, 207–232. Oxford & New York: Oxford University Press.

Berman, Ruth A. & Dan Isaac Slobin. 2013. *Relating events in narrative: A crosslinguistic developmental study*. East Sussex: Psychology Press.

Bochnak, M. Ryan & Lisa Matthewson. 2020. Techniques in complex semantic fieldwork. *Annual Review of Linguistics* 6 (1). 261–283.

Bogal-Allbritten, Elizabeth, Elizabeth Coppock & Golsa Nouri-Hosseini. 2018. What matters. Totem Field Storyboards. URL http://www.totemfieldstoryboards.org/stories/what_matters/ (accessed 4 September 2020).

Bohnemeyer, Jürgen. 2015. A practical epistemology for semantic elicitation in the field and elsewhere. In M. Ryan Bochnak & Lisa Matthewson (eds.), *Methodologies in semantic fieldwork*, 13–46. Oxford & New York: Oxford University Press.

Borjian, Habib & Maryam Borjian. 2008. The last Gālesh herdsman: Ethno-linguistic materials from south Caspian rainforests. *Iranian Studies* 41 (3). 365–401.

Borjian, Maryam. 2005. Bilingualism in Mazandaran: Peaceful coexistence with Persian. In Zeena Zackaria & Tammy Arstein (eds.), *Languages, communities, and education*, 65–74. New York: Society for International Education.

Burton, Strang & Lisa Matthewson. 2015. Targeted construction storyboards in semantic fieldwork. In M. Ryan Bochnak & Lisa Matthewson (eds.), *Methodologies in semantic fieldwork*, 135–156. Oxford & New York: Oxford University Press.

Chafe, Wallace L. (ed.). 1980. *The pear stories: Cognitive, cultural, and linguistic aspects of narrative production*. Norwood, NJ: Ablex.

Chen, Sihwei, Vera Hohaus, Rebecca Laturnus, Meagan Louie, Lisa Matthewson, Hotze Rullmann, Ori Simchen, Claire K. Turner & Jozina Vander Klok. 2017. Past possibility cross-linguistically: Evidence from twelve languages. In Ana Arregui, María Luisa Rivero & Andrés Salanova (eds.), *Modality across syntactic categories*, 235–287. Oxford: Oxford University Press.

Cinque, Guglielmo. 1999. *Adverbs and functional heads: A cross-linguistic perspective*. Oxford: Oxford University Press.

Condoravdi, Cleo. 2002. Temporal interpretation of modals: Modals for the present and for the past. In David I. Beaver, Luis D. Casillas Martinez, Brady Z. Clark & Stefan Kaufmann (eds.), *The Construction of Meaning*, 59–88. Stanford, CA: CSLI Publications.

Davis, Henry, Carrie Gillon & Lisa Matthewson. 2015. Diversity driven but cognitively constrained: Boas meets Chomsky (response to commentators). *Language* 91 (3). e127–e143.

Deal, Amy Rose. 2015. Reasoning about equivalence in semantic fieldwork. In M. Ryan Bochnak & Lisa Matthewson (eds.), *Methodologies in semantic fieldwork*, 157–174. Oxford: Oxford University Press.

Eberhard, David M., Gary F. Simons & Charles D. Fennig. 2020. Ethnologue: Languages of the world, twenty-first edition. Dallas, Texas: SIL International. URL https://www.ethnologue.com/language/mzn (accessed 13 August 2020).

Featherston, Sam. 2007. Data in generative grammar: The stick and the carrot. *Theoretical Linguistics* 33 (3). 269–318. URL https://doi.org/10.1515/TL.2007.020.

Hacquard, Valentine. 2006. *Aspects of modality*. Boston, MA: Massachusetts Institute of Technology dissertation.

Himmelmann, Nikolaus P. 2002. Documentary and descriptive linguistics. In Osamu Sakiyama & Fubito Endo (eds.), *Lectures on endangered languages*, volume 5, 37–83. Kyoto: Endangered Languages of the Pacific Rim.

Hock, Hans Henrich & Brian D. Joseph. 2019. *Language History, language Change, and language relationship: An introduction to historical and comparative linguistics*. Berlin: Mouton de Gruyter. URL https://doi.org/10.1515/9783110613285-008.

Izvorski, Roumyana. 1997. The present perfect as an epistemic modal. In Aaron Lawson (ed.), *Proceedings of semantics and linguistic theory VII*, 222–239. Ithaca, NY: Cornell University.

Klamer, Marian & Francesca R. Moro. 2020. What is "natural" speech? Comparing free narratives and frog stories in Indonesia. *Language Documentation & Conservation* 14. 238–313.

Kolagar, Zahra. 2018a. The delicious lunch. URL https://fieldworkhub.wordpress.com/2018/05/23/the-delicious-lunch/ (accessed 12 March 2022).

Kolagar, Zahra. 2018b. The poetry contest. URL https://fieldworkhub.wordpress.com/2018/05/23/the-poetry-contest-english-version/ (accessed 12 March 2022).

Kolagar, Zahra. 2019. Crosslinguistic variation in modal systems: Semantic field-work on Tabari. Tübingen: Eberhard Karls Universität Tübingen MA thesis. https://uni-tuebingen.de/en/research/core-research/collaborative-research-centers/crc-833/research-projects/b1/theses/.

Kratzer, Angelika. 1981. The notional category of modality. In Hans J. Eikmeyer & Hannes Rieser (eds.), *Words, Worlds, and Contexts: New Approaches in Word Semantics*, 38–74. Berlin: Mouton de Gruyter. URL https://doi.org/10.1515/9783110842524-004.

Kratzer, Angelika. 1991. Modality. In Arnim von Stechow & Dieter Wunderlich (eds.), *Semantics: An international handbook of contemporary research*, 639–650. Berlin: Mouton de Gruyter. URL https://doi.org/10.1515/9783110126969.7.639.

Krifka, Manfred. 2011. Varieties of semantic evidence. In Claudia Maiernborn, Klaus Von Heusinger & Paul Portner (eds.), *Semantics: An international handbook of natural language meaning*, 242–267. Berlin: Mouton de Gruyter.

Louie, Meagan. 2015. The problem with no-nonsense elicitation plans (for semantic fieldwork). In M. Ryan Bochnak & Lisa Matthewson (eds.), *Methodologies in semantic fieldwork*, 47–71. Oxford & New York: Oxford University Press.

Matthewson, Lisa. 2004. On the methodology of semantic fieldwork. *International journal of American linguistics* 70 (4). 369–415.

Matthewson, Lisa. 2016. Modality. In Maria Aloni & Paul Dekker (eds.), *Cambridge handbook of formal semantics*, 525–559. Cambridge, UK: Cambridge University Press.

Matthewson, Lisa, Henry Davis & Hotze Rullmann. 2007. Evidentials as epistemic modals: Evidence from St'át'imcets. *Linguistic Variation Yearbook* 7 (1). 201–254.

Meunier, Meagan & Qingcheng Zen. 2020. A Wug's journey. URL https://fieldworkhub.wordpress.com/2020/06/16/wug-journey/ (accessed 6 September 2020).

Narrog, Heiko. 2012. *Modality, subjectivity, and semantic change: A cross-linguistic perspective*. Oxford: Oxford University Press.

Nouri-Hosseini, Golsa. 2018. Experimenting with picture-based methods for semantic fieldwork: A case study on quantity superlatives in Persian. Gothenburg: University of Gothenburg MA thesis. URL http://hdl.handle.net/2077/58149.

Portner, Paul. 2009. *Modality*. Oxford: Oxford University Press.
Rullmann, Hotze & Lisa Matthewson. 2018. Towards a theory of modal-temporal interaction. *Language* 94 (2). 281–331.
Strömqvist, Sven & Ludo Verhoeven. 2004. *Relating events in narrative: Typological and contextual perspectives*. Ahwah, NJ: Lawrence Erlbaum Associates, Inc.
TFS Working Group. 2011a. Bake-off. Totem Field Storyboards. URL http://www.totemfieldstoryboards.org/stories/bake_off/ (accessed 26 August 2020).
TFS Working Group. 2011b. Chore girl. Totem Field Storyboards. URL http://www.totemfieldstoryboards.org/stories/chore_girl/ (accessed 26 August 2020).
TFS Working Group. 2011c. On the lam. Totem Field Storyboards. URL http://www.totemfieldstoryboards.org/stories/on_the_lam/ (accessed 4 September 2020).
TFS Working Group. 2011d. Sick girl. Totem Field Storyboards. URL http://www.totemfieldstoryboards.org/stories/sick_girl/ (accessed 26 August 2020).
TFS Working Group. 2012. Feeding Fluffy. Totem Field Storyboards. URL http://www.totemfieldstoryboards.org/stories/feedingfluffy/ (accessed 26 August 2020).
Vander Klok, Jozina. 2013. Pure possibility and pure necessity modals in Paciran Javanese. *Oceanic Linguistics* 52 (2). 341–374.
Vander Klok, Jozina. 2014. Questionnaire on modality for cross-linguistic use. URL http://www.eva.mpg.de/lingua/tools-at-lingboard/questionnaires.php (accessed 5 February 2018).
Vander Klok, Jozina. 2019. Exploring modality and temporality interactions through the storyboard Bill vs. the weather. *Semantic Fieldwork Methods* 1 (1). 1–29.
Yoshie, Satoko. 1996. *Sari dialect*. Tokyo: Institute for the Study of Languages and Cultures of Asia and Africa.

Appendices

The appendices present a sample transcription of the stories *The delicious lunch* (see Appendix A) and *The poetry contest* (see Appendix B) as told by Ms. Maryam Tajandi, one of the Tabari consultants whom Zahra Kolagar consulted during her four-week fieldwork trip to Iran in 2018. Ms. Tajandi is from Mazandaran province residing in Babolsar, and is proficient in both Persian and Tabari. For each storyboard, the (a) examples illustrate how the story was presented using the contact language Persian and the (b) examples is the transcribed narration, as told by Ms. Tajandi in Tabari. The transcription of the narratives was done by Zahra Kolagar, herself a native speaker of Tabari.

A The delicious lunch

(1) a. *In   Ali   ast.*
    this Ali   exist.3SG.PRS.IND
    'This is Ali'

 b. *Ve   Ali   haste.*
    3SG Ali   exist.3SG.PRS.IND
    'He is Ali'

(2) a. *Ali   dar   rahe   raftan   be   khane   az   madrese*
    Ali   in   way   go.INF.PRS to   home   from   school
    mi-bashad.
    DUR-be.3SG.PRS.PROG.IND
    'Ali is on his way home from school.'

 b. *Ali dare   madrese-je   shune   sere.*
    Ali DUR.PRS   school-LOC   go.3SG.PFV.IND   home
    'Ali is going home from school.'

(3) a. *Ali   ba   khod   mi-andishad:*   "**shayad** emruz*
    Ali   with   REFL   DUR-think.3SG.PRS.PROG.IND   EPIS.POS   today
    ghaza-ye   khoshmazze-i   dashte   bashim."
    food-LK   delicious-LK   have.PTCP   be.1PL.PFV.PROG.SBJV
    'Ali thinks to himself: "Maybe there will be something delicious for lunch today."'

b. *Ve she pahli fek kande* **"shayed** *emruz*
3SG REFL beside think do.3SG.PRS.IND EPIS.POS today
khashmazze gheza dashte bibuim."
delicious food have.PTCP BE.1PL.PFV.PROG.SBJV
'He thinks to himself: "Maybe there will be something delicious for lunch today."'

(4) a. *U mi-andishad:* **"shayad**, *emruz hatta baraye*
3SG DUR-think.3SG.PRS.PROG EPIS.POS today even for
nahar Ghorme sabzi dashte bashim."
lunch Ghorme sabzi have.PTCP be.1PL.PFV.PROG.SBJV
'He thinks: "Maybe there's even Ghorme Sabzi for lunch today."'

b. *Ve fek kande:* **"shayed**, *atte kam amru*
3SG think do.3SG.PRS.IND EPIS.POS one less.COMP today
nehar-e-ve ghaza Ghorme sabzi dashtbibuim."
lunch-LK-for food Ghorme sabzi have.3SG.PST.IPFV.SBJV
'He thinks: "Maybe, at least we have Ghorme Sabzi for lunch today."'

(5) a. *Ali buye ghaza-ra ke az ashpazkhane*
Ali smell food-OBJMAR that from kitchen
mi-ayad hes mi-konad.
DUR-come.3SG.PRS.PROG feel DUR-do.3SG.PRS.PROG
'Ali can already smell the food coming from the kitchen.'

b. *Ali gheza-ye bu-re ke ashpezkhane-e dele-je*
Ali food-LK smell-LK that kitchen-LK inside-LOC
ene garne.
come.3SG.PRS.IND get.3SG.PRS.IND
'Ali can already smell the food coming from the kitchen.'

(6) a. *Se-ta dig dar ashpazkhane hast; abi, zard,*
three.QP pot in kitchen exist.SG.PRS.IND blue yellow
va sabz.
and green
'There are three pots in the kitchen; blue, yellow, and green.'

b. *Ashpezkhane-ye dele se-ta lave dare; abi,*
kitchen-LK inside three.QP POT be.3SG.PRS.IND blue
zard, o sabz.
yellow and green
'There are three pots in the kitchen; blue, yellow, and green.'

(7) a. *Ali mi-andishad: "**shayad** ghaza dar dig-e*
Ali DUR-think.3SG.PRS.PROG EPIS.POS food in pot-LK
zard rang bashad." Amma dig-e zard rang
yellow colour be.3SG.PRS.IND but pot-LK yellow colour
khali ast.
empty exist.3SG.PRS.IND
'Ali thinks: "Maybe the food is in the yellow pot." But, the yellow pot is empty.'

b. *Ali fek kande: "**shayad** gheza zard-e lave-e*
Ali think do.3SG.PRS.IND EPIS.POS food yellow-LK pot-LK
dele davashe." Emma, zard-e lave khali
inside.LOC be.3SG.PRS.SBJV but yellow-LK pot empty
haste.
exist.3SG.PRS.IND
'Ali thinks: "Maybe the food is in the yellow pot." But, the yellow pot is empty.'

(8) a. *Ali mi-andishad: "**shayad** ghaza dar dig-e abi*
Ali DUR-think.3SG.PRS.IND EPIS.POS food in pot-LK blue
bashad." Amma, dig-e abi khali ast.
be.3SG.PRS.SBJV but pot-LK blue empty exist.3SG.PRS.IND
'Ali thinks: "Maybe the food is in the blue pot." But, the blue pot is empty.'

b. *Ali fek kande: "**shayad** gheza abi lavi-e*
ALI think do.3sg.PRS.IND EPIS.POS food blue pot-LK
dele davashe." Emma, abi lavi khali
inside.LOC be.3SG.PRS.SBJV but blue pot empty
haste.
exist.3SG.PRS.IND
'Ali thinks: "Maybe the food is in the blue pot." But, the blue pot is empty.'

(9) a. *Ali   mi-andishad:*   "*khob, pas* **hatman** *ghaza dar*
       Ali   DUR-think.3SG.PRS.IND   well   then EPIS.NEC   food   in
       dig-e   sabz   hast."   *Bale! ghaza dar dig-e*
       pot-LK   green-LK   exist.3SG.PRS.IND yes   food   in   pot-LK
       sabz   hast.
       green   exist.3SG.PRS.IND
       'Ali thinks: "Well, then the food must be in the green pot." Yes! There is food in the green pot...'

   b. *Ali   fek   kande:*   "*kha, pas   gheza* **hatmen** *sabz-e*
      Ali   think   do.3SG.PRS.IND   well   then food   EPIS.NEC   green-LK
      lave-ye   dele   dare.   *are! gheza sabz-e   lave-ye*
      pot-LK   inside.LOC   be.3SG.PRS.IND   yes   food   green-LK   pot-LK
      dele   dare.
      inside.LOC   be.3SG.PRS.IND
      'Ali thinks: "Well, then the food must be in the green pot." Yes! There is food in the green pot...'

(10) a. ... *Va   ghaza   Ghorme   sabzi   hast.*
         ... and   food   Ghorme   sabzi   exist.3SG.PRS.IND
         '... And it is Ghorme Sabzi.'

    b. ... *Va,   gheza   Ghorme   sabzi   haste.*
         ... and   food   Ghorme   sabzi   exist.3SG.PRS.IND
         '... And it is Ghorme Sabzi.'

B The poetry contest

(1) a. *In   Maryam   hast.*   *U   daneshamuz-e   sal-e*
       this   Maryam   exist.3SG.PRS.IND   3SG   student-LK   year-LK
       aval-e   dabirestan   hast   *va   u   kheili   ba*
       first-LK   high.school   exist.3SG.PRS.IND   and   3SG   very   with
       talash   hast.
       effort   exist.3SG.PRS.IND
       'This is Maryam. She is a junior high school student and she makes a lot of efforts.'

b. *Ve Maryem haste. Ve daneshamuz*
3SG Maryam exist.3SG.PRS.IND 3SG student
haste, sal-avel-e dabirestan dars
exist.3SG.PRS.IND year-first-LK high.school study
khundene, va ve khale ba telash haste.
do.3SG.PRS.IND and 3SG very with effort exist.3SG.PRS.IND
'This is Maryam. She is a student, she is a junior high school student and she makes a lot of efforts.'

(2) a. *In Khanum-e Rahimi, moallem-e adabiyat-e Maryam*
this Mrs.-LK Rahimi teacher-LK literature-LK Maryam
hast.
exist.3SG.PRS.IND
'This is Mrs. Rahimi, Maryam's Persian literature teacher.'

b. *Ve moallem-e adabiyat-e Maryem khanum-e Rahimi*
3SG teacher-e literature-LK Maryam Mrs.-LK Rahimi
haste.
exist.3SG.PRS.IND
'This is Maryam's Persian literature teacher, Mrs. Rahimi.'

(3) a. *Maryam mi-khahad dar mosabeghe-ye*
Maryam DUR-want.3SG.PRS.PROG.IND in contest-LK
moshaere sherkat konad (va u kheili delash
poetry participate do.3SG.PRS.IND and 3SG very heart
mi-khahad barande shavad).
DUR-want.3SG.PRS.PROG win.3SG.PRS.SBJV become.3SG.PRS.SBJV
'Maryam wants to participate in the poetry contest (and she really wants to win).'

b. *Maryem khane moshaere-e meshabeghe dele*
Maryam want.3SG.PRS.PROG poetry-LK contest-LK in
sherkat hakane, (ve khane barande
participate do. 3SG.PRS.IND 3SG want.3SG.PRS win
bavashe).
be.3SG.PRS.SBJV
'Maryam wants to participate in the poetry contest, (she really wants to win).'

(4) a. *Amma,   u   dar   dars-e   adabiyat-e   Farsi   zaif*
       but   3SG   in   subject-LK   literature-LK Farsi weak
       hast.
       exist.3SG.PRS.IND
       'However, she is weak in Persian literature.'

   b. *Emma,   ve-ne   adabiyat   zaif   haste.*
       but   3SG-POSS.ADJ   literature weak   exist.3SG.PRS.IND
       'However, she is weak in *Persian) literature.'

(5) a. *Maryam   az   madar-ash   mi-porsad:*
       Maryam   from   mother.POSS.ADJ   DUR-ask.3SG.PRS.PROG
       *"Madar,   aya   man   **mi-tavanam**   dar*
       mother   Q   I   DUR-ROOT.POS.3SG.PRS.PROG   in
       mosabeghe-ye   moshaere   sherkat   konam?   Aya   fek
       contest-LK   poetry   participate do.3SG.PRS.SBJV Q   think
       *mi-koni   man   **mi-tavanam***
       DUR-do.2SG.PRS.PROG   I   DUR-ROOT.POS.3SG.PRS.PROG
       barande   beshavam?"
       win   be.3SG.PRS.SBJV
       'Maryam asks her mom: "Mom, can I sign up for the poetry contest? Do you think I can win?"'

   b. *Maryam   she   mar-je   persene: "Mar,   man*
       Maryam   POSS.ADJ   mother-LOC   ask.3SG.PRS.PROG mother I
       betombe   *moshaere-e   mosabeghe-e   dele*
       ROOT.POS.3SG.PRS.PROG   poetry-LK   contest-LK   in
       sherkat   hakenem?   Fekr   kandi   man
       participate   do.1SG.PRS.SBJV think   do.2SG.PRS.PROG   I
       betombe   *barande   bavasham?"*
       ROOT.POS.1SG.PRS.PROG   win   be.1SG.PRS.SBJV
       'Maryam asks her mom: "Mom, can I sign up for the poetry contest? Do you think I can win?"'

(6) a. *Madar-ash   be   madrese   mi-ravad   va   az*
       mother-POSS.ADJ   to   school   DUR-go.3SG.PRS.PROG   and   from
       moallem-e   adabiyat-e   Maryam   mi-porsad: "Aya
       teacher-LK   literature-LK Maryam   DUR-ask.3SG.PRS.PROG Q
       shoma   fekr   mi-konid
       you.PL(respectful)   think   DUR-do.3PL.PRS.PROG(respectful)

        ke   Maryam **mi-tavanad**   dar   mosabeghe-ye
        that   Maryam DUR-ROOT.POS.3SG.PRS.PROG in   contest-LK
        moshaere   sherkat   konad?"
        poetry   participate do.1SG.PRS.SBJV
        'Her mom goes to school and asks Maryam's literature teacher: "Do you think that Maryam can take part in the poetry contest?"'

   b. *Ve-ne   mar   mardese   shune   o*
       3SG-POSS.ADJ mother   school   go.3SG.PRS.PROG and
       Maryam-e   moallem-e   adabiyat-je   persene:
       Maryam-LK   teacher-LK   literature-LOC ask.3SG.PRS.PROG
       "she-man   fek   kandini
       you.PL(respectful) think   do.3PL.PRS.PROG(respectful)
       *Maryam **betonde**   moshaere-e   mosabeghe-e*
       Maryam   ROOT.POS.3SG.PRS.PROG   poetry-LK   contest-LK
       dele   sherkat   hakene?
       in   participate do.1SG.PRS.SBJV
       'Her mom goes to school and asks Maryam's literature teacher: "Do you think that Maryam can take part in the poetry contest?"'

(7) a. *Moallem mi-guyad:*   *"Dar ebteda, Maryam*
       teacher   DUR-say.3SG.PRS.PROG at   first   Maryam
       ***bayad**   say konad   dar dars-e   adabiyat*
       ROOT.NEC try do.3SG.PRS.IND in   subject-LK literature
       nomre-ha-ye   beh-tar-i   begirad."
       grade-PL-LK good-COMP-LK get.3SG.PRS.SBJV
       'The teacher says: "First, Maryam should improve her grades in literature."'

   b. *Ve-ne   moallem gane:*   *"avel, Maryem*
       3SG-POSS.ADJ teacher say.3SG.PRS.PROG.IND first   Maryam
       ***vene**   she   nomre-e   adebiyat-re   beh-tar*
       ROOT.NEC.NON-PST   REFL   grade-LK literature-LK good-COMP
       hakene."
       do.3SG.PRS.SBJV
       'The teacher says: "First, Maryam should improve her grades in literature."'

(8) a. *Baad moallem mi-guyad:*   *"Hamchenin,*
       then   teacher   DUR-say.3SG.PRS.PROG.IND also
       *Maryam **bayad**   darmorede shaer-an-e mashhur*
       Maryam   ROOT.NEC   about   poet-PL-LK famous

bish-tar   motale'e   konad."
more-COMP   study   do.3SG.PRS.SBJV
'Then the teacher says: "Also, Maryam should read up more on famous poets."'

b. *Baad, moallem gane:*   "*Hamchenin, Maryem*
   then   teacher say.3SG.PRS.PROG.IND   also   Maryam
   vene   *shenas-e   shaer-a-e   mored   motale'e*
   ROOT.NEC   famous-LK   poet-PL-LK about   study
   hakene."
   do.3SG.PRS.SBJV
   'Then the teacher says: "Also, Maryam should read up on famous poets."'

(9) a. *Dar akhar, moallem mi-guyad:*   "*Maryam*
       at end   teacher DUR-say.3SG.PRS.PROG.IND   Maryam
       bayad   *bish-tar   tamrin   konad*   *va*
       ROOT.NEC   more-COMP   practice   do.3SG.PRS.SBJV   and
       she'er-ha-ye   bish-tari   az   hefz   konad."
       poem-PL-LK   more-COMP from memory   do.3SG.PRS.SBJV
       'At last, the teacher says: "Maryam should also practice and recite a lot of poems."'

   b. *Akher-sar, moallem gane:*   "*Maryem*
      end-head   teacher say.3SG.PRS.PROG.IND   Maryam
      vene   *tamrin   hakene*   *o   she'er-a-ye*
      ROOT.NEC.NON-PST practice do.3SG.PRS.SBJV   and poem-PL-LK
      ziyad-i-re   hefz   hakene.
      many-LK-OBJMAR memory   do.3SG.PRS.SBJV
      'At last, the teacher says: "Maryam should practice and recite a lot of poems."'

(10) a. *Madar   mi-guyad:*   "*Khob, Maryam*
        mother DUR-say.3SG.PRS.PROG.IND   well   Maryam
        mi-tavanad   *nomre-ha-ye   beh-tar-i*
        DUR-ROOT.POS.3SG.PRS.PROG.IND   grade-PL-LK good-COMP-LK
        begirad."
        get.3SG.PRS.SBJV
        'The mother says: "So, Maryam can get better grades."'

b. *Ve-ne   mar   gane:*   "*Kha,   Maryem*
   3SG-POSS.ADJ mother   say.3SG.PRS.PROG.IND well   Maryem
   betonde   *she   nomre-ha-re   beh-tar*
   ROOT.POS.3SG.PRS.PROG   REFL   grade-PL-OBJMAR   good-COMP
   hakene."
   do.3SG.PRS.SBJV
   'The mother says: "So, Maryam can get better grades."'

(11) a. *U   ezafe   mi-konad:*   "*Motmaennan, Maryam*
        3SG   add   DUR-do.3SG.PRS.PROG.IND   sure   Maryam
        mi-tavanad   *bish-tar   darmored-e*
        DUR-ROOT.POS.3SG.PRS.PROG   more-COMP   about-LK
        sha'er-ha-ye   mashhur   motale'e   konad."
        poet-PL-LK   famous   study   do.3SG.PRS.SBJV
        'She adds: "Sure, Maryam can read more on famous poets."'

   b. *Ve   hamchenin   gane:*   "*Motmaen*
      3SG   also   say.3SG.PRS.PROG.IND   sure
      *bash,   Maryem   **betonde**   bishtar*
      be.3SG.PRS.IND Maryam ROOT.POS.3SG.PRS.PROG   more.COMP
      shenas-e   shaer-a-e   mored   motale'e   hakene."
      famous-LK   poet-PL-LK   about   study   do.3SG.PRS.SBJV
      'She adds: "Sure, Maryam can read more on famous poets."'

(12) a. "*Khob,   Maryam   **bayad**   bish-tar   tamrin*
        okay   Maryam   ROOT.NEC   more-COMP   practice
        konad   va   she'er-ha-ye   bish-tar-i-ra
        do.3SG.PRS.SBJV   and   poem-PL-LK   more-COMP-LK-OBJMAR
        az   hefz   konad."
        from   memory   do.3SG.PRS.SBJV
        "'Okay, and Maryam should practice and recite a lot of poems."'

   b. "*Kha,   va   Maryem   **vene**   tamrin*
      okay   and   Maryam   ROOT.NEC.NON-PST   practice
      hakene   o   she'er-a-ye   ziyad-i-re
      do.3SG.PRS.SBJV   and   poem-PL-LK   more-COMP-LK-OBJMAR
      hefz   hakene."
      memory   do.3SG.PRS.SBJV
      "'Okay, and Maryam should practice and recite a lot of poems."'

(13) a. *Maryam hame-ye in kar-ha-ra anjam*
Maryam all-LK this task-PL-OBJMAR accomplish
mi-dahad, va sal-e baad, dar
DUR-give.3SG.PRS.PROG.IND and year-LK after in
mosabeghe-ye mosha'ere barande
contest-LK poetry winner
mi-shavad.
DUR-become.3SG.PRS.PROG.IND
'Maryam does all that, and then next year, she wins at the poetry contest.'

b. *Maryem hame-ye in kara-re anjam*
Maryam all-LK this task-OBJMAR accomplish
dene, o atte sal baad, mosabeghe-ye
give.3SG.PRS.PROG.IND and one year after contest-LK
she'er-e dele barande vune.
poetry-LK inside.LOC winner become.3SG.PRS.PROG.
'Maryam does all that, and then next year, she wins at the poetry contest.'

Jozina Vander Klok
3 Discourse contexts targeting modality in fieldwork: A revised modal questionnaire

Abstract: This chapter critically evaluates and expands on the discourse contents in a questionnaire created to target and identify different expressions of modality within a language from a typological perspective. Originally developed to elicit expressions of modality in Javanese (Austronesian), the questionnaire has been adapted and disseminated for cross-linguistic use, and since been used in research on 30 languages across six different language families. Based on these results and further fieldwork on Javanese, I consider the successes and failures of several discourse contents in the original questionnaire, thereby building new ones to overcome the previous failures and widening the coverage of the modal questionnaire to target a further range of modal expressions connected to modal strength. This chapter also presents an overview of different applications of how this revised questionnaire can be conducted within and across languages.

1 Introduction

This chapter offers a revised version of the modal questionnaire (Vander Klok 2014b), designed to be used as a cross-linguistic tool for uncovering modal expressions of a given language, and thereby adding to how modal systems are lexically specified and/or grammatically encoded from a wider typological perspective. In particular, the modal questionnaire offers controlled discourse contexts that are created to target a specific type of modality, and can be implemented in a variety

---

Acknowledgments: Many thanks to all the previous studies on modality that have been conducted using the original modal questionnaire (Vander Klok 2014b), which allowed me to create a revised, more inclusive version that has been 'field-tested'. Thank you to the reviewers for helpful comments that have improved the clarity of this chapter, and I especially thank Pablo Fuentes for discussion of the discourse contexts of the revised questionnaire as well as Daniel Reisinger and Hotze Rullmann for discussion of the TO/TP. Any errors are my own. Lastly, thank you to my fellow editors for sharing the excitement of investigating modality!

Jozina Vander Klok, Humboldt-Universität zu Berlin, Unter den Linden 6, 10099 Berlin, Germany, e-mail: jozina.vander.klok@hu-berlin.de

https://doi.org/10.1515/9783110721478-004

of ways according to the language consultants and researchers' expectations and goals alike.

This chapter is structured as follows. In section 2, I first provide the relevant background on the terms concerning modality used in this chapter. Section 3 summarizes the main contributions of the original modal questionnaire, and section 4 introduces the revised questionnaire, showing how this version addresses a number of limitations of the original one. Section 5 then illustrates different discourse contexts from the revised modal questionnaire, discussing how these contexts target specific modal types while excluding others. Section 6 illustrates how the discourse contexts can be adapted based on the language under study, and section 7 demonstrates how the modal questionnaire can be implemented, drawing on and learning from the experiences and published results of previous fieldwork across 30 languages from diverse language families. Section 8 concludes.

The full version of the revised modal questionnaire is included as an appendix to this chapter, and can also be freely downloaded at TulQuest as well as the Max Planck Institute for Evolutionary Anthropology website *Typological tools for field linguistics*.[1]

2 Background on modality

The primary aim of the modal questionnaire is to investigate the kinds of grammatical strategies that modal expressions in a given language may use across the semantic dimensions of modal flavour, modal force, and modal strength. What does this mean? This section provides a brief descriptive background to the terminology used in this chapter.

Modality allows speakers to talk about non-actual states-of-affairs. Talking about the 'non-actual' is a property unique to human language, universal across all languages, and acquired early (Matthewson 2016: 726). Research in formal and typological semantics has identified at least two main semantic dimensions of modality: modal force and modal flavour (e.g., Kratzer 1981, 1991; Palmer 1986; Bybee et al. 1994).

Modal force concerns the difference between possible or necessary states-of-affairs, corresponding to existential ($\exists$) and universal ($\forall$) quantificational force in a standard model of formal semantics. In English, for instance, *may* expresses

---

[1] TulQuest: http://tulquest.huma-num.fr/en/node/70 and MPI EVA Typological tools: https://www.eva.mpg.de/lingua/tools-at-lingboard/questionnaires.php

only possibility, while *must* expresses only necessity, thus indicating a lexical specification of modal force.

In addition to these two quantificational forces, modal strength or graded modality has recently been an important third semantic dimension in how modality is expressed in natural language. Modal strength concerns differences such as weak vs. strong necessity, or weak vs. strong possibility. For instance, English lexicalizes the expression of weak necessity with the modals *ought* and *should*, compared to the (strong) necessity modals *must* or *have to*. For weak necessity modal strength, two main approaches are a domain restriction or a degree-based approach. The domain restriction approach takes the prejacent (the proposition without the modal) of a weak necessity modal to be true in a smaller domain of quantification (by some measure) than the prejacent of a strong necessity modal. The degree-based approach takes weak modal strength to be akin to the more general phenomenon of gradability in language. For these different approaches, see e.g., Kratzer (1981), Portner (2009), Yalcin (2007, 2010), Rubinstein (2012), Lassiter (2017), Vander Klok and Hohaus (2020), among others.

Modal flavour concerns what type of modality a modal expression is compatible with. There are a plethora of terms and ways to categorize modal flavours; see for instance a comparison of terminology in Portner (2009: 140) as well as in Narrog (2012: 287). Nevertheless, cross-linguistic research has shown that there are at least the following modal flavours that languages distinguish. Here, I introduce descriptive terms, using terminology from e.g., Kratzer (1977, 1981). Epistemic modality concerns reasoning according to a body of knowledge or available evidence, (1a); deontic modality concerns reasoning according to a body of rules, (1b); circumstantial modality concerns reasoning according to the facts of the actual world, (1c); teleological modality concerns reasoning according to someone's goals, (2a); and bouletic modality concerns reasoning according to someone's wishes or desires, (2b). As shown in (1)–(2), the necessity modal *must* (or *have to*) in English is compatible across all modal flavours. (Bouletic modality is lexically encoded by the verb *want* in English.)

(1) a. *The ancestors of the Maoris **must** have arrived from Tahiti.* [epistemic]
 b. *The Maori children **must** learn the names of their ancestors.* [deontic]
 c. *If you **must** sneeze, at least use your handkerchief.* [circumstantial]
 (Kratzer 1977: 338, (2)–(3))

(2) a. *You **must** turn at the next light.* [teleological]
 b. *I **must** have that painting.* [bouletic]
 (Portner 2009: 72, (106c))

These various modal flavours have been typically categorized into two broad groups between epistemic and root (or non-epistemic) (cf. Palmer 1986; Brennan 1993; van der Auwera and Plungian 1998; Nauze 2008; Portner 2009). Epistemic types of modality includes epistemic, as one would expect, as well as evidential modal flavours, a type of modality which also indicates the source of evidence (e.g., Izvorski 1997). However, note that not all evidentials are claimed to be epistemic modals (e.g., Faller 2019). Evidentials are not discussed in this chapter, but see Huijsmans (this volume) for a discussion on diagnostics to distinguish evidential markers as epistemic or not.

Root (or non-epistemic) types of modality include all the other above-mentioned modal flavours: deontic, teleological, circumstantial, and bouletic. Furthermore, non-epistemic modality has been sub-divided into 'participant-external' modality, which includes deontic and teleological modal flavours, and 'participant-internal' modality, which includes circumstantial and bouletic modal flavours (e.g., van der Auwera and Plungian 1998). These distinctions are summarized in Table 1:

Table 1: Categorization of modal flavours across necessity and possibility (adapted from Nauze 2008: 18; based on van der Auwera and Plungian 1998).

EPISTEMIC	ROOT / NON-EPISTEMIC			
	PARTICIPANT-EXTERNAL		PARTICIPANT-INTERNAL	
Epistemic	Deontic	Teleological	Circumstantial	Bouletic
necessity	'obligation'	necessity	'needs'	'want'
possibility	'permission'	possibility	'ability'	'wish'

Gluckman and Bowler (2020: 200, fn 7) provide a nice overview of how this typology relates to different proposals in the literature:

> [O]ther works that propose similar modal classifications include Palmer (1986), Bybee et al. (1994), Hengeveld (2004), Nuyts (2006), and Portner (2009). However, not all of these authors use the same terminology as van der Auwera and Plungian (1998) and Nauze (2008); moreover, there is variation among authors as to which modal concepts the terms are meant to cover. For instance, participant-internal modality is termed "dynamic modality" in Palmer (1986, 2001) and covers the internal abilities and desires of an Agent. In Portner (2009), participant-internal modality is a sub-type of "dynamic modality" (dynamic-volitional) but it covers the concepts of Agent-oriented ability, opportunity, and disposition. In contrast, participant-internal modality is called "participant-oriented" in Hengeveld (2004), and it includes the internal abilities, needs, and desires of an Agent.

Thus, in the latter two works, bouletic modality is included as a sub-type of participant-internal modality, as adapted in Table 1. Note that bouletic 'wish' is not considered to have possibility modal force (i.e., on par with *may* in English), but rather a force weaker than strong necessity (see, e.g., von Fintel and Iatridou 2008; Fuentes, this volume).

Modal-temporal interaction is another facet of studying modality, although this is not the main focus of the modal questionnaire. Nevertheless, it is important to be aware of this interaction in a given language since modal expressions can often co-occur with aspect or tense marking. Temporality in language interacts with modality in that the temporal perspective indicates the time at which the modal base is calculated (past, present, future), and temporal orientation establishes the relation between the temporal perspective and the time of the event (Condoravdi 2002; Matthewson 2012). For example, Homer (2013) provides a context to elicit an epistemic modal claim (either possibility with *pouvoir* 'can' or necessity with *devoir* 'have.to' in French) with a present temporal perspective and a past temporal orientation, (3).² Since modals are verbs and indicate tense and aspect in French, the past temporal orientation is overtly seen through suffixation on the verb.

(3) Epistemic context: On the day of the utterance D0, the speaker's grandfather asks her why she panicked and stormed out of the house yelling on D-6, when she saw him lying on the floor. The man is 90 years old but the speaker knows at D0 that he has never had any health problem; right after her fit of panic on D-6, the speaker realized that her grandfather was in fact meditating on the floo*r*.

Tu ***pouv**$_{epis}$-**ais*** *très* *bien* / ***dev**$_{epis}$-**ais*** *sûrement* *avoir* *eu*
You might-PST very well / must-PST surely have had
une crise cardiaque.
a attack cardiac
'It was held very likely/certain (by me) that you had had a heart attack.'
(Homer 2013: 3, (4))

In the literature, it has been debated whether different modal flavours may or may not be restricted to a subset of temporal interactions, such as whether English (among other languages) disallows a past temporal perspective with an epistemic modal base (e.g., Condoravdi 2002 vs. von Fintel and Gillies 2008, among

---

2 The abbreviated glosses used in this chapter are: AC anticausative; APPL applicative; AV Actor Voice; COMP complementizer; DEM demonstrative; DEON deontic modality; EPIS epistemic modality; FV final vowel; FUT future; NEC necessity; NMLZ nominalizer; POS possibility; PST past; RECP reciprocal; ROOT root modality; SBJV subjunctive; SG singular; SM subject marker; VBLZ verbalizer.

others). Recently, Rullmann and Matthewson (2018) propose that cross-linguistically there is no such gap, and more generally, tense supplies the temporal perspective, and aspect indicates the temporal orientation, as based on data from Dutch, English, Gitksan, and St'át'imcets. Reisinger, Matthewson, and Rullmann (this volume) test this hypothesis more in-depth using corpus data, one study on English and one on St'át'imcets, thereby illustrating an avenue to study modality through corpora.

Beyond modal-temporal interactions, modality has also been studied in connection with mood (cf. Bybee, Perkins, and Pagliuca 1994; Narrog 2012; Portner 2018). The term *mood* is used here broadly to include verbal and sentential mood, such as subjunctive, optative, irrealis, interrogative, or imperative. In (4) from French, the subjunctive mood of the verb *vienne* 'come' in the subordinate clause is "triggered by" the modal *possible* 'possible' in the main clause.

(4) Il   est possible que je vienne.
     it   is   possible that I   come.subjunctive
     'It is possible that I'll come.' (Portner 2009: 258, (329))

Portner (2009: 258) writes that: ". . . one of the main empirical challenges is to describe the range of triggers for each language and to understand the patterns of variation in the types of triggers relevant to different languages." This questionnaire is limited to identifying grammatical strategies for expressing specific modal flavour/force combinations and therefore is not intended to address mood categories, which nonetheless may be prominent in the language under study. See, for instance, Agostinho and Rech (this volume) on the irrealis marker *ka* in Lung'Ie, which is found with possibility modals (among other contexts).

3 Overview of the original modal questionnaire

In order to facilitate fieldwork on modality that precisely targets the semantic distinctions across modal flavour and force and some sub-types of gradable modality, Vander Klok (2014b) developed a 'Modal questionnaire for cross-linguistic use'. In this section, I first provide an overview of the original modal questionnaire, while also discussing its strengths and limitations. In section 4.2, I then turn to how these limitations are broadly addressed in the revised version.

The modal questionnaire is designed to be a fieldwork tool to investigate the modal expressions in a given language and to identify possible grammaticalized strategies. That is, does a given modal expression grammaticalize both modal force and modal flavour? Only modal force? Only modal flavour? Neither modal force nor modal flavour? The questionnaire presents a number of discourse contexts that target one cross-section of modal force or strength (e.g., necessity, weak necessity, or possibility) and modal flavour (e.g., epistemic, deontic, circumstantial, or teleological). In addition, most discourse contexts are intended to be contrasted with one type of modality or modal force. For example, the context in (5) targets 'deontic possibility', and contrasts with 'deontic necessity', which is not compatible given this context. In English this contrast is overtly seen wherein the target sentence in (5a) is felicitous with the possibility modal *may*, but not with the necessity modal *must* in (5b) (the infelicity indicated by #).

(5) Deontic possibility context: The ferris wheel ride at WBL [Wisata Bahari Lamongan] is only for children under 15 years old. Tutus is 12 years old. It is not obligatory for Tutus to go on the ride if she doesn't want to.
    a.   *Tutus may ride the ferris wheel.*
    b.   # *Tutus must ride the ferris wheel.* (Vander Klok 2014b: 3, (16))

Section 5 will go into further detail on the discourse contexts. In the original questionnaire, which comprised of 37 total contexts, some cross-sections had more discourse contexts than others; these numbers were arbitrary. Table 2 provides a summary of the coverage in Vander Klok (2014b).

Table 2: Overview of discourse contexts in Vander Klok (2014b).

	Epistemic	Deontic	Circumstantial	Teleological
Necessity	6	4	3	1
Weak necessity	3	3	–	2
Possibility	3	7	5	Not included

Among the strengths of the original questionnaire are that it has broad coverage of different types of modal flavor and force, and that it includes weak necessity as part of the modal strength dimension. Additionally, the questionnaire provides discourse contexts that target a specific type of modality and force/strength, and in many cases, excludes another minimally different type in order to allow for easily generating minimal pairs in a given language, such as in (5). From a methodological perspective, a questionnaire should have the flexibility in that it can be implemented in various ways, as further demonstrated in section 7 for the modal questionnaire.

The original modal questionnaire was also limited in scope. Chiefly among the limitations are that it does not include discourse contexts that target teleological possibility or circumstantial weak necessity (indicated by the shaded cells in Table 2, although the latter may be difficult to identify; see section 4.2). Further, the original questionnaire does not include other types of gradable modality besides weak necessity, such as strong vs. weak possibility; and it does not include bouletic modality. Other types of modal flavours that were not included are evidentials or future modality. As indicated by the categorization in Table 2, the original questionnaire does not explicitly tie in the different discourse contexts with some divisions made in the typological literature, in particular with distinguishing participant-internal vs. participant-external types of modality, but it could be compatible with this division. Lastly, the original questionnaire does not identify which modal-temporal interactions are targeted.

4 Overview of the revised modal questionnaire

In the revised version of this questionnaire, many of the above limitations are addressed. It now includes discourse contexts that target teleological possibility modality and bouletic modality (necessity modal force). Further, it explicitly identifies participant-internal vs. participant-external types of modality, tying into broader divisions, and identifies which modal-temporal interactions are targeted. In this way, the revised questionnaire has a fuller and broader coverage, while also tying in with the literature on modality types and their relation with temporality. The overall coverage of the revised questionnaire is summarized in Table 3. The modal-temporal interactions are specified in the questionnaire itself; see the Appendix.

Table 3: Overview of discourse contexts targeting modality types in the revised questionnaire.

	EPISTEMIC	ROOT / NON-EPISTEMIC			
		PARTICIPANT-EXTERNAL		PARTICIPANT-INTERNAL	
	Epistemic	Deontic	Teleological	Circumstantial	Bouletic
Necessity	5	4	4	4	3
Weak Necessity	3	3	3	–	–
Possibility	4	5	3	5	–

The revised modal questionnaire now comprises of 46 total discourse contexts, with a more even distribution across modal force/modal flavour. For instance, teleological modality was under-represented in comparison with the other modal flavours in the original questionnaire, but now has more contexts, and is on par with these other flavours. Multiple discourse contexts for each cross-section also will allow the researcher to pick and choose the contexts that may work best for them. I illustrate some of the discourse contexts in section 5. First, I turn to how insights from fieldwork on modality led to some of these changes (section 4.1), and then discuss how the remaining limitations in scope are addressed (section 4.2).

4.1 Revised modal questionnaire: Lessons from the field

Some discourse contexts from the original have been revised (see also section 7), while others are new in order to address previous gaps. The new discourse contexts that are now included in the revised version of the modal questionnaire target teleological possibility and bouletic modality (only 'want').

One of the revised contexts is given in (6) (as example (4) in the Appendix.) In the original modal questionnaire, the following sentence was included at the end of the context (before "Mas Hakim thinks..."): *He looks all over again, but the cat is nowhere to be found.* A reviewer comments that this discourse context seems to also equally allow for the non-modal assertion "The cat is not in the house" as the target sentence. In order to create a discourse context where epistemic necessity is still felicitous, while also distancing it from the seemingly equally possible non-modal assertion, the pieces of evidence that the cat is not in the house is reduced.[3]

(6) [Target: epistemic necessity] Mas Hakim is calling for his cat. The cat is not coming. Mas Hakim looks for the cat in the kitchen, but the cat is not there. Then he looks in the living room, and in the bathroom, and in his sister's bedroom. The cat is not in any of those rooms. Mas Hakim thinks... (*The cat MUST NOT be in the house.*)

Concerning the gaps in the original questionnaire, one cross-section of modality that was not included was teleological possibility, as illustrated in (7). This may have been due to how it was first set up as discourse contexts which minimally contrast with other modality flavours or modal force.

---

[3] As the same reviewer notes, this raises the point whether *must p* is as strong as *p* (cf. von Fintel and Gillies 2010). While this revised modal questionnaire does not address this point, contexts such as these may be useful for cross-linguistic comparison on this issue.

(7) *John **can** take the subway.* [teleological possibility]
    (Portner 2009: 185, (225c))

Kolagar (2018), in her study on modality in Tabari (Indo-Iranian) provides an adapted context from one of the teleological weak necessity contexts to make it compatible with possibility modal force, as in (8). A version of this context is now included in the revised version.

(8) Teleological possibility context: There are two different ways to get to Sari from Tehran. Both take around 7 hours by bus and they are equally beautiful. '*You can / #must take the Haraz road.*' (Kolagar 2018: 52, (37))

Concerning the gap of bouletic modality, Gluckman and Bowler (2020: 199) note that bouletic modality was necessary to add as it was relevant to the Logoori (Bantu) modal system in connection with the expression of weak necessity with the verbal modal *kwenya*. That is, with the impersonal use of the modal *kwenya*, this modal is compatible across all types of modal flavour, as illustrated in in (9) for deontic modality, while the plain use of *kwenya* in (10) expresses bouletic modality 'want' (as well as *need to* or *about to*) (see Gluckman and Bowler 2020 for details).[4]

(9) Deontic weak necessity context: Sira wants to go to town but he doesn't have a bike. He wants to borrow his brother's bike, and he thinks that he could do so without his brother knowing, but:
    ga-eny-ek-a   Sira   a-sav-e   amu-aavo
    6SM-ENY-AC-FV 1.Sira 1SM-ask-SBJV 1-brother
    'It should be that Sira asks his brother.' (Gluckman and Bowler 2020: 229, (64a))

(10) *Sira   y-eny-a   ku-li-a   ma-barabandi*
     1.Sira 1SM-ENY-FV 15-eat-FV 6-loquat
     'Sira wants to eat loquats.' (Gluckman and Bowler 2020: 226, (59c))

von Fintel and Iatridou (2008) also show that in a number of languages, the expression of desire as 'wish' is transparently derived with a bouletic modal ('want') plus counterfactual morphology (i.e., the same morphology used in counterfactual contexts). This is also the same strategy for deriving weak neces-

---

[4] In the Logoori examples, the numbers in the glosses refer to noun classes (see Gluckman and Bowler 2020: 235).

sity from other strong necessity modals of different modal flavours (e.g., deontic). For instance, in French, the bouletic modal verb *vouloir* 'want', when combined with "counterfactual morphology" expresses a wish; e.g., *je voudrais* 'I wish'. Other modal verbs, such as *devoir* 'have to', express weak necessity with the same morphology, as *je devrais* 'I ought to'. Thus, bouletic modality was important to include in the revised version to capture possible broader grammaticalization patterns of a modal system (but the reader is referred to Fuentes, this volume, for creating discourse contexts for eliciting 'wish').

The revised version was also inspired by Gluckman and Bowler's (2020) insights on Logoori that the typological distinction between participant-external and participant-internal (cf. Nauze 2008; van der Auwera and Plungian 1998) should be included as a cross-linguistic point of possible grammaticalized strategy within a modal system. That is, Gluckman and Bowler (2020) show that Logoori grammatically distinguishes between participant-internal (root) modality, on one hand, and participant-external (root) and epistemic modality on the other hand. The modal *kunyala* can be used in the impersonal form in the latter, as in (11)–(12), but not the former, as shown by the infelicity in (13).[5]

(11) Deontic possibility context: According to the rules of the hospital, only family members are allowed to enter the patient's room during visiting hours. You came to visit your sister, but it was after visiting hours. However, the nurse gives you permission to see her, anyway. She says:
ga-nyal-ek-a   u-zi-a   mu
6SM-NYAL-AC-FV   2SG-go-FV   in
'It's possible to go in.' (Gluckman and Bowler 2020: 208, (17))

(12) Epistemic possibility context: The police in Kisumu are looking for Sira, and they've been given a tip that he's traveled to one of the other major cities in Kenya. Therefore, they say:
ga-nyal-ek-an-a   ndee   Sira   a-zi-i   Nairobi
6SM-NYAL-AC-RECP-FV   that   1.Sira   1SM-go-FV   9.Nairobi
'It's possible that Sira went to Nairobi.' (Gluckman and Bowler 2020: 210, (22))

---

5 The contexts in (11) and (13) are based on discourse contexts in the modal questionnaire (original and revised).

(13) Circumstantial possibility context: Sira is quite old now, but he is still strong. His children are scared that he will hurt his back if he does any intense labor, so they told him that he is forbidden to lift heavy things. But one day Sira's friend Maina asked to help him in the field, because Maina knows Sira is still strong. So when Maina saw a large rock that had to be moved, he asked Sira straightaway for help (but he didn't tell Sira's children!). Maina knew that:
ga-nyal-ek-a   ndee   Sira   a-sad-a   li-gena
6SM-NYAL-AC-FV that   1.Sira   1SM-lift-FV   5-rock
('It's possible that Sira lift the rock.') (Gluckman and Bowler 2020: 206–207, (12))

Gluckman and Bowler (2020: 202) write that they "... take the felicity of impersonal *kunyala* in PE [participant-external] modal contexts, and the infelicity of impersonal *kunyala* in PI [participant-internal] modal contexts, to support the distinction between PI and PE modal categories made in the typological literature." However, given that the impersonal *kunyala* can also be used in epistemic contexts (and there seems to be a gap for bouletic possibility), one could also argue that this shows that impersonal *kunyala* cannot occur in circumstantial possibility contexts without making a claim for a broader grammatical characterization of modal systems. Nevertheless, I agree that the inclusion of participant-internal and participant-external in the modal questionnaire provides a useful broader characterization of the typology of modal systems, as included in Tables 1 and 3. More research is needed, however, to claim that this broader characterization is grammaticalized in a language or more generally across languages.

4.2 Addressing the limitations of the revised modal questionnaire

While there remain some limitations of the revised questionnaire concerning modal strength, modal-temporal interactions, and evidentiality, each of these can be supplemented by additional resources, as identified below. Moreover, both the original and the revised questionnaire were not designed to ask about any cross-linguistic trends concerning the syntax-semantics of modal expressions, but this would be an important research question in light of different proposals between epistemic and non-epistemic (or root) modality (cf. Cinque 1999; Nauze 2008; Hacquard 2010; Rullmann and Matthewson 2018).

First, the modal questionnaire investigates weak necessity across different modal flavours, but does not extend to more fine-grained differences relating to weak necessity, such as counterfactuality (cf. von Fintel and Iatridou 2008) or frustratives (Kroeger 2017; Fuentes to appear). However, there are a number of resources that already cover these additional meanings. The interested researcher can use the discourse contexts in Fuentes (this volume), which also covers desires and wishes (bouletic modality). In addition, counterfactuality can also be elicited with the storyboards *Party food* (Rolka and Cable 2014) or *The Fortune Teller* (TFS Working Group 2010). Several storyboards developed by the MelaTAMP project also target different aspects of counterfactuals: *Bananas* (von Prince 2018a) elicits counterfactual complement clauses; *Festival* (von Prince 2018b) elicits counterfactual future conditionals; *Garden* (Krajinović 2018a) elicits counterfactual present conditionals; and *Making laplap* (Krajinović 2018b) elicits counterfactual past conditionals.

Beyond the discourse contexts of this questionnaire, the tests developed by Rubinstein (2021) that relate this modal strength with necessity and possibility as based on semantic entailment can also be used to accompany this questionnaire. Vander Klok and Hohaus (2020) also illustrate these tests with Javanese data and contribute further discourse contexts to tease apart weak necessity from necessity and possibility modal force.

Note that in the revised version, there is a gap for targeting circumstantial weak necessity. It seems that this cross-section is only marginally tenable: the circumstantial modality type concerns facts about the actual world from a participant-internal perspective, and this seems to only be felicitous with possibility or necessity modal force. But with weak necessity modal strength, it seems that only with some participant-internal circumstantial events that can be somewhat controlled by the agent, it is possible to manipulate the modal strength. Compare the difference between *going to the washroom* vs. *sneeze, cough*. In the former, in which the bodily function can be somewhat controlled, it seems felicitous to use a weak necessity modal, as in (14), while with the latter predicates which are uncontrollable, it seems infelicitous to use *should* or *ought* in English, as in (15) (without it shifting to a (weak) epistemic interpretation).

(14) Context: My bladder is full.
 I **{should/ought to}** urinate (now), but I just want to finish writing this paragraph first.

(15) Context: The fresh ground pepper is tickling my nasal passages.
 ??/# I **{should/ought to}** sneeze (now).
 ??/# I **{should/ought to}** cough (now).

In another attempt to elicit circumstantial weak necessity, Gluckman and Bowler (2020: 227) offer the discourse context in (16), with the target sentence in Loogori paraphrased as "the speaker expresses that the internal needs of their body are such that they should pee".

(16) Circumstantial weak necessity context: This is going to be a long bus ride, therefore:
 ni-n-la-niin-a   e-basi   nzi-eny-ek-a   nzi-nyal-e
 COMP-1SG-FUT-board-FV   9-bus   1SG-*ENY*-AC-FV   1SM-urinate-SBJV
 'Before getting on this bus, I should pee.' (Gluckman and Bowler 2020: 227, (61a))

However, I find that this context is also naturally compatible with teleological modality, such as based on the speaker's goal to sustain the long bus ride. Further, not only because in Logoori weak necessity is expressed by *kwenya*, which in its plain form expresses bouletic modality, Gluckman and Bowler (2020: 228) also raise the same issue as above whether circumstantial weak necessity can be independently distinguished as a cross-section of modal flavour and modal force/strength. They write (p. 228): "This category seems to inherently overlap with the subject's desires (when the subject is animate). [...] As a result, it is difficult to distinguish PI [participant-internal] weak necessity from bouletic modality in general – if in fact such a distinction exists at all." Although I leave these contexts aside in the modal questionnaire, it still could be worthwhile to check these contexts, especially if the language under study has dedicated lexical morphology or a grammaticalized strategy for weak necessity modality. Concerning these types of discourse contexts targeting obligation and desire, see also Fuentes (this volume) for a guideline to create such controlled scenarios.

A further gap regarding modal strength in the revised modal questionnaire concerns the possible cross-linguistic lexicalization or grammaticalization of different degrees of possibility. This notion is brought up in examples like (17) in English, where the adjective *possible* is modified by different adverbs indicating a strong or weak possibility. Similarly, the possibility modal *can* in English could also be modified.

(17) a. *It is barely possible to climb Mount Everest without oxygen.*
     b. *It is easily possible to climb Mount Toby.*
        (Kratzer 1991: 643, (18a,b))

In English, *could* is observed to express a weaker possibility than with *can*, according to the Cambridge dictionary, see (18).[6] While many languages, such

---

[6] "English Grammar Today" <https://dictionary.cambridge.org/grammar/british-grammar/can-could-or-may>

as French, use counterfactual marking with possibility modals that seem to indicate a weaker possibility, there also seems to be an effect of politeness. I do not address these contexts here.

(18) a. *It could be dangerous to cycle in the city.*
 b. *It can be dangerous to cycle in the city.*

Based on Javanese, which does not have a lexicalized or grammatical strategy to express weak or strong possibility, Vander Klok and Hohaus (2020: 42–43) raise the question whether there might be a cross-linguistic gap in expressing weak/strong possibility as a grammaticalized modal concept. While gradable possibility strength is not included in the revised modal questionnaire, it would be worthwhile to explore such contexts.

Second, additional types of modal-temporal interactions are not included in this modal questionnaire because I assume these are related to how tense and grammatical aspect is expressed in the language under study (cf. Rullmann and Matthewson 2018). In particular, this interaction has been studied in connection with epistemic vs. circumstantial modality, with Condoravdi's (2002) seminal paper on English *might have*, and across many different languages focusing on interactions with epistemic modality. For the interested researcher, discourse contexts that distinguish past possibility epistemic modal claims across past, present and future temporal orientation can be found in Chen et al. (2017). Further, these contexts can be complemented with two storyboards on past epistemic possibility claims: *Feeding Fluffy* (TFS Working Group 2012) targets a past temporal perspective and present temporal orientation, and *Bill vs. the weather* (Vander Klok 2013b) targets a past temporal perspective with a future temporal orientation. Studying these interactions will be important to further developing cross-linguistic predictions concerning how modality interacts with tense and grammatical aspect in a language, but it may be useful to start with the modal questionnaire that focuses only on a subset of these interactions to understand the basic paradigm of grammatical strategies concerning modal force and modal flavour.

Third, the revised modal questionnaire does not include evidential modality. This may be an important feature of the language under study, and so the modal questionnaire can be complemented with the *Evidentiality, inferentiality, and speaker's attitude questionnaire,* which is available on TulQuest, developed primarily for Tibetic languages, and is contextualized for Ladakhi dialects (Zeisler 2016). Other sources for replicating discourse contexts to elicit evidential modality markers can be found in Aikhenvald (2004), Wiemer (2019), Matthewson (2020), or Huijsmans (this volume), among others. As with the current modal questionnaire, the discourse contexts for evidentiality can be adapted to the relevant culture and research interests (see section 6).

In sum, despite there still being some limitations in scope of the revised questionnaire, these gaps can be supplemented through other questionnaires or storyboards, as well as discourse contexts from the current literature.

5 Discourse contexts to target expressions of modality

This section takes a closer look at some examples of the discourse contexts in the revised modal questionnaire, which draw from the previous literature on modality as well as the scholarly works that have used the original questionnaire. Here, I illustrate with the discourse contexts that target necessity modal force across different modal flavours in (19)–(23); see the Appendix for the full questionnaire. The target sentences are given in italics, with the modal expression in English in capitals.

(19) Epistemic necessity context: Ramadon routinely has coffee at Lisa's *warung kopi* (café) every day. It's not obligatory for Ramadon; he just goes for coffee there all the time. It's coffee time now, so...*Ramadon MUST be at Lisa's café*.

(20) Deontic necessity context: You are going to visit your friend in the hospital. When you enter into the hospital, you stop at the information desk to inquire what room your friend is in. But the woman at the information desk tells you that you can't visit your friend now because it's already 8pm! She says, "I'm sorry, the hospital regulations say that...*visitors MUST leave by 6pm*."

(21) Teleological necessity context (adapted from von Fintel and Iatridou 2008): There is only one main road, Deandles, along the northern coast of Java to get to Semarang from Paciran. *If you go to Semarang from Paciran, you HAVE TO take this road.*

(22) Circumstantial necessity context: You are on a bus to Yogya. You have not had a chance to go to the toilet for 4 hours, and your bladder is full. You text your friend: *I HAVE TO pee so badly!*

(23) Bouletic necessity context: Your friend asks what you want to do today since it is a holiday and you both are not required to do any tasks today. You say: *I WANT to go to the cinema.*

Many discourse contexts in the questionnaire are intended to target one crosssection of modality and contrast with one type of modality or modal force to allow for possible minimal pairs. For instance, (5) above contrasted deontic necessity vs. deontic possibility, differing along the modal force dimension. The context in (19) contrasts along the modal flavour dimension: the target is epistemic necessity modality, while disallowing a deontic interpretation since the context explicitly states that it is not obligatory for Ramadon to go have coffee at Lisa's coffee shop. The contexts in (20)-(22) contrast along the modal force dimension: each target sentence is felicitous with necessity modal force, but infelicitous with possibility force (although it is entailed in each case). For example, in (20), the hospital regulations are not advice, but rules, and assuming that the woman at the information desk adheres to these regulations, she states that these are obligatorily followed. It would be infelicitous in this context to utter "Visitors may leave by 6pm" since it opens up the possibility for visitors to stay, which is against the regulations. Similarly, in (21), since the discourse context sets up only one route to get from one place to another: in order to meet the goal of arriving at that destination, it is necessary to take that one route. Using a weaker modal force such as the one expressed by *should* or *ought to* (or even *can*) in English given this discourse context is infelicitous because it suggests that there is more than one way to fulfil the goal of traveling to Semarang from Paciran. In this way, the discourse contexts can often set up for judgment tasks of multiple target sentences with different modal expressions or constructions, where some may be hypothesized to be felicitous and others infelicitous given the context.

The advantage of using the discourse contexts of the modal questionnaire is that they have been designed to target only one cross-section of modality. In corpora of natural discourse, it is often difficult to extrapolate what exactly is the type of modality (e.g., Rubinstein et al. 2013). Nevertheless, in conducting the modal questionnaire, it is sometimes the case that a consultant can imagine another reading, (silently) augmenting the discourse context (cf. Bochnak and Matthewson 2020), which results in possible ambiguity. For this reason, it is important to have feedback, either through discussion during elicitation or a written prompt on the questionnaire, so both the researcher and the consultant are on the same page as to the reading(s) of the modal expression (see also Vander Klok and Conners 2019: 89). Beyond feedback, multiple applications of the questionnaire with the same consultant or different consultants may also be helpful to understand whether judgments are confirmed or altered (possibly because of a different interpretation of the discourse context). Vander Klok and Conners (2019: 75–77) demonstrate how application of the original modal questionnaire across 15 participants of Paciran Javanese speakers helped to confirm judgments. At the same time, allowing for written feedback aided to clarify the judgment of individual speakers when there were cases of different judgments across speakers as based on the same discourse contexts.

6 How the discourse contexts can be adapted: More lessons from the field

This section illustrates how the discourse contexts of the modal questionnaire can be adjusted to the local context and culture, without compromising the target sentences. Semantic elicitation requires concentration on the part of the speaker to judge the target sentence within the given discourse context; if this context is already easily imaginable from their perspective, it facilitates the judgment task. The original modal questionnaire (Vander Klok 2014b) has been adapted to thirty languages across six language families: Niger-Congo, Austronesian, Arawak, Indo-European, and Uralic, as shown in Table 4.

Table 4: Cross-linguistic use of the original modal questionnaire (Vander Klok 2014b).

Language [ISO 639-3 code] (Family)	Reference
Manda [mgs] (Tanzanian Bantu; East Bantu; Niger-Congo)	Bernander (2017)
Mpoto [mpa], Matengo [mgv], Ikoma, Nata, Isenye [ntk] Ngoreme [ngq] (Tanzanian Bantu; East Bantu; Niger-Congo)	Bernander (in progress)
Luganda [lug], Lusoga [xog], Lugwere [gwr], Runyoro-Rutooro [ttj], Runyankore [nyn]-Rukiga [cgg], Kihaya [hay], Kinyambo [now], Kikerewe [ked], Kizinza [zin] (West Nyanza Bantu cluster; Bantu; Niger-Congo)	Kawalya, de Schryner, and Bostoen (2018)
Logoori [rag], Lubukusu [bxk], Lunyore [nyd], Lusaamia [lsm], Lutiriki [ida], and Luwanga [lwg] (Luhya; East Bantu; Niger-Congo)	Gluckman et al. (2017a, 2017b)
Logoori [rag] (Luhya; East Bantu; Niger-Congo)	Gluckman and Bowler (2020); Bowler and Gluckman (2021)
Javanese [jav] (Western Malayo-Polynesian; Austronesian)	Vander Klok (2013); Vander Klok and Conners (2019)
Samoan [smo] (Oceanic; Austronesian)	Hohaus (2020)
Paresi [pab] (Arawak)	Rech, Brandão, and Wit (2018)
Tabari/Mazandarani [mzn] (Indo-Iranian; Indo-European)	Kolagar (2018)
Bulgarian [bul] (Indo-European)	Lyufti (2021)
Bosnian [bos], Serbian [srp], Croatian [hrv] (Indo-European)	Veselinović (2019)
Saami [smi] (Uralic)	Kalábová (2017)
Tlingit [tli] (Athabaskan)	Burge (2017)

The modal questionnaire was originally designed for Javanese (Austronesian), and thus is primarily culturally relevant for Javanese speaker communities as living on Java Island, Indonesia, and would need to be changed to be appropriate for the language under study. Here I give some examples of contexts that only required minimal adjustments, such as changing the proper name in (24), the law in (25), the mode of transport in (26), or the names of the cities in (27) (in southern vs. northern Tanzania) (each indicated in **bold**). The language under study is indicated for each context, and each of the changes aim at being relevant to the world knowledge of the native speaker participants.

(24) Tlingit; Na-Dene, Athabaskan
Epistemic necessity context: **Dzéiwsh** goes to the restaurant every morning at the same time of day. It's 9AM and so . . .
'*Dzéiwsh must be at the restaurant.*' (Burge 2017: 54–55)

(25) Paresi, Arawak
Deontic necessity context: According to **article 244 of the Brazilian Traffic Code** when you ride a motorcycle
'*You have to wear a helmet.*' (Rech, Brandão, and Wit 2018: 237)

(26) Logoori; Luhia, Bantu
Circumstantial possibility context: The **matatus** have a limit of 13 people by law. But the drivers don't care, and stop for more than 13 people. Also, the **matatus** are bigger than you think.
'*Matatus can carry 20 people.*' (Gluckman and Bowler 2020: 206, (11))

(27) Manda; Bantu
Epistemic weak necessity context: You are not living in **Tukuyu** anymore. You notice how diffferent it is with the weather in **Musoma**, where you live right now. You know that in **Tukuyu** it's the rainy season now, and there's often rain every afternoon. Now it's 3p.m. so . . .
'*It should be raining now in Tukuyu.*' (Rasmus Bernander, pers. comm.)

Two additional examples of contexts that are more substantially adapted are demonstrated in (28) and (29). The first changes the context from a person who broke her arm, and even though now it is healed and she has permission from the doctor to lift her baby, she is too weak. The second changes the context from not finding the right ingredients for a Javanese dish (*dudoh menir*) in Canada; and also provides more information about 'Mina' and her situation, giving a fuller picture.

(28) Tlingit; Na-Dene, Athabaskan
Deontic possibility context: A person has been ill for a long time, and was having stomach problems. For a while he was not allowed by his doctor to have solid food. Yesterday he got permission from his doctor to eat food again, but he's not able to because he's too weak.
'*He can eat [solid food].*' '*. . . but he doesn't.*' (Burge 2017: 60–61)

(29) Tabari/Mazandarani; Indo-Iranian, Indo-European
Circumstantial possibility context: Mina is from Shiraz, however she has married Daovod who is from Rasht. As she travels back to Shiraz to visit her family over the Nowrouz holidays, she decides to make the *Baghalighatogh* for them. But no matter how much she searches, she cannot find fava beans in Shiraz. She is really unhappy as she wanted to impress her parents.
She can / #might make Baghalighatogh. (Kolagar 2018: 56, (45)).

As illustrated by these examples, the discourse contexts of the modal questionnaire provide a framework that sets up the target sentence with a modal claim. It is at the discretion of the researcher to change the contexts so that it is most appropriate for the speakers of the language under study. These changes may only be minimal or require a more substantial revision.

Note that some of the scholars who have used the original modal questionnaire (Vander Klok 2014b) do not (always) include the discourse contexts in publications, such as Bernander (2017) or Kawalya, de Schryner, and Bostoen (2018). While Kawalya, de Schryner, and Bostoen (2018: 15) report that the questionnaire was "greatly modified to fit into Nuyts' typology of modality [. . .] and to make it culturally relevant", the reader does not get a sense of how different the discourse contexts are without the examples. Since the discourse contexts are central to targeting only one cross-section of modal flavour and modal force/strength, where it is possible, I suggest including the discourse contexts in the publications where the results are on establishing the semantics of a modal expression in the language under study.

7 How the modal questionnaire can be implemented

One of the main advantages of the modal questionnaire is that its implementation is flexible, depending on the researcher's goals and the experiences of the community of speakers. Table 5 shows the different ways that the original modal questionnaire (Vander Klok 2014b) has been used. The revised version has the same possibilities.

Table 5: Overview of various implementations of the modal questionnaire, adapted based on Vander Klok (2014b).

Type of implementation	Language(s) (Reference)
Elicitation + Translation task	Manda (Bernander 2017) West Nyanza Bantu cluster (Kawalya, de Schryner, and Bostoen 2018)
Elicitation + Felicity judgment task	Malang Javanese (Vander Klok and Conners 2019) Bulgarian (Lyutfi 2021)
Elicitation + Translation task + Felicity judgment task	Samoan (Hohaus 2020) Tlingit (Burge 2017) Logoori (Gluckman and Bowler 2020) Tabari (Kolagar 2017)
Questionnaire + Translation task	Paresi (Rech, Brandão, and Wit 2018)
Questionnaire + Semi-forced choice task	Paciran Javanese (Vander Klok 2013a)
Questionnaire + Likert rating task	Paciran Javanese (Vander Klok 2013a) Bosnian, Serbian, Croatian (Veselinović 2019)

Overall, there are two main ways that the modal questionnaire can be conducted, as elicitation or as a written questionnaire. *Elicitation* refers to the researcher working together with a speaker or multiple speakers, either one-on-one or with a small group, where (usually) the researcher presents the discourse context and the target sentence, and then asks for different tasks concerning the target sentence. A *written questionnaire* for semantic fieldwork refers to a set of discourse contexts plus target sentence(s) and asks participants to complete some task concerning the target sentence.[7] Questionnaires, I assume, are presented to participants who respond on their own time without necessarily having discussion with the researcher after receiving instructions, thus differing from elicitation in which the researcher is always present and there is ongoing discussion. Of course, the written questionnaire presupposes that the participants are literate. For working with speakers of primarily oral cultures, elicitation is possible. The various tasks that could be implemented across either elicitation or questionnaires are translation, felicity judgment task, (semi-)forced choice task, or Likert rating task, each

---

[7] See Vander Klok and Conners (2019) on the role of written questionnaires within a typology of questionnaires, and also for use in comparative field research.

illustrated in the following by past experiences of conducting the modal questionnaire. This list is non-exhaustive; other implementations could be a fill-in-the-blank task or adapting the questionnaire as a production experimental task (see Cournane and Hacquard, this volume, for ideas in this direction).

First, for translation, the target sentence is asked to be translated from the contact language (a language shared by both the researcher and the participant(s)) into the object language (the language under study). The study by Kawalya, de Schryner, and Bostoen (2018) on West Nyanza languages provides an excellent example of the translation task in one-on-one elicitation, and furthermore, illustrates the use of different contact languages depending on the ability of the researcher. English was directly used as the contact language for the Ugandan languages. For languages spoken in Tanzania, the situation was more complex because of a lack of a shared contact language between the researcher and the speaker. Kawalya, de Schryner, and Bostoen (2018: 15) explain:

> For the interviews in Tanzania, where most of the respondents did not understand English well, the interviewer worked with an assistant, who understood both Luganda (for communication with the interviewer) and Kiswahili (for communication with the respondents). The interviewer would read a sentence to the assistant in Luganda and explain the context of the sentence to him. The assistant would then explain that context to the speaker(s) in Kiswahili, after which he would read to them the particular sentence in Kiswahili. The speaker(s) would then provide the appropriate sentence in the object language, to be written down by the interviewer.

Kawalya, de Schryner, and Bostoen (2018) thus illustrate how one can get around the challenge of lacking a shared contact language in elicitation.

The translation task can also be used in a written questionnaire. Rech, Brandão, and Wit (2018) conducted two short questionnaires on deontic modality to investigate modality across tense in Paresi. The questionnaire was presented in Brazilian Portuguese, and bilingual Paresi-Brazilian Portuguese speakers were asked to translate the target sentence.

One potential pitfall of the translation task is that speakers may translate the target sentence without it being embedded within the discourse context, thus potentially losing the intended meaning. In order to avoid this pitfall, written questionnaires can include an open question concerning possible alternate forms which may corroborate the translated version (Vander Klok and Conners 2019: 89). For instance, in the modal questionnaire for Paresi, Rech, Brandão, and Wit (2018: 237) note that ". . .besides the translation task, there is a question about whether there are other ways in Paresi to express this same content." Rasmus Bernander (pers. comm.) explains that he had some hesitation from speakers with the translation task in elicitation, and how he overcame it in his current project:

> there were some insecurity, despite all the context given, if the consultant understood the exact flavor/force that was targeted. I got the feeling that the consultants were mostly just translating the final sentence without paying so much attention to the context after all. This is probably connected to the fact that direct-translation sentence for sentence is what these consultants are used to [. . .]. During the transcription stage, however, I was able to double-check this.

See also Ferreira and Müller (this volume) and references therein on semantic elicitation tasks beyond translation.

A second way the modal questionnaire can be implemented is by using a felicity judgment task in elicitation or within a questionnaire format. A felicity judgment task is where the target sentence is asked to be judged in terms of how acceptable it fits within the discourse context (cf. Matthewson 2004). It differs from an acceptability judgment task in that the target sentence is known to be grammatical: what is being asked about is the acceptability of the semantic or pragmatic content of the sentence within the discourse context. A number of previous studies (cf. Table 5) have used this method, in both elicitation and questionnaire form (via Likert rating, explained below). With elicitation, for instance, Burge (2017: 50–51) shows how this task was useful to understand different verb modes in Tlingit and their compatibility with different modality types. She writes that a translation task of the target sentence was first used, where "[t]he consultant was asked to provide ways to express a similar notion in Tlingit, [. . .] before then being asked to judge the felicity of the main verb in the prospective, hortative, and potential verb modes."

Third, a (semi-)forced choice task presents the discourse context along with two (or more) target sentences. In a forced choice task, the language consultant must choose only one of the target sentences as the most appropriate (i.e., felicitous) given the context. The semi-forced choice task offers more flexibility in that the consultant could, e.g., choose one or more of the target sentences, or none. An example of the semi-forced task is illustrated in (30), as applied to Javanese (Vander Klok 2013a: 355). The two target sentences differed in the modal expression; one with the root necessity modal *kudu* 'have.to', and one with the deontic possibility modal *oleh* 'allow'. In this case, the aim was to distinguish Javanese expressions for necessity vs. possibility modal force. The discourse context targets necessity modal force, so it was hypothesized that only the target sentence with *kudu* 'have.to' would be felicitous. This was borne out, with 13/15 participants choosing (30a), and the additional two participants offering alternatives with *kudu*, but with a different verb (*ngepasno* 'to make sth just fit') or adding the definite enclitic to *luwehan=e* 'more', essentially choosing (30a) with minor modifications. None of the participants chose the target sentence in (30b) with *oleh* 'allow', a possibility modal.[8]

(30) Teleological necessity context: One bag of rice is usually enough for 3 days. There are still 2 bags left. I don't have time to buy more rice at the market because it's far away. So . . .

a. Aku **kudu**   nyukup-no   luweh-an   beras   iki
    1SG ROOT.NEC AV.enough-APPL   more-NMLZ   uncooked.rice DEM
    gawe enem dino.
    make six   day
    'I have to make this rice last for 6 days.'

b. # Aku **oleh**   nyukup-no   luweh-an   beras
    1SG   DEON.POS AV.enough-APPL   more-NMLZ   uncooked.rice
    iki gawe enem dino.
    DEM make six   day
    'I am allowed to make this rice last for 6 days.'

A second example is given in (31), where discourse context targets teleological weak necessity. The two target sentences were also minimal pairs; one with a root weak necessity modal *kudune* 'ought' and one with the epistemic weak necessity modal *mesthine* 'should' (each bi-morphemic, composed of the corresponding necessity modal plus the suffix *-ne*, see Vander Klok and Hohaus 2020). It was hypothesized that only the target sentence with *kudune* 'ought' would be felicitous. This was confirmed by the majority, with 9/15 participants choosing (31a) alone. Additionally, one participant chose (31b) and one participant chose both (a) and (b) target sentences, suggesting that 2/15 participants found the epistemic modal to be compatible in this discourse context, and differing from the main hypothesis. Finally, 4/15 participants offered a different alternative, with the expression *enak-e* 'it is nice', as shown in (31c). In this case, more research is

---

8 Note that in the original questionnaire, this context was intended to target 'deontic necessity' modality. However, as a reviewer correctly points out, this context rather targets teleological modality, based on the goal of avoiding to run out of food – as there is no 'rule or regulation' to make the rice last for 6 days. In hindsight, this context should have been used with a target sentence including *iso* 'can' in Javanese, which can be used to express teleological possibility. The modal *oleh* 'may' is only compatible with deontic possibility modality (Vander Klok 2013a). In the revised modal questionnaire, this context (also edited) is now under 'teleological necessity' modality (see the Appendix).

necessary to understand this expression, which derives from the adjective *enak* 'pleasing, pleasant (of voice, sounds, seat)'.[9]

(31) Teleological weak necessity context: There are different ways to get to the market in Blimbing. You can go by horse-carriage, rickshaw, public van, or just go by motorcycle by yourself. You are not sure how to go. Patrus advises you to take the horse-carriage because it is traditional. . .

    a.   Nek   sampeyan   reng   pasar   Blimbing,   **kudu-ne**
         if   2   to   market   Blimbing   ROOT.NEC-NE
       numpak   dokar.
       AV.ride   horse.carriage
       'If you go to Blimbing market, [you] should take the horse-carriage.'

    b. # *Nek   sampeyan   reng   pasar   Blimbing,   **mesthi-ne***
         if   2   to   market   Blimbing   EPIS.NEC-NE
       numpak   dokar.
       AV.ride   horse.carriage
       'If you go to Blimbing market, [you] should take the horse-carriage.'

    c.   *Nek   sampeyan   reng   pasar   Blimbing,   **enak-e**   numpak*
         if   2   to   market   Blimbing   pleasant-NE   AV.ride
       dokar.
       horse.carriage
       'If you go to Blimbing market, it is pleasant to take the horse-carriage.'

As shown by these examples, in both the forced or semi-forced choice task, it is advantageous for the researcher to allow the consultant to offer alternatives in cases they feel that none of the target sentences are felicitous in the discourse context, or to allow the consultant to provide additional felicitous examples which can corroborate the target sentences (see also Vander Klok 2014a, Vander Klok and Conners 2019).

The semi-forced choice task, in my experience, has also revealed contexts to not be robust in targeting only one cross-section of modal flavour and force/strength. Originally the discourse contexts were tested in elicitation before conducting the semi-forced choice task as a written questionnaire, and the contexts were chosen based on their success in elicitation. However, some contexts showed that in fact both target sentences are possible, as confirmed by multiple speakers.

---

[9] Among other descriptions of *enak*, see the entry in Robson and Wibisono (2002), accessed online at: http://sealang.net/java/

This result could suggest that either (i) both modal expressions in the language are compatible with that modal flavour/force combination or (ii) the discourse context can be understood as allowing a different type of modal flavour/force combination, and is therefore compatible with more than one combination. For example, (32) in the original modal questionnaire aims to target a deontic weak necessity modal (with *kudune* 'ought' in Javanese), and in the semi-forced choice task, this was contrasted with a target sentence with the epistemic weak necessity modal (*mesthine* 'should'). However, results for Paciran Javanese were that 7 participants chose (a) with *mesthine*, 5 chose (b) with *kudune*, and 3 chose both (a) and (b) target sentences.

(32) Weak necessity context: Diki's parents are really concerned about how well he does in school. They want him to succeed in all the subjects. But Diki wants to play football all the time instead of doing schoolwork. His parents order him:

a. *Kowe* **mesthi-ne**   *marek-no*   *PR-mu*   *disek*
   2   EPIS.NEC-NE AV.finish-APPL homework-your first
   sa'durunge *balbal-an.*
   before   football-VBLZ
   'You should finish your homework first before playing football.'

b. *Kowe* **kudu-ne**   *marek-no*   *PR-mu*   *disek*
   2   ROOT.NEC-NE AV.finish-APPL homework-your first
   sa'durunge *balbal-an.*
   before   football-VBLZ
   'You ought to finish your homework before playing football.'

It is only with independent research on what the modal expressions lexically specify for that scenario (i) can be ruled out. In the case for Javanese, the weak necessity modal *mesthine* 'should' only allows for epistemic modal flavour, while *kudune* 'ought' is only compatible with root (non-epistemic) modality (Vander Klok and Hohaus 2020). This follow-up research showed that the scenario (ii) held, in that actually this context is compatible with both epistemic and deontic modal flavours. Thus, for targeting the distinction between weak necessity epistemic and root, this was not a good discourse context, but perhaps could be still appropriate to target weak necessity in general. (Note that this example is no longer included in the revised modal questionnaire, among others.)

The fourth and last type of task illustrated here, a Likert rating task, is wherein participants are requested to rate the felicity of the target sentence given the discourse context between, e.g., 1 and 5. This task (or other similar ones, such as Magnitude Estimation Task, Featherston 2005) is appropriate if the researcher wants to use statistics to analyze the results. Veselinović (2019) used this task in order to gain robust results on how adult speakers of Bosnian, Croatian, Serbian differentiated syntactic constructions in epistemic vs. root modal contexts. Veselinović (2019: 184) adapted the modal questionnaire in Vander Klok (2014b) to include several target sentences to be rated within each discourse context: "The number of sentences per context varied between 3 (n=5, necessity circumstantial, possibility deontic and possibility circumstantial) and 6 (n=7)." These results were then compared with results from children, using a different task in Veselinović (2019). Vander Klok (2013a) also used a Likert rating task to check the robustness of individual target sentences in Javanese, which were judged using the semi-forced choice task.

In sum, the modal questionnaire can be used in a manner appropriate for working with the language consultants and the goals of the researcher, conducted via elicitation or as a written questionnaire through various tasks. The most common in previous scholarship included translation and felicity judgment tasks (or a combination); other choices used were the semi-forced choice or Likert rating tasks.

8 Conclusion

This chapter has examined the discourse contexts of a questionnaire to investigate the expression of modality in a given language, with the primary aim towards better understanding the cross-linguistic typology of lexical or grammatical strategy of modal expressions across modal flavour and modal force/strength. This chapter surveyed how the original modal questionnaire (Vander Klok 2014b) has been adapted and conducted for 30 languages, and offered a revised version of the questionnaire (see Appendix), building on the insights of this previous scholarship that is more comprehensive than the original. The current limitations of the revised version were addressed. Lastly, this chapter considered how the questionnaire can be implemented in a variety of ways, and as illustrated by the cross-linguistic use, each adapted to the research population and framework.

As a final note, I emphasize that the modal questionnaire is designed to facilitate the study of modality cross-linguistically, but it is not meant as a 'one-size-fits-all' method or the only type of methodology that can be used in fieldwork. Other studies have primarily used a mix of storyboards and corpus-based analysis, such as on the expression of possibility modality in two Oceanic languages (von Prince and Margetts 2019); or a mix of storyboards and targeted fieldwork, such as on Atayal (Austronesian) (Chen 2019), Washo (Isolate) (Bochnak 2015a,b) or Gitksan (Tsimshianic) (Matthewson 2013), or simply using elicitation (e.g., Deal 2011 on Nez Perce). Other studies have used a mix of picture books, semi-structured interviews and natural conversation, such as on Suriname Javanese (Austronesian) and Surinamese creole languages (Borges et al. 2017). These studies can provide further inspiration for developing discourse contexts. Overall, it is hoped that the revised questionnaire will enable fieldworkers, especially working on underdescribed languages, to better describe the expression of modality, and continue to be adapted in future studies across different languages.

References

Aikhenvald, Alexandra. 2004. *Evidentiality*. Oxford: Oxford University Press.
Bernander, Rasmus. 2017. *Grammar and grammaticalization in Manda: An analysis of the wider TAM domain in a Tanzanian Bantu language*. Gothenburg, Sweden: University of Gothenburg dissertation.
Bochnak, M. Ryan. 2015a. Variable force modality in Washo. In Thuy Bui & Deniz Özyıldız (eds.), *NELS 45: Proceedings of the Forty-Fifth Annual Meeting of the North East Linguistic Society: Volume 1*, 105–114. CreateSpace Independent Publishing Platform.
Bochnak, M. Ryan. 2015b. Underspecified modality in Washo. In Natalie Weber & Sihwei Chen (eds.), *Proceedings of the Eighteenth and Nineteenth Workshop on Structure and Constituency in the Languages of the Americas* (WSCLA), 3–17. Vancouver, BC: UBCWPL.
Bochnak, M. Ryan & Lisa Matthewson. 2020. Techniques in complex semantic fieldwork. *Annual Review of Linguistics* 6. 261–283.
Borges, Robert, Pieter Muysken, Sophie Villerius & Kofi Yakpo. 2017. The tense-mood-aspect systems of the languages of Suriname. In Kofi Yakpo & Pieter Muskyen (eds.), *Boundaries and bridges: Language contact in multilingual ecologies*, 111–132. Berlin: Mouton de Gruyter. https://www.degruyter.com/document/doi/10.1515/9781614514886-012/html
Bowler, Margit & John Gluckman. 2021. Gradability across grammatical domains. *Linguistic Variation* 21 (2). 281–321. https://doi.org/10.1075/lv.20003.bow
Burge, Heather. 2017. *Prospective aspect in Tlingit*. Vancouver, BC: University of British Columbia MA thesis.
Brennan, Virginia Mary. 1993. *Root and epistemic modal auxiliary verbs*. Amherst, MA: University of Massachusetts, Amherst dissertation.
Bybee, Joan, Revere Perkins & William Pagliuca. 1994. *The evolution of grammar: Tense, aspect and modality in the languages of the world*. Chicago: University of Chicago Press.
Chen, Sihwei. 2019. Graded possibility: Distinguishing epistemic modals in Atayal. In Sae-Youn Cho (ed.), *Proceedings of the 12th Generative Linguistics in the Old World & the 21st Seoul International Conference on Generative Grammar*, 419–428. Seoul, Republic of Korea: Hankook Munhwasa.
Chen, Sihwei, Vera Hohaus, Rebecca Laturnus, Meagan Louie, Lisa Matthewson, Hotze Rullmann, Ori Simchen, Claire K. Turner & Jozina Vander Klok. 2017. Past possibility cross-linguistically: Evidence from 12 languages. In Ana Arregui, Maria-Luisa Rivero &

Andrés Salanova (eds.), *Modality across syntactic categories*, 235–287. Oxford: Oxford University Press.
Cinque, Guglielmo. 1999. *Adverbs and functional heads: A cross-linguistic perspective*. New York & Oxford: Oxford University Press.
Condoravdi, Cleo. 2002. Temporal interpretation of modals: Modals for the present and for the past. In David Beaver, Stefan Kaufmann, Brady Clark & Luis Casillas (eds.), *The construction of meaning*, 59–88. Stanford: CSLI Publications.
Deal, Amy Rose. 2011. Modals without scales. *Language* 87. 559–585.
Faller, Martina. 2019. The discourse commitments of illocutionary reportatives. *Semantics & Pragmatics* 12 (8). http://dx.doi.org/10.3765/sp.12.8
Featherston, Stan. 2005. Magnitude estimation and what it can do for your syntax: Some wh-constraints in German. *Lingua* 115. 1525–1550.
von Fintel, Kai & Anthony S. Gillies. 2008. CIA leaks. *Philosophical Review* 117. 77–98.
von Fintel, Kai & Anthony S. Gillies. 2010. Must... stay... strong! *Natural Language Semantics* 18 (4). 351–383.
von Fintel, Kai & Sabine Iatridou. 2008. How to say 'ought' in foreign: The composition of weak necessity modals. In Jacqueline Guéron & Jacqueline Lecarme (eds.), *Time and modality*, 115–141. Dordrecht: Springer.
Fuentes, Pablo. To appear. Mapudungun frustrative *-fu-*: A modal analysis. Accepted in *Canadian Journal of Linguistics*.
Gluckman, John & Margit Bowler. 2020. The expression of modality in Logoori. *Journal of African Languages and Linguistics* 41 (2). 195–238.
Gluckman, John, Margit Bowler, Michael Diercks, Maurice Sifuna & Kelvin Alulu. 2017a. A typological study of modality in Luhya languages. Paper presented at the Association of Contemporary African Linguistics 48th meeting (ACAL 48), Indiana University, 30 March–2 April.
Gluckman, John, Margit Bowler, Maurice Sifuna & Michael Diercks. 2017b. Modality in Luhya: A typological study. Paper presented at the Linguistics Society of America 91st annual meeting, Austin, Texas, 5–8 January.
Hacquard, Valentine. 2010. On the event relativity of modal auxiliaries. *Natural Language Semantics* 18. 79–114.
Hohaus, Vera. 2020. Flavours of Samoan modality: The split between epistemic and root. Paper presented at the 27th Annual Meeting of the Austronesian Formal Linguistics Association, The National University of Singapore, 20–22 August 2020.
Homer, Vincent. 2013. Epistemic modals: High ma non troppo. In Seda Kan, Claire Moore-Cantwell & Robert Staubs (eds.) *Proceedings of NELS 40*. Amherst, MA: GLSA.
Hengeveld, Kees. 2004. Illocution, mood, and modality. In Geert Booij, Christian Lehmann, Joachim Mugdan & Stavros Skopeteas (eds.), *Morphology: An international handbook on inflection and word-formation*, vol. 2, 1190–1201. Berlin: Mouton de Gruyter.
Izvorski, Roumyana. 1997. The present perfect as an epistemic modal. *Semantics and Linguistic Theory* 7. 222–239.
Kalábová, Hana. 2017. *Materiály k popisu inarijské sámštiny* [Materials for the description of Inari Sami]. Prague, Czech Republic: Karlova University BA thesis.
Kawalya, Deo, Gilles-Maurice de Schryver & Koen Bostoen. 2018. Reconstructing the origins of the Luganda (JE15) modal auxiliaries *-sóból-* and *-yînz-*: A historical-comparative study across the West Nyanza Bantu cluster. *South African Journal of African Languages* 38 (1). 13–25.

Kolagar, Zahra. 2018. *Crosslinguistic variation in modal systems: Semantic fieldwork on Tabari*. Tübingen, Germany: Eberhard Karls Universität Tübingen MA thesis.

Krajinović, Ana. 2018a. Garden (MelaTAMP storyboards). https://doi.org/10.5281/zenodo.1421237 (accessed 16 February 2021).

Krajinović, Ana. 2018b. Making laplap (MelaTAMP storyboards). https://doi.org/10.5281/zenodo.1421185 (accessed 16 February 2021).

Kratzer, Angelika. 1977. What 'must' and 'can' must and can mean. *Linguistics and Philosophy* 1. 337–355.

Kratzer, Angelika. 1981. The notional category of modality. In Hans-Jurgen Eikmeyer & Hannes Rieser (eds.), *Words, worlds, and contexts: New approaches in word semantics*, 38–74. Berlin: Mouton de Gruyter.

Kratzer, Angelika. 1991. Modality. In Armin von Stechow & Dieter Wunderlich (eds.), *Semantics: An international handbook of contemporary research*, 639–650. Berlin: Mouton de Gruyter.

Kroeger, Paul. 2017. Frustration, culmination, and inertia in Kimaragang grammar. *Glossa* (2)1. https://doi.org/10.5334/gjgl.146

Lassiter, Dan. 2017. *Graded modality: Qualitative and quantitative perspectives*. Oxford: Oxford University Press.

Lyutfi, Sizen Ertan. 2021. *Modal verbs in Bulgarian: Their lexical specification and interaction with tense, aspect and evidentiality*. Oslo, Norway: University of Oslo MA thesis.

Matthewson, Lisa. 2004. On the methodology of semantic fieldwork. *International Journal of American Linguistics* 70. 369–415.

Matthewson, Lisa. 2012. On the (non-)future orientation of modals. *Proceedings of Sinn und Bedeutung* 16 (2). 431–446.

Matthewson, Lisa. 2013. Gitksan modals. *International Journal of American Linguistics* 79. 349–394.

Matthewson, Lisa. 2016. Modality. In Maria Aloni & Paul Dekker (eds.), *Cambridge handbook of formal semantics*, 726–775. Cambridge: Cambridge University Press.

Matthewson, Lisa. 2020. Evidence type, evidence location, evidence strength. In Chungmin Lee & Jinho Park (eds.), *Evidentials and modals*, 82–120. Current Research in the Semantics/Pragmatics Interface 39. Leiden: Brill.

Narrog, Heiko. 2012. *Modality, subjectivity, and semantic change*. Oxford: Oxford University Press.

Nauze, Fabrice. 2008. *Modality in typological perspective*. Amsterdam: Universiteit van Amsterdam dissertation.

Nuyts, Jan. 2006. Modality: Overview and linguistic issues. In William Frawley, Erin Eschenroeder, Sarah Mills & Thao Nguyen (eds.), *The expression of modality*, 1–26. Berlin: Mouton de Gruyter.

Palmer, Frank R. 1986. *Mood and modality*. Cambridge & New York: Cambridge University Press.

Palmer, Frank R. 2001. *Mood and modality*, 2nd edn. Cambridge & New York: Cambridge University Press.

Portner, Paul. 2009. *Modality*. Oxford & New York: Oxford University Press.

Portner, Paul. 2018. *Mood*. Oxford & New York: Oxford University Press.

Rech, Núbia Ferreira, Ana Paula Brandão & Marina Wit. 2017. The relationship between irrealis mood and deontic modality in Paresi (Arawak). *LIAMES* 18 (2). 229–252.

Rolka, Matthew & Seth Cable. 2014. Party food (Totem Field Storyboards). http://totemfieldstoryboards.org/stories/party_food/ (accessed 16 February 2021).

Robson, Stuart & Singgih Wibisono. 2002. *Javanese-English dictionary*. Singapore: Periplus.

Rubinstein, Aynat. 2012. *Roots of Modality*. Amherst, MA: University of Massachusetts, Amherst dissertation.

Rubinstein, Aynat. 2020. Weak necessity. In Lisa Matthewson, Cécile Meier, Hotze Rullmann & Thomas Ede Zimmermann (eds.), *Companion to semantics*. Oxford: Wiley-Blackwell.
Rubinstein, Aynat, Hillary Harner, Elizabeth Krawczyk, Daniel Simonson, Graham Katz & Paul Portner. 2013. Toward fine-grained annotation of modality in text. *Proceedings of IWCS 2013 Workshop on Annotation of Modal Meanings in Natural Language* (WAMM). http://www.aclweb.org/anthology/W13-0306
Rullmann, Hotze & Lisa Matthewson. 2018. Towards a theory of modal-temporal interaction. *Language* 94 (2). 281–331.
TFS Working Group. 2010. The fortune teller (Totem Field Storyboards). http://totemfieldstoryboards.org/stories/fortune_teller/ (accessed 16 February 2021).
TFS Working Group. 2012. Feeding Fluffy (Totem Field Storyboards). http://totemfieldstoryboards.org/stories/feeding_fluffy/ (accessed 16 February 2021).
van der Auwera, Johan & Vladimir Plungian. 1998. Modality's semantic map. *Linguistic Typology* 2. 79–124.
Vander Klok, Jozina. 2013a. Pure possibility and pure necessity modals in Paciran Javanese. *Oceanic Linguistics* 52 (2). 341–374.
Vander Klok, Jozina. 2013b. Bill vs. the weather (Totem Field Storyboards). http://totemfieldstoryboards.org/stories/bill_vs_the_weather/ (accessed 16 February 2021).
Vander Klok, Jozina. 2014a. On the use of questionnaires in semantic fieldwork: A case study on modality. In Aicha Belkadi, Kakia Chatsiou & Kirsty Rowan (eds.), *Proceedings of Language Documentation and Linguistic Theory* 4 (LDLT 4), 1–10. London: SOAS.
Vander Klok, Jozina. 2014b. Questionnaire on modality for cross-linguistic use. http://www.eva.mpg.de/lingua/tools-at-lingboard/questionnaires.php & http://tulquest.huma-num.fr/fr/node/70 (accessed 16 February 2021).
Vander Klok, Jozina & Thomas J. Conners. 2019. Using questionnaires as a tool for comparative linguistic field research: Two case studies on Javanese. In Aimée Lahaussois & Marine Vuillermet (eds.), *Methodological tools for linguistic description and typology*, 62–96. (Language Documentation & Conservation Special Publication 16). Honolulu: University of Hawai'i Press. http://hdl.handle.net/10125/24858
Vander Klok, Jozina & Vera Hohaus. 2020. Weak necessity without weak possibility: The composition of modal strength distinctions in Javanese. *Semantics & Pragmatics* 13 (12). https://doi.org/10.3765/sp.13.12
Veselinović, Dunja. 2019. *The syntax and acquisition of modal verb flavors*. New York, NY: New York University dissertation.
von Prince, Kilu. 2018a. Bananas (MelaTAMP storyboards). https://doi.org/10.5281/zenodo.1230385 (accessed 16 February 2021).
von Prince, Kilu. 2018b. Festival (MelaTAMP storyboards). https://doi.org/10.5281/zenodo.1231804 (accessed 16 February 2021).
von Prince, Kilu & Ana Margetts. 2019. Expressing possibility in two Oceanic languages. *Studies in Language* 43 (3). 628–667. https://doi.org/10.1075/sl.18051.pri
Wiemer, Björn. 2019. *Catching the elusive: Lexical evidentiality markers in Slavic languages (A questionnaire study and its background)*. Bern, Switzerland: Peter Lang D.
Yalcin, Seth. 2007. Epistemic modals. *Mind* 116. 983–1026.
Yalcin, Seth. 2010. Probability operators. *Philosophy Compass* 5. 916–937.
Zeisler, Bettina. 2016. Evidentiality, inferentiality, and speaker's attitude, questionnaire, or exemplary set. http://tulquest.huma-num.fr/en/node/41

Appendix: Revised modal questionnaire for cross-linguistic use

Example of how to cite this questionnaire:

Vander Klok, Jozina. 2022. Revised modal questionnaire for cross-linguistic use. http://www.eva.mpg.de/lingua/tools-at-lingboard/questionnaires.php (Accessed on DATE).

or
Vander Klok, Jozina. 2022. Revised modal questionnaire for cross-linguistic use. http://tulquest.huma-num.fr/fr/node/70 (Accessed on DATE).

Notes for using this revised questionnaire:

- This revised modal questionnaire builds on the first modal questionnaire (Vander Klok 2014b), through new discourse contexts and expanding its coverage to additional modality types to encompass a wider and more inclusive typological perspective. Its goals and aims as well as the versatility in its implementation are the same as the original (cf. the discussion of how to use the original questionnaire in Vander Klok 2014a).
- Vander Klok (this volume) is a paired resource that further explains the terminology in this modal questionnaire, and also brings together the results of a number of previous studies of the original modal questionnaire to explain the current expansion.
- This revised questionnaire is designed to be a fieldwork tool to investigate what might be the grammaticalized strategies of modal expressions in that language. For instance, does a given modal expression have the same grammaticalization for both modal force and modal flavour? for only modal force? for only modal flavour? for neither modal force or modal flavour? Some strategies could be, for example, lexical specification or underspecification, specific morphology, complementation strategies, the combination of a particle and mood, etc..
- Depending on the researchers' goals and timeline, this method can easily be paired with other fieldwork tools such as interviews, naturalistic recordings, or storyboards, etc. to corroborate the results of the questionnaire.

- The aim of this revised questionnaire is to provide discourse contexts that target one cross-section of modal force/strength (e.g. necessity, weak necessity, or possibility) and modal flavour (e.g. plain epistemic, deontic, circumstantial, teleological, and bouletic). It does not test for evidentiality or future modals, nor does it include how modal expressions may or may not overlap with mood (e.g., subjunctive, optative, imperative, etc.). Table 1 provides an overview.

Table 1: Overview of discourse contexts targeting specific modality types.

	Epistemic	Root / Non-epistemic			
		Participant-external		Participant-internal	
	Epistemic	Deontic	Teleological	Circumstantial	Bouletic
Necessity	5	4	3	4	3
Weak Necessity	3	3	3	–	–
Possibility	4	5	3	5	–

- The revised questionnaire also includes the *temporal perspective* (TP) and the *temporal orientation* (TO) of each of the target sentences, given the discourse context. Temporality in language interacts with modality in that the temporal perspective indicates the time at which the modal base is calculated (past, present, future), and temporal orientation establishes the relation between the temporal perspective and the time of the event (Condoravdi 2002; Matthewson 2012). Since the main purpose of the questionnaire is not to research possible differences in TP and TO (across different modal flavours), I have simply identified the TP and TO so that the researcher is aware of possible temporal-modal interactions in the language under study.
- I have created most of the contexts; some contexts are adapted from the literature on modality. These references are indicated below.
- The questionnaire contexts are given in English; depending on your fieldwork situation, it will be necessary to translate the contexts into the object language. It is very important that the translation is culturally specific to the language being studied (see e.g., Matthewson 2004). As this questionnaire was originally designed for Javanese (Austronesian), you will have to change a number of lexical items (proper names, times, etc.) to make the contexts culturally relevant. If you have translated the contexts, it is also important to conduct pilot tests beforehand to ensure that the main points of the contexts were not lost in translation.

Versatility of questionnaires

The following are examples of the ways in which this questionnaire can be used:
- elicitation with only one or a small group of speakers
- translation exercise (cf. Dahl 1985)
- fill-in-the-blank (this requires knowledge of the morpho-syntax of the object language)
- truth-value judgment task
- felicity judgment task
    - semi-forced choice task
    - forced choice task
    - rating task
- Following standard practices in experimental methodology, it is best to have fillers and practice examples in the implementation of the questionnaire.
- It is also ideal to be able to have feedback from the language consultants.
- Some contexts might not be as clean as possible; I would be very happy to hear of other construals, additional contexts, or comments on your experience in using these contexts.
Please feel free to email me at: jozina.vanderklok@mail.mcgill.ca

Test items

- Each context is intended to target one cross-section of modality. In addition, many contexts can be directly contrasted with one type of modality or modal force/strength. The target cross-section is indicated in square brackets at the beginning of the context (e.g., [Target: deontic necessity], and if there can be a direct contrast, this is also indicated as, e.g., [vs. epistemic necessity].
- The target sentence is indicated in rounded parentheses at the end of the context with the modal expression in capital letters. Where appropriate for English, I have indicated the infelicitous English modal expression (using the symbol #).
- The temporal orientation (TO) and temporal perspective (TP) is also indicated in square brackets following each discourse context.

The discourse contexts are organized in the following headings, shown in Table 2:

Table 2: Overview of the headings.

	EPISTEMIC	ROOT / NON-EPISTEMIC			
		PARTICIPANT-EXTERNAL		PARTICIPANT-INTERNAL	
	Epistemic	Deontic	Teleological	Circumstantial	Bouletic
Necessity	A1	B1	C1	D1	E1
Weak Necessity	A2	B2	C2	–	–
Possibility	A3	B3	C3	D3	–

A Epistemic

A1 Epistemic necessity

(1) [Target: epistemic necessity vs. deontic necessity] Ramadon routinely has coffee at Lisa's *warung kopi* (café) every day. It's not obligatory for Ramadon; he just goes for coffee there all the time. It's coffee time now, so. . . (Ramadon MUST be at Lisa's warung.)

[present TP; present TO]

(2) [Target: epistemic necessity vs. deontic necessity] You know that Mida goes to the market every morning after *subuh* (first prayer)/dawn, even though she is not required to. Right now, you wonder where Mida is. You check the clock: it's 5:30am. (Mida MUST be at the market.)

[present TP; present TO]

(3) [Target: epistemic necessity] (adapted from von Fintel and Gillies 2007; see also Peterson 2010: 129 on evidential component and logical inference)
The math teacher says: The ball is in A or in B or in C. It is not in A. It is not in B. So (it MUST be in C)

[present TP; present TO]

(4) [Target: epistemic necessity] Mas Hakim is calling for his cat. The cat is not coming. Mas Hakim looks for the cat in the kitchen, but the cat is not there. Then he looks in the living room, and in the bathroom, and in his sister's bedroom. The cat is not in any of those rooms. Mas Hakim thinks . . . (The cat MUST NOT be in the house.)

[present TP; present TO]

(5) [Target: epistemic necessity] Joko went to his friend's house last night, but when he arrived, he saw that the lights were off. Joko returned to his own house without bothering to knock because he thought at that time that . . . ('My friend MUST NOT be at home.') (. . .but he/she was!)

[past TP; present TO]

Note: *at that time* in the context refers to the time Joko decided not to knock.

A2 Epistemic weak necessity

(6) [Target: epistemic weak necessity vs. deontic weak necessity] You know that Pak Sari works from 8am–12pm every morning. Most of the time he goes to the office, but you know that once in a while he works at school. It is now 9am. You say to your friend: ('Pak Sari SHOULD be at the office now.')

[present TP; present TO]

(7) [Target: epistemic weak necessity vs. deontic weak necessity] You are not living in Yogya anymore. You notice how different it is with the weather in Malang, where you live right now. You know that in Yogya it's the rainy season now, and there's often rain in the afternoon, but not necessarily everyday. Now it's 3pm, so, you think: (It SHOULD / #OUGHT TO be raining now in Yogya.)

[present TP; present TO]

Note: This context is also compatible with epistemic possibility. Thus, the target sentence in English 'It MAY be raining now in Yogya.' is also felicitous.

(8) [Target: epistemic weak necessity vs. deontic weak necessity] When the light is on at Bu Alisma's house, it is usually a sign that she is home. You want to go visit Bu Alisma, and walking by her house, you see that the light is on right now. But you also see sandals by the front door that could be Alisma's sister. You think to yourself: (Bu Alisma SHOULD / #OUGHT TO be at home, . . .but it's not for sure/for certain.)

[present TP; present TO]

A3 Epistemic possibility

(9) [Target: epistemic possibility vs. epistemic necessity] Professor Farihi is not consistent. The students never know if he's going to come or not to give a lecture. Today, it's time to start class and the students are waiting again. (He MIGHT / #MUST be coming to the university today.)
[present TP; future TO]

(10) [Target: epistemic possibility vs. epistemic necessity] Dewi's necklace is missing, and she is looking for her necklace. She looks in her wardrobe and on top of the wardrobe. It's not there. She looks on top of the tv. It's not there. She looks in her backpack; it's not there. Wait! She hasn't checked her sister's wardrobe yet, but Dewi really isn't sure if it would be there . . . (Dewi's necklace MIGHT / #MUST be in her sister's wardrobe.)
[present TP; present TO]

(11) [Target: epistemic possibility vs. epistemic (weak) necessity] Bambang is looking for his pet cat, but cannot find it. Bambang knows that his cat is very elusive/mysterious. Bambang tells his sister:
(The cat MAY be inside. The cat MAY also be outside.)
(The cat MAY be inside and the cat MAY be outside.)
(#The cat MUST be inside and the cat MUST be outside.)
(#The cat SHOULD be inside and the cat SHOULD be outside.)
[present TP; present TO]

Note: if the language does not allow sentential conjunction, the additive particle (*also* in English) could be substituted instead.

(12) [Target: epistemic possibility vs. deontic possibility] Amin's parents told him that he is not allowed to go to see his friend in Jakarta because it is too far away. You heard that Amin is leaving Paciran next week, but you don't know where he will go. Amin is a daring type of guy that usually does things that he is not permitted to do. You think: (Amin MAY/MIGHT/ #is allowed to go to Jakarta.)
[present TP; future TO]

B Deontic

B1 Deontic necessity

(12) [Target: deontic necessity] In Indonesia, the law states that when you ride a motor bike... (You MUST wear a helmet.)

[present TP; present TO]

(13) [Target: deontic necessity] (adapted from von Fintel 2006, von Fintel & Gillies 2007) You are going to visit your friend in the hospital. When you enter in the hospital, you stop at the information desk to inquire what room your friend is in. But the receptionist at the information desk tells you that you can't visit your friend now because it's already 8pm! She says, "I'm sorry, the hospital regulations say that... (Visitors MUST leave by 6pm.)"

[present TP; present TO]

(14) [Target: deontic necessity vs. deontic weak necessity] When Agus went to the hospital, he was confused at first because he tried to get a doctor's appointment, but he couldn't! But then, the nice lady at the information desk explained that he didn't yet have a hospital ID card to be a patient here, and if you don't have one, there are no exceptions. This is because the regulations at the hospital state: (Patients MUST/#SHOULD have a hospital ID card to use the hospital services.)

[present TP; present TO]

(15) [Target: deontic necessity] Tomo's boss is very strict about getting tasks completed on time. Today, the boss ordered Tomo to finish fixing the motorbike by the end of work day. Now, it is noon. Tomo thinks to himself: (I HAVE TO finish fixing the motorbike this afternoon/today.)

[present TP; future TO]

B2 Deontic weak necessity

(16) [Target: deontic weak necessity] Waiq is the oldest child, and he is not yet married. His younger brother, Hakim, wants to get married. But according to some family members... (the oldest OUGHT TO marry first.)

[present TP; future TO]

(17) [Target: deontic weak necessity] (based on von Fintel and Iatridou 2008) Your friend tells you that the rules of the restaurant state that employees must wash their hands after going to the bathroom. You reply to your friend: (Non-employees OUGHT TO wash their hands too!)
[present TP; future TO]

(18) [Target: deontic weak necessity vs. deontic necessity] Your aunt says that the Sultan's son has to speak *krama* (High Javanese) since he is part of the royal family. She also thinks that in order to show the correct respect and honour to others, (all Javanese people OUGHT TO speak *krama*).
[present TP; future TO]

B3 Deontic possibility

(19) [Target: deontic possibility vs. deontic necessity] The ferris wheel ride at WBL [an amusement park] is only for children under 15 years old. Tutus is 12 years old. It is not obligatory for Tutus to go on the ride if she doesn't want to. (Tutus MAY/#must ride the ferris wheel.)
[present TP; future TO]

(20) [Target: deontic possibility vs. deontic necessity] According to the rules of the hospital, only family members are allowed to enter the patient's room during visiting hours. You came to visit your sister, but it was after visiting hours. But the really nice nurse says. . . (You MAY/#MUST enter.)
[present TP; future TO]

(21) [Target: deontic possibility vs. deontic (weak) necessity] You are making plans for tomorrow night to get together with your friend. Your friend says:
(You CAN stay overnight and you CAN go home.)
(You CAN stay overnight. You CAN also go home.)
(#You OUGHT to stay overnight and you OUGHT to go home.)
(#You HAVE to stay overnight and you HAVE to go home.)
[present TP; future TO]

Note: if the language does not allow sentential conjunction, the additive particle (*also* in English) could be substituted instead. Disjunction could also be used (*or* in English), but it would not then work to elicit minimal pairs with necessity modals.

(22) [Target: deontic possibility vs. circumstantial possibility] Ria fell down the stairs and broke her arm a while ago. She hasn't been lifting her baby while her arm was hurt because the baby is heavy. Finally, she has recovered, and she went to the doctor for a final check-up. The doctor gave her permission to lift her baby. But when she got home after her visit to the doctor, Ria found that she is still too weak to lift her baby.
(Ria CAN/MAY/ #able to lift her baby.)

[present TP; future TO]

(23) [Target: deontic possibility vs. circumstantial possibility] Kana's teacher told her class that it was okay/they were allowed to go swimming, but Kana doesn't want to because she cannot swim! (Kana CAN go swimming.)

[present TP; future TO]

C Teleological

C1 Teleological necessity

(24) [Target: teleological necessity] (adapted from von Fintel and Iatridou 2008) There is only one main road, Deandles, along the northern coast of Java to get to Semarang from Paciran. (If you go to Semarang from Paciran, you HAVE TO/ #SHOULD take this road.)

[present TP; future TO]

(25) [Target: teleological necessity] (based on Gluckman and Bowler 2020) Semarang is playing in a tournament. In order to advance: (Semarang HAS TO/MUST/ #SHOULD beat Yogyakarta.)

[present TP; future TO]

(26) [Target: teleological necessity] The best fried rice in town is made by Pak Bambang. You have invited your sister for dinner, and decide to have fried rice. You tell your sister: We HAVE TO order from Bambang to eat the best fried rice.

[present TP; future TO]

(27) [Target: teleological necessity] (adapted from Horne 1961: 269) A pound of rice usually lasts for three days, and there are two pounds left now. I don't have time to go to the market because I am away fishing for the next

6 days... (So I HAVE TO/??CAN make the remaining rice last for six more days.)

[present TP; future TO]

C2 Teleological weak necessity

(28) [Target: teleological weak necessity] (adapted from von Fintel & Iatridou 2008) There are different ways to get to the market in Blimbing. You can go by horse-carriage, rickshaw, public van, or just go by motorcycle by yourself. You are not sure how to go. Patrus advises you to take the horse-carriage because it is traditional. (To get to the market in Blimbing, you SHOULD take a horse-carriage.)

[present TP; future TO]

(29) [Target: teleological weak necessity] (adapted from von Fintel & Iatridou 2008) There are three ways to get to Yogya: the Semarang Route, the Bojonegero route, and the Surabaya route. Cak Khuluq says that the Bojonegero route is very beautiful. So according to him, (If you go to Yogya, you SHOULD take the Bojonegero route.)

[present TP; future TO]

(30) [Target: teleological weak necessity vs. teleological necessity]. Your friend wants to buy a new shirt for her new job at a reasonable price. There are many nice shops for professional clothes in the area, and you work at one of them and think it offers good prices. You say: You SHOULD / #HAVE TO go to my shop to buy a new shirt.

[present TP; future TO]

C3 Teleological possibility

(31) [Target: teleological possibility] (based on Kolagar 2018: 52) There are two different ways to get to Sari from Tehran. Both take around 7 hours by bus and they are equally beautiful. (You CAN / #MUST take the Haraz road.)

[present TP; future TO]

(32) [Target: teleological possibility]. There are two swimming pools in the town with the exact same design and both are equal distance from your house. You plan to go swimming later on, but have no specific desire for which

pool to go to. But you know that more people swim at the pool to the west for some reason. You tell your sister: ('We CAN go to the swimming pool to the west (to meet more people).')

[present TP; future TO]

(33) [Target: teleological possibility] Your friend wants to buy a new shirt for her new job. Since there are many nice shops for professional clothes in the area, you say: ('You CAN go to Maula's boutique.')

[present TP; future TO]

D Circumstantial

D1 Circumstantial necessity

(34) [Target: circumstantial necessity] You are on a bus to Yogya. You have not had a chance to go to the toilet for 4 hours, and your bladder is full. You text your friend: (I HAVE to pee so badly!)

[present TP; future TO]

(35) [Target: circumstantial necessity] Normally at *ngaji* (Holy Qu'ran reading), it is time to be serious. But then we saw Bu Yeni had fallen asleep in a funny position/with her mouth wide open. (Our friend Bu Siti HAD TO laugh.)

[past TP; present/future TO]

(36) [Target: circumstantial necessity] (cf. Kratzer 1991, von Fintel 2006, Gluckman & Bowler 2020) In the middle of a conversation, you feel a sneeze coming on. You say: (Excuse me! I HAVE TO sneeze.)

[present TP; future TO]

(37) [Target: circumstantial necessity with inanimate subject] (from Gluckman & Bowler 2020: 216) You have an old car. Because it is old: (The car NEEDS/ HAS TO have oil.)

[present TP; present TO]

D2 Circumstantial possibility

(38) [Target: circumstantial possibility vs. epistemic possibility] (Adapted from Kratzer 1991) Context: Ani came to visit a small island in the Philippines. She noticed that the climate and many of the plants are similar to some places she visited in Sulawesi, Indonesia. For example, the temperature is the same, the rainfall is the same, the types of rocks and the soil are the same. But when she looked around, she didn't find any *duku* trees anywhere. But because the temperature, rainfall, and soil are the same, she thinks that: (Duku trees CAN/#might grow here.)

[present TP; future TO]

(39) [Target: circumstantial possibility vs. epistemic possibility] Jozi knows how to make *dudoh menir* [a kind of sauce]. Now she is back in Canada, and she wants to make *dudoh menir*, but the right kind of ingredients are not sold where she lives! So she's unhappy because she wanted to show her parents how to make *dudoh menir*. (Jozina CAN / #might make *dudoh menir*.)

[present TP; future TO]

(40) [Target: circumstantial possibility vs. deontic possiblity] Budi was in a motorbike accident 3 weeks ago, and he sprained his ankle. Budi is able to walk now. However, the doctor told Budi that he is not allowed to walk until 5 weeks after the accident. (Budi CAN / #may walk now.)

[present TP; present TO]

(41) [Target: circumstantial possibility vs. deontic possibility] (adapted from Kratzer 1991:640) Pak Diki is quite old now, but he is still strong. His children are scared that he will hurt his back if he does any intense labour, so they told him that he is forbidden to lift heavy things. But one day Diki's friend Roshid asked to help him in the field, because Roshid knows Diki is still strong. So when Roshid saw a large rock that had to be moved, he asked Diki straightaway for help (but he didn't tell Diki's children!). Roshid knew that... (Diki CAN lift that rock)

[present TP; present TO]

(42) [Target: circumstantial possibility vs. deontic possibility] The 'travel' vans have a limit of 13 people by law. But the drivers don't care, and stop for more than 13 people. Also, the vans are bigger than you think. (Travel vans CAN / #may fit 20 people.)

[present TP; present TO]

E Bouletic

E1 Bouletic necessity

(43) [Target: bouletic necessity] (based on Gluckman & Bowler 2020: 217): You love designer shoes. You see beautiful Gucci shoes in a store window, and you say: (I WANT/NEED TO buy them.)

[present TP; future TO]

(44) [Target: bouletic necessity vs. deontic necessity] Your friend asks you what you desire to do today since it is a holiday and you both are not required to do any tasks today. You say: (I WANT to go to the cinema.)

[present TP; future TO]

(45) [Target: bouletic necessity] A daughter tells her parent: (My friend WANTS to visit me. I also WANT my friend to visit.)

[present TP; future TO]

References

Dahl, Östen. 1985. *Tense and aspect systems*. Oxford & New York: B. Blackwell.
von Fintel, Kai. 2006. Modality and Language. In Donald M. Borchert (ed.), *Encyclopedia of philosophy*, 20–27. 2nd edn. Detroit: MacMillan Reference USA.
von Fintel, Kai & Anthony S. Gillies. 2007. An opinionated guide to epistemic modality. In Tamar Gendler & John Hawthorne (eds.), *Oxford studies in epistemology, vol. 2*, 32–62. Oxford: Oxford University Press.
von Fintel, Kai & Sabine Iatridou. 2008. How to say *ought* in foreign: The composition of weak necessity modals. In Jacqueline Guéron & Jacqueline Lecarme (eds.), *Time and modality*, 115–141. Dordrecht: Springer.
Gluckman, John & Margit Bowler. 2020. The expression of modality in Logoori. *Journal of African Languages and Linguistics* 41 (2). https://doi.org/10.1515/jall-2020-2010.
Horne, Elinor C. 1961. *Beginning Javanese*. New Haven, London: Yale University Press.
Kratzer, Angelika. 1991. Modality. In Armin von Stechow & Dieter Wunderlich (eds.), *Semantics: An international handbook of contemporary research*, 639–650. Berlin: Mouton de Gruyter.
Matthewson, Lisa. 2004. On the methodology of semantic fieldwork. *International Journal of American Linguistics* 70. 369–415.
Peterson, Tyler. 2010. *Epistemic modality and evidentiality in Gitksan at the semantics-pragmatics interface*. Vancouver, BC: University of British Columbia dissertation.
Rullmann, Hotze, Lisa Matthewson & Henry Davis. 2008. Modals as distributive indefinites. *Natural Language Semantics* 16. 317–357.

Vander Klok, Jozina. 2012. *Tense, aspect, and modality in Paciran Javanese*. Montreal, QC: McGill University dissertation.

Vander Klok, Jozina. 2014a. On the use of questionnaires in semantic fieldwork: A case study on modality. In Aicha Belkadi, Kakia Chatsiou & Kirsty Rowan (eds.), *Proceedings of Language Documentation and Linguistic Theory* 4 (LDLT 4), 1–10. London: SOAS.

Vander Klok, Jozina. 2014b. Questionnaire on modality for cross-linguistic use. http://www.eva.mpg.de/lingua/tools-at-lingboard/questionnaires.php & http://tulquest.huma-num.fr/fr/node/70 (accessed 16 February 2021).

Daniel Reisinger, Lisa Matthewson & Hotze Rullmann
4 Using corpora to investigate modal-temporal interactions

Abstract: Two corpus-based studies are described that focus on the temporal interpretation of modals: a larger case study using English data from *COCA*, and a smaller pilot study on an underdescribed language, St'át'imcets (Salish), with data drawn from a story collection (Alexander 2016). The two parameters of temporal perspective and temporal orientation (Condoravdi 2002) are investigated, testing hypotheses developed in an earlier theoretical study (Rullmann and Matthewson 2018). Preliminary results show that the theoretical predictions are largely confirmed. Advantages and shortcomings of the corpus-based approach are evaluated, and the importance of consulting with native speakers to interpret corpus data is emphasized.

1 Introduction

1.1 The plan

In this chapter we report on two corpus-based studies on modality: a larger one focusing on English data, and a smaller pilot study focusing on an underdescribed language, St'át'imcets (a.k.a. Lillooet; Salish). Our studies target a topic that so far has not, to our knowledge, been addressed in the corpus-based literature: modal-temporal interactions. Thus, for each corpus item in our sample, we investigate

---

Acknowledgments: We would like to thank Henry Davis, Bronwyn Bjorkman, and the members of the UBC TAP Lab (Tense and Aspect in the Pacific Lab) for helpful feedback. We are also grateful to three anonymous reviewers and to Jozina Vander Klok for detailed comments on an earlier draft of this paper. Thanks also to Carl Alexander for his wonderful collection of stories that formed the corpus for the St'át'imcets study reported on here. The research reported in this paper was funded in part by the Social Sciences and Humanities Research Council of Canada (grant #435-2016-0381).

Daniel Reisinger, University of British Columbia, 2613 West Mall, Vancouver, BC, Canada V6T 1Z4, e-mail: daniel.reisinger@ubc.ca
Lisa Matthewson, University of British Columbia, 2613 West Mall, Vancouver, BC, Canada V6T 1Z4, e-mail: lisa.matthewson@ubc.ca
Hotze Rullmann, University of British Columbia, 2613 West Mall, Vancouver, BC, Canada V6T 1Z4, e-mail: hotze.rullmann@ubc.ca

https://doi.org/10.1515/9783110721478-005

its temporal properties, and where appropriate we test hypotheses about the interactions between modal flavour, modal force, and temporal properties. Our goal is not to make a direct (quantitative or qualitative) comparison between the two languages; this would require further research, given the vast grammatical contrasts in the modal and tense-aspect systems of the two languages, as well as the differences in the availability and size of texts, and the non-identity of genres (written fiction for English, and oral narratives for St'át'imcets). However, by applying the same theoretical framework and annotation scheme to both languages, we hope to gain insight into the extent to which well-resourced languages like English and underdescribed languages like St'át'imcets can be investigated using the same approach.

Our goals in the paper are two-fold: first, to describe our methodology and evaluate its advantages and shortcomings, and second, to report our preliminary results. We will show that it is possible to test theoretical hypotheses about modal-temporal interactions via a corpus study, and we will also show that the theoretical proposals in prior literature about both English and St'át'imcets are mostly confirmed in our data, although there are some wrinkles as well. We will also show that the investigation of corpus data led to the discovery of new empirical phenomena that had not been discussed in prior literature; this was particularly true in the St'át'imcets pilot study. Finally, we will re-affirm a point that has been (implicitly or explicitly) assumed in much of the existing literature: when working on subtle semantic questions such as modal-temporal interactions, it is important to have native speakers to interpret the corpus data. This makes it more challenging to conduct such studies on minority and/or endangered languages such as St'át'imcets, and the challenge is further exacerbated by the smaller size of the available corpora on such languages, and the potentially smaller range of available genres. However, we hope to convince readers that the challenges are worth it for the insights that result.

In the remainder of this section, we briefly overview some of the literature involving corpus studies of modality. In section 2, we provide theoretical background on modal-temporal interactions and lay out our hypotheses and their predictions. Section 3 presents our English case study, outlining our methodology and results, and section 4 does the same for our St'át'imcets case study. Section 5 concludes with some discussion of the advantages and challenges of this type of corpus-based study.

1.2 Previous corpus studies on modals

Our goal in this section is not to provide a comprehensive review or evaluation of prior literature. Instead, we merely introduce some examples to give an impression of the types of corpus-based modality research that has been, and is being, carried out. For relevant general overviews, see also Katz (2019) on corpus methods in semantics, and van der Auwera and Diewald (2012) on a range of methods for studying modality.

There is a reasonably sizable body of prior research that uses corpus methods to investigate the semantics of modal elements. The majority of the prior research is on large, well-studied languages, predominantly English and German, although see for example Matsuyoshi et al. (2010), Al-Sabbagh, Diesner, and Girju (2013), Mendes et al. (2016), and references therein, for studies on other (still large) languages such as Japanese, Arabic, or Portuguese. Recently, researchers have begun investigating modality in underdescribed languages using corpus data; see in particular work by Kilu von Prince and colleagues on various Oceanic languages (e.g., von Prince et al. 2019; von Prince and Margetts 2019). Mberamihigo (2014) is a corpus-based study of modality in Kirundi; Jasionyte (2012) targets Lithuanian necessity modals. There are steadily increasing possibilities for corpus-based research on underdescribed languages these days, due to a growing number of open access corpora on many underdescribed languages: the EDLP archive (https://www.elararchive.org/), PARADISEC (https://catalog.paradisec.org.au/), and the Jakarta Field Station archive (https://lingweb.eva.mpg.de/archive/jakarta/data.php.html), among others.

A central theme in many corpus-based studies on modality is the identification of modal flavour, and correlations of modal flavour with other phenomena. Examples of studies investigating the modal flavour of English or German modals include Diewald (1999), Mortelmans (2000), Recski (2002), de Haan (2011), Ruppenhofer and Rehbein (2012), and Rubinstein et al. (2013). For example, de Haan (2011) uses the Brown and Switchboard corpora to probe deontic vs. epistemic readings of English *must*; the goal is to create an automatic tagging mechanism to predict modal flavour using features of the surrounding constructions (such as the subject of the sentence, declarative vs. interrogative sentence type, and so on). Register differences are found, such that in the written Brown corpus *must* has predominantly deontic meanings, while in the spoken Switchboard corpus epistemic meanings are more prevalent. Rubinstein et al.'s (2013) study using the MPQA corpus (Wiebe, Wilson, and Cardie 2005) reveals an interesting finding about annotations of modals in corpora: they find that when it came to modal flavour, their two annotators reliably agreed only on the highest-level distinctions (between priority and non-priority modal flavours),[1] and there was a lack of reliable inter-annotator agreement on the fine-grained distinctions.

---

[1] In the modal literature, the concept of *priority* refers to those modals that identify some possibility as more preferable than another (cf. Portner 2009). This usually includes modals with bouletic, deontic, and teleological interpretations.

Another research question that can be probed using corpus data is the semantic embeddability of epistemic modals, as in Hacquard and Wellwood (2012). These authors examine *might, can, must,* and *have to* in embedded environments (conditional antecedents, questions, and complements of attitude verbs) using the New York Times section of the English Gigaword Corpus. They establish that epistemic modal readings are embeddable, but in a restricted way as compared with root modals; the particular embedding environment also plays a role (e.g., epistemic modals are rare in the antecedents of conditionals, and resist embedding under attitude verbs of desire or command).

Modal flavour can also be investigated using historical corpora, to trace diachronic developments. For example, Dollinger (2006) traces the development of *must* and *have to* in the Canadian, American, and British English of the late 18th and early 19th centuries. He investigates the rise of epistemic readings of these modals, and the extent of 'colonial lag' (where first-generation settlers retain older features of the language). Diachronic studies of modal force also exist, including for example Yanovich (2006). Yanovich investigates the modal force of the precursors of English *must*. He argues that Old English **motan* was a variable-force modal, which developed into a modal that was ambiguous between necessity and possibility in Early Middle English.

While many corpus studies of modality focus on a single language, comparative investigations include for example Mortelmans (2012), who compares English *must*, Dutch *moeten*, and German *müssen*. Using a three-way translation corpus of fictional texts, she finds that English *must* covers a wider range of meanings than its Dutch or German counterparts. Van der Auwera et al. (2005) use parallel corpora in English and Slavonic languages (consisting of a Harry Potter novel) to compare verbal with adverbial strategies to express epistemic uncertainty (e.g., *may, might, could* vs. *maybe, perhaps*). See also Wärnsby (2006) on Swedish vs. English, and Šoliene (2012) on Lithuanian vs. English.

The acquisition of modals can also be investigated using corpora. There is much work on the acquisition of modal flavour and modal force; see for example Papafragou (1998), Cournane (2014, 2015, 2021), van Dooren et al. (2017), Dieuleveut et al. (2019), as well as the discussion in Cournane and Hacquard (this volume). Not all of this research is solely on English; see for example van Dooren et al. (2019), which compares Dutch with English.

As we have seen, a wide range of different specific research questions are posed in the existing corpus-based literature. However, except for research on L1 acquisition showing that temporal orientation may serve as an important cue for children in detecting the distinction between epistemic and non-epistemic modal flavour (van Dooren et al. 2017, 2019; Cournane 2021), to our knowledge, there has not been a corpus study so far that specifically focuses on the temporal properties of modals. That is where our project comes in. Before presenting our two case studies, we provide some necessary theoretical background.

2 Theoretical background

2.1 Temporal perspective and temporal interpretation

The theoretical basis for this study is provided by the model of modal-temporal interaction proposed by Rullmann and Matthewson (2018), which builds on a long line of research in formal semantics, most notably Condoravdi (2002). Condoravdi pointed out that the interpretation of modals is sensitive to time in (at least) two different ways, which she calls Temporal Perspective (TP) and Temporal Orientation (TO). Roughly speaking, TP is the time at which the modal claim is assessed, whereas TO is the temporal relationship between the modal's TP and the time of the eventuality described by the complement of the modal. For example, the epistemic *must have* in (1) has present TP, because the sentence makes a claim about the speaker's knowledge at the time of utterance, whereas it has past TO because the grading of the papers took place at some time prior to that. Paraphrasing loosely in possible-worlds semantics, (1) says "In every world that is compatible with what the speaker believes *at the utterance time* (= present TP), the speaker graded more than 20 papers *at some previous time* (= past TO)."

(1) I **must have** graded more than 20 papers today.   (present TP, past TO)

By contrast, the deontic semi-modal *had to* in (2) has past TP and future TO, because it makes a claim about the speaker's obligations at a time in the past (10 a.m. on the day of utterance), but the grading is in the future relative to the TP (some time after 10 a.m.). A rough paraphrase would be: "In every world compatible with the speaker's obligations *at 10 a.m. on the day of utterance* (= past TP), the speaker grades more than 20 papers *at a time later than that* (= future TO)."

(2) [Context: It is 5 p.m.]
     At 10 a.m. today, I still **had to** grade more than 20 papers.   (past TP, future TO)

Condoravdi (2002) further observed a systematic ambiguity in the temporal interpretation of the expression *might have* in English: (3) can have either present TP and past TO, or past TP and future TO. This ambiguity is resolved by the continuations in (3a) and (3b). (3a) brings out the present TP, past TO reading: in this context, the sentence makes an epistemic claim expressing the speaker's current uncertainty about a past event. With the continuation (3b), on the other hand, the sentence is interpreted with past TP and future TO: it expresses a counterfactual claim about how, if circumstances had been different, events would have unfolded in the future from a vantage point located in the past. In (3a,b) this difference in the temporal interpretation of the modal seems tied to a difference in modal flavour: (3a) is epistemic, whereas (3b) has circumstantial modality (of which we take counterfactuality to be a subtype).

(3) *The teaching assistant **might have** graded this paper already* ...
    a. ... *but I'm not sure if they did.*   (epistemic: present TP, past TO)
    b. ... *if they had procrastinated less.*   (counterfactual: past TP, future TO)

However, Rullmann and Matthewson (2018) argue that temporal properties and modal flavour are independent of each other, and that in principle any modal flavour can go with any temporal profile (TP and TO), although there may be certain lexical restrictions on individual modals. In particular, they show that contrary to what is often assumed in the literature, epistemic modals can have past TP. A case in point would be (4), inspired by an example from von Fintel and Gillies (2008: 87, ex. (21a), *There might have been ice cream in the freezer*). In the context provided, (4) has an epistemic modal with past TP because it makes a claim about the speaker's epistemic state at a time preceding the utterance time, namely the time at which she texted the teaching assistant. At that time, she considered it possible that the teaching assistant had already graded the paper, but at the utterance time this is no longer the case. (For further details and extensive empirical evidence, see Rullmann and Matthewson 2018.)

(4) [Context: Prof. A is grading a stack of papers. She picks a paper from the pile, looks at it, and puts it aside. Prof. A then sends a text message and proceeds to grade the other papers. After a while, Prof. A receives a text, picks up the first paper, and starts to grade it. Prof. B, who has observed all this, asks: "Why did you send a text just now?" Prof. A answers:]

*The teaching assistant **might have** graded that paper already, but he says he didn't, so I guess I'll have to do it myself.*   (epistemic: past TP, past TO)

To account for modal-temporal interactions, Rullmann and Matthewson (2018) hypothesize that universally, TP is determined by temporal operators that scope immediately above a modal, whereas TO is determined by temporal operators below it. Assuming a syntactic hierarchy as in (5) where modals are sandwiched between tense and aspect, this means that typically TP will be determined by tense, and TO by aspect.

(5) Tense > Modal > Aspect

Rullmann and Matthewson (2018) apply this framework to give an analysis of modal-temporal interactions in four languages: English, Dutch, St'át'imcets (Salish), and Gitksan (Tsimshianic). These languages differ in the details of both their temporal and modal systems. In English and Dutch, past and present tense is marked overtly, whereas St'át'imcets and Gitksan have a covert non-future tense. Rullmann and Matthewson further point out that St'át'imcets and Gitksan also differ from the two Germanic languages in that their modals are lexically specified for modal flavour (i.e., different modals are used for epistemic, deontic, and other types of modality), and in the way they encode TO: they mark future TO by means of prospective aspect in the complement of the modal,[2] whereas English and Dutch overtly mark past TO using the perfect (with the auxiliary *have*). Examples illustrating this for Gitksan are given in (6)–(7); see section 4 for St'át'imcets modal data. In (6), there is no prospective aspect under the modal and the TO is either past or present; in (7) the prospective aspect enforces future TO.[3]

(6) *Yugw=**imaa/ima'**=hl* wis.
     IPFV=**EPIS**=CN   rain
     'It might have rained.' / 'It might be raining.' / ≠ 'It might rain (in the future).'
     ✓ Context: You see puddles, and the flowers looking fresh and damp.
     ✓ Context: You hear pattering on the roof.
     # Context: You hear thunder, so you think it might rain soon.
     (Matthewson 2013: 364–365)

---

2 This prospective marking appears overtly for all modals in Gitksan and for epistemic modals in St'át'imcets, but for circumstantial modals in St'át'imcets the prospective semantics is folded into the lexical semantics of the modals.
3 Glossing abbreviations follow the Leipzig Glossing Rules where possible. Additional glosses: CIRC circumstantial modality; CRED consonant reduplication; DIR directive transitivizer; EXCL exclusive marker; EXIS existential; FRED final reduplication; INDEP independent pronoun; INVIS invisible; MID middle intransitivizer; POS possibility; PROSP prospective; REM remote; TRED total reduplication; VIS visible.

(7) Yugw=**imaa/ima'**=hl **dim** wis.
     IPFV=**EPIS**=CN   **PROSP** rain
     ≠ 'It might have rained.' / ≠ 'It might be raining.' / 'It might rain (in the future).'
     # Context: You see puddles, and the flowers looking fresh and damp.
     # Context: You hear pattering on the roof.
     √ Context: You hear thunder, so you think it might rain soon.
     (Matthewson 2013: 365)

As for TP, this is never marked overtly in St'át'imcets and Gitksan (since these languages do not distinguish past from present tense), whereas in Dutch it is marked by means of overt tense inflection on modal verbs (which inflect just like main verbs do). Examples showing this are given in (8)–(9). In the Gitksan example in (8), past vs. present TP is not encoded, while in Dutch in (9), it is.

(8) **Da'a̱khlxw**-i-s   Henry   **dim**   jam-t.
     CIRC.POS-TR-PN   Henry   **PROSP** cook-3.II
     'Henry is able to cook.' / 'Henry was able to cook.'   (past or present TP, future TO)
     (Rullmann and Matthewson 2018: 305)

(9) a. Henry **kan**   koken.
         Henry **can.PRS.SG** cook.INF
         'Henry is able to cook.'

     b. Henry **kon**   koken.
         Henry **can.PST.SG** cook.INF
         'Henry was able to cook.'

English modal auxiliaries are inflectionally impoverished, in that they are not inflected for tense (at least not productively). As a result, English modal-temporal interactions are less transparent than in the other three languages. Because English cannot overtly mark modal auxiliaries for tense, it sometimes has to resort to a *have* following the modal in order to encode TP rather than TO; hence the ambiguity of *might have* in examples like (3). Rullmann and Matthewson argue that the reading where *might have* has past TP (as in (3b) or (4)) is due to a fixed lexical, non-compositional interpretation of this combination. Because of such lexical idiosyncrasies, the English modal auxiliary system is quite 'messy', with different subclasses of modals behaving in different ways. Since our first corpus-based study is about English, we will now give a more detailed overview of the determination of TP and TO in English modals.

2.2 Temporal properties of English (semi-)modals

2.2.1 Temporal orientation and modal flavour

As far as the determination of TO is concerned, the English modal system is quite uniform, in that TO is determined by the aspectual properties of the prejacent (i.e., the complement of the modal). This is illustrated in (10) for *may*, but other (semi-)modals show the same pattern. If the prejacent is in the perfect (i.e., the modal is followed by *have* plus a past participle), TO is past, as in (10a). (The only exceptions are fixed lexicalized combinations like *might have*, as in (3b) and (4), where the perfect marks past TP and the TO can be past, present, or future.) If the prejacent is in the progressive or lexically stative, as in (10b,c), the TO is usually present, although future TO is also possible with future temporal adverbials or in the right discourse context (e.g., *Tomorrow, it may be sunny*). If the prejacent is eventive and non-progressive, as in (10d,e), TO is always future.

(10) a. *It **may have** rained.* (past TO)
 b. *It **may** be raining.* (present/future TO)
 c. *It **may** be sunny.* (present/future TO)
 d. *It **may** rain.* (future TO)
 e. *You **may** leave.* (future TO)

It has often been observed (Condoravdi 2002, among many others) that TO constrains the flavour of the modal; i.e., whether the modal is epistemic, deontic, bouletic, teleological, etc. The main division is between epistemic modals on the one hand, and non-epistemic or root (a.k.a. circumstantial) modals on the other. Roughly speaking, modals with past or present TO can only be epistemic, whereas modals with future TO can in principle be either epistemic or non-epistemic (although future epistemic modality may be hard to tell apart from future circumstantial modality; see, e.g., Vander Klok 2019). However, the correlation between TO and modal flavour is not perfect, and there appear to be some exceptions. For instance, sometimes a deontic modal with a stative prejacent could be interpreted as having present TO (e.g., *According to the rules, he must be in his office at this time*).

Various proposals have been made to explain the correlation between TO and modal flavour (for instance, the Diversity Condition of Condoravdi 2002), but there is no consensus on this issue, nor on the proper classification of modal flavours (for discussion, see Portner 2009: 134–144, and references cited there). In our English corpus study, we only annotated a broad distinction between epistemic and non-epistemic interpretations, which is not only relatively straightforward, but also the crucial distinction for the different TO patterns; yet, we stay neutral on what might account for constraints on the relation between TO and flavour.

Modal flavour is also constrained by lexical properties of individual (semi-)modals. Modal auxiliaries are generally liberal in the range of flavours they allow; *may* can have either epistemic or deontic (or another non-epistemic) flavour, whereas *be allowed to* can only be non-epistemic. But even modal auxiliaries can have idiosyncratic restrictions on flavour; for example, when *may* is used in a yes-no question, it can only have the sense of permission (i.e., deontic flavour), as in *May I leave now?* And *can* is normally not epistemic, but its negation *can't* can be (e.g., *Where is Prof. Sorenson? She might/*can/can't be in her office*); see, e.g., Iatridou and Zeijlstra (2013: 563), who suggest that epistemic *can* is a negative polarity item.

2.2.2 Temporal perspective

English (semi-)modals show much greater variability with respect to the determination of TP than they do for TO. Semi-modals, such as *have to*, *be able to*, and *be allowed to*, inflect overtly for (past or present) tense, which transparently reflects their TP, as shown in (11a,b).

(11) a. *I **have to** leave.* (present TP)
    b. *I **had to** leave.* (past TP)

Things get more interesting when we look at modal auxiliaries, which are not inflected productively for tense. Some modals inherently have present TP (e.g., *may*, *can*).[4] This is shown for a main clause in (12a). The fact that the present tense is inherent to these modals is demonstrated even more clearly in embedded clauses like (12b): if the matrix clause is in the past tense, these modals only allow for a so-called 'double access' reading, analogous to that of a non-modal embedded clause in the present tense in (13a); i.e., Mary is in Ottawa both at the utterance time and at the time of Sue's saying so (Ogihara 1996; Abusch 1997, among others). These modals lack the 'simultaneous' or 'backshifted' readings of past-under-past embedded clauses such as (13b), where Mary is in Ottawa at the time of Sue's saying, or at a time before that.

(12) a. *Mary **may** be in Ottawa.* (present TP)
    b. *Sue said that Mary **may** be in Ottawa.* (present TP; double access)

---

4 Arguably this also applies to *will* if we follow Abusch (1985) in analyzing *will* as 'woll' + present tense.

(13) a. *Sue said that Mary **is** in Ottawa.*   (double access)
    b. *Sue said that Mary **was** in Ottawa.*   (simultaneous or backshifted)

Rullmann and Matthewson call such modals with inherent present tense 'class I modals', and analyze them as containing a present tense morpheme in their lexical representation.

It should be noted that for *may* there appears to be a dialect split, perhaps reflecting a change in progress (Denison 1992; Huddleston and Pullum 2002: 202–203; Rullmann and Matthewson 2018). The judgement in (12b) reflects what appears to be the more conservative variety, in which *may* has obligatory present TP. For many (younger?) speakers, however, (12b) can have a simultaneous reading as well. For more on this issue, see below.

Other English modals (Rullmann and Matthewson's classes II and III, including *must, might, could, should,* and arguably *would*) always seem to have present TP in matrix clauses as in (14a) (but see below for discussion of a systematic exception). In embedded clauses, however, they behave as if they have past tense in that they get a 'simultaneous' reading, as in (14b). What Sue said in (14b) is that Mary was necessarily/possibly in Ottawa at the time of Sue's saying; whether she is still in Ottawa at the utterance time of (14b) is irrelevant. This means that the modal in (14b) has past TP.

(14) a. *Mary **must/might** be in Ottawa.*   (present TP)
    b. *Sue said that Mary **must/might** be in Ottawa.*   (past TP; simultaneous)
    c. *Sue said that Mary **had to** be in Ottawa.*   (past TP; simultaneous or backshifted)

It is important to note that (14b) does not allow a backshifted reading, unlike the semi-modal *had to* in (14c), which carries overt past-tense inflection. The pastness of *must* and *might* (and other modals in the same class) may therefore be called "defective" in that it is dependent on a matrix past tense, and is not able to shift time backwards in either matrix (14a) or embedded (14b) clauses. In embedded clauses, it still behaves as if it is a past tense, though, in that it allows the simultaneous reading which for non-modals and semi-modals is only possible with overt past-tense inflection.[5] The "defective" pastness of *might* can also be

---

[5] There are certain modals in class III that do allow for backshifting, although they otherwise behave just like *might*, namely *could* and *would*, but interestingly only on a non-epistemic interpretation (see Huddleston and Pullum 2002: 196–197; Portner 2009: 224ff; and Rullmann and Matthewson 2018: 320). This apparently idiosyncratic behaviour of individual lexical items shows that an even more fine-grained classification of English modals is called for, taking into account

observed from the fact that it acts as the past-tense counterpart of *may* when it appears in indirect speech. In the same way that the direct speech event in (15a) is reported in indirect speech as (15b), with past tense in the embedded clause, (16b) with *might* is the indirect-speech counterpart of direct-speech (16a) with *may* (at least in the more conservative variety). Thus, the so-called "Sequence of Tense" (SOT) rules of English treat *might* as if it was the result of inflecting *may* with past tense (and this reflects its diachronic origin). There is no similar alternation for *must*, or perhaps more accurately, *must* is its own past/present counterpart. (Historically, *must* was a past-tense form.)

(15) a. *Sue said: "Mary **is** in Ottawa."*
 b. *Sue said that Mary **was** in Ottawa.*

(16) a. *Sue said: "Mary **may** be in Ottawa."*
 b. *Sue said that Mary **might** be in Ottawa.*

Rullmann and Matthewson (2018) account for the exceptional behaviour of modals like *might* and *must* by analyzing them as lexically having either a present tense or a "zero" tense morpheme (the latter being equivalent to the "zero" tense that results in non-modal sentences from deletion under SOT).

There is an important further distinction between *must* on the one hand (class II) and *might* (as well as *could, would,* and *should*) on the other (class III). This difference emerges when we look at the temporal interpretation of the modals in combination with *have*. Whereas *must have* can only have present TP (or past TP in SOT contexts) and past TO, *might have* allows for additional readings with past TP, even in main-clause (i.e., non-SOT) environments; TO can then be either past, present, or future. Cases where this occurs include counterfactuals such as (3b) or (17a), as well as past-TP epistemics like (4) or the original 'ice cream' example from von Fintel and Gillies (2008: 87) on which it was modeled, a variant of which is given here in (18). As the (b) examples show, the corresponding cases with *must have* lack the intended past-TP interpretation.

(17) a. *If our goalie had been injured, we **might have** lost the game.*
 b. #*If our goalie had been injured, we **must have** lost the game.*
  (past-TP counterfactual reading impossible in (b))

---

modal flavour as well. Since *could* and *would* were not included in the corpus study reported in this paper, we leave this as an issue for future research.

(18) [Context: Why did you look into the freezer a moment ago?]
   a. There **might have** been ice cream in there.
   b. #There **must have** been ice cream in there.
                                (past-TP epistemic reading impossible in (b))

Condoravdi (2002) argues that the possibility of past TP with *might have* results from *have* optionally scoping over *might*, yielding past TP rather than past TO. Rullmann and Matthewson instead argue for a lexical analysis, in which past-TP *might have* is treated as a fixed non-compositional combination. The fact that only certain combinations (such as *might have*) allow for past TP, whereas others (like *must have*) do not, supports a lexical analysis.[6] For further arguments, the reader is referred to Rullmann and Matthewson (2018).

Coming back to *may* for a moment, we can now characterize the difference between the "conservative" and the "innovative"' varieties that was noted above by saying that in the latter, *may* belongs to class III (and hence is essentially equivalent to *might*); it therefore allows for past TP in SOT environments, as well as the additional non-compositional interpretation of *might have*, which occurs in counterfactual and past-TP epistemic contexts. Some examples are given in Rullmann and Matthewson (2018: 320), as well as in our corpus data below. However, treating this as a binary dialect split may be a gross oversimplification. In reality the sociolinguistic situation is likely to be more complicated, and we can't exclude the possibility that some speakers are somewhere in between these two idealized extremes, allowing *may (have)* to have past TP in some cases but not others. We will come back to this in the discussion of our corpus results in section 3.3.

2.3 Summary of TP and TO in English modals

The organization of TP and TO in English is summarized in Table 1. The table contains the six modal forms that are the focus of our English case study: bare *may*, *must*, and *might*, as well as *may have*, *must have*, and *might have*. For *may* and *may have* only the "conservative" dialect is represented. *May have* and *must have* can only be interpreted compositionally, with the perfect in the scope of the modal resulting in past TO. *Might have* has an additional non-compositional

---

6 Interestingly, counterfactual *must have* apparently did occur in older stages of English, and can be found in George Eliot, for instance (Huddleston and Pullum 2002: 109; Rullmann and Matthewson 2018: 320). Such idiosyncratic behaviour of individual modals that is subject to dialect variation and diachronic change is broadly an argument in favour of a lexicalist approach.

interpretation in which it has past TP, and TO is essentially free (i.e., can be past, present, or future). *May* and *may have* have inherent present TP, whereas *must* and *must have* as well as *might* and the compositional interpretation of *might have* normally have present TP, except in SOT contexts, where they can have past TP. The next section discusses another context where these modals allow for past TP, namely Free Indirect Discourse (FID).

Table 1: The English modal system according to Rullmann and Matthewson (2018).

		TP	TO
Class I	*may* (conservative dialect)	present	present/future
	may have (conservative dialect; compositional)	present	past
Class II	*must*	present (or past in SOT/FID)	present/future
	must have (compositional)	present (or past in SOT/FID)	past
Class III	*might*	present (or past in SOT/FID)	present/future
	might have (compositional)	present (or past in SOT/FID)	past
	might have (non-compositional)	past	past/present/future

2.4 Free Indirect Discourse and narrative perspective

Above, we saw that class II and III modals (i.e., *must* and *might* and their kin) can get a past-TP interpretation under SOT in embedded clauses when the tense of the matrix clause is past. This past tense is "defective" in the sense that it doesn't allow for backshifting, unlike a real past tense. In main clauses, these modals normally only allow for present TP. However, under certain circumstances *must* and *might* can actually have past TP in main clauses (Hacquard 2006, 2010, 2011; Rullmann and Matthewson 2018, among others). This occurs in narrative discourse when the sentence represents the perspective (i.e., thoughts or other mental attitude) of the protagonist in the story, as opposed to that of the narrator. Two attested examples are reproduced here (= Rullmann and Matthewson's (ex. 138a,b)):

(19) *Today, turning the corner of Pepys Road, she caught the smell of burning wood, of hot ash, and was suddenly back on the outskirts of Harare [. . .]. An odd time for someone to be burning wood in London; it **must** be a fire someone had held back because of the terrible weather.*
(John Lanchester: *Capital*, ch. 73)

(20) *Patrick had not wanted to betray his own anxieties by asking too many questions about what Freddy really felt. The end result was that now, [. . .] he had no reliable idea about Freddy's state of mind. He **might** be panicking, just as Patrick was.*
(John Lanchester: *Capital*, ch. 16)

Similar cases of past TP with what we will call "protagonist perspective" were found in our corpus study. Such cases can plausibly be regarded as instances of Free Indirect Discourse (FID), the phenomenon by which certain indexicals (for instance, adverbs like *now* or *today*), but not others (e.g., pronouns like *I*), can be shifted in narrative discourse to reflect the perspective of a protagonist in the story rather than that of the narrator. Overt tense patterns with pronouns in that it is not shiftable.

FID has been studied extensively in both formal linguistics (Banfield 1982; Schlenker 2004; Sharvit 2008; Maier 2014, 2015; Eckardt 2015, 2021, among others) and literary studies (Cohn 1978; Fludernik 1995; Palmer 2004; Herman 2011, among others). In formal semantics, various approaches to FID have been proposed. Probably the most influential has been the context-shifting approach as worked out in most detail by Eckardt (2015). In Eckardt's analysis the interpretation of FID involves two contexts: the "external" context of the narrator and the "internal" context of the protagonist. But other approaches to FID have been proposed in the formal-semantic literature, for instance treating it as a type of mixed quotation (Maier 2015) or assimilating it to syntactic embedding (Hacquard 2006, 2010, 2011).[7]

If we adopt Eckardt's two-context theory, we could re-analyze the "defective past tense" of *must* and *might* as actually being a *present* tense that is *shiftable* in FID in the same way that adverbs like *now* can be shifted, unlike a normal, overt (present or past) tense, which can't be shifted. This means that in FID the tense of *must* and *might* does not refer to the utterance time of the external context (i.e., the time of narration; that is, the "now" of the narrator),

---

[7] See Rullmann and Matthewson (2018) for some arguments against Hacquard's approach in terms of syntactic deletion of a matrix clause.

but rather to the time of the internal context (i.e., the protagonist's "now"). This idea can then be extended to SOT contexts, where shifting takes place to the context of a matrix attitude holder (see Sharvit 2008 for important observations about the parallelism between SOT and FID). However, working out the formal details of such an approach would go beyond the scope of this paper. For the purposes of our corpus study, we stay theoretically neutral about the analysis of FID and SOT. The main empirical generalization to be tested is that in both SOT and FID contexts (but not elsewhere), modals like *might* and *must* can have a TP that is in the past relative to the time of narration (the utterance time of the external context). (We will continue to refer to this as "past TP", even though, if our suggestion to analyze *must* and *might* as having a shiftable present tense is on the right track, it might be more accurate to call it a "protagonist's present" TP.)

3 Describing the English corpus project

3.1 Introduction

In this section, we present a quantitative case study, which tests Rullmann and Matthewson's (2018) predictions about modal-temporal interactions with corpus data in English. In particular, we investigate the predictions presented in Tables 2 and 3 below, where checkmarks indicate which temporal properties a modal is predicted to be compatible with, while dashes indicate temporal properties that should not be available for the respective modals.

Table 2: Predictions concerning the temporal orientation.

	Past TO	Pres TO	Fut TO
may	—	✓	✓
must	—	✓	✓
might	—	✓	✓
may have	✓	—	—
must have	✓	—	—
might have	✓	if in past TP contexts	if in past TP contexts

Table 3: Predictions concerning the temporal perspective.

	Past TP in SOT/FID contexts	Past TP available in other contexts
may	—	—
may have[8]	—	—
must	✓	—
must have	✓	—
might	✓	—
might have	✓	✓

3.2 Methodology

3.2.1 Data source

As data source for our case study, we selected the *Corpus of Contemporary American English* (COCA) – a large-scale synchronic corpus which includes tagged data from a variety of genres (e.g., academic, fiction, magazines, news, spoken). Specifically, we focused on the fiction portion of this corpus, which contains 81 million words from book chapters, short stories, and plays that were published between 1990 and 2019. Compared to the other available genres, this subcorpus seemed particularly suitable for the purposes of our investigation, which (among other things) seeks to examine whether and how narrative perspective affects modal-temporal interactions. Specifically, fiction is the genre in which FID is most likely to occur. This does not mean that FID is an exceptional type of language that falls outside the normal rules of grammar. Rather, literary authors exploit already existing resources of the language. Further, FID is not restricted to the high literary style of authors of the canon of 19th and 20th century literature.[9] We therefore have good reasons to think that the study of modals and tense in fiction can provide important insights into modal-temporal interaction in narratives.

---

8 As noted in section 2.2.2, past TP may be available for *may (have)* in certain innovative varieties of English.
9 Clement (2014) shows that examples of (an early form of) FID can already be found in Dutch popular novels of the 17th century, although direct discourse was still the most prevalent way of representing a character's speech or thought until the disappearance of the authorial narrator in the 19th century. And as Meier (2015) points out, FID occurs commonly in fan-fiction written by non-professional writers. Likewise, many of the cases of FID in our sample occur in "low" literary genres such as science fiction.

3.2.2 Data retrieval and data filtering

In May 2019, the first author searched the corpus for *may_v**, *might_v**, and *must_v** (where *v** represents the part-of-speech tag for "verb") and retrieved a randomized sample of 500 data points for each of the three modal verbs. Each of the data points included some meta-information on the publication as well as the textual excerpt containing the respective modal, as illustrated in Figure 1.

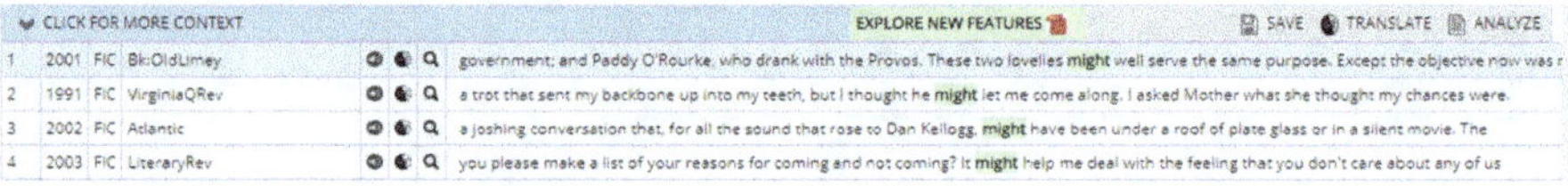

Figure 1: Excerpt of a query for *might_v**.

Subsequently, the first author manually went through each of the three modal data sets, removed problematic data points (e.g., false positives, incomplete constructions), and separated utterances with a bare modal (e.g., *may*) from utterances in which a modal was used with *have* (e.g., *may have*).[10] We did this until we had gathered 100 data points for each construction, resulting in the six data sets shown in Table 4:[11]

Table 4: Data sets used for the present investigation.

bare modal	tokens	modal + *have*	tokens
may	100	may have	100
might	100	might have	100
must	100	must have	100

3.2.3 Annotation

The English study was conducted primarily by the first and third authors (native speakers of German and Dutch respectively; both fully fluent in English), with assistance of the second author (a native speaker of English).

---

10 Utterances where *have* acted as a full verb, as in (i), were classified as instances exhibiting a bare modal use.

(i) You **must** have your guesses, your speculations. (Kim Magowan: *Nothing in My Mouth*)

11 The original data set resulting from the query for *may_v** contained an unexpectedly high proportion of bare *may* tokens, and an unexpectedly small proportion of *may have* tokens. To get 100 tokens for *may have*, we thus had to retrieve another batch of data from COCA, following the same procedure.

The first author annotated the modal data for the categories listed in Table 5 (among others). All potentially ambiguous data points were discussed with the other authors.[12]

Table 5: Some of the categories used in the annotation process.

categories	Annotation options
modal base	epistemic	circumstantial (= non-epistemic)	ambiguous
embedded	yes	no
▷ type of embedding	complement clause	relative clause	adjunct clause	other
▷ tense of the matrix verb	past	present
temporal perspective	past	present	future	ambiguous
temporal orientation	past	present	future	ambiguous
narrative perspective	narrator	protagonist (≈ FID)	ambiguous

In the following paragraphs, we address some of the main issues we encountered during the annotation process and present some pointers on how these issues can be mitigated.

First, given the limited context provided by the original *COCA* queries, the annotation of concepts like TP, TO, or narrative perspective often proved to be difficult. To make solid judgments for these categories, we often had to retrieve larger chunks of the surrounding context. While the added context solved this issue in most cases, some data points remained impossible to classify with certainty, as exemplified in (21).

(21) Ambiguous data points

    a. Ambiguity between Past TP, Past TO and Pres TP, Past TO
It was a surprised presence. The soul who had been trapped in that green bottle for so long didn't know where she was or what had happened. It was like being awakened from sleep. It pleased me to realize her time inside the bottle hadn't been hellish. It had been little more than a long nap.
*She **must have** remembered her husband and the monks and the house on the river where she was exorcised. I had no doubt that she knew she was a long way from home.*
(Tim Sullivan: *Under Glass*)

---

[12] The triangles (▷) in Table 5 indicate that these categories were only considered for annotation when the answer to the superior category (i.e., "embedded") was positive.

b. Ambiguity between Past TP, Past TO, FID and Past TP, Fut TO (counterfactual)
*Other people thought it was a shameful abdication of his rights as a man. Even in Queensland, they wouldn't say "white man," but that's what many of them were thinking. The scandal **might have** retarded his advance at JCU, so when an offer came for a full professorship at the University of Hawaii, Jimmy snapped it up like the hungry shark he used to be, on weekends.*
(Joe Haldeman: *Camouflage – Part II*)

Secondly, since English core modals do not carry overt tense inflection, determining their TP sometimes proved to be difficult. This issue was exacerbated by the fact that the role of time in fiction and narratives, and the relation between "narration time" and "narrated time", is an extremely complex topic. In this study, we have assumed a relatively naive approach in which we equate the UT (utterance time) with the time of narration, i.e., the time at which the story is told (or at least pretended to be told) by the narrator (i.e., the time of the external context in the theory of Eckardt 2015). Most of the examples in our sample occur in what appear to be straightforward past-tense narratives where the story is told in retrospect and therefore the protagonist's "now" (the time of Eckardt's internal context) precedes the time of narration (except for direct speech quotations within the story).[13] Modals occurring in such past-tense narratives can have either present TP (if they reflect the narrator's perspective) or past TP (if they reflect the protagonist's perspective).

We also found a couple of examples of narratives told in the present tense, where the story is told "as it happens", so to speak. In such cases of "historical present", we assume that the UT (the time of narration, i.e., the time of the external context) coincides with the protagonist's "now". For such cases we have assumed that the modal has present TP. Examples are given in (22):[14]

---

[13] It is important to note that the narration time (the time of the external context) may not be the actual time at which the story is written by the real-life author of the novel or story (who should not be confused with the fictional narrator). For instance, as a reviewer pointed out, a science fiction story set in the future may be written in the past tense. We would analyze such cases by taking the narration time to be the (fictional) time in the future from whose temporal vantage point the story is pretended to be told, which is some (usually unspecified) point in time *following* the events of the story. A full analysis of this and other complex cases of time in fiction goes beyond the scope of this paper.

[14] For the purposes of this paper, we set aside the theoretical analysis of the historical present. For formal analyses, see Schlenker (2004), Eckardt (2015), Anand and Toosarvandani (2018), and Toosarvandani (2020).

(22) Modals in present-tense narratives
   a. *"It was probably too hard a scramble for me anyway,"* Elaine says. She **must have** *inherited the martyr skills from Mom. "Did Rob make it?"*
   (Karen Rosenbaum: *The River Rerun*)

   b. *"Yeah, it's really very intricate," Harry tells her, "all those little slopes and curves, the way they fit. It's on the principle of a wedge, an inclined plane, the same way the Pyramids were built." Feeling he* **may have** *wandered rather far, venturing into the terrible empty space where the Pyramids were built, he announces, "Also, Edison had backing. Look at who his friends were down there. Ford. Firestone. The giant fat cats.*
   (John Updike: *Rabbit at Rest*)

Since English modals lack overt tense inflection, the identification of the TP is often difficult because it has to be based on contextual cues about narrative perspective, which may be ambiguous or hard to interpret. One test we used to mitigate this issue was to substitute the modal with a semi-modal which overtly marks tense, taking care to keep the same modal force and flavour as much as possible (e.g., replacing *must* with *has to / had to*), as exemplified in (23), which shows that the TP for (23a) must be present, not past. Among the authors, intuitions about this were very clear.

(23) Determining TP via the semi-modal substitution test
   a.   *The warden laughed. "You* **must** *be kidding."*
                                                     (unknown author: *Contraband*)
   b.   *The warden laughed. "You* **have to** *be kidding."*
   c.   # *The warden laughed. "You* **had to** *be kidding."*

In SOT contexts, the tense of the matrix verb proved to be a useful cue for determining the temporal perspective of the embedded modal.

(24) Determining TP in SOT contexts via the tense of the matrix verb
   a. Past matrix verb, past TP modal
      I regretted the loss, but by this time my father's illness had become severe and I **imagined** *that my deprivation* **might have** *been ordained as a way of making me pay attention to him and take up the role, as directed by my mother, of man of the family.*
      (Robert Love Taylor: *My Mother's Shoes*)

b. Present matrix verb, present TP modal
   "*They're investigating. He **thinks** it **might have** been a murder/suicide. The husband might have killed his wife, tossed her over, then jumped himself.*"
   (Colleen Coble: *Twilight at Blueberry*)

Third, the annotation of narrative perspective proved equally challenging in many cases. However, we found that the presence of ideational expressions, interjections, and other similar cues can often help distinguish protagonist perspective from narrator perspective.

(25) Cues for distinguishing narrator and protagonist perspective
   a. Protagonist perspective, highlighted by an ideational expression
   *Emile didn't want to see anyone. **All he could think about** was his old Chief calmly making a decision to kill himself and an entire crew of prisoners. David Rimbeau would do it rationally, carefully, being sure that the majority of those on the Lowsten were in agreement. Not like Catherine **might have**, in a fury, but a gentle and considered operation that was no more than sense.*
   (S. N. Lewitt: *Blind Justice*)

   b. Protagonist perspective, highlighted by an interjection
   *A desperate, grasping-at-straws gamble formed in his mind. **What the hell** – he **might** as well go for it. He rose to his feet.*
   (Robin Wells: *Ooh, la la!*)

Lastly, annotating TO posed a particular challenge, as it was difficult to avoid approaching it with theoretical biases (e.g., when the prejacent is in the perfect, the modal will have past TO). As a result, there is a risk of circular reasoning (i.e., the results confirm the predictions because the annotation relied on the predictions). We believe that in future studies, this issue could be mitigated by having multiple naive, but trained, annotators annotate the corpus data and by introducing a systematic measurement of inter-annotator reliability (cf., Spooren and Degand 2010; Fuoli and Hommerberg 2015; Hoek and Scholman 2017, among others).

3.2.4 Measurements

Once all the tokens had been annotated, we calculated how frequently each modal-temporal configuration occurred with each modal expression. While the frequency measurements we will present in the results section (Section 3.3) are merely descriptive, we hope to use the annotated data from this case study for more sophisticated statistical analyses in the future (cf. Gries 2008 and Brezina 2018 for an overview of statistical measurements of corpus data).

3.3 Results and discussion

In the following subsections, we present the results of our corpus analysis and compare them to the predictions we offered in section 3.1.

3.3.1 Temporal orientation

We will show in this section that the corpus analysis generally supports the predictions we laid out in section 3.1 – with a few caveats.

Table 6 documents the TO of the modals in our corpus data. Note that in the tables we group present and future TO together, since, even though TO is constrained by the aspectual properties of the prejacent (stative or progressive vs. eventive), the difference between present and future TO is often hard to decide in practice. (For example, does *You must be quiet now* have present or future TO?)

Table 6: Temporal orientation of the English modals *may (have)*, *might (have)*, *must (have)*.

	Past TO	Pres / Fut TO	Ambiguous TO
bare *may* (n = 100)	0	100	0
bare *might* (n = 100)	0	100	0
bare *must* (n = 100)	0	100	0
may + *have* (n = 100)	59	0	41
might + *have* (n = 100)	54	45	1
must + *have* (n = 100)	94	0	6

Our prediction that *may*, *might*, and *must* should always occur with present or future TO is fully confirmed by the corpus data (100% each). Examples illustrating this are given in (26).

(26) *May*, *might*, and *must* with present/future TO
    a. "And you can't tell who's sick! They **may** look like you or me," Mother told us, "but they don't DO like we do."
       (Kit Reed: *Precautions*)

b. *"I draw a blank,"* he said, *"but Herman **might** know. He's retired now, but he's still pretty sharp. He **might** just remember."*
(Donald Barr: *Sam*)

c. *"She's a jewel, dear boy. You **must** bring her to our dinners and teas. I demand it! She's Tolstoy's grandniece."*
(Jerome Charyn: *Tatiana & T.S. Eliot*)

The data also seem to support our prediction that *must have* should always occur with past TO. For this modal, we observe a strong, almost exclusive, preference for past TO (94%), illustrated by (27a). However, we also have to acknowledge that 6% of the *must have* cases appear to be ambiguous in terms of their TO, i.e., they could represent present TP with past TO, as predicted, or past TP with present TO, which was not predicted. One such example is given in (27b).

(27) TO for *must have*
 a. Past TO
 *"That **must have** been some conversation you had with Potemkin this afternoon,"* said the Mouse.
 (Mike Resnick: *Soothsayer*)

 b. Indeterminable TO
 *Kicker is, I saw one of the fellas responsible for the artwork – this scrawny man in filthy dungarees was doing the honors. **Must've** been eighty years old; His ribs stuck out and his eyes were milky. Blind as hell.*
 (Laird Barron: *Hallucigenia*)

For *may have*, we also expected that it should always exhibit past TO. Our preliminary results, however, seem to challenge this prediction. While 59% of the *may have* tokens can be classified as unambiguously exhibiting past TO, as exemplified in (28a), we had to classify the remaining 41% of the data as "ambiguous" because judgments seemed particularly unclear. One such problematic case is given in (28b). This might be an instance of present TP and past TO if epistemic *may have* is taken to represent the narrator's perspective, but it could also be understood as protagonist perspective (i.e., FID) with past TP and present TO.

(28) TO for *may have*
 a. Past TO
 *"Well, the former simply **may have** been a trompe l'oeil, dear, while the latter may indeed have a very sound explanation – grounded in mischief, perhaps?"*
 (Michael Libling: *Timmy Gobel's Bug Jar*)

b. Indeterminable TO
*The Seor was straightening one end of his moustache, and half-smirking to himself, while the Seora was using a handkerchief (or it **may have** been a hotel face-cloth) to wipe her mouth. (Of the taste of hungry kisses, I supposed.) Their clothes were a bit dishevelled, but chamber-maids weren't born yesterday.*
(Ronald Frame: *Critical Paranoia*)

Among other things, the annotation was complicated by the innovative dialect issue (cf. section 2.2). Likewise, it was not clear whether SOT and FID pattern the same for *may have*. Either way, these ambiguous cases may pose a potential problem for Rullmann and Matthewson's (2018) theory, but they might also reflect a language change in process. Resolving this issue would require careful experimental and sociolinguistic investigation, however. For now, we set the *may have* data aside, and hope to return to it in future research.

Lastly, we hypothesized for *might have* that if it has present TP, it can only have past TO (29), but if it has past TP, it can have past, present, or future TO (30).[15]

(29) *Might have* with present TP and past TO
"*If what you remember about his youth was true, our families **might have** come from the same place. In northeastern Poland is this huge forest – the forest where the bison live, where this vodka comes from. That **might have** been the forest your mother meant in her stories.*"
(Andrea Barrett: *The Forest*)

(30) *Might have* with past TP and past (a), present (b), or future (c) TO.
a. *Gabi rested a hand on her belly, felt the faint stirring there. The first time she'd felt that tiny life inside her, she'd fallen in love. Being pregnant might be inconvenient. It might not have been the result of a love match. It **might have** cost her a job, but she already loved this baby more than anything.*
(Sherry Woods: *Wind Chime Point*)

b. "*That **might have** been the end of it, until the day before Danner's visit, when Axel noticed Ross heading up to the attic and followed him.*"
(Richard Chwedyk: *The Man Who Put the Bomp*)

---

15 In our data, all past TP cases of *might have* with present or future TO turned out to be counterfactual.

c. *Maybe if he had been more scrupulous about taking his medication, or maybe if his body had been a bit stronger, or maybe if he hadn't been so fond of malts and spirits and the hubbub of bars, he **might have** done even more good work.*
(Paul Auster: *Timbuktu*)

As shown in Table 7, the corpus data support this hypothesis: all present TP instances of *might have* have past TO, while the past TP instances of this modal are more flexible in terms of their TO.

Table 7: Temporal orientation and perspective of the English modal *might have* (n = 100).

	Past TO	Pres / Fut TO	Ambiguous TO
Past TP	27	45	1
Pres TP	27	0	0

3.3.2 Temporal perspective

Table 8 documents the TP of the modals in our corpus. As we will detail in the following paragraphs, the data support our predictions for this notion as well.

Table 8: Temporal perspective of the English modals *may (have)*, *might (have)*, *must (have)*.

	Past TP	Pres TP	Ambiguous TP
bare *may* (n = 100)	0	100	0
may have (n = 100)	0	59	41
bare *must* (n = 100)	17	80	3
must have (n = 100)	33	60	7
bare *might* (n = 100)	36	63	1
might have (n = 100)	73	27	0

We hypothesized that *may* and *may have* can never have past TP. While the corpus data fully support this prediction for bare *may* – which occurs exclusively with present TP, see (31)[16] – our tentative results for *may have* are, once again, much messier than anticipated. While 59% of the data fit our hypothesis and unambiguously exhibit present TP, as exemplified by (32), the remaining 41% of the data are less clear, if not problematic for our original analysis. One such example is given in (33), which seems to allow past TP in an FID context.

(31) *May* with present TP
   *She is single and lives outside of Tucson, in Buckeye, Arizona. I always planned on telling you, but then Mick and I split up, and there was always a reason I couldn't. Now, it **may** be too late.*
   (Bonnie Hearn Hill: *If Anything*)

(32) *May have* with present TP
   *"I'm still keeping an open mind. Her death **may have** been connected to the missing jewelry and made to look like a copycat murder."*
   (Mary Higgins Clark: *Loves Music, Loves to Dance*)

(33) *May have* with past TP reading in FID
   *On my way, I put more of the mental puzzle together. Indeed, there **may have** been more than one treasure buried, but the one the Gordons were looking for, and may well have found, was buried on Plum Island. I was reasonably certain of that.*
   (Nelson DeMille: *Plum Island*)

For *must* and *must have*, we predicted that they can only have past TP if they occur in FID or SOT contexts. The corpus study confirms this hypothesis. Of the 17 instances of *must* with past TP, 5 occur in FID contexts and the remaining 12 in SOT contexts. Likewise, of the 33 *must have* tokens with past TP, 17 exhibit FID effects and the remaining 16 SOT effects. Examples are given in (34) and (35), respectively.[17]

---

[16] However, we have come across some cases of *may* with past TP outside of the corpus data for this study, so although they may be rare, they do seem to exist. This further complicates the issue of dialect variation. An attested example is given in (i):

(i) *"The first day she was there, there was actually some discussion that she **may** not survive," he said. "Every report we've had since then has been updated to where it's much more encouraging. So we are holding her and her family in our prayers."*
(CBC News Online, July 24, 2013)

[17] The three ambiguous cases for *must* as well as the seven ambiguous cases for *must have* (see Table 8) allow a present TP or a past TP interpretation. Crucially, in the past TP readings, they convey the protagonist's perspective – which fits our predictions.

(34) Past TP *must (have)* in FID contexts
    a. *That phrase was a code well-known to the cardinal, but to assure himself he began to ask, "By which you mean to say – " # "These tapestries are elegant, are they not?" Clement looked away. # The cardinal understood: His Holiness* **must** *not say the name of his chief assassin – his avenging angel.*
    (Elizabeth Aston: *Mr. Darcy's Dream*)

    b. *"You smoke drugs?" "Not anymore," Loring shrugged. "Sorry." He thought of the bag of weed his sister-in-law had unearthed in June. Gloria had smoked it at the end, to escape the excruciating pain; at some point this summer, Loring* **must have** *finished it.*
    (Elise Juska: *Transfer Station*)

(35) Past TP *must (have)* in SOT contexts
    a. *Yet as the days and weeks went by, I couldn't bring myself to believe it. I dreamed about him almost every night, and there was something so real about those dreams that I came to believe that he* **must** *be alive somewhere.*
    (Douglas Niles: *The Coral Kingdom*)

    b. *The police insisted that she* **must have** *used martial arts training or that Kane* **must have** *broken his own skull, spine, and neck in the straggle.*
    (Mary A. Turzillo: *Miranda's Monster*)

We also hypothesized that bare *might* can only have past TP in SOT or FID contexts. Again, this prediction seems to be borne out by our corpus data. Of the 36 past TP cases of bare *might*, 24 can be categorized as SOT contexts and the remaining 12 as FID contexts, as exemplified in (36) and (37), respectively.

(36) Past TP *might* in SOT contexts:
    a. *They kept... afflicted people in the cells. All sorts. Fever addled, demented, crippled. They'd been assigned there, told there* **might** *be cures. There weren't cures. They were specimens. We prodded and cut and dosed, not to cure them but to satisfy our curiosity. Eventually, they died. Eventually, we killed them.*
    (Madeline Smoot: *One Thousand Words for War*)

    b. *He figured that, after the waste bucket incident, a few games of Bricks* **might** *calm him and avert a physical crisis. And it did, for a time.*
    (Nathaniel Rich: *Blue Rock*)

(37) Past TP *might* in FID contexts:
   a. *That's why he couldn't call the police. He needed time to think everything through, to work out the best way to handle it, and for that he needed a cigarette. It could be hours, even days, before the old guy's body was discovered. He was retired, reclusive, lived alone. Chess had time. It **might** be the only thing he had going for him. Before he left, Chess bent over the body and dug into Dial's pockets for his keys – just in case he wanted to come back.*
   (Ellen Hart: *The Cruel Ever After*)

   b. *She knew it was only a matter of time before the rest of her Claflin clan found them. Money, they always needed money. Her father Buck had taken her on the revival circuit since she was old enough to stand, project her voice and fascinate a crowd; then Tennie with her clairvoyant act had taken over. The family cooked up patent medicines and practiced magnetic healing. Both sisters were good at the laying on of hands, which **might** prove useful if their plans, worked out in the Midwest, came to fruition – as they must.*
   (Marge Piercy: *Sex Wars*)

Our last prediction stated that the complex form *might have* is less restricted than plain *might*, allowing it to have past TP, regardless of whether it occurs in an FID or SOT context or not. This is borne out by the corpus data. The 73 past TP tokens for *might have* include – in addition to instances of FID or SOT – also numerous counterfactual uses. Illustrative examples are given in (38).

(38) Past TP *might have* in (a) FID, (b) SOT, and (c) counterfactual contexts
   a. *Almost immediately there was the fierce yipping of a dog, frantic and high-pitched. She thought she heard someone call, "Come in!" but she hesitated. They **might have** been calling, "Coming!" And small dogs could bite, too.*
   (Judi Culbertson: *The Nursery*)

   b. *Tom walked faster after he said, "She's on the way," but Axel still had to run back to him two more times, like he thought Tom **might have** lost his way and had to be shown where the library was.*
   (Richard Chwedyk: *Orfy*)

   c. *If I hadn't convinced you to take that semester abroad, the two of you **might** never **have** met.*
   (Marie Bostwick: *Apart at the Seams*)

We did not find any cases in our corpus data of epistemic *might* have with past TP and present TO analogous to von Fintel and Gillies' (2008) 'ice cream' case (see (18)). Note that they presented this example in a dialogue and not in a narrative FID context. As Rullmann and Matthewson (2018) argue, cases like the 'ice cream' example are due to the special non-compositional interpretation of the fixed combination *might have* with past TP and past/present/future TO (see the bottom row of Table 1), which does not involve the shiftable present tense dependent on an FID or SOT context. This distinguishes them from cases like (38a) and (38b) involving a shiftable present tense, which are compositional and where the presence of *have* therefore can only result in *past* TO (see the second row from the bottom in Table 1). Since cases of epistemic *might have* with past TP and *present* TO (like the 'ice cream' example) do not involve a shiftable tense, they are not expected to have a special affinity for FID/SOT contexts. See Rullmann and Matthewson (2018, section 2.6, pp. 18–20) for some discussion of why epistemic modals with past TP that do not rely on FID/SOT are relatively rare and need strong contextual support in order to be licensed, which may account for their absence in our data.

3.4 Summary

Our analysis of 600 modal tokens from *COCA* by and large lends support to the predictions made by Rullmann and Matthewson (2018), with some notable complications with respect to *may (have)* in particular. However, this case study also highlights the interesting challenges of determining modal-temporal interactions in "real life" data, even for a very well-studied language like English. Reliable annotations often require large chunks of context and native speaker judgments, and even then, some utterances may remain ambiguous in terms of temporal perspective, temporal orientation, or narrative perspective.

4 Analyzing corpus data from underdescribed languages

4.1 Introduction to the St'át'imcets modal and temporal systems

In this section we discuss a pilot attempt to apply the same approach used in the English corpus project to corpus data from an underdescribed language, St'át'imcets. The modal system of St'át'imcets has been analyzed as being structured differently from that of English: rather than lexically encoding modal force, St'át'imcets modals lexically encode modal flavour (Rullmann, Matthewson, and Davis 2008). The three most common modals (apart from the prospective modal *kelh*) are *k'a*, *ka*, and *ka-...-a*. These have been analyzed as encoding the modal flavours listed in (39):

(39) *ka*   deontic or irrealis
      ka-...-a   circumstantial
      k'a   epistemic (inferential evidential)

For *ka*, the term "irrealis" should not be taken to mean that it is an irrealis mood marker within a mood system. Rullmann, Matthewson, and Davis (2008: 330) characterize the "irrealis" uses of *ka* as follows: "These include counterfactual conditionals and certain kinds of future conditionals, as well as counterfactual wishes. Roughly speaking, in all its irrealis uses, *ka* requires that the embedded proposition be false at the evaluation time." Importantly, under both deontic and irrealis interpretations, *ka* is a circumstantial modal. The circumfix *ka-...-a* is also circumstantial, but tends towards pure circumstantial and ability readings (see section 4.3.2 for more details).

With regard to modal force, all these modals have been shown to be acceptable in contexts supporting both necessity and possibility readings. They have been analyzed as introducing universal quantification over possible worlds, with weaker readings being captured via domain restriction (restriction on the set of worlds picked out by the modal base) (Rullmann, Matthewson, and Davis 2008).

Turning to temporal properties, St'át'imcets does not encode the difference between past and present tense (van Eijk 1997; Matthewson 2006). The prediction of Rullmann and Matthewson's (2018) system is therefore that TP will not be overtly marked in this language, and they argue that this is in fact the case (see also Chen et al. 2017). With respect to TO, there is overt prospective marking in the language (the second-position clitic *kelh*, and an auxiliary *cuz'*), and Rullmann and Matthewson argue that St'át'imcets clauses without overt marking for prospective aspect contain a covert non-prospective aspect. This therefore predicts that past- and present-oriented modals will have no overt aspectual marking, while future-oriented ones will co-occur with prospective *kelh* or *cuz'*. Rullmann and Matthewson show that this prediction is upheld for epistemic modals, but that circumstantial modals appear with no aspectual marking. Since circumstantial modals are always future-oriented, they propose that these modals are lexically specified as having future TO (see also Chen et al. 2017).

Our corpus-based pilot study of St'át'imcets modals was designed to test these proposals. In particular, we aimed to test the following predictions:

(40) i. The modals *ka, ka-...-a,* and *k'a* have the modal flavours listed in (39).
  ii. The modals *ka, ka-...-a,* and *k'a* are compatible with contexts supporting a range of modal forces.
  iii. All the modals can have past or present temporal perspective.
  iv. Temporal perspective is not overtly encoded on any modals.
  v. All the modals can have future temporal orientation; epistemic modals (but not circumstantial ones) can have past or present temporal orientation.
  vi. Circumstantial modals do not co-occur with any aspectual marking.
  vii. For epistemic modals, past and present temporal orientation is not encoded, but future temporal orientation is marked by prospective aspect.

In this paper we report on a very small study that tests the predictions in (35), and also discuss the extent to which we are able to feel confident that our St'át'imcets corpus provides enough information to annotate these factors.

4.2 Methodology

The St'át'imcets corpus used for this pilot project is a collection of stories told by Carl Alexander (Alexander 2016). The collection contains approximately 9,000 words of narrative. The stories include legends, recountings of historical events, and personal memories. The St'át'imcets text is fully glossed and translated into English. We worked with an electronic, searchable .pdf version of the book.

The choice to use a collection of narratives as our corpus is motivated by availability. There is no corpus of St'át'imcets conversational data, and there is essentially no fiction published in the language. In general, the genres of material that are available for St'át'imcets, in either published or online formats, are exactly those represented in Alexander (2016).[18] Narratives of this kind are the closest we can get to fiction in English. At the same time, it should be pointed out that one could not form an equivalent corpus of oral narratives in English by simply asking English speakers to tell stories, given the cultural differences in the status of stories and story-telling. The notion of genre is inherently culture-bound, and the matching of narrative genres across languages and cultures is always going to be imperfect; any comparisons should therefore always be approached with caution.

---

18 For example, the First Voices website (https://www.firstvoices.com/home) has a collection of personal stories in St'át'imcets. See also Matthewson (2005), Matthewson, Davis, and Rullmann (2009), and Edwards, LaRochelle, Mitchell (2017) for collections of St'át'imcets narratives.

The methodology for the St'át'imcets pilot study was identical to that for the English study. The second author, who has been doing fieldwork on St'át'imcets since the early 1990s, inspected each modal and annotated its modal flavour, temporal perspective, and temporal orientation. The same spreadsheet categories were used as in the English study, with a couple of alterations to enable us to test predictions that were specific to the St'át'imcets modal-temporal system. First, a category for 'modal force' was added (with annotation options 'possibility', 'necessity' and 'weak necessity'); this was not necessary in the English study as modal force is lexically encoded. Second, instead of a category 'modal base' (with options 'epistemic', 'circumstantial', 'ambiguous'), for St'át'imcets there was a category 'modal flavour' with options 'epistemic', 'deontic', 'irrealis', and 'circumstantial'. Within the class of modals annotated as 'circumstantial', we distinguished several sub-types of circumstantial modality, to be listed below in section 4.3.2, example (46). The second author made notes about any difficulties in the annotation.

For this pilot study, we annotated 20 instances of each of the three modals *ka* (deontic/irrealis), *ka-. . .-a* (circumstantial), and *k'a* (epistemic), for a total of 60 elements. We chose simply the first 20 instances of each modal that appeared in Alexander (2016).

4.3 Results and discussion

4.3.1 Deontic/irrealis *ka*

The predictions for *ka* are that it will have either deontic or irrealis modal flavours, that it is compatible with both strong and weak modal force, that it can have either past or present temporal perspective, that TP is not overtly marked, that it can only have future temporal orientation, and that TO is not overtly marked.

Of the 20 tokens of *ka* examined, six were deontic and 14 were irrealis. Examples of each are given in (41)–(42).

(41) Deontic *ka*
"*Ao,*"   *wa7*   *tsut*   *ta=smúlhats=a.*   "*Án'was=**ka**   láti7*
NEG   IPFV   say   DET=woman=EXIS   two=**IRR**   at+there.VIS
kw=s=ts'íla=s   *áti7*   *ku=s-q'weláw'-su*
DET=NMLZ=like=3POSS   to+there.VIS   DET=NMLZ-pick-2SG.POSS
i=tákem=a   *láti7.*"
PL.DET=all=EXIS   at+there.VIS
"'No,' says the woman. "You should pick twice as much as everything you've got there.'" (Alexander 2016: 16)

(42) Irrealis *ka*
   Wa7   tsut   n-sqátsez7=a,   "lh=wá7=as=**ka**   máwal'
   IPFV   say   1SG.POSS-father=EXIS COMP=IPFV=3SBJV=**IRR**   alive
   ta=sw'úw'h=a,   kanm=ás=**ka**?
   DET=cougar=EXIS do.what=3SBJV=**IRR**
   'My father said, "If the cougar were still alive, what would it have done? [...]"'
   (Alexander 2016: 145)

Looking at modal force, all six of the deontic uses of *ka* are translated into English with *should*, and seem in their contexts to be compatible with weak necessity interpretations. However, the pure textual evidence does not fully pin down the modal force. For example, in (41) just above, the woman is speaking to an owl and she is demanding that he pick more and more berries each time he comes back. It's unclear whether a strong necessity interpretation (translatable as 'You have to pick twice as much ...') would be inappropriate. (A possibility interpretation *can* be ruled out, as it would not make sense in the context: it is an order or a request, not a suggestion or permission.) The absence of deontic possibility (permission) cases in the pilot study is not unexpected. Rullmann, Matthewson, and Davis (2008: 329) observe that "In texts, it is difficult to find clear examples of unambiguously existential deontic *ka*." However, they also note that *ka* is in general rare in texts, and this is confirmed here: of the approximately 9,000 words in this corpus, there were in total only 22 instances of *ka*).[19]

Of the 14 irrealis cases, six are translated into English with *would*, one with subjunctive *were*, and one with *will*. These eight tokens all seem to be compatible with necessity interpretations of the modal. The remaining six irrealis tokens are translated into English with possibility modals (one *can*, and five *coulds*). The *can* example is given in (43).[20]

(43) "Kan   kw=s=mets-en-ácw   láti7
   whether DET=NMLZ=get.written-DIR-2SG.ERG   at+there.VIS
   kw=s=plán=s=tu7   na=qátsk-sw=a?
   DET=NMLZ=already=3POSS=REM   ABS.DET=older.brother-2SG.POSS=EXIS
   Nílh=**k[a]**=t'u7   s=tsukw=s   wi=snímulh
   COP=**IRR**=EXCL   NLMZ=finish=3POSS PL=1PL.INDEP

---

[19] This compares with 99 instances in the corpus of circumstantial *ka-...-a*, and 108 instances of epistemic *k'a*.
[20] The reader may notice that there is an instance of English *can* also in the interrogative sentence that begins this excerpt. This sentence is more literally 'Is it the case that you will sign the papers...?'

kw=s=cwíl'-em=lhkalh."
DET=NMLZ=look.for-MID=1PL.POSS
"'Can you sign the papers saying that your older brother has passed away? Then we can quit looking for him.'"
(Alexander 2016: 344)

It seems equally felicitous to translate this example with 'Then we could quit looking for him,' which would clearly accord with it being a possibility irrealis modal. Interestingly, the five tokens that were translated with *could* all involve ability readings, and all contain in addition the circumstantial modal *ka-...-a*, which is used by itself to convey ability. An example of this modal doubling is given in (44). All these cases involve counterfactual ability, which accounts for the presence of the modal *ka* in such cases.

(44) Wá7=as=**ka**   **ka**-qwal'út-**a**   i=sráp=a, ...
     IPFV=3SBJV=IRR   CIRC-speak-CIRC   PL.DET=tree=EXIS
     'If the trees could talk, ...'
     (Alexander 2016: 411)

None of the 20 instances of *ka* examined contain any overt marking of TP, consistent with our prediction, and none contain any prospective aspect marking for TO, also consistent with predictions. All six deontic cases had present TP and future TO; an example can be seen in (41) above, where the speaker (the woman) is imposing a present obligation for a future action on the addressee. The irrealis cases mostly seemed to have past TP, although sometimes it is difficult to tell from the context (for example in (42) above); (45) is a clear example of past TP and future TO.

(45) *Ka* with past TP and future TO
     [We ran away. Peter almost went towards the stable.]
     *Kwán·en=**ka**   pináni7   lh=ts'ítem=as   áku7,*
     take·FRED=IRR   at.that.time COMP=go.towards=3SBJV   to+there.INVIS
     t'u7   p'elk'-ús-em   láti7,   nílh=t'u7
     but   get.turned.around-face-MID   at+there.VIS   COP=EXCL
     s=q'ílhil=lhkalh   tákem   ulhcw   áku7   tsitcw-kálh=a.
     NMLZ=run=1PL.POSS   all   enter   to+there.INVIS house-1PL.POSS=EXIS
     'He would've been caught if he had gone that way, but he turned around, and we all ran inside our house.'
     (Alexander 2016: 137)

All this is consistent with our predictions. It would be interesting to see if examination of a larger corpus would reveal deontic cases with past TP.

4.3.2 Circumstantial *ka-...-a*

The analysis of *ka-...-a* as a circumstantial modal comes from Davis, Matthewson, and Rullmann (2009). This was advanced as a way to unify the apparently five different readings this modal allows, namely:

(46) a. ability
 b. manage-to
 c. accidentally
 d. suddenly
 e. non-controllable (in principle not controllable by an agent)

Davis, Matthewson, and Rullmann unify the ability and the manage-to readings as both being ability readings, by showing that the "manage-to" reading lacks an actuality entailment (i.e., it is merely a past-tense ability reading with an actuality implicature). They unify the "accidentally", "suddenly", and "non-controllable" readings as being "no-choice" readings – something had to happen, given the relevant facts at the relevant time. These readings also lack an actuality entailment. The "ability" and "no-choice" readings are both analyzed as involving circumstantial modality, with the modal force being weaker in the former.

Of the 20 tokens of *ka-...-a* in the pilot study, eight had "ability" interpretations, one had an "accidentally" interpretation, nine had "non-controllable" interpretations, and two had "permission" interpretations.[21] Examples of each of these are given in (47)–(50).

---

[21] One of the tokens we annotated as 'non-controllable' requires further investigation; it is given in (i). It is not actually clear that the decider had no choice about her decision, but it is also unclear which of the other circumstantial interpretations could be at play here.

(i) *ka-ptínus-em-a,* "aoz."
 CIRC-think-MID-CIRC NEG
 '... [she] then decided, "No."' (Alexander 2016: 63)

(47) Ability *ka-...-a*
N'án'atcw   aylh   láti7,   nílh=t'u7   ses
morning   then   at+there.VIS   COP=EXCL   NLMZ+IPFV+3POSS
kens-tcús-em   ta=skalúl7=a,   aoz   kwas
want.to-look-MID   DET=owl=EXIS   NEG   DET+NMLZ+IPFV+3POSS
***ka**-pegw·pigw-alús-**a**   láti7.*
CIRC-TRED·open-eye-**CIRC**   at+there.VIS
'Then in the morning, when the owl tried to look around, he couldn't open his eyes.'
(Alexander 2016: 41)

(48) Accidentally *ka-...-a*
*Nílh=t'u7   s=tqílh=ts=k'a   **ka**-n-tsqám'-**a***
COP=EXCL   NMLZ=almost=3POSS=EPIS   **CIRC**-LOC-fall.back-**CIRC**
láti7   ta=skalúl7=a ...
at+there.VIS   DET=owl=EXIS
'So the owl almost fell backwards ...'
(Alexander 2016: 17)

(49) Non-controllable *ka-...-a*
*Wá7=t'u7   aylh,   nilh   s=(a...)   **ka**-7a·7·ma-s-ás-**a***
IPFV=EXCL   then   COP   NMLZ=   **CIRC**-good·CRED·CAUS-3ERG-**CIRC**
láti7   ta=sm'é·m'·lhats=a   láku7.
at+there.INVIS   DET=woman·CRED·=EXIS   at+there.INVIS
'So then he fell in love with a girl over there.'
(Alexander 2016: 11)

(50) Permission *ka-...-a*
Wa7   láti7,   sáwlhen   láti7   ta=skalúl7=a: "Kan
be   at+there.VIS ask.question   at+there.VIS   DET=owl=EXIS   whether
*kw=s=**ka**-kwan·en-s-án-**a***
DET=NMLZ=**CIRC**-take·FRED-CAUS-1SG.ERG-**CIRC**
ta=sm'é·m'·lhats=a   lts7a?
DET=woman·CRED=EXIS   at+here.VIS
'The owl was there, so he asked: "Can I take your daughter? [...]"'
(Alexander 2016: 12)

The corpus data thus largely support the predictions about the modal flavour of *ka-...-a*. The only slightly unexpected finding is the "permission" readings; these were not identified by Davis, Matthewson, and Rullmann (2009) as being a feature of *ka-...-a*, and according to Rullmann, Matthewson, and Davis (2008), permission would more usually be expressed by deontic/irrealis *ka*. However, data elicited independently via a storyboard confirm the use of *ka-...-a* for "permission" readings.[22] This is shown in (51). The context for this sentence is that Mary has obtained her mother's permission to go out and play, but isn't physically able to do so because her leg is broken. The first use of *ka-...-a* in (51) conveys permission, and the second conveys (negated) ability.

(51) Tsut   kw=s=Mary,   "Tsut   ti=n-skícez7=a
     say   DET=NMLZ=Mary   say   DET=1SG.POSS-mother=EXIS
     kw=s=áma,   kwenswá   **ka**-nás-**a**   sáy'sez',
     DET=NMLZ=good   DET+1SG.POSS+NMLZ+IPFV   **CIRC**-go-**CIRC**   play
     t'u7   cw7aoz   kwenwá   **ka**-sáy'sez'-**a**,   xán'=lhkan,
     but   NEG   DET+1SG.POSS+NMLZ+IPFV   **CIRC**-play-**CIRC**   get.hurt=1SG.SBJ
     nilh   s=qácw·ecw   n-sq'wáxt=a."
     FOC   NMLZ=get.broken·FRED   1SG.POSS-leg=EXIS
     'Mary said, "My mother said okay, I'm allowed to go out and play, but I can't play, I hurt myself and my leg is broken."'
     (Gertrude Ned, from *Chore Girl* (TFS Working Group 2011))

This suggests that the range of circumstantial modal readings for *ka-...-a* must be expanded to include deontic possibility. This in turn raises further research questions, including when (i.e., in which discourse contexts) permission is rendered by *ka* and when it is rendered by *ka-...-a*. Another interesting question is why *ka-...-a* does not also allow deontic necessity readings (obligation), even though according to Rullmann, Matthewson, and Davis (2008) and Davis, Matthewson, and Rullmann (2009), all St'át'imcets modals allow variable modal force. Another possibility is that the apparent permission interpretations of *ka-...-a* are simply ability readings: if one is able to do something, that could be either because of physical abilities, or more generally because there are no impediments to one's doing it, including no deontic prohibitions.

Apart from this caveat, the claims in the literature about modal force are upheld in the pilot corpus study: we find both strong interpretations ("acciden-

---

[22] The storyboard methodology involves the presentation of a series of pictures, in response to which the consultant tells a story in their own words. The storyboards are designed to elicit specific linguistic phenomena; they thus differ from all-purpose narrative-elicitation, which is exemplified by the Pear Stories (Chafe 1980) or Frog Stories (Berman and Slobin 1994). See Burton and Matthewson (2015) for an introduction to the use of storyboards in semantic elicitation, and see Kolagar and Vander Klok, this volume, on the use of storyboards to study modality.

tally" and "non-controllable") and weaker interpretations (ability and permission).

The temporal perspective of the 20 *ka-...-a* examples in the pilot study is usually past (as in (47), (48), and (49) above). The two cases of present TP both involve direct speech (one is given in (42) above). There was never any overt marking of TP, as expected.

Nor was there any overt marking of TO. As with the English corpus-based study, it seems difficult to have clear theory-independent judgments about TO in the St'át'imcets pilot study also.

4.3.3 Epistemic *k'a*

The existing literature presents a substantial amount of evidence that *k'a* has exclusively epistemic modal flavour (Matthewson, Davis, and Rullmann 2007; Rullmann, Matthewson, and Davis 2008). It is therefore interesting that of the 20 tokens of *k'a* in the pilot study, only nine are translated into English with some marker of epistemic modality (which is usually *must*, with one *seemed* and one *looked like*). One example is given in (52).

(52) Epistemic *k'a*
 Nilh s=tsut=s, "O, nílh=kelh ts7a, wá7=**k'a**=ti7
 COP NMLZ=say=3POSS oh COP=PROSP this.VIS IPFV=**EPIS**=that.VIS
 qwits, wa7 sq'uq'wts."
 rich IPFV fat
 'She said, "This will be the one, he must be rich since he's fat."'
 (Alexander 2016: 64)

Four of the 20 tokens are very likely epistemic, but the modality is rendered in the translation only by the hedge 'about', as in (53).

(53) Epistemic *k'a*
 T'ák=**k'a** e=t7ú pála7 sxetspásq'et láti7 elh
 go.along=**EPIS** to=that.VIS one week at+there.VIS and.then
 qwéts-p=tu7 ta=skalúl7=a píxem'.
 move-INCH=REM DET=owl=EXIS hunt
 'About a week passed before the owl set out to hunt.'
 (Alexander 2016: 34)

Four of the tokens involve cases where the narrator is likely guessing about what happened, or is relying on a report from a third person, as in (54); these are thus plausibly epistemic. For the remaining three tokens, the data are *consistent* with an epistemic interpretation, but there is no actual evidence for epistemic modality in the context or the translation; see (55) for an example, where the English translation lacks any epistemic or other modal marker corresponding to *k'a*.

(54) Epistemic *k'a*
 *Nílh=**k'a**=ti7 s-kéla7-s láti7 iz', 1900.*
 COP=**EPIS**=that.VIS NMLZ-first-3POSS at+there.VIS those.VIS 1900
 'That's when they first did that, 1900.'
 (Alexander 2016: 95)

(55) Epistemic *k'a*?
 *Láku7=**k'a** zam', láti7 lh=wá7=as láti7*
 at+there.INVIS=**EPIS** after.all at+there.VIS COMP=be=3SBJV at+there.VIS
 ta=smúlhats=a wa7 es=[s]kúza7, ta=sm'é·m'·lhats=a.
 DET=woman=EXIS IPFV have=offspring DET=woman·CRED·=EXIS
 'A woman lived there that had a young daughter.'
 (Alexander 2016: 52)

Even for this last type of case, there is no other modal flavour these instances of *k'a* could reasonably have, so perhaps the lack of a modal in the English translations is merely an artefact of the fact that strong epistemic modality can easily be omitted in translation. Here is a case where discussion with a native speaker of St'át'imcets is critical to fully understanding the interpretation of the corpus data.

As for modal force, there is no evidence for epistemic possibility in the 20 tokens of *k'a* in the study; they all seem to involve necessity (or weak necessity) interpretations. However, there are several cases of *k'a* in the rest of the corpus that are translated into English with *maybe* or *might (have)*, so a larger corpus study would likely support the prediction that *k'a* is compatible with a range of modal forces. Of course, relying only on translations to determine modal force is fraught, since an English sentence containing *maybe* or *might* could be compatible with a situation that also supports a strong epistemic modal. Moreover, the cases in the rest of the corpus where *k'a* is translated into English with a weak modal element all seem to involve subjunctive marking, and some involve the polar question marker *kan* 'whether'; these constructions require further research. One example is given in (56).

(56) **Kán=as=k'a**   láti7   kw=s=tqilh=ts
     whether=3SBJV=EPIS at+there.VIS   DET=NLMZ=almost=3POSS
     xetspqíqin'kst   i=tsícw=a   káku7   cwíl'-em.
     one.hundred   PL.DET=get.there=EXIS around+there.INVIS look.for-MID
     'There might have been nearly 100 people who came around there to look for him.'
     (Alexander 2016: 338)

Turning to the temporal properties of *k'a*, 19 out of the 20 tokens of *k'a* in our study seem to have present TP (including all the examples given above) and one may have past TP, as shown in (57):

(57) Past TP *k'a*?
     Tákem=**k'a**   ti=sq'ít=a   kw=s=q'weláw'-em=s.
     all=**EPIS**   DET=day=EXIS   DET=NMLZ=pick-MID=3POSS
     'He picked what seemed like all day.'
     (Alexander 2016: 13)

The reason this potentially has past TP is because in the larger context of the story, the subject of (57), the owl, is being asked to do lots of tasks that seem arduous and difficult to him. The larger context for this example is given in the English translation in (58):

(58) *"Can I take your daughter? How much do you want?"*
     "Oh," the woman said, "Go pick me lots of tsáqwem *(saskatoon berries). Fill a bunch of baskets, and then bring them to me."*
     So the owl went berry picking. **He picked what seemed like all day**, *and he filled two baskets. He took them to the woman.*
     "Oh," said the woman, "that's not enough. Go pick that much more again."

It is plausible that the 'seemed' here refers to the owl's perspective. Notice also that in English, it would be infelicitous in this discourse context to say 'He picked what seem<u>s</u> like all day'.

With regard to TO, the results were as follows: of the 20 tokens of *k'a* in the pilot study, four seem to have present TO, and 16 past TO. The 'fat' case above (52) is an example of present TO, and the 'week passed' case (53) is past TO. In accordance with our predictions, there was no overt marking of TO for either the present or past cases. It would be interesting in a larger corpus study to see whether future-TO cases of *k'a* arise.

4.4 Summary

This pilot study of three St'át'imcets modals (deontic/irrealis *ka*, circumstantial *ka-...-a*, and epistemic *k'a*) largely supported the predictions found in existing literature with respect to modal flavour, modal force, and temporal properties. There were no obvious counterexamples to the expected modal flavours, although the corpus revealed a previously unnoticed use of circumstantial *ka-...-a* for permission (which raises intriguing questions for future research), and there were also cases where epistemic *k'a* was translated only with "about to" or not at all.

In terms of modal force, deontic/irrealis *ka* and epistemic *k'a* seemed to overwhelmingly favour (weak) necessity readings. This tendency was already noticed by Rullmann, Matthewson, and Davis (2008), and their impression was confirmed in the corpus data. It would be interesting to see whether a larger corpus study would find instances of these modals with weak modal force, and also to see whether there are generalizations about what facilitates or licenses this (such as the possible relevance of subjunctive marking).

We found no counterexamples to any of the predictions about modal-temporal interactions; that is, we found that (a) all modals could have either past or present TP without any overt marking; (b) circumstantial modals do not co-occur with any aspectual marking; and (c) epistemic modals can have past or present TO without any overt marking. There were some gaps in the attested combinations in this study: we found no instances of deontic readings of *ka* with past TP, and no cases of epistemic *k'a* with future TO. With respect to the second point, if it turns out to be rare even in a larger study to find epistemic *k'a* with future TO, it could be because there is another way to express future epistemic readings, namely the prospective marker *kelh*. An example from the corpus of an epistemic use of *kelh* is given in (59).

(59) "*[Lh]=cúz'=acw   kwan-ts,   áoz=**kelh***
      COMP=PROSP=2SG.SBJV   take+DIR-1SG.OBJ   NEG=**PROSP**
      kwásu   qwenqwánt."
      DET+NMLZ+IPFV+2SG.POSS poor
      "'If you choose me, you'll never be poor.'"
      (Alexander 2016: 59)

The largest caveat to the success of the empirical predictions is with TO; as noted above, with both the circumstantial modals there is very little theory-independent evidence in the corpus data about TO.

5 Conclusion and outlook

What have we learned from this corpus investigation of modal-temporal interactions in two languages? First of all, that this is an enterprise that is definitely worth doing. Looking at corpus data has by and large provided confirmations of our theoretical predictions (based on theories which were in part grounded in and inspired by isolated attested examples drawn from corpora), but it has also provided further nuance and qualification of our generalizations, and highlighted problems to be investigated in future research. Confronting theories with real-life examples reveals challenges and can lead to important modifications and refinements.

We also ran into several obstacles, and there are methodological lessons to be drawn for the future, especially when it comes to corpus work on underdescribed languages, although most of these points hold for "bigger" languages like English as well. Most importantly, the kind of semantic distinctions we have focused on in this study can be extremely subtle and hard to determine. Things like modal flavour, temporal orientation and perspective, and protagonist vs. narrator perspective do not leap off the page. There are often no obvious markers present in the corpus that can be used as unambiguous indicators of these semantic distinctions.[23] Instead, researchers have to rely on speaker intuitions, either their own or those of speaker-consultants. The discourse context plays an important role in this, and it may be necessary to take a much larger amount of surrounding text into consideration than is usual in corpus studies.

The necessity of examining larger chunks of text when annotating modal data is a good thing in the sense that it shows the importance of context (in the widest sense of the word) for semantic and pragmatic interpretation, and in that it forces us to focus on whole texts rather than isolated sentences. But even if the entire story can be inspected, there are many cases where TP or TO may still be ambiguous or indeterminate, or where a sentence could be interpreted as reflecting either the narrator's or the protagonist's perspective (or even both or neither).

Something else our two case studies have shown is that it is a lot easier to extract valuable information from corpus data if one has at least a preliminary hypothesis or analysis going into the study. For example, take the case of St'át'imcets *ka-...-a,* which in prior literature was found to have five apparent readings,

---

23 This has been observed by prior researchers, of course, and it holds in spite of the research that specifically seeks to predict things like modal flavour from other features of the environment; see the references in section 1.2 above. We suspect that the issues with interpreting corpus data are potentially even more acute when modal-temporal interactions are the focus of the research.

which Davis, Matthewson, and Rullmann (2009) argued can be unified under a single analysis as a strong circumstantial modal. One of the five interpretations of *ka-...-a* is "non-controllable", and we analyzed example (49) above ('So he fell in love with a girl over there') as an instance of that interpretation. After all, it seems in the context of the story that the owl had no choice but to fall in love with the girl. However, if one began the investigation of *ka-...-a* by looking at this corpus, it would probably be difficult to detect that there was even any modality at all based on the translation of this example. In fact, *ka-...-a* is not reflected at all in the translation. Of course, being driven by a hypothesis could also lead to a self-fulfilling prophecy whereby it is assumed that the interpretation is what one predicts it should be, even if there is no independent evidence specifically for that interpretation in the corpus. This leads to our next point: the importance of working with native speakers to interpret and annotate the corpus wherever possible.

It's clear that to alleviate the issues raised here as much as possible, researchers should work with native speakers. For a language like English, ideally the data would be annotated by several trained annotators, who have been given clear instructions but who are "naive" as to the theories that are being tested.[24] We have not done this yet in these two case studies, but it is an obvious goal for future research. The main challenge that we see for this is the development of clear and consistent criteria that the annotators can be instructed to use. In some cases, there may be straightforward tests, like substitution with a semi-modal to determine TP (see section 3.2.3 above). For other factors (like TO or protagonist perspective) such relatively clear criteria may be harder to come by, because these notions are more theory-dependent or "subjective".

For less well-resourced languages like St'át'imcets, the available corpora are much smaller and harder to come by. If the researcher is not themselves a fluent speaker, they will have to largely rely on working with native speaker-consultants of the language, for instance asking whether a sentence in a given context may felicitously be paraphrased in one way or another without changing the meaning. In other words, corpus work such as this study has to be integrated with more traditional fieldwork methodologies.

Overall, we think there are (at least) two important conclusions to be drawn here. First, we want to emphasize the methodological similarities, rather than the differences, between corpus-based work on English and other well-studied languages on the one hand, and on less-resourced languages like St'át'imcets on

---

24 See for example Rubinstein et al. (2012) for discussion of how to use Mechanical Turk participants in modality research (although note that this was not a corpus study).

the other, despite the obvious practical differences. There was a clear parallel between our two studies: in both, a prior theoretical analysis was needed, and ideally one should work with one or more native speakers. Moreover, paraphrases are a good technique (e.g., the substitution test with semi-modals in English), and also one can do further elicitation and testing inspired by examples in the corpus (up to and including psycholinguistic experimentation where this is practically feasible).

Our second take-home message is a plea for methodological pluralism. No single methodology (be it native speaker intuitions, corpora, traditional fieldwork elicitation, psycholinguistic experiments, and so on) can provide the researcher with direct access to the truth – there simply is no methodological magic bullet. Rather, different approaches are complementary to each other and should be used in combination (see, for example, the results in Chen, this volume, and Agostinho and Rech, this volume, which both use a combination of two different methods). The best and most certain results are obtained from converging evidence obtained by applying a range of different methodological paradigms.

References

Abusch, Dorit. 1985. *On verbs and time*. Amherst, MA: University of Massachusetts dissertation.
Abusch, Dorit. 1997. Sequence of tense and temporal *de re*. Linguistics and Philosophy 20. 1–50.
Alexander, Carl. 2016. *Sqwéqwel' mûta7 sptakwlh: St'át'imcets narratives by Qwa7yan'ak (Carl Alexander),* transcribed, translated and edited by Elliot Callahan, Henry Davis, John Lyon & Lisa Matthewson. Vancouver & Lillooet: UBCOPL & USLCES.
Al-Sabbagh, Rania, Jana Diesner & Roxana Girju. 2013. Using the semantic-syntactic interface for reliable Arabic modality annotation. In Ruslan Mitkov & Jong C. Park (eds.), *Proceedings of the Sixth International Joint Conference on Natural Language Processing*, 410–418. Nagoya, Japan: Asian Federation of Natural Language Processing.
Anand, Pranav & Maziar Toosarvandani. 2018. No explanation for the historical present: Temporal sequencing and discourse. In Uli Sauerland & Stephanie Solt (eds.), *Proceedings of Sinn und Bedeutung 22*, 73–90. Berlin: ZAS.
Banfield, Ann. 1982. *Unspeakable sentences: Narration and representation in the language of fiction*. London: Routledge and Kegan Paul.
Berman, Ruth & Dan Slobin. 1994. *Relating events in narrative: A cross-linguistic developmental study*. Hillsdale, NJ: Erlbaum.
Brezina, Vaclav. 2018. *Statistics in corpus linguistics: A practical guide*. Cambridge: Cambridge University Press.
Burton, Strang & Lisa Matthewson. 2015. Targeted construction storyboards in semantic fieldwork. In M. Ryan Bochnak & Lisa Matthewson (eds.), *Methodologies in semantic fieldwork*, 135–156. Oxford: Oxford University Press.

Chafe, Wallace (ed.). 1980. *The pear stories: Cognitive, cultural, and linguistic aspects of narrative production*. Norwood, NJ: Ablex.

Chen, Sihwei, Vera Hohaus, Rebecca Laturnus, Meagan Louie, Lisa Matthewson, Hotze Rullmann, Ori Simchen, Claire K. Turner & Jozina Vander Klok. 2017. Past possibility cross-linguistically: Evidence from 12 languages. In Ana Arregui, Maria-Luisa Rivero & Andrés Salanova (eds.), *Modality across syntactic categories*, 236–287. Oxford: Oxford University Press.

Clement, Marja. 2014. The development of free indirect constructions in Dutch novels. *Journal of Literary Semantics* 43 (2). 127–141.

Cohn, Dorrit. 1978. *Transparent minds: Narrative modes for presenting consciousness in fiction*. Princeton, NJ: Princeton University Press.

Condoravdi, Cleo. 2002. Temporal interpretation of modals: Modals for the present and the past. In David Beaver, Luis Casillas Martinez, Brady Clark & Stefan Kaufmann (eds.), *The construction of meaning*, 59–88. Stanford, CA: CSLI Publications.

Cournane, Ailís. 2014. In search of L1 evidence for diachronic reanalysis: Mapping modals. *Language Acquisition* 21 (1). 103–117.

Cournane, Ailís. 2015. *Modal development: Input-divergent L1 acquisition in the direction of diachronic reanalysis*. Toronto, ON: University of Toronto dissertation.

Cournane, Ailís. 2021. Revisiting the epistemic gap: It's not the thought that counts. *Language Acquisition* 28 (3). 215–240.

Davis, Henry, Lisa Matthewson & Hotze Rullmann. 2009. 'Out of control' marking as circumstantial modality in St'át'imcets. In Lotte Hogeweg, Helen de Hoop & Andrey Malchukov (eds.), *Cross-linguistic semantics of tense, aspect, and modality*, 205–244. Amsterdam & Philadelphia: John Benjamins.

Davies, Mark. 2008. *The Corpus of Contemporary American English*. www.english-corpora.org/coca/ (last accessed 26 September 2021).

De Haan, Ferdinand. 2011. Disambiguating modals: Constructions and *must*. Manuscript. https://www.academia.edu/756730/Disambiguating_modals_constructions_and_must (last accessed 26 September 2021).

Denison, David. 1992. Counterfactual *may have*. In Marinel Gerritsen & Dieter Stein (eds.), *Internal and external factors in syntactic change*, 229–256. Berlin: Mouton de Gruyter.

Dieuleveut, Anouk, Annemarie van Dooren, Ailís Cournane & Valentine Hacquard. 2019. Learning modal force: Evidence from children's production and input. In Julian J. Schlöder, Dean McHugh & Floris Roelofsen (eds.), *Proceedings of the 2019 Amsterdam Colloquium*, 111–122. Amsterdam: ILLC, University of Amsterdam.

Diewald, Gabriele. 1999. *Die Modalverben im Deutschen: Grammatikalisierung und Polyfunktionalität* [Modal verbs in German: Grammaticalization and polyfunctionality]. Tübingen: Niemeyer.

Dollinger, Stefan. 2006. The modal auxiliaries *have to* and *must* in the Corpus of Early Ontario English: Gradient change and colonial lag. *The Canadian Journal of Linguistics / La revue canadienne de linguistique* 51 (2). 287–308.

Dooren, Annemarie van, Anouk Dieuleveut, Ailís Cournane & Valentine Hacquard. 2017. Learning what *can* and *must* can and must mean. In Alexandre Cremers, Thom van Gessel & Floris Roelofsen (eds.), *Proceedings of the 2017 Amsterdam Colloquium*, 225–235. Amsterdam: ILLC, University of Amsterdam.

Dooren, Annemarie van, Maxime Tulling, Ailís Cournane & Valentine Hacquard. 2019. Discovering modal polysemy: Lexical aspect *might* help. In Megan M. Brown & Brady Dailey (eds.), *Proceedings of BUCLD 43*, 203–216. Somerville, MA: Cascadilla Press.

Eckardt, Regine. 2015. *The semantics of Free Indirect Discourse: How texts allow us to mind-read and eavesdrop*. Leiden: Brill.

Eckardt, Regine. 2021. The parameters of indirect speech. In Daniel Gutzmann, Lisa Matthewson, Cécile Meier, Hotze Rullmann & Thomas Ede Zimmermann (eds.), *The Wiley Blackwell companion to semantics*, Vol. IV, 2213–2237. Hoboken, NJ: Wiley.

Edwards, Bill, Martina LaRochelle & Sam Mitchell 2017. *Sqwéqwel's nelh skelkekla7lhkálha: Tales of our elders*. Transcribed, translated & edited by Henry Davis, John Lyon, Jan van Eijk & Rose Agnes Whitley. Vancouver: UBCOPL & USLCES. https://lingpapers.sites.olt.ubc.ca/sqweqwels-nelh-skelkekla7lhkalha-tales-of-our-elders/.

von Fintel, Kai & Anthony Gillies. 2008. CIA leaks. *Philosophical Review* 117. 77–98.

Fludernik, Monika. 1994. *The fictions of language and the languages of fiction: The linguistic representation of speech and consciousness*. London: Routledge.

Fuoli, Matteo & Charlotte Hommerberg. 2015. Optimising transparency, reliability and replicability: Annotation principles and inter-coder agreement in the quantification of evaluation expressions. *Corpora* 10 (3). 315–349.

Gries, Stefan Th. 2009. *Quantitative corpus linguistics with R*. London & New York: Routledge.

Hacquard, Valentine. 2006. *Aspects of modality*. Cambridge, MA: Massachusetts Institute of Technology dissertation.

Hacquard, Valentine. 2010. On the event relativity of modal auxiliaries. *Natural Language Semantics* 18. 79–114.

Hacquard, Valentine. 2011. Modality. In Claudia Maienborn, Klaus von Heusinger & Paul Portner (eds.), *Semantics: An international handbook of natural language meaning*, 1484–1515. Berlin: Mouton de Gruyter.

Hacquard, Valentine & Alexis Wellwood. 2012. Embedding epistemic modals in English: A corpus-based study. *Semantics and Pragmatics* 5. 1–29.

Herman, David (ed.). 2011. *The emergence of mind: Representations of consciousness in narrative discourse in English*. Lincoln, NE: University of Nebraska Press.

Hoek, Jet & Merel C.J. Scholman. 2017. Evaluating discourse annotation: Some recent insights and new approaches. In Harry Bunt (ed.), *Proceedings of the 13th Joint ACL-ISO Workshop on Interoperable Semantic Annotation*, 1–13. Tilburg University, The Netherlands: TiCC (Tilburg Center for Cognition and Communication).

Huddleston, Rodney & Geoffrey Pullum (eds.). 2002. *The Cambridge grammar of the English language*. Cambridge: Cambridge University Press.

Iatridou, Sabine & Hedde Zeijlstra. 2013. Negation, polarity, and deontic modals. *Linguistic Inquiry* 44. 529–568.

Jasionyte, Erika. 2012. Lithuanian impersonal modal verbs *reik(ė)ti* 'need' and *tekti* 'be gotten': A corpus-based study. In Aurelija Usoniene, Nicole Nau and Ineta Dabašinskiene (eds.), *Multiple perspectives in linguistic research on Baltic languages*, 206–228. Newcastle upon Tyne: Cambridge Scholars Publishing.

Katz, Graham. 2019. Semantics in corpus linguistics. In Klaus von Heusinger, Claudia Maienborn & Paul Portner (eds.), *Semantics: Typology, diachrony and processing*, 409–443. Berlin & Boston: De Gruyter Mouton.

Maier, Emar. 2014. Language shifts in free indirect discourse. *Journal of Literary Semantics* 43 (2). 143–167.

Maier, Emar. 2015. Quotation and unquotation in Free Indirect Discourse. *Mind & Language* 30. 345–373.
Matsuyoshi, Suguru, Megumi Eguchi, Chitose Sao, Koji Murakam, Kentaro Inui & Yuji Matsumoto. 2010. Annotating event mentions in text with modality, focus, and source information. In Nicoletta Calzolari, Khalid Choukri, Bente Maegaard, Joseph Mariani, Jan Odijk, Stelios Piperidis, Mike Rosner & Daniel Tapias (eds.), *Proceedings of the Seventh Conference on International Language Resources and Evaluation (LREC'10)*, 1456–1463, Valletta, Malta: European Language Resources Association (ELRA).
Matthewson, Lisa. 2005. *When I was small – I wan kwikws: A grammatical analysis of St'át'imcets oral narratives*. Vancouver, BC: UBC Press.
Matthewson, Lisa 2006. Temporal semantics in a supposedly tenseless language. *Linguistics and Philosophy* 29. 673–713.
Matthewson, Lisa. 2013. Gitksan modals. *International Journal of American Linguistics* 79. 349–394.
Matthewson, Lisa, Henry Davis & Hotze Rullmann. 2007. Evidentials as epistemic modals: Evidence from St'át'imcets. *Linguistic Variation Yearbook* 7. 201–254.
Mberamihigo, Ferdinand. 2014. L'expression de la modalité en Kirundi: Exploitation d'un corpus électronique [The expression of modality in Kirundi: Use of an electronic corpus]. Brussels: Université libre de Bruxelles dissertation.
Mendes, Amália, Iris Hendrickx, Luciana Ávila, Paulo Quaresma, Teresa Gonçalves & João Sequeira. 2016. Modality annotation for Portuguese: From manual annotation to automatic labeling. *LiLT – Language Issues in Language Technology* 14 (5). 1–35.
Mortelmans, Tanya. 2000. On the 'evidential' nature of the 'epistemic' use of the German modals *müssen* and *sollen*. *Belgian Journal of Linguistics* 14. 131–148.
Mortelmans, Tanya. 2012. Epistemic MUST and its cognates in German and Dutch. The subtle differences. *Journal of Pragmatics* 44. 2150–2164.
Ogihara, Toshiyuki. 1996. *Tense, attitudes and scope*. Dordrecht: Kluwer.
Palmer, Alan. 2004. *Fictional minds*. Lincoln, NE: University of Nebraska Press.
Papafragou, Anna. 1998. The acquisition of modality: Implications for theories of semantic representations. *Mind and Language* 13 (3). 370–399.
Portner, Paul. 2009. *Modality*. Oxford: Oxford University Press.
von Prince, Kilu, Ana Krajinović, Anna Margetts, Nick Thieberger & Valérie Guérin. 2019. Habituals in four Oceanic languages of Melanesia. *STUF – Language Typology and Universals* 72 (1). 21–66.
von Prince, Kilu & Anna Margetts. 2019. Expressing possibility in two Oceanic languages. *Studies in Language* 43 (3). 628–667.
Recski, Leonardo Juliano. 2002. The English modal auxiliary *must:* A corpus-based syntactic-semantic account. *Revista da ABRALIN* 1 (2). 99–122.
Rubinstein, Aynat, Dan Simonson, Joo Chung, Hillary Harner, Graham Katz & Paul Portner. 2012. Developing a methodology for modality type annotations on a large scale. Paper presented at the Modality Workshop, University of Ottawa, 20 April.
Rubinstein, Aynat, Hillary Harner, Elizabeth Krawczyk, Daniel Simonson, Graham Katz & Paul Portner. 2013. Toward fine-grained annotation of modality in text. In Paul Portner, Aynat Rubinstein, Graham Katz (eds.), *Proceedings of IWCS 2013 Workshop on Annotation of Modal Meanings in Natural Language (WAMM)*, 38–46. Association for Computational Linguistics.

Rullmann, Hotze, Lisa Matthewson & Henry Davis. 2008. Modals as distributive indefinites. *Natural Language Semantics* 16. 317–357.

Rullmann, Hotze & Lisa Matthewson. 2018. Towards a theory of modal-temporal interaction. *Language* 94 (2). 281–331.

Ruppenhofer, Josef & Ines Rehbein. 2012. Yes we can!? Annotating the senses of English modal verbs. In Nicoletta Calzolari, Khalid Choukri, Thierry Declerck, Mehmet Uğur Doğan, Bente Maegaard, Joseph Mariani, Asuncion Moreno, Jan Odijk & Stelios Piperidis (eds.), *Proceedings of the Eighth International Conference on Language Resources and Evaluation (LREC-2012)*, 1538–1545. European Language Resources Association (ELRA).

Schlenker, Philippe. 2004. Context of thought and context of utterance: A note on free indirect discourse and the historical present. *Mind & Language* 19 (3). 279–304.

Sharvit, Yael. 2018. The puzzle of free indirect discourse. *Linguistics and Philosophy* 31 (3). 353–395.

Šoliene, Audrone. 2012. Epistemic necessity in a parallel corpus: Lithuanian vs. English. In Aurelija Usoniene, Nicole Nau & Ineta Dabašinskiene (eds.), *Multiple perspectives in linguistic research on Baltic languages*, 10–42. Newcastle upon Tyne: Cambridge Scholars Publishing.

Spooren, Wilbert & Liesbeth Degand. 2010. Coding coherence relations: Reliability and validity. *Corpus Linguistics and Linguistic Theory* 6 (2). 241–266.

TFS Working Group. 2011. *Chore Girl*. http://www.totemfieldstoryboards.org (accessed 7 September 2021).

Toosarvandani, Maziar. 2020. Encoding time in tenseless languages: The view from Zapotec. In D.K.E. Reisinger & Marianne Huijsmans (eds.), *Proceedings of the 37th West Coast Conference on Formal Linguistics*, 21–41. Somerville, MA: Cascadilla Proceedings Project.

van der Auwera, Johan & Gabriele Diewald. 2012. Methods for modalities. In Andrea Ender, Adrian Leemann & Bernhard Wälchli (eds.), *Methods in contemporary linguistics*, 121–142. Berlin & Boston: de Gruyter Mouton.

van der Auwera, Johan, Ewa Schalley & Jan Nuyts. 2005. Epistemic possibility in a Slavonic parallel corpus – a pilot study. In Björn Hansen & Petr Karlík (eds.), *Modality in Slavonic Languages, New Perspectives*, 201–217. München: Sagner.

Van Eijk, Jan 1997. *The Lillooet language: Phonology, morphology, syntax*. Vancouver: UBC Press.

Vander Klok, Jozina. 2019. Exploring the interaction of modality and temporality through the storyboard *Bill vs. the weather*. *Semantic Field Methods* 1 (1). 1–29.

Wärnsby, Anna. 2006. (De)coding modality: The case of *must*, *may*, *måste* and *kan*. *Lund Studies in English 113*. Lund, Sweden: Department of English Centre for Languages and Literature, Lund University.

Wiebe, Janyce, Theresa Wilson & Claire Cardie. 2005. Annotating expressions of opinions and emotions in language. *Language Resources and Evaluation* 39 (2). 164–210.

Yanovich, Igor 2016. Old English *motan*, variable-force modality, and the presupposition of inevitable actualization. *Language* 92 (3). 489–521.

Ailís Cournane & Valentine Hacquard

5 Adapting acquisition methodologies to study modality in underdescribed languages

Abstract: This chapter focuses on methods used to test modality in child language acquisition. Acquisition and fieldwork approaches are united by the goal to understand the representational systems of the grammars under inquiry (developing or adult). They differ in what is known and unknown. In language acquisition we typically know a lot about language specific target constructions, but not the development of full competency, while in fieldwork we don't know as much about those targets, but we can trust that adult speakers have full competency. When we design child studies, we create replicable sets of carefully controlled contexts and stimuli. Focusing on a few methodological paradigms that have been successful for deepening our understanding of modal development, we consider the advantages and challenges associated with adapting these methods to study underdescribed languages. We speculate on how fieldworkers might be able to make the best use of these methods, in a way that complements existing methods.

1 Introduction

Fieldworkers and acquisitionists studying modality both aim to accurately describe and explain modal systems: for their syntax, semantics and pragmatics. A common ultimate goal is to learn how much variation and similarity exists in

---

Acknowledgements: We are indebted to Anouk Dieuleveut, Annemarie van Dooren, and Paloma Jeretič for helpful discussions about these acquisition materials, working on modality with language consultants (in Kaqchikel (Mayan), Georgian (Kartvelian), and Siona (Tucanoan), respectively), and similarities and differences between language acquisition and fieldwork. We are also grateful for comments and helpful suggestions from two anonymous reviewers and the editors of this volume.

Ailís Cournane, New York University, 10 Washington Pl., New York, NY, 10003, USA, e-mail: cournane@nyu.edu
Valentine Hacquard, University of Maryland, College Park, 1401 Marie Mount Hall, College Park, MD, 20742, USA, e-mail: hacquard@umd.edu

https://doi.org/10.1515/9783110721478-006

cross-linguistic modal systems. We ask, how can this notionally defined area of language get packaged into grammars? What is yet unknown is quite different, however, between fieldwork and acquisition work. In fieldwork on underdescribed languages we don't yet know the (full) modal system for adult grammatical competence. In acquisition work, we typically know the modal system of the target language very well (as for e.g., English or Spanish), but don't yet know the developmental path children take to arrive at adult grammatical competency. Given the particular challenges of working with children, and isolating and characterizing grammatical competence in development (as distinct from conceptual and processing development), we have to be creative and careful to arrive at useful methodologies. Our successes may translate well to understudied languages, when considering the common goals of fieldworkers and acquisitionists, so long as we bear in mind the differing unknowns (target grammar vs. developmental grammar). In this paper, we: (a) share our carefully controlled first language acquisition materials for modal language, and the insights we've learned about modal development from using these materials, (b) relate and compare our methods to existing semantic fieldwork methods, (c) offer suggestions about adapting our materials for research on understudied languages, noting that our materials are suitable for working with adults or children, and (d) advocate for an increased back-and-forth between our two subfields: fieldwork on underdescribed languages has helped us understand better what children entertain as possible for modal language systems (see Cournane 2020), and acquisition work on modals helps us understand how learning shapes adult modal systems.

In fieldwork, the question of how modal concepts are grammatically expressed is addressed by seeing what patterns are actually attested in the language under study. For the fieldworker, the main goal is describing a language whose modal properties are not yet known from a linguistics perspective. The question is: how is modality expressed in the language, and how does that fit into the known typology of modal systems? We have learned more about the kinds of modals and modal systems languages may have from this work, especially on understudied languages (Bochnak 2015; Deal 2011; Matthewson 2010; Peterson 2010; Rullmann, Matthewson and Davis 2008; Rullmann and Matthewson 2018; Vander Klok 2012, i.a.). In acquisition work, the question of how modal concepts are grammatically expressed is addressed by seeing what hypotheses children entertain or fail to entertain along their learning path. For the acquisitionist, the main goal is describing when and how children acquire the target system (usually well-known), and understanding aspects of the input and changes within the child that drive development. The question is: how is the target system learned? Acquisitionists must be attuned to social, conceptual and other non-linguistic developments that may affect children's modal language use or their ability to perform certain tasks (i.e. "task effects"). Contrast that to the fieldworker, who can trust that speakers have developed adult competence in linguistic and non-linguistic domains, that there are no conceptual or socio-pragmatic deficits due to immature development (though there may be sociocultural differences which can affect tasks).

In our projects on modal acquisition, we have primarily worked with English-learning children (our "convenience sample" when working with monolingual populations in North American cities, though working with small children is rarely convenient), but have also done experiments with Bosnian/Croatian/Serbian-learning children (Veselinović 2019; Cournane and Veselinović *accepted*), and worked on corpora in Dutch (van Dooren et al. 2019), French (Cournane and Tailleur, 2021), and Bosnian/Croatian/Serbian (Veselinović and Cournane 2020). None of these languages is underdescribed, but in acquisition that is often seen as an advantage. Knowing the language well is helpful when characterizing the target language, the input the child receives, and the learning path more generally. There are fewer unknowns. However, this real advantage for understanding the dynamics of development has contributed to acquisition work being even more narrowly centered on a few well-studied languages than linguistics research is more broadly.

Adapting methods specifically designed for one population and language will always involve creativity and effort to make sure the method maintains its integrity for addressing the desired research questions and hypotheses. That said, adapting from acquisition to fieldwork is a reasonably good match, despite on-the-surface major differences between our populations. We share many of the same challenges, many that researchers working with mature speakers of well-studied and widely spoken language do not.

First, few speakers and small sample size is common in both fields (see Bochnak and Matthewson 2015: 3–5). In acquisition work it is often difficult to get participants who fit the eligibility requirements of a study. Even working on widely spoken languages, recruiting and testing children is much more challenging than with adult participants from the same communities. Children cannot consent for themselves, so there are many more steps and individuals (i.e., caregivers, teachers, daycare directors, etc.) involved in the consent and assent[1] process. The process involves

---

[1] Children cannot give informed consent to participate in a research study (Parental/Guardian informed consent is required), so to adhere to legal and ethical requirements and best practices, we instead need them to give oral assent before we run an experiment with them. This involves a short conversation where we explain, in an age-appropriate way, that we want to learn more about how children talk and that to do that we're asking for their help. We ask them if they are willing to play the language game with us, and if they agree, we continue.

heavy recruiting effort for each participant that is successfully recruited. This leads to the problem of a "small n", that is, samples which lack power for statistical analysis. In brief, we usually do not have the resources (time, personnel, money) to devote to collecting large ns, before sharing our work and bringing it to publication (contrast this with studies conducted with adults online, where hundreds of participants are collected within a matter of days and costs are relatively low). And, adding to the small n challenge, many participants' data need to be excluded from analysis because children have a higher likelihood of being non-compliant participants. Work on understudied languages also usually faces issues related to limited data. Because of small ns, methods and analysis may in some ways be a closer fit from acquisition work than from psycholinguistics more broadly.

Second, in both fields we need to be extremely careful about making assumptions from what we know as linguists or speakers. This comes down to not being a member of the population. Many linguists are not native speakers of the understudied languages under inquiry, and we are never children. Compare this to when linguists work with mature speakers of a language that they are a native speaker of – their implicit biases about the phenomena are much more likely to be inconsequential to a clear view of facts, because they are a member of the broad population of study (abstracting away from sociolinguistic variation). In acquisition and fieldwork, we run a high risk of tacitly imposing our knowledge as linguists or speakers into the materials, data, or analysis. This issue can be particularly insidious in acquisition, as researchers often are native speakers of the language they are studying in development: it is very easy to assume that if a child learning our own language behaves a certain way, they are using the same knowledge or abilities that mature speakers like us do. Or if a child gives a somewhat opaque response, we may overinterpret it, filling in missing information from our own knowledge (and ironically, can end up measuring ourselves rather than the participant). The first author often teaches her students to pretend that child English (or whatever language we are looking at) is a different language or dialect from what they speak, to gain a healthy distance from making these kinds of tacit assumptions that can muddy a clear view on the facts.

And, lastly, looking at semantic and pragmatic areas of languages, controlling the context for acceptability and felicity is essential, because "[u]tterances are only true or false, felicitous or infelicitous, in context." (Bochnak and Matthewson 2020: 262; see also Bochnak and Matthewson 2015; Burton and Matthewson 2015; Cover 2015; Ferreira and Müller, this volume, §3.1; Vander Klok 2014, 2019). Here too, we cannot assume that because the context we created supports our own interpretation for e.g., an epistemic possibility modal, that participants or speakers will have the same interpretation of that context. To combat these challenges, as in fieldwork, we try to use multiple methods on the same phenomenon to triangulate to the truth about the phenomenon under inquiry. And, we carefully monitor participants throughout testing, and probe for qualitative data and explanation where possible, to shed further light on responses to our materials. And, during development, we extensively pilot our materials out on others, both adults and children in person, to hone the materials to where we need them to be so we can be as confident as possible about the data they will garner. These practices help mitigate both the small n issue and the insidious effects of context interpretation. We will discuss some further, more specific, ways we deal with these challenges for the specific methodologies we cover.

We will not cover the literature on modal development (see Papafragou 1998; Hickmann and Bassano 2016; Cournane 2020 for overviews). Instead, we highlight some key questions that motivate acquisition studies and their potential relevance for fieldwork, and provide references for the interested reader here (1–5). In Section 2, we use our materials to showcase some new findings our methods have revealed even for relatively well-studied English learners. There are several aspects of modality that makes it particularly interesting from an acquisition standpoint:

1. Modal expressions are used to describe abstract concepts, which children may or may not grasp innately or early in development (possibility, necessity, desire, knowledge, etc.) (Leahy and Carey 2020; Shtulman and Phillips 2018; i.a.).
2. Modal expressions are abstract vocabulary or constructions with no obvious physical correlates, whose acquisition may thus need to rely heavily on syntactic and pragmatic cues (Dieuleveut et al. 2019; van Dooren et al. 2017; i.a.; see also Gleitman 1990; Hacquard and Lidz 2018).
3. The same modal words can express different flavors (in about ¼ of the world's languages according to van der Auwera and Amman 2005,[2] including those languages where acquisition has been most extensively studied), raising the question of how children figure out this one-to-many mapping (Cournane 2015; Papafragou 1998; van Dooren et al. 2017; i.a.).
4. Modals (at least in those languages where acquisition has been extensively studied) are often used in pragmatically enriched ways: they can be used to perform indirect speech acts like requests, and with scalar implicatures. These pragmatically enriched uses both raise the question of how children disentangle semantic and pragmatic contributions of modal statements,

---

[2] Variable-force modals were not counted in van der Auwera and Ammann (2005), therefore the one-fourth of the typological report reflects only flavour-variability, underestimating meaning-variability more generally (Matthewson 2013).

and provide a rich testing ground to probe children's pragmatic abilities (Dieuleveut et al. 2019, 2022; Noveck 2001; Ozturk and Papafragou 2015; i.a.).
5. Modals don't all behave in a uniform way in how they scope relative to negation (Iatridou and Zeijlstra 2013), and, controversially, to tense and aspect (see Hacquard 2009; Klecha 2016; Rullmann and Matthewson 2018, i.a.), raising the question of when and how children figure out these scopal constraints, and how these scopal constraints affect modal acquisition (Jeretič 2018; Koring, Meroni and Moscati 2018; Moscati and Crain 2014; Dieuleveut et al. 2022; i.a.).

Because the fieldworker can rely on informants having mature conceptual and pragmatic abilities, some of the acquisition studies designed to test children's conceptual and pragmatic competence with modals may be less relevant. However, the fieldworker faces some of the issues that make both the acquisition of modals *and* its investigation by acquisitionists challenging: can the same modal expressions be used to express different forces or flavors? How do they interact with elements like negation, tense, aspect or evidentiality? How does one tease apart the semantic and pragmatic contributions of a modal utterance? We will look at three methods that have helped us understand more about modal development, and consider how these relate to existing fieldwork methodology, and how they may be adapted for work on underdescribed languages.

Sharing our successes continues a long tradition of adapting acquisition methods for use in fieldwork contexts: notably, truth-value judgment tasks (Crain and Thornton 1998; Gordon 1998) and frog stories (Berman and Slobin 1994, using Mercer Mayer's "Frog, Where Are You?"). Here we aim to offer more materials and methods, specifically about modality, to the important and pressing enterprise of learning more about the semantics and pragmatics in understudied languages.

2 Case studies: Acquisition methodologies for modal language

We'll present three studies: one production study to elicit modals from participants, and two comprehension studies, to test understanding of certain modal expressions, one focused on flavour, the other on force. We begin by explaining our methods, and then compare and contrast them to existing fieldwork methods, exploring similarities and differences. For each method, we lay out potential gain from adapting these methods to the field, while acknowledging several challenges that fieldworkers may face in adapting our materials to use on underdescribed languages. Where possible, we make suggestions for adaptations and applications. We provide comparisons, comments and suggestions that apply to all three studies we present in the General Discussion (§3). We make our materials available at OSF (https://osf.io/v9ure/) and welcome inquiries for further information or resources to the NYU Child Language Lab, www.childlanguagelab.com.

2.1 A sentence-repair task: Modal production task

Cournane, Hirzel and Hacquard (submitted) use a sentence repair task (see also Cournane 2014) to see what lexical preferences speakers have for expressing modal meanings to match particular carefully controlled situational contexts, and how children's preferences differ from adults' preferences. This method elicits modal productions for a 2x2 set of contexts, crossing modal flavour (teleological (=root), epistemic) and force (possibility, necessity) giving 4 unique situational combinations (Figure 1). This acquisition study was informed by the work on understudied languages. Namely, our 'modal meaning space' is inspired by Nauze (2008) and Vander Klok (2012), and our research questions are directly inspired by the variable-force modal literature (Bochnak 2015; Deal 2011; Peterson 2010; Rullmann, Matthewson and Davis 2008; Yanovich 2013). We explore the possibility that our English-learning children may entertain non-English, but cross-linguistically available, semantic representations for modals in their input. Acquisition research prior to this study had taken for granted that modal verbs are either possibility or necessity, probably because both possibility and necessity modals exist in English and other common languages which have provided the vast majority of evidence for child linguistic development. However, the comprehension literature for modal force shows non-adult behaviours through early school age (Byrnes and Duff 1989; Hirst and Weil 1982; Noveck 2001; Noveck, Ho and Sera 1996; Ozturk and Papafragou 2015, i.a.), which have been attributed to conceptual or pragmatic immaturity, without also considering that learners may hypothesize variable-force modals, especially if they fail to identify clear necessity modals (Dieuleveut et al. 2022).

In our study, children (3- and 4-year-olds, n= 46) and adults (n= 24) heard stories about going to stores via different coloured roads (teleological) and hiding in different coloured boxes (epistemic) (similar to Ozturk and Papafragou 2015's Experiment 1). Each flavour-force pairing is maximally similar to the others, with variation (e.g., boxes vs. roads) of only the critical type to clearly support flavour and force distinctions. These scenarios thus provide us with confidence that our scenes will be interpreted as intended, so that we can trust that participants' uses of modal lexemes are in keeping with how they can grammatically encode each of the modal force-flavor combinations of interest. There were 4 items per condition (each cell in Figure 1). The stories provided a natural and supportive narrative for all four types of test sentences. Note that when there are two equally salient possibilities, it is pragmatically strange to only highlight one (*She can go down the red road*), so we mention the other possibility before the target.

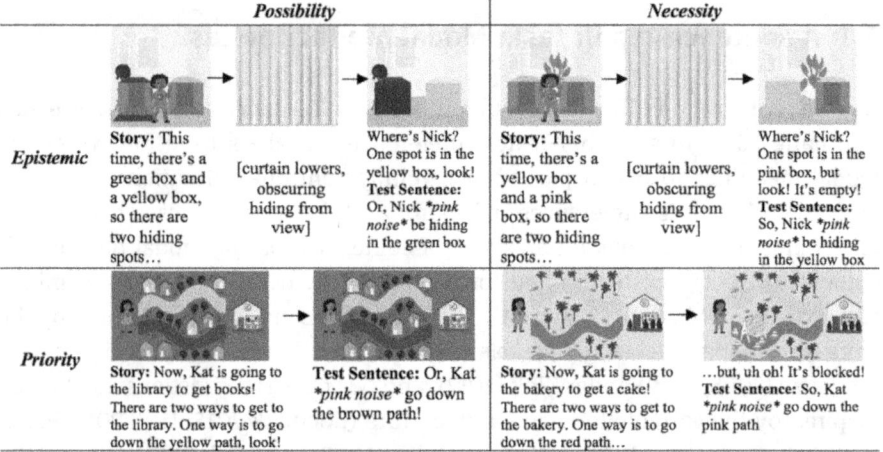

Figure 1: Sample trials in each condition crossing FORCE (POSSIBILITY, NECESSITY) and FLAVOUR (EPISTEMIC, TELEOLOGICAL). Arrows indicate changes from one scene to the next on a tablet. (Drawings by Mina Hirzel; Stories by Ailís Cournane, Mina Hirzel & Valentine Hacquard. 2018. https://osf.io/v9ure/).

The task was to repeat story sentences with obscured modals to a shy snail puppet called Mr. Drooly, who was listening alongside the participant, so he could hear them. Pink noise blocked the modal but preserved the syntactic frame in which the modal occurs. This frame contains aspectual cues consistent with the intended flavour: eventive *go* for teleological (1a) and stative *be* for epistemic (1b) in the prejacent (see Condoravdi 2002; Portner 2009). Participants corrected the glitch with a modal of their choosing. This method works well for giving a choice to the speaker for how to repair the sentence, because multiple distinct modals can be used in the same slot in the English sentence, between the subject and bare verb complement: e.g., *can, must, might, have to, should*. This methodology is innovative for testing modal development because it targets both force and flavour together as the dependent variable, and prompts participants to produce modals of their own choosing but in an experimenter-constrained manner. In short, it allows us to get snapshots of how individuals can use modal forms to express their 'modal meaning space'.

(1) a. Kat <<noise>> go down the red path (given goal to get to the bakery)   TELEOLOGICAL
    b. Nick <<noise>> be hiding in the red box (given evidence the other is empty)   EPISTEMIC

Our results show that adults behave as expected for English, using different lexical items for the force dimension: in epistemic contexts, they primarily produced *could* for possibility, and *must* for necessity. In teleological contexts adults produced mostly *could* for possibility and *should* or *have to* for necessity. Thus, in necessity contexts adults tended to differentiate by both force and flavour. And, adult uses showed flavour-variability, especially for *could* across teleological and epistemic possibility conditions. Children produced fewer modal sentence-repairs than adults did (36% vs. 99%). This is a risk with any production task, as participants may respond in non-compliant or unexpected ways, and children usually yield higher rates of non-target data. However, children's non-modal and non-frame-compliant material (i.e., modal, but not fitting the syntactic frame in the prompt) were usually also informative about modal language knowledge and preferences. For example, if a child produced "*Maybe* Nick is hiding in the red box" this supplies a semantically appropriate modal repair (*maybe*) but also alters the frame (*be* > *is*). Child modal results are provided in Figure 2. We've shaded modal forms as follows: possibility modals in light grey, necessity in dark grey, and future in medium grey. Children tend to produce possibility modals for all 4 conditions, but appear to differentiate by flavour: they use more *might* in epistemic contexts, but more *can* in teleological contexts. Some children used *have to*, but they used it for both possibility and necessity conditions. Children also use many future modals, but similarly across flavours and forces. One interesting finding for our purposes here is that English-learning children appear to use particular modals for both forces (cf. variable-force modals), contra English-speaking adults.

Results are informative for child modal systems, as children generally use the same modal words as adults, but this study reveals how these map differently to the 2x2 modal meaning space we set-up. These results suggest children may not yet have the adult linguistic representations for the modal verbs of English. Child productions of possibility modals are more in line with adult productions than their uses of necessity modals, consistent with similar asymmetries in spontaneous corpus data (Dieuleveut et al. 2019, 2022), and experimental comprehension data (Ozturk and Papafragou 2015; Cournane et al. *in prep*). Children tend

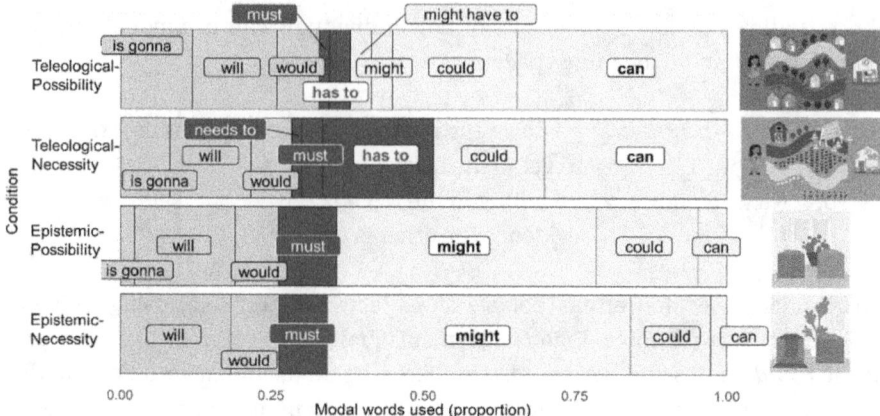

Figure 2: Children's modal word responses by condition. Possibility = Light Grey. Necessity = Dark Grey. Future = Medium Grey.

to prefer using different modals for different flavours, but, unlike their adult counterparts, they do not as readily distinguish by force, using the same modals across both possibility and necessity conditions (a pattern remarkably like variable-force modals, at least on the surface, but seen in 4-year-old English learners).

2.1.1 Comparison to existing methods, potential added value, and adaptation challenges

These materials may not be culturally or age-appropriate for everyone. Possible adaptations include superficial changes like recasting characters, locations and hiding locales to be more culturally or age relevant, or changing what noise obscures the portion of audio (e.g., we used pink noise and Cournane (2014) used a dog's bark, but a bird call or car honk should be equally effective). For older children and adults, the shy snail may be a fun childhood throwback or could be infantilizing or confusing. We explicitly tell adult controls who do our child studies (typically college students) that the materials are designed to work with young children. Easy ways to mature the materials are to change the signal to a radio transmission that gets obscured at some points, or if available, to use writing and have smudges or blanks for key words or morphemes (an option mentioned in Vander Klok 2014 as well). This could add to the fun of the task – perhaps building a backstory where someone's notebook was found but with water damage and we need to decode the content. The recorded components could be scrapped in favour of live narration if the fieldworker is confident with elicited production prompts; This change would be especially useful for underdescribed languages with a primarily oral culture.

This study is a type of targeted elicited production task (for use in semantic fieldwork, see e.g., *The BowPed Topological Relations Picture Series,* Bowerman and Pederson 1992, discussed in Bochnak and Matthewson 2020), using contextualizing stimuli to constrain speaker productions to a desired area of language. More specifically, this is a sentence-repair/completion task. The basic method involves obscuring a portion of an utterance (or text) to elicit production of a piece of language, of the speaker's choosing, to fit a context of the researcher's choosing. With this methodology, many questions related to productive possibilities and preferences can be addressed, although adapting the method to linguistic properties of individual languages may require some adaptability and creativity.

This methodology also has elements of existing storyboarding fieldwork methods for semantic research (see Burton and Matthewson 2015). Storyboards provide a narrative series of images (or videos) to contextually (conceptually, semantically and pragmatically) support a targeted language use (see e.g., Matthewson 2013; Vander Klok 2014, 2019; Ferreira and Müller this volume, §3.2; and Kolagar and Vander Klok this volume, for storyboards targeting modal meanings). They "combine the advantages of spontaneous speech with the benefit of being able to test hypotheses about particular linguistic elements or constructions." (Burton and Matthewson 2015: 135). The images encourage speakers to talk about particular topics and distinctions. Deconstructing the items of a child behavioural experiment of the type described here essentially gives us multiple, minimally different, short storyboards. Like storyboards, each experimental item has a short series of images and supporting storyline designed to semantically and pragmatically support the use of modal language along two major dimensions that languages are known to grammatically distinguish (force,[3] flavour). These scenarios, with richly controlled and maximally similar contexts across forces and flavour, may be a useful extension from storyboards because they provide multiple slight variations on a theme – in brief, our materials could be adapted into many similar storyboards.

Similar to storyboards, our materials are visually presented, and the visual scenes for each storyline are carefully controlled for force and flavor distinctions. Being visually supported, these scenarios can thus serve as non-translation-based materials for targeted modal fieldwork (important in semantic fieldwork, see Matthewson 2004; Zhornik and Pokrovskaya 2018). The shared language can be used

---

[3] We are sketching force as possibility or necessity, but bear in mind that modals may also be gradable (e.g., Lassiter 2010).

to help set up the stories and context, with a reduced risk of priming for the test language due to using modal expressions in the set-up (this is equally important to avoid in child experimental work, so we have made the set-up modal-free for English[4]). And, unlike contexts that are presented orally or via text, the visual scenes reduce working memory load. This is critical for work with small children to reduce unwanted task effects. With fieldwork, this is also helpful, as reducing memory load or room-for-imagination/enrichment allows greater trust that the language facts collected are actually of the type the researcher sought to collect (Bochnak and Matthewson 2020: 276).

Different from storyboards, these do not incorporate a fun twist to make the experience more enjoyable for the consultant (common though not essential for storyboards, Burton and Matthewson 2015: 145), though they are happy, child-friendly, and relatively short (for children's attention spans and to get multiple items into a short period of time). Also, if we treat every item as a mini-storyboard, then each story lacks a resolution. Because we repeat multiple items within participants, we need to avoid learning or expectations affecting perception of the task goals, so we don't provide resolution (e.g., imagine we revealed which box Nick was hiding in in an epistemic possibility scenario, and it was red, children might then expect Nick to like red boxes, and reframe the study as a guessing game rather than a scene-describing game). Instead, at the end of the story we provide a wrap-up of the whole experience. Likewise, at the beginning of the experiment we provide a general intro for the epistemic hiding scenes and the around town shopping scenes. The overall storyline arc (see Louie 2015) thus "bookends" the multiple story items per teleological and epistemic experimental block.

For direct adaptation of this sentence-repair method to understudied languages – including the trick of obscuring a portion of the target utterance to elicit very targeted productions – substantial challenges may arise because of linguistic differences. English is a language with many free modal words (auxiliaries and semi-auxiliaries) that fit the same linear slot between the subject and bare verb, so this method is a good fit for English because speakers can choose from among many modals to repair the glitch in the sentence, thus revealing something about the meanings they have for those modals through how they use them. If in the target language, modal meaning is carried by a very short duration morpheme or by suprasegmentals, or when the language's modal vocabulary is

---

[4] The potential exception is the use of future *going to* in setting up the teleological stories, but this was necessary to make the scenario clear as to the future goal (teleological modality).

not concentrated in the same linear position or morphosyntactic category,[5] this method may be more difficult to adapt, or indeed not possible to adapt in its full form. However, it may be possible to obscure a larger portion of the utterance that contains the modal variation of interest (e.g., perhaps the entire verb or verb phrase for mood variation). If the construction of interest has the modal element (or covarying element, e.g., one could have constant modals in the test sentence and obscure tense marking, to test what tense is compatible with what modal uses) at the end of the utterance, the fieldworker can start the sentence and ask the consultant to complete it as they think best. This can be done with a hanging sort of prosody, as in "The girl went to the bakery to pick up *a* . . .", feeding the sentence for the participant to complete. In brief, one may find it useful to only partially prompt the test sentence.

Our scenarios may be also be adopted partially, rather than with the full experimental design or linguistic manipulations. When deconstructed, the scenarios we created are similar to components of the Modal Questionnaire (Vander Klok 2014; see also the revised version by Vander Klok, this volume), and could be used in a similar way to explore the modal expressions of a language. For example, a fieldworker may hypothesize that a particular modal element is a possibility modal from hearing it used in contexts compatible with that meaning, but be uncertain as yet as to whether it is flavour-variable or force-variable (under certain conditions). Furthermore, since necessity entails possibility, it may also be a necessity modal. The fieldworker could use our visually supported scenarios to test out which flavours and forces the modal is compatible with, particularly to try to see which scenarios its use is not acceptable for (if any). The consultant may offer alternatives as they tune-in to the dimensions of variation being probed – like whether there is more than one open possibility, or the temporal orientation of the scene (achieving the goal of reaching the location in the near future, or being in a hiding space in the present). As discussed in the modal fieldwork methodology literature, targeted follow-ups are an important way to learn more from a particular task (e.g., Bochnak and Matthewson 2020; Vander Klok 2019); If the participant offers one modal construction in response, ask them "are there other ways you could say this?".

In these sentence-repair studies (Cournane 2014; Cournane, Hirzel and Hacquard, submitted) participants often recast epistemic necessity as a simple declarative with *is*. And for root modals, they sometimes recast as imperatives ("Go down

---

[5] English also has modal meanings expressed by many different syntactic categories, but crucially for this method there is a critical mass of modal verbs that express different forces and flavors and all occur in the same position.

the red road!"). Knowing the landscape of English, it is straightforward to see how these unanticipated strategies for responding to the task items (unanticipated because they don't use the provided syntactic frame) nonetheless capture the relevant meanings of the scenarios. In a child experimental study these kinds of responses cannot be included in the quantitative assessment (though are considered qualitatively), which could be considered a disadvantage. But unanticipated strategies may also be an advantage in fieldwork in the case that they reveal alternative grammatical ways of expressing the "same" meanings (see Vander Klok 2019, §4.3). Targeted follow-ups may be useful here as well. They may get consultants or participants to provide alternative ways of saying things, and perhaps talk about subtle differences in acceptability or felicity or usage patterns, that will help better understand the modal expressions (and related elements) of the language.

Finally, a putative drawback of production task is that they don't directly provide negative data: our study allows us to learn what linguistic expressions speakers prefer to use in the contexts we set-up, but not about which expressions they cannot use in those contexts. This could be seen as a problem, as often noted in discussion of experimental design practices for linguistics, "the methodology must allow the researcher to probe for negative data: contexts where a well-formed utterance is not acceptable." (Bochnak and Matthewson 2020: 3). However, the method also allows us to probe for speaker's own preferences and avoids certain disadvantages of comprehension tasks – there is little room for a *yes*-bias or guessing strategies, as in most types of comprehension task (e.g., forced-choice or judgment tasks). So, while responses are less predictable and attest only positive data, they are rich in their own right, and get at questions and hypotheses about language production that comprehension-based methods do not. Production tasks are an important tool for our methodological toolbox, and are especially useful when methods are compared against other types of methods, to help triangulate to the facts about the phenomenon.

2.2 Comprehension task 1: Modal force study

Regarding modal force, children need to figure out both what the underlying force of a modal is (e.g., possibility vs. necessity), whether their language has modal expressions for both possibility and necessity, and when the use of one might be more appropriate than the other (e.g., necessity modals are often more appropriate in necessity contexts than their possibility counterparts, even if the latter are logically true in these contexts). One challenge is that necessity entails possibility. On the semantic end of things, what prevents an English-learning child from treating *must* or *have to* as encoding possibility, if a possibility meaning is true whenever *must p* or *have to p* is uttered? Perhaps all children need is to observe these modals in downward entailing environments (Gualmini and Schwarz 2009), since they reverse entailment patterns. However, in speech to children, necessity modals rarely appear with negation, let alone other downward entailing environments (Dieuleveut et al. 2019, 2022). Moreover, some necessity modals like *must* outscope negation, while others, like *have to*, scope under it (Zeijlstra and Iatridou 2013), making it difficult to use negation to figure out force (see Jeretič 2018; Dieuleveut et al. 2019, 2022). On the pragmatic end of things, how do children figure out that a modal like *might* is true, but underinformative in necessity situations? To pick up on the underinformativity of *might*, one must be aware of the existence of *must*, but as we saw, acquiring necessity modals faces its own challenges. Moreover, not all languages have modals with scalemates (e.g., Nez Perce, Deal 2011), so children cannot bank on their language having duals. Learning the semantics and pragmatics of modal force involves overcoming many learning challenges, analogous to the fieldwork challenges of discovering the modal force facts of an underdescribed language (for further discussion of the learnability of modal force, and its possible resolution, see Dieuleveut et al. 2019, 2022).

Prior studies on modal force development have primarily used epistemic paradigms, involving a hidden object or character to test child interpretations (as in the hiding-in-boxes scenarios in Figure 1) (for overview, see Ozturk and Papafragou 2015). Earliest work (Hirst and Weil 1982; see also Bascelli and Barbieri 2002) also included a deontic scenario but children performed much more poorly than in the epistemic task (guessing the location of a peanut), likely due to task complexity effects (selecting between two puppet teachers, who gave differing orders to a puppet student for no clear reason) (Hirst and Weil 1982). Children tend to overaccept underinformative modal uses (*can* when *have to* is felicitous), apparently making logical judgements rather than pragmatic ones. This type of non-adult behaviour is consistent with children having pragmatic difficulties with generating scalar implicatures (e.g., Noveck 2001). However, under the right circumstances, adults can also be made to behave logically and accept possibility modals in necessity contexts. Moreover, when the alternatives are provided or made very salient children perform better (see Ozturk and Papafragou 2015). Together these findings suggest that children's difficulties may reside more with knowing which alternatives are relevant in context, rather than with the pragmatic reasoning itself (see also Barner, Brooks and Bale 2011; Skordos and Papafragou 2016).

For example, Experiment 1 in Ozturk and Papafragou (2015) involved characters hiding in boxes onstage (hiding while curtains were drawn), followed by the curtains opening on a test scenario (four distinct scenarios: (a) a single closed box, (b) two closed boxes, (c) one closed and one open box and the sentence targets the closed box, (d) one closed and one open box and the sentence targets the open box). An experimenter produced statements (e.g., The cow *may/has to* be in the red box) or questions (e.g., *Can* the cow be in the red box? vs. Does the cow *have to* be in the red box?) for participants to judge or answer. Results showed that both adults and children accepted *can/may* when underinformative (in scenarios (a) and (c)), both groups apparently not computing scalar implicatures under these circumstances. More surprisingly, children also accepted uses of necessity *have to* in possibility scenarios (scenario (b)) about half of the time, unlike adults who judged these statements false or responded "no" to the questions. Ozturk and Papafragou (2015) argued for a conceptual explanation, essentially that children struggle with reasoning about more than one open possibility at the same time (Acredolo and Horobin 1987; Piéraut-Le Bonniec 1980). In possibility scenarios (two closed boxes) children randomly commit to one of the possibilities to rapidly resolve the uncertainty, and this results in *have to* being true about half the time (essentially children flip a coin on which open possibility to choose; though see Moscati et al., 2017).

Cournane, Dieuleveut, Repetti-Ludlow and Hacquard (in prep) extended the methods from Ozturk and Papafragou (2015) to test teleological scenarios, adapting the materials from Hirzel, Hacquard, and Cournane (submitted). Do children perform similarly for force with a root modality, which they have more experience with for *can* and *have to* from the input (see Shatz and Wilcox 1991; van Dooren et al. 2017)? We chose to test force in teleological scenarios because they are a subtype of root modality that is more readily imageable than deontic (permission, obligation), and allows us to maintain the same experimental structure as the epistemic hidden-box tasks, using open and closed roads. We are testing 3-to-4-year-olds and adult controls in this study, which involves a protagonist (Kat) going to different shops to prepare for a friend's birthday party. A pre-recorded narrator describes onscreen pictures (Figure 3: A, B), and a puppet (Logan) says the test sentence (Figure 3: C). The narrator then prompts the child to judge whether Logan is right or wrong. We ran (or are running) three experiments: Experiment 1 tests *can* and *have to* between subjects, Experiment 2 tests *can, can't* and *have to, doesn't have to* between subjects, and Experiment 3 tests *can* and *have to* within subjects. To make Logan's negative statements felicitous in Experiment 2, we systematically added a line to the Narrator's set-up, asking Logan a question (e.g., Narrator: "Logan, to get to the pizzeria, can Kat go down the green road?", Logan: "No, Kat can't . . .").

A Narrator: *Cat is going to the pizzeria to get a pizza for the party.*
B Narrator: *There are two ways to get to the pizzeria: the green road and the yellow road.*
[Animation – construction drops on] *But uh oh! The green road is blocked!*
C Logan [Animation – mouth moves] *To get to the pizzeria, Cat has to go down the yellow road.*
Prompt (Narrator): *Is Logan right?*

Figure 3: Sample item for Modal Force Study (Experiment 1), illustrating a *has to* use in a necessity scenario. (Drawings by Mina Hirzel & Chiara Repetti-Ludlow; Stories by Ailís Cournane, Anouk Dieuleveut, Chiara Repetti-Ludlow & Valentine Hacquard. 2019. https://osf.io/v9ure/).

Our results on Experiment 1 (*can* and *have to* tested between subjects) show that both children (n= 24, 12 per modal) and adults (n= 20, 10 per modal) accept *can* in both possibility and necessity contexts, apparently not computing scalar implicatures in the necessity contexts (just as with uses of *may/can* in epistemic necessity scenarios in Ozturk and Papafragou 2015). Most children uniformly accept *have to* in possibility scenarios, contra adults who reject it in these scenarios, and contra Ozturk and Papafragou (2015) where children were at chance. For Experiment 2, adults behave as we expected – the same as Experiment 1 for the positive items, and the expected reversed judgements for the negated items. Child data collection is ongoing (at time of writing, n= 17). So far, children behave more or less as expected with *can/can't*, but not with *have to/doesn't have to*, although this task shows more noise[6] than Experiment 1. Our method of supporting negation adds an unanticipated challenge for children: they appear to have especial difficulty when the target is that Logan is wrong for saying "yes", or right for saying "no". This mismatch appears to confuse some children. We have not yet begun data collection on Experiment 3 at time of writing. Our overall results so far suggest preschoolers are adult-like for *can*, but they tend to treat *have to* like *can*. This suggests that children may have a possibility meaning for *have to*.

The teleological task results for *have to* in Experiment 1 differ from the parallel epistemic results from Ozturk and Papafragou (2015). The children in the teleological study (Cournane et al. *in prep*) are about a year younger on average

---

[6] In reference to experimental results, *noise* refers to more variance in responses among individuals, including from extraneous sources (factors that were not controlled for, or not under study).

than those in the epistemic study (Ozturk and Papafragou 2015). In teleological possibility contexts children accept *have to* the majority of the time, while in epistemic possibility contexts they accept *have to* only about half the time. One possible explanation for this discrepancy is that in the epistemic task children may interpret *have to* as root (consistent with how *have to* is predominantly used in the input, as root). Consider that if one hears 'the cow has to be in the red box' in a scene with two closed boxes (red and blue), the adult-like response is 'no (because the cow could also be in the blue box)'. But, on a root reading of *have to* (~ 'The cow *is obliged to* be in the red box'), children's acceptance of necessity in possibility situations is force-appropriate. That is, children may not always interpret the flavour of the modal in line with researchers' intent, unlike adults who are more accommodating and savvier. Another possible explanation is that children initially think that *have to* is a possibility modal, consistent with our teleological results for 4-year-olds. Then by age 5, some children may have learned that *have to* is a necessity modal, consistent with the mixed results for *have to* with Ozturk and Papafragou's epistemic results. The differing results between epistemic and teleological paradigms for testing modal force, and the inherent overlap of possible flavours in particular situations, underscore that flavour construals can affect judgments about the truth and felicity of the modal force.

2.2.1 Comparison to existing methods, potential added value, and adaptation challenges

First, relatively straightforward possible adaptations to fieldwork include superficial changes like recasting characters, locations and story topics to be more age or culturally appropriate, perhaps changing the birthday party preparation to preparing for a wedding, or to travel to another city or country. The roles of the narrator and the puppet can be carried out live with two researchers (or one, perhaps using a translation language for the set-up and then asking for judgement on target language test sentences to draw the contrast between set-up and judgement).

This task is a variation on the classic truth-value judgment task (Crain and Thornton 1998; Gordon 1998), which has already been widely adopted from child language research to other populations, including to understudied languages. In these tasks we set-up careful scenarios that support more than one possible interpretation, and ask participants to judge whether something a puppet says is true or false relative to the scenario. The participant's judgement sheds light on how they interpret the test sentences. Ideally, the design should make the critical sentences false, as a rejection is stronger than an acceptance, and the follow-up of "Why not?" or "What really happened?" works well to get the reasoning behind the rejection. For example, adults who reject *have to* sentences (e.g., "To get to the Pizzeria, Kat has to go down the red road") in the possibility scenarios with two open roads, say things like, "No, she doesn't have to because the yellow road is open too." In fieldwork, truth-value judgments can be done singly, but in work with children we try to have at least 4 items of the same type (e.g., judgments of *can* with necessity scenarios).

Results from this study complement those from our Modal Repair Task (§2.1). These studies cover roughly the same age group, and with children from similar communities (English-speaking children from the New York City and Washington, D.C. areas). The Modal Repair Task gives production data, and we saw that children use the same modals across both forces (e.g., *can* and *have to* show up for both teleological possibility and necessity contexts). In this Modal Force Study, using a truth-value judgment task, we can test acceptability of those same modals with the same population of children and adult controls to see what patterns hold and improve our understanding of children's modal representations. This is parallel to how fieldworkers use multiple methodological strategies for the same phenomenon, with the same consultant(s), to best understand the semantics and pragmatics of the expression (see Bochnak and Matthewson 2015).

These materials were designed to test force interpretation for particular English modals (*can, have to*), for which we know the semantic and pragmatic facts. And, relevant for our Experiment 2, we know the relative scope of the modals with and without negation (*can't* = not > possible; *doesn't have to* = not > necessary) which can vary by modal (in particular for necessity modals, see Iatridou and Zeijlstra 2013), which allows us to interpret non-adult child patterns for negative test sentences as possibly relating to different relative scope. For example, a couple children tested on the *have to/doesn't have to* condition for Experiment 2 rejected both positive and negative sentences. These children may have a necessity semantics for *have to* because they behave like adults in necessity contexts (contra the majority of children tested thus far), but they may erroneously assume *have to* outscopes negation (necessary > not; akin to *mustn't*), causing them to reject *doesn't have to* in possibility contexts. These challenges may make this task (at least Experiment 2) too "late-stage" for some fieldwork settings, if certain facts about the modals under study are still unknown. However, these materials may be used in a partial way (i.e., adopting some components and not others), to help gather more information, which can be compared against other targeted inquiry. As with other methods, we often probe participants with follow-up questions after they have made their judgement, e.g., "Why is Logan wrong?" and these responses can help interpret participants' quantitative responses.

Multiple items per test condition allows multiple repetitions of the same kinds of scenarios (we have 4 items per condition here). This may be useful for seeing patterns of acceptance/rejection for variable-force modal items (cf. patterns of picture-selection for the Modal Flavour Task in Cournane and Pérez-Leroux 2020, for English variable-flavour modal *must*, covered in §2.3). And, repeating the same kind of scenario could potentially be helpful to diagnose these variable-force expressions in carefully constructed usage contexts. That said, pragmatic factors and the entailment relationship – e.g., *may* is true wherever *must* is – complicate modal force inquiry, so targeted diagnostics are also necessary (see Bochnak 2015; Deal 2011; Peterson 2010; Rullmann, Matthewson and Davis 2008; Yanovich 2013).

In both acquisition and fieldwork, one has to keep in mind that participants/consultants may not necessarily hone in on the intended force/flavor, given the frequent overlap in both force (possibility true in necessity contexts), and flavor (ability/teleological). For example, what prevents participants from interpreting *have to* in the epistemic contexts of Ozturk and Papafragou (2015) as deontic instead? Or, in our contexts, what prevents participants from interpreting *can* as about Kat's ability as opposed to about the possible roads to get to the pizzeria? We tried to mitigate this issue by making the question under discussion (see e.g., Roberts 2012) explicit in the overall set-up (Kat needs to get to different stores to prepare for a birthday party), and within each item by having the puppet repeat "To get to the pizzeria, ..." before every test sentence (note that we varied shops for each item).

In this task, the test sentence is judged as a whole, so it would be easy to manipulate the test sentence as needed. For example, stories can be reused with different modal elements (e.g., this study could be re-run with no substantive changes just by swapping *have to* out for *must*; this would give the same judgement predictions except for when negated, as *have to* scopes below negation but *must* above) or with modalized sentences using different kinds of modal elements (particles, adverbs, etc.) as the whole sentence is judged by the participant/speaker. It is important to maintain the set-up to support the test sentence usage and make as clear as possible the intended flavour of the scenario. To ensure this, consider how we mention all possibilities in the scene to set up both possibility and necessity readings, how we used a polar question before the test sentence to license the use of negation, and how we explicitly state the goal and attempt to control the question under discussion.

Having a consultant judge another speaker, in this classic child-directed version of the truth-value judgment task, could be problematic. For children this is essential to avoid introspection and to reduce a type of child yes-bias where they are inclined to agree with adult teacher-figures, but more ok with telling puppets they are "silly", but for adults who are capable of metalinguistic introspection this may invite vagueness into the judgements – perhaps there is some variation among speakers, and the consultant has heard someone say something like what the puppet said, but would not say it themselves. The first author recalls this happening when doing fieldwork in Inuktituk (Inuit) (Consultant: Oleekie Etungat), where the consultant sometimes said sentences were fine, but then divulged that they were how people in a different region of Baffin Island spoke, not how she spoke in her regional variety. The puppet can be eliminated in favour of having more direct judgements, either spoken by the fieldworker or written down.

2.3 Comprehension study 2: Flavour preference task

This method involves a Picture Choice Task targeting deontic (root) and epistemic interpretations of modalized sentences. It is from Cournane (2015) and Cournane and Pérez-Leroux (2020), and adapted to Bosnian/Croatian/Serbian in Veselinović (2019) and Veselinović and Cournane (*accepted*) (see also Fond 2005; Heizmann 2006). We will focus on the English study, but also note how it was adapted to grammatical properties of Bosnian/Croatian/Serbian. In English (and Bosnian/Croatian/Serbian) a modal verb's interpretation differs by syntactic construction. In English, the availability of root and epistemic flavour is constrained by interaction with aspect (e.g., Hacquard 2009; Ramchand 2018). Specifically, when a modal auxiliary verb like *must* is followed by a bare eventive verb like *vote* (2a), both a root and epistemic interpretation are possible. Note that the epistemic interpretation with a bare eventive verb has a habitual construal. With grammatical aspect marking (perfect or progressive), *must* has an epistemic interpretation (2b, c).[7] Given the syntactic construction (*Modal + Bare Eventive Verb* or *Modal + Grammatical Aspect*), what interpretation will child and adult speakers prefer – deontic or epistemic? The participant chooses between two pictures (the dependent variable), one portraying a deontic interpretation and one an epistemic (see Figure 4). This method allows the researcher to test what interpretations are available for specific modal constructions, and what preferences speakers have when both interpretations are available (Cournane and Pérez-Leroux 2020, use this method in part to study change-in-progress for modal *must*).

---

[7] A root interpretation is possible, but requires making the sentence future-in-the-past, as by adding the adverbial "by tonight" to (2c). This is related to how root modalities are restricted to future-oriented prejacents (see Condoravdi 2002; Rullmann and Matthewson 2018; Werner 2006); perfect and progressive marking render prejacents past and present-oriented, respectively, so root modality is ruled out without additional temporal operators or a strong context to the same effect.

(2) a. *Annemarie* **must** *vote* ...
 ... because it's her civic duty. (Root)
 ... because she's really interested in politics. (Epistemic)

 b. *Anouk* **must** *be voting* ...
 ... because she left the house with her I.D. (Epistemic)

 c. *Anouk* **must** *have voted* ...
 ... because she is wearing an "I voted" sticker (Epistemic)

Figure 4 summarizes the materials and design, using a sample story, and our Appendix provides the full list of materials for the English study. We introduced participants to a Penguin telling stories from a book (presented pre-recorded on a laptop). Penguin sets the scene for each mini-story with an initial picture and comment, then turns the book back to himself, turns the page (we play a page-turning noise), and says the test sentence. Then, after saying the test sentence, Penguin turns the book back towards the participant and says, "See look!", showing two possible pictures (we counterbalanced which side the epistemic and deontic pictures appeared on). The participant is then prompted to select the picture "Penguin was looking at" when he said the test sentence. We ran 54 children (aged 3–6) and 19 adults, all speakers of the local dialect in Toronto, Canada. In Figure 4 we also see the English test sentences, our independent variable: MODAL ONLY with the auxiliary modal *must* followed by a bare eventive verb, and MODAL ASPECT, with *must* followed by grammatical aspect marking (perfect, progressive). We expected adults to prefer epistemic interpretations for the modal aspect sentences, and deontic interpretations for the modal only sentences (these are ambiguous, but the mini-stories don't explicitly support a habitual reading of the bare verb to give an epistemic interpretation of *must*). We expected children to begin with a (a) deontic bias (in line with root biases observed in child spontaneous production data, e.g., Papafragou 1998; van Dooren et al. 2017, 2019), (b) to gradually become more adult-like (differentiate interpretations by construction), and (c) to show more epistemic interpretations for modal only sentences than adults (in line with language change-in-progress, see Cournane and Pérez-Leroux 2020, for details).

Results are given in Figure 5. Adults behaved as expected, strongly preferring epistemic interpretations for MODAL ASPECT sentences, and variably selecting both deontic and epistemic pictures for MODAL ONLY sentences, but with a preference for deontic interpretations (adult responses are mostly in the d-quadrant in Figure 5). Adults differentiated for interpretations by construction. Small children had a slight overall deontic bias (3-year-old responses were mostly in the c-quad-

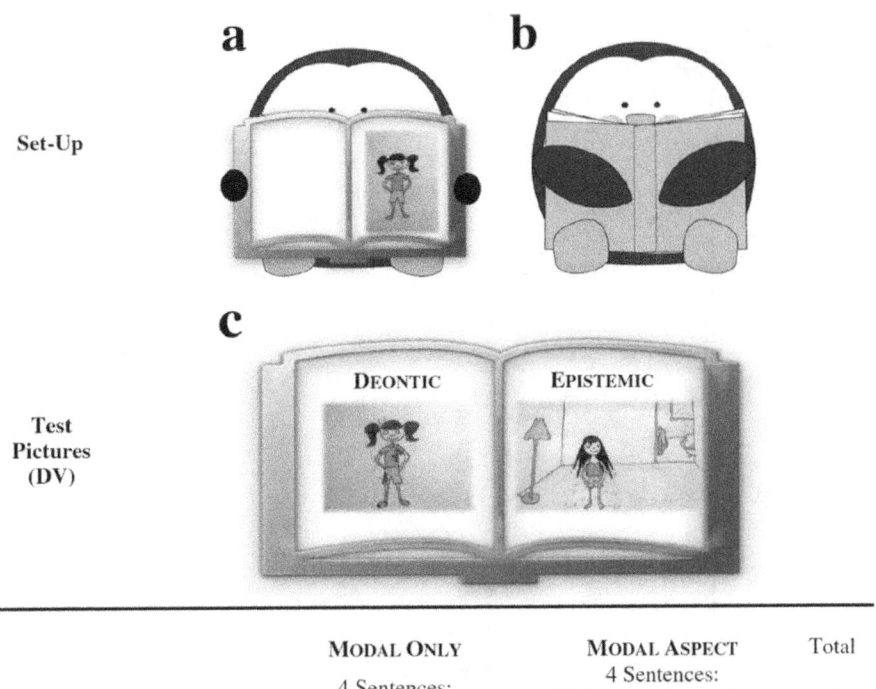

Figure 4: Flavor preference task, sample stimuli, and design. Narration for each image: (a) Penguin: This is Jada. She likes to play in the mud, but she also likes to be clean. (b) [Page turning noise]. Penguin: Oh! [Test Sentence]. (c) Penguin: See look! Experimenter: Penguin said, [repeat test sentence]. Which picture was penguin looking at? Each participant saw eight stories with MODAL ONLY sentences and eight MODAL ASPECT sentences, four each of which were progressive and perfect. The participant was prompted to pick either the deontic or the epistemic picture. (Drawings by Ailís Cournane; Stories by Ailís Cournane & Ana Teresa Pérez-Leroux. 2013. https://osf.io/v9ure/).

rant), but were otherwise close to chance. No child group differentiated for interpretations by construction, unlike adults. And, 5-year-olds show a strongly significant epistemic bias (their responses are mostly in the b-quadrant). This epistemic picture-selection bias is adult-like for the modal aspect sentences, but not for the modal-only sentences (it is in line with the child-driven change-in-progress hypothesis). This study allowed us to see what interpretations speakers have for

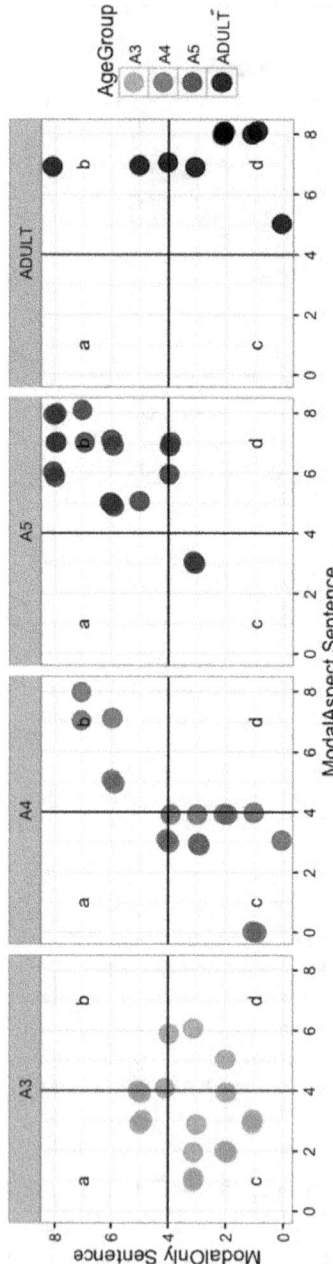

Figure 5: Results for all age groups (A3 = 3-year-olds, A4 = 4-year-olds, A5 = 5-year-olds). Individual speakers are plotted by the number of epistemic picture choices given to the MODAL ONLY (y-axis) and MODAL ASPECT (x-axis) sentences.

particular modal sentences, in a constrained way. Because of the 8 items per construction condition (modal only, modal aspect (4 each perfect and progressive) it also allowed us to assess individual interpretive preferences for variable-flavour modal *must*, and how those pattern within our age groups.

In Bosnian/Croatian/Serbian, modal verbs like *morati* 'must' (citation form) are also variable-flavour, but the syntactic properties of root vs. epistemic uses of the modal verbs differ from English. Briefly, Bosnian/Croatian/Serbian has categorically different constructions for root and epistemic uses of the modal verbs (Veselinović 2017, 2019). When the modal appears in a biclausal structure, with the modal verb in default agreement form, and the embedded main verb in imperfective the interpretation is epistemic (3a). When the modal appears in a monoclausal structure, with the modal verb agreeing with the subject, and the main verb in perfective form, the interpretation is root (3b) (see Veselinović 2019 for details and experimental results confirming this distinction for adult speakers of Bosnian/Croatian/Serbian).[8]

(3) a. **Mora**-∅   da se[9] mede   kupa-ju
     must-3SG DA SE little.bear.PL bathe-3PL
     'The bear cubs must be bathing'   *Root, ✓Epistemic

    b. Mede   **mora**-ju da se o-kupa-ju
     little.bear.PL must-3PL DA SE PFV-bathe-3PL
     'The bear cubs must bathe'   ✓Root, *Epistemic
                                                     (Veselinović 2019: 190)

Some story items from the English study were straightforward to translate into Bosnian/Croatian/Serbian. Others were problematic because the main verb aspect was not of the right base aspectual class in Bosnian/Croatian/Serbian. New verbs (and corresponding stories) had to be selected, according to the following criteria: (i) the aspectual pair of verbs had to exist, and (ii) the imperfective had to be of a form termed 'simple' in the BCS literature, while the perfective had to be formed via prefixation from the imperfective. Also, the default agreement for the modal verb *morati* is only clearly present when the subject is plural, so all subjects were made plural. We used *mede* "little bears/bear cubs" throughout. The materials were all re-created so they would be by the same

---

8 The following abbreviations will be used here: 3 third person; SG singular; PL plural; PFV perfective.
9 The functional morphemes *da* and *se* have differing analyses in the literature, see Veselinović (2019) for overview.

hand, have uniform verb types, and have consistent subjects. The scenarios and deontic and epistemic pictures were then experimentally normed with Bosnian/Croatian/Serbian native speakers prior to conducting the actual study. Norming of this kind is done in order to see if the scenarios we'd created were good enough renditions of deontic and epistemic scenarios to use in the main study. For details and results see Veselinović (2019). Results were very like those in English, despite input and syntactic differences between *must* and *morati* (see Veselinović 2019; Cournane and Veselinović *accepted*)

2.3.1 Comparison to existing methods, potential added value, and adaptation challenges

First, possible adaptations to the fieldwork setting include superficial changes like recasting characters, locations and story topics to be more culturally appropriate, and changing the book reading arrangement to instead involve looking at photographs, videos or drawings, or even looking at scenes out the window. What is critical is that the scene is out of view at the time the participant hears the test sentence, and only later do they see the options. The assumption is that participants will arrive at an interpretation prior to seeing the scenes, and that interpretation will guide their selection. Another adaptation would be to add more possible interpretations. We opted for only two because it was reasonable for *must*-interpretations to get at the broad, syntactically-mediated distinction between root and epistemic, and to reduce memory and attention load of stories for small children.

This is a type of forced choice task. Forced choice tasks are common in L1A and more broadly in psycholinguistics (see e.g., Ambridge and Rowland 2013), and are also used in fieldwork (e.g., which sentences is better for a given context? Or, which context is better for a given sentences? See e.g., Vander Klok 2014). More specifically, this is a picture choice task aimed at assessing interpretative possibilities or preferences (dependent variable, the choice between pictures) for single sentences (independent variable). There is some similarity here to acceptability judgment tasks used in fieldwork (see Bochnak and Matthewson 2020: 263–265 for an overview), but the pairings are expanded beyond a one-to-one match-up. In this study we offer two possible interpretations (operationalized as pictures) for one sentence. We used only two pictures to limit visual load and task complexity, but providing up to 4 pictures is fairly common for forced choice tasks, and increases the power associated with each selection type (chance behaviour becomes ¼ instead of ½, so consistent).

There is considerable flexibility to this method as pictures can be reused with different modal elements (e.g., the English study could be re-run with very little change just but swapping *must* out for *have to*). If picture adaptations are required for the language (as happened for Bosnian/Croatian/Serbian, due to verbal aspectual classes), we recommend norming the new pictures independently (i.e., running them online on MTurk or similar for their feasibility as good examples of e.g., an epistemic scene) so one can trust that the pictures are good examples of the desired interpretation (see Cournane 2015; Veselinović 2019; for norming processes). Each predicate brings its own slight idiosyncrasies to bear, making this norming especially important.

The multiple items per test condition allows repetitions. This may be useful for seeing patterns of preference by construction for variable-flavour modal items, and could be helpful to diagnose these items. However, one should be aware that the implicature that a deontic obligation will get carried out (i.e., if something must be done, it will be; see Traugott and Dasher 2002) may allow participants to select epistemic pictures with deontic modal sentences. To diagnose this and also to generally garner more insights into responses, it is helpful to ask follow-up prompts (as we did in the child studies), such as, "How did you know it was that picture?" (after the participant chooses a picture). Qualitative data that arises spontaneously during testing is often very informative, and can be increased by explicitly asking follow-up questions about test items at least some of the time (we aim for at least one prompt per unique condition). For example, children who picked the epistemic picture for the MODAL ONLY sentences regularly followed-up this prompt with a brief discussion of the evidence, e.g., how Jada's hair is wet or how she's in her pajamas ready for bed. Because fieldworkers also work one-on-one with consultants, these follow-up prompts can be an integral part of using this method, as they are in acquisition.

These materials were designed to test flavour interpretation for particular necessity modals, and so the scenarios make a contrast not only between deontic and epistemic, but between deontic obligation and epistemic necessity. This means that possibility modals could be tested using this method, but the materials would need to be altered to support open possibilities in root and epistemic flavours (see the sample scenarios in Figure 1, for Cournane, Hirzel, and Hacquard, submitted). The picture selection could be an array of all four major flavour-force combinations (Figure 1) to assess which are possible interpretations. A mix-and-match approach to the methods presented here may help solve some adaptation issues.

These materials could be deconstructed into storyboards, as mentioned for the other methods we have presented as well. The forced-choice picture prompts could be integrated into broader stories, creating a combination storyboard and picture choice task. For example, one could set up a story like Vander Klok (2019), and then provide a test sentence to the speaker and give them two possible continuation pictures for the story. The question would be, which picture better illustrates the test sentence? This could be useful to do targeted work on constructions to rule out close alternative interpretations, or to learn about meaning variability or ambiguity.

Along the same lines, this method can easily be "flipped" to a sentence choice task (another type of forced choice task), where the researcher provides just one picture context (independent variable), and then two minimally different sentences that the researcher should select between on semantic or pragmatic grounds (dependent variable). Instead of addressing the question, "which pictures depicts your interpretation of the test sentence?" (picture choice task) this method addresses the question, "which construction (or form) better expresses what is happening in the picture?". The set-up and prompt question can help target either semantic (e.g., Which sentence is right?) or pragmatic (e.g., Who said it better?) interpretations, and the opportunity for follow-up discussion is rich, as there are minimally different sentences to discuss in reference to a picture scenario.

This sentence choice method was used in two other studies with *must* reported in Cournane and Pérez-Leroux (2020), comparing *must* sentences to unmodalized counterparts in deontic (children, n= 52; adults, n= 10) and epistemic scenarios (children, n= 35; adults, n= 9). In these tasks, using the epistemic version as an example, participants heard short introductions the same as for the picture choice task, but then they saw just one continuation picture (either epistemic, showing indirect evidence for the prejacent, or actual, showing direct evidence for the prejacent). For every test item they heard two sentences, one with *must* (e.g., *Scott must be wearing his rainboots*) and one without (e.g., *Scott is wearing his rainboots*), spoken by two puppets. Participants were trained to pick the puppet who was "paying closer attention to the story" and who "said it better". For further example experiments and discussion of judging one sentence versus selecting between two for semantic and pragmatic meaning with modals see Ozturk and Papafragou (2015). More broadly for different methods in pragmatic tasks, especially for scalar implicatures, see Skordos and Papafragou (2016).

3 General discussion

We discussed three distinct methods we have used to learn more about child modal language development: an elicited production task involving sentence repairs, and two comprehension tasks: a truth-value judgment task and a picture selection task, to probe children's grasp of modal flavour and force, and usage preferences. All of these studies test predictions about modal language and different methodological choices are fitted to the properties of the target language and the conceptual domain. Methods and materials can also be combined as researchers see fit, to address questions differing from those addressed in each of the studies described above. Just as fieldworkers must triangulate to semantic representations and pragmatic felicity patterns from using multiple different methods (Bochnak and Matthewson 2015), so must acquisitionists. This "the more the merrier" approach is required even to address basic questions about the domain of inquiry because every method invites different task effects, and children are developing multiple cognitive and linguistic abilities and knowledge in parallel, making interpretation challenging, even for well-controlled experiments. Each methodology is just a tool for addressing research questions in a controlled way, taking into consideration the subtleties of the linguistic domain, the strengths and limitations of the method, and the particular challenges of the population (e.g., working memory limitations with children).

Our methodologies may help contribute to the general push for more experimental methods in field linguistics and work on understudied languages (e.g., Clemens et al. 2015; Li et al. 2011; Rech et al. this volume; Tollan, Massam and Heller 2019; Whalen and McDonough 2015). This work can help increase understanding of the languages under study, and contribute to psycholinguistic and sociolinguistic theories, which have been overwhelmingly built on English and other commonly studied languages. And, because our child-friendly experiments are designed to rely neither on reflection nor metalinguistic ability, they are suitable for work with all ages, including small children (for acquisition work on underscribed languages see Courtney 2008; Demuth, Moloi and Machobane 2010; de Villiers et al. 2009; Eisenbeiß 2006; Gagliardi and Lidz 2014; Lima 2014; Pye 2017; Pye and Pfeiler 2014; Viau and Lidz 2011; among others).

All of our studies are experimental in nature. Wholesale adaptation of experimental work from well-studied languages to understudied languages is often thought to be untenable because of the necessity of multiple participants (see Bochnak and Matthewson 2015, Introduction, for discussion). The languages we have worked on for exploring modal development have millions of native speakers, and are being acquired by children. For many understudied languages, unfortunately these markers of an unendangered language are not true: often there are few native speakers, or the language is no longer being transmitted to children. In these cases, either standard experimental methods, child acquisition research, or both, are not possible. Psycholinguistics work, and experimental methods for human behaviour more broadly, rely on population sampling: getting enough data for statistical power, to infer findings from the sample to the population more generally. That said, child language work has notoriously "small ns" in the wider psycholinguistics and developmental psychology world, and researchers have had to be particularly savvy to develop best practices for working with small datasets. For this reason, while acknowledging additional challenges, we suggest fieldworkers interested in doing experimental work, but with constraints on how many participants they can test, may rely more readily on child studies for ways to get the most from small datasets. For example, as suggested above for each of our studies, we also gather qualitative data from participants, to try to better understand their selection or judgment behaviours.

One pillar of experimental design is repetition (for statistical power) and reproducibility. Our methods for child studies involve running multiple trials of the same condition (e.g., four trials of the epistemic possibility condition for the sentence repair task) with multiple children, in order to sample enough from the population to do inferential statistics. While this kind of experimental method may not be feasible with many understudied languages, the many similar scenarios, with minor variations on the same recipe, may be useful for repetitions with the same speaker in the same or different sessions. Intra-speaker reproducibility of this type is a practicable alternative to population (re)sampling methods of reproducibility (Bochnak and Matthewson 2015: 5). With many similar items (i.e., all the stories we develop for each condition of each of our studies) portions of our tasks can be repeated at different intervals over time without repeating identical items.

Retesting participants or consultants on the same items risks them memorizing their way of responding to the task item(s), inviting task effects which obscure the facts of interest. We try to reduce this in experimental work by introducing variation that we are confident will be inconsequential. When one is doing intra-speaker replication, there is the possibility that speakers remember how they responded last time and are primed by themselves (see also Burton and Matthewson 2015: 145). This could be problematic because they may not be tapping in to their grammar directly, but into the task memory and this may reduce variation in responses, which perhaps the language can allow. For example, in English speakers may give *have to* to all necessity items in our Modal Repair task because they self-prime, when in fact their grammar has a many-to-one form-to-meaning mapping for those items (allowing also *should, must, need to*, etc.). This self-priming can also be lessened by inconsequential variations in stimuli, in addition to employing targeted follow-ups and multiple methodologies. In sum, acquisitionists and fieldworkers are both interested in grammatical competence of individuals, but must work with less-than-ideal circumstances from the standpoint of best practices of experimental design and statistical sampling. That said, they work on particularly interesting and important populations, and so must find creative ways to do sound science.

Semantic judgements can be subtle and are highly context-dependent, notably so for variable-flavour or variable-force modals, so carefully controlled stories with vetted conditions (e.g., workshopped, piloted, normed) are important (Bochnak and Matthewson 2015). All of our studies involve visual scenes, which provide the simplest, most direct way, to set up reliable contexts (videos or animations are likewise good, and sometimes even better, see Bar-El 2015; Bochnak and Matthewson 2020: 271–272). For our visual scenes and story narratives, we workshop the details of our materials extensively in our lab groups and ask around to linguists and/or psychologists working in related areas for their expertise, making adjustments as needed. Then we pilot our tasks on adults and children, making further adjustments as needed before entering the actual data collection phase. We can be confident that adults interpret them as intended, as the English-speaking adult participants behaved as expected for well-studied English modals in our studies – adult controls often serve as both the baseline and the proof of utility of the methods in child studies. Since we are confident about many aspects of the adult patterns for English, if adults perform as expected we can be confident that our task is working the way we intended it to.

It bears stressing that for all L1A experiments it is always best practice to run adults on the same exact studies as children – even in a well-studied language like English and even when the researchers speak the language – as a way to verify that the task is testing what we expect it to, and that the linguistic description is characteristic of the sample population. For example, in running Cournane and Pérez-Leroux (2020), the first author learned that working with a different variety of Canadian English than her own, speakers had different preferences for *must* vs. *have to* in epistemic contexts. In other words, her judgements when creating the materials were not the same as those of the test population, even though she speaks an only minimally different dialect. Working on underdescribed languages without the benefits of (as much) sociolinguistic and change knowledge, it may be harder to work out the nature of observed intra- or inter-speaker variations, and between children and adults (Are they due to developmental changes? Changes in progress? Or, stable semantic or pragmatic distinctions?). Running multiple adults on the same studies, and running adults on the same studies as children may help to disentangle (or perhaps discover?) distinct contributions to variation, like interspeaker variation (related to dialect differences and language change) vs. intraspeaker meaning variability.

Furthermore, another advantage of adapting child experimental work, rather than much other psycholinguistic work with adult speakers, is related to this fact that the "Fieldworker-consultant relationship is not fully parallel to the investigator-subject relationship" (Bochnak and Matthewson 2015: 5). The fieldwork-consultant relationship is more parallel with investigators and *child* subjects, as we nearly always test one-on-one in person, and we check in with the child regularly. This is much less often the case with adult participant studies, where we either set them up and leave them to it in the lab, or we simply provide written instructions for online tasks. With child participants, we also sit "face-to-face and assess the situation in real time" (Bochnak and Matthewson 2015: 5) and thus garner extra qualitative data to help us make decisions about which data to exclude (i.e., if the child was clearly distracted or said something to make us think they were not doing the task as intended, such as repeatedly telling us they really like Frogs when the task involves choosing between two puppets, one a frog). Adapting to challenges in advance and on-the-fly is also something both fieldworkers and child acquisitionists surely know better than most other sub-types of linguist, as each fieldwork situation is unique and each phenomenon studied with children has added challenges. With child participants, unlike with consultants, we rarely have a longstanding relationship so individual characteristics are not as readily assimilated into qualitative interpretations as with typical fieldwork.

Finally, one constant concern we have in interpreting our results is whether children differ from adults (and the researcher's intentions for the stimuli) by how they interpret aspects of our scenarios, or how they pragmatically enrich our stories, rather than how they use modal verbs. For example, in our modal force task, could children – like adults – know that *have to* a necessity modal, but be pragmatically enriching possibility contexts to make it felicitous? This issue is also present in fieldwork (and indeed any study using constructed stimuli to explore interpretation or felicity), and has been extensively discussed in the semantics fieldwork methods literature (e.g., Bochnak and Matthewson 2020; Matthewson 2004; Vander Klok 2019). Our strategies to try to mitigate these risks has been similar: (a) workshop, pilot and norm materials in advance, (b) run studies on control groups to improve confidence that the materials are working as intended (or to know when to go back to the drawing board), (c) gather qualitative responses to supplement selection or judgment data and provide evidence either that participants are or are not interpreting materials as intended, and (d) remain mindful of implicit biases with respect to materials interpretation – we want to measure the participants' interpretations of the materials not our own.

4 Conclusion

In this chapter we have discussed three methodological paradigms used in first language acquisition studies on modality: a sentence-repair modal production task, a picture preference forced-choice modal flavour comprehension task, and a truth-value judgment modal force comprehension task. These methods have helped us better understand child modal interpretations and have proven useful for shedding new light on modal development (see Cournane 2020 for a recent and more language acquisition centered discussion). For all three paradigms outlined, if adaptations for underdescribed languages maintain the overall procedure, it would be possible to work both with adults and with children because these tasks are designed to not require meta-knowledge nor meta-judgements. We hope that the methodological challenges we have faced and found solutions for can be helpful not just in the usual developmental work on well-studied languages, but also in work on speakers of underdescribed languages. Developmental work on underdescribed languages is of particularly great value, though involves both the challenges of working on underdescribed languages and working with children. We hope that sharing our materials and experiences can contribute to facilitating at least some of the developmental research aspects of the tasks.

Acquisitionists and fieldworkers working on modality share a common goal of describing and explaining possible modal systems. Extant modals and modal systems are all examples of how this conceptual domain can be encoded into language. So, as increased cross-linguistic fieldwork on modality has helped us better understand linguistic modality, it has in turn helped us better consider hypotheses that child learners may entertain during acquisition. For example, foundational work on modal force development (overwhelmingly on well-studied Indo-European languages, primarily English) predates the semantic description of languages with variable-force modals. Going forward, we now know that languages can have variable-force modals, and so we can now consider this as a viable possibility for development (even if not present in the target input language). Can the tools we have used to learn more about modal development for a particular target language be flipped, to help learn more about adult modal (=target, in child studies) grammars? Building on a long tradition of adapting acquisition materials to the field, we think there is promise and that sharing our materials and insights from modal acquisition may be a way to give back to the linguistic subfield that has helped us expand and clarify our hypothesis space for child learners.

References

Ambridge, Ben & Rowland, Caroline F. 2013. Experimental methods in studying child language acquisition. *WIREs Cognitive Science* 4 (2). 149–168.
Acredolo, Curt & Horobin, Karen. 1987. The child's relational reasoning and tendency toward premature closure. *Developmental Psychology* 23 (1). 13–21.

Bar-El, Leora. 2015. Documenting and classifying aspectual classes across languages. In M. Ryan Bochnak & Lisa Matthewson (eds.), *Methodologies in semantic fieldwork*, 75–109. Oxford, UK: Oxford University Press.

Barner, David, Neon Brooks & Alan Bale. 2011. Accessing the unsaid: The role of scalar alternatives in children's pragmatic inference. *Cognition* 118 (1). 84–93.

Bascelli, Elisabetta & Maria Silvia Barbieri. 2002. Italian children's understanding of the epistemic and deontic modal verbs *dovere* (must) and *potere* (may). *Journal of Child Language* 29 (1). 87–107.

Bochnak, M. Ryan. 2015. Variable force modality in Washo. In Thuy Bui & Denis Özyildiz (eds.), *Proceedings of 45th North-East Linguistics Society*, 105–114. (NELS45). Cambridge, MA: Massachusetts Institute of Technology.

Bochnak, M. Ryan & Lisa Matthewson (eds.). 2015. *Methodologies in semantic fieldwork*. Oxford, UK: Oxford University Press.

Bochnak, M. Ryan & Lisa Matthewson. 2020. Techniques in complex semantic fieldwork. *Annual Review of Linguistics* 6 (1). 261–283.

Bowerman, Melissa & Erik Pederson. 1992. Topological relations picture series. In Stephen C. Levinson (ed.), *Space Stimuli Kit 1.2: November 1992,* 51. Nijmegen, the Netherlands: Max Planck Institute for Psycholinguists.

Burton, Strang & Lisa Matthewson. 2015. Targeted construction storyboards in semantic fieldwork. In M. Ryan Bochnak & Lisa Matthewson (eds.), *Methodologies in Semantic Fieldwork*, 135–156. Oxford, UK: Oxford University Press.

Byrnes, James P. & Michelle A. Duff. 1989. Young children's comprehension of modal expressions. *Cognitive Development* 4 (4). 369–387.

Clemens, Lauren Eby, Jessica Coon, Pedro Mateo Pedro, Adam Milton Morgan, Maria Polinsky, Gabrielle Tandet & Matthew Wagers. 2015. Ergativity and the complexity of extraction: A view from Mayan. *Natural Language and Linguistic Theory* 33 (2). 417–467.

Condoravdi, Cleo. 2002. Temporal interpretation of modals: Modals for the present and the past. In David Beaver, Luis Casillas Martinez, Brady Clark & Stefan Kaufmann (eds.), *The construction of meaning*, 59–88. Stanford, CA: CSLI Publications.

Cournane, Ailís. 2015. *Modal development: Input-divergent L1 acquisition in the direction of diachronic reanalysis*. Toronto, ON: University of Toronto dissertation.

Cournane, Ailís. 2020. Learning modals: A grammatical perspective. *Language and Linguistics Compass* 14 (10). 1–22.

Cournane, Ailís, Mina Hirzel & Valentine Hacquard. submitted. Mapping modal verbs to meanings: An elicited production study on 'force' and 'flavor' with young preschoolers.

Cournane, Ailís & Ana Teresa Pérez-Leroux. 2020. Leaving obligations behind: Epistemic incrementation in preschool English. *Language Learning and Development* 16 (3). 270–291.

Cournane, Ailís & Sandrine Tailleur. 2021. La production épistémique chez l'enfant francophone: Une étude comparative. [Epistemic production in francophone children: A comparative study]. *Arboressences* 10. 47–72.

Cournane, Ailís & Dunja Veselinović. accepted. If they must, they will: Children overcommit to likeliness inferences from deontic modals. *Glossa*. https://doi.org/10.16995/glossa.5802

Courtney, Ellen H. 2008. Child production of Quechua evidential morphemes in conversations and story retellings. El Paso, TX: University of Texas manuscript.

Cover, Rebecca Tamar. 2015. Semantic fieldwork on TAM. In M. Ryan Bochnak & Lisa Matthewson, *Methodologies in semantic fieldwork*, 233–268. Oxford, UK: Oxford University Press.

Crain, Stephen & Rosalind Thornton. 1998. *Investigations in universal grammar*. Cambridge, MA: The MIT Press.
De Villiers, Jill G., Jay L. Garfield, Harper Gernet-Girard, Tom Roeper & Margaret Speas. 2009. Evidentials in Tibetan: Acquisition, semantics, and cognitive development. *New Directions for Child and Adolescent Development* 2009 (125). 29–47.
Deal, Amy Rose. 2011. Modals without scales. *Language* 87 (3). 559–585.
Demuth, Katherine, Francina Moloi & Malillo Machobane. 2010. 3-Year-olds' comprehension, production, and generalization of Sesotho passives. *Cognition* 115 (2). 238–251.
Dieuleveut, Anouk, Annemarie van Dooren, Ailís Cournane & Valentine Hacquard. 2019. Acquiring the force of modals: Sig you guess what sig means? In Megan M. Brown & Brady Dailey (eds.), *Proceedings of the 43nd Annual to the Boston University Conference on Language Development,* 189–202. (*BUCLD* 43). Somerville, MA: Cascadilla Press.
Dieuleveut, Anouk, Annemarie van Dooren, Ailís Cournane & Valentine Hacquard. 2022. Finding out modal force: evidence from children's production and input. *Natural Language Semantics*. https://doi.org/10.1007/s11050-022-09196-4
Eisenbeiß, Sonja. 2006. Documenting child language. *Language Documentation and Description* 3. 106–140.
Fond, Marissa Joanne. 2003. *Deontic and epistemic modal expression: Theory and acquisition in English and Spanish*. Northampton, MA: Smith College BA thesis.
Gagliardi, Annie C. & Jeffrey Lidz. 2014. Statistical insensitivity in the acquisition of Tsez noun classes. *Language* 90 (1). 58–59.
Gordon, Peter. 1998. The truth-value judgment task. In Dana McDaniel, Cecile McKee & Helen Smith Cairns (eds.), *Methods for Assessing Children's Syntax,* 211–235. Cambridge, MA: The MIT Press.
Gualmini, Andrea & Bernhard Schwarz. 2009. Solving learnability problems in the acquisition of semantics. *Journal of Semantics* 26 (2). 185–215.
Hacquard, Valentine. 2009. On the interaction of aspect and modal auxiliaries. *Linguistics and Philosophy* 32 (3). 279–315.
Heizmann, Tanja. 2006. Acquisition of deontic and epistemic readings of *must* and *müssen*. In Tanja Heizmann (ed.), *University of Massachusetts occasional papers in linguistics* 34. 21–50. Amherst, MA: GLSA, University of Massachusetts.
Hirst, William & Joyce Weil. 1982. Acquisition of epistemic and deontic meaning of modals. *Journal of Child Language* 9 (3). 659–666.
Iatridou, Sabine & Hedde Zeijlstra. 2013. Negation, polarity, and deontic modals. *Linguistic Inquiry* 44 (4). 529–568.
Jeretič, Paloma. 2018. Evidence for children's dispreference for weakness: A corpus study. New York, NY: New York University qualifying paper.
Klecha, Peter. 2016. Modality and embedded temporal operators. *Semantics and Pragmatics* 9. 1–55.
Koring, Loes, Luisa Meroni & Vincenzo Moscati. 2018. Strong and weak readings in the domain of worlds: A negative polar modal and children's scope assignment. *Journal of Psycholinguistic Research* 47 (6). 1193–1217.
Lassiter, Daniel. 2010. Gradable epistemic modals, probability, and scale structure. *Semantics and Linguistic Theory* 20. 197–215.

Leahy, Brian P. & Susan E. Carey. 2020. The acquisition of modal concepts. *Trends in Cognitive Sciences* 24 (1). 65–78.

Li, Peggy, Linda Abarbanell, Lila Gleitman & Anna Papafragou. 2011. Spatial reasoning in Tenejapan Mayans. *Cognition* 120 (1). 33–53.

Lima, Suzi. 2014. All notional mass nouns are count nouns in Yudja. *Semantics and Linguistic Theory* 24. 534–554.

Louie, Meagan. 2015. The problem with no-nonsense elicitation plans for semantic fieldwork. In M. Ryan Bochnak & Lisa Matthewson (eds.), *Methodologies in semantic fieldwork*, 47–71. Oxford: Oxford University Press.

Matthewson, Lisa. 2004. On the methodology of semantic fieldwork. *International Journal of American Linguistics* 70 (4). 369–415.

Matthewson, Lisa. 2010. On apparently non-modal evidentials. *Empirical Issues in Syntax and Semantics* 8. 333–357.

Matthewson, Lisa. 2013. On how (not) to uncover cross-linguistic variation. In Stefan Keine & Shayne Sloggett (Eds.), *Proceedings of the North East Linguistic Society* 42, 323–342.

Moscati, Vincenzo & Stephen Crain. 2014. When negation and epistemic modality combine: The role of information strength in child language. *Language Learning and Development* 10 (4). 345–380.

Moscati, Vicenzo, Likan Zhan & Peng Zhou. 2017. Children's on-line processing of epistemic modals. *Journal of Child Language* 44 (5). 1025–1040.

Nauze, Fabrice Dominique. 2008. *Modality in typological perspective*. Amsterdam, NL: Institute for Logic, Language and Computation: Universiteit van Amsterdam dissertation.

Noveck, Ira A., Simon Ho & Maria Sera. 1996. Children's understanding of epistemic modals. *Journal of Child Language* 23 (3). 621–643.

Noveck, Ira A. 2001. When children are more logical than adults: Experimental investigations of scalar implicature. *Cognition* 78 (2). 165–188.

Ozturk, Ozge & Anna Papafragou. 2015. The acquisition of epistemic modality: From semantic meaning to pragmatic interpretation. *Language Learning and Development* 11 (3). 191–214.

Papafragou, Anna. 1998. The acquisition of modality: Implications for theories of semantic representation. *Mind and Language* 13 (3). 370–399.

Peterson, Tyler Roy Gösta. 2010. *Epistemic modality and evidentiality in Gitksan at the semantics-pragmatics interface*. Vancouver, BC: University of British Columbia dissertation.

Piéraut-Le Bonniec, Gilberte. 1980. *The development of modal reasoning*. New York, NY: Academic Press.

Portner, Paul. 2009. *Modality*. Oxford, UK: Oxford University Press.

Pye, Clifton. 2017. *The comparative method of language acquisition research*. University of Chicago Press.

Pye, Clifton & Barbara Pfeiler. 2014. The comparative method of language acquisition research: A Mayan case study. *Journal of Child Language* 41 (2). 382–415.

Ramchand, Gillian. 2018. *Situations and syntactic structures*. Cambridge, MA: The MIT Press.

Roberts, Craige. 2012. Information structure: Towards an integrated formal theory of pragmatics. *Semantics and Pragmatics* 5. 1–69.

Rullmann, Hotze & Lisa Matthewson. 2018. Towards a theory of modal-temporal interaction. *Language* 94 (2). 281–331.

Rullmann, Hotze, Lisa Matthewson & Henry Davis. 2008. Modals as distributive indefinites. *Natural Language Semantics* 16 (4). 317–357.

Shatz, Marilyn, and Sharon A. Wilcox. 1991. Constraints on the acquisition of English modals. In Susan A. Gelman & James P. Byrnes (eds.), *Perspectives on language and thought: Interrelations in Development,* 319–353. Cambridge, UK: Cambridge University Press.

Shtulman, Andrew & Jonathan Phillips. 2018. Differentiating "could" from "should": Developmental changes in modal cognition. *Journal of Experimental Child Psychology* 165. 161–182.

Skordos, Dimitrios & Anna Papafragou. 2016. Children's derivation of scalar implicatures: Alternatives and relevance. *Cognition* 153. 6–18.

Tollan, Rebecca, Diane Massam & Daphna Heller. 2019. Effects of case and transitivity on processing dependencies: Evidence from Niuean. *Cognitive Science* 43 (6). e12736.

Traugott, Elizabeth C. & Richard B. Dasher. 2002. *Regularity in semantic change.* Cambridge, UK: Cambridge University Press.

van Dooren, Annemarie, Anouk Dieuleveut, Ailís Cournane & Valentine Hacquard. 2017. Learning what *must* and *can* must and can mean. In Alexandre Cremers, Thom van Gessel & Floris Roelofsen (eds.), *Proceedings of the 21st Amsterdam Colloquium,* 225–234. Amsterdam, the Netherlands: Institute for Logic, Language and Computation (ILLC), University of Amsterdam.

van Dooren, Annemarie, Maxime A. Tulling, Ailís Cournane & Valentine Hacquard. 2019. Lexical Aspect and Modal Flavor in Dutch. In Megan M. Brown and Brady Dailey (eds.), *Proceedings from the 43nd Annual Boston University Conference on Language Development,* 203–216. (BUCLD 43). Somerville, MA: Cascadilla Press.

Vander Klok, Jozina. 2012. *Tense, aspect, and modality in Paciran Javanese.* Montreal, QC: McGill University dissertation.

Vander Klok, Jozina. 2014. On the use of questionnaires in semantic fieldwork: A case study on modality. *Proceedings of Language Documentation and Linguistic Theory* 4. 1–11.

Vander Klok, Jozina. 2019. Exploring modality and temporality interactions through the storyboard Bill vs. The weather. *Semantic Field Methods* 1 (1). 1–29.

Veselinović, Dunja. 2019. *The syntax and acquisition of modal verb flavors.* New York, NY: New York University dissertation.

Veselinović, Dunja & Ailís Cournane. 2020. The grammatical source of missing epistemic meanings from modal verbs in child BCS. In Tania Ionin & Jonathan Eric MacDonald (eds.), *Formal approaches to Slavic linguistics 26,* 417–436. Ann Arbor, MI: Michigan Slavic Publications.

Viau, Joshua & Jeffrey Lidz. 2011. Selective learning in the acquisition of Kannada ditransitives. *Language* 87 (4). 679–714.

Werner, Tom. 2006. Future and non-future modal sentences. *Natural Language Semantics* 14 (3). 235–255.

Whalen, Doug & Joyce McDonough. 2015. Taking the laboratory into the field. *Annual Review of Linguistics* 1 (1). 395–415.

Yanovich, Igor. 2013. *Four pieces for modality, context and usage.* Cambridge, MA: Massachusetts Institute of Technology dissertation.

Zhornik, Daria & Sophie Pokrovskaya. 2018. Modelling visual stimuli for descriptive fieldwork among the Upper Lozva Mansi: Metalanguage vs. target language. Paper presented at *Fieldwork: Methods and Theory" Workshop,* University of Gothenburg, Sweden, December 13–14, 2018.

Appendix: Flavor preference task stimuli, English (Cournane & Pérez-Leroux 2020)

(Drawings by Ailís Cournane; Stories by Ailís Cournane & Ana Teresa Pérez-Leroux. 2013. https://osf.io/v9ure/)

1–8 Progressive stories, 9–16 Perfect stories

1. INTRO: *This is Iryna; she doesn't like to be dirty.*
   MODAL-ONLY: *Iryna must take a bath*
   MODAL-ASPECT: *Iryna must be taking a bath*

   Intro   Picture Choice (shown: deontic left, epistemic right)

2. INTRO: *This is Joanna and her cat, Slushie. Slushie loves to hunt mice. Joanna is scared of mice!*
   MODAL-ONLY: *Slushie must hunt a mouse*
   MODAL-ASPECT: *Slushie must be hunting a mouse*

   Intro   Picture Choice (shown: deontic left, epistemic right)

3. INTRO: *Alex wants to make snowmen in the snow, but it's very very cold outside!*
   MODAL-ONLY: *Alex must be wearing her warm winter clothes*
   MODAL-ASPECT: *Alex is wearing her warm winter clothes*

   Intro   Picture Choice (shown: deontic left, epistemic right)

4. INTRO: *Michelle doesn't know how to swim. Her mom wants her to learn*
   MODAL-ONLY: *Michelle must swim*
   MODAL-ASPECT: *Michelle must be swimming*

   Intro   Picture Choice (shown: deontic left, epistemic right)

5. INTRO: *Baby Chipmunk wants to eat candy. Her mom wants her to eat healthy acorns!*
   MODAL-ONLY: *Baby Chipmunk must eat her acorns*
   MODAL-ASPECT: *Baby Chipmunk must be eating her acorns*

   Intro   Picture Choice (shown: deontic left, epistemic right)

6. INTRO: *Scott wants to go play in the rain; but he doesn't want to wear any clothes!*
   MODAL-ONLY: *Scott must wear his rain boots*
   MODAL-ASPECT: *Scott must be wearing his rain boots*

   Intro   Picture Choice (shown: deontic left, epistemic right)

7. INTRO: *Matt was mean to his sister. Their mom is mad.*
   MODAL-ONLY: *Matt must say sorry to his sister*
   MODAL-ASPECT: *Matt must be saying sorry to his sister*

   Intro   Picture Choice (shown: deontic left, epistemic right)

8. INTRO: *Becky has never ridden a bike before. Her mom wants her to learn safely.*
   MODAL-ONLY: *Becky must ride a bike with training wheels*
   MODAL-ASPECT: *Becky must be riding a bike with training wheels*

   Intro   Picture Choice (shown: deontic left, epistemic right)

9. INTRO: *Mark is in his painting class. His teacher shows him what to paint*
   MODAL-ONLY: *Mark must paint a flower*
   MODAL-ASPECT: *Mark must have painted a flower*

   Intro Picture Choice (shown: deontic left, epistemic right)

10. INTRO: *This is Jada. She likes to play in the mud, but she also likes to be clean*
    MODAL-ONLY: *Jada must take a bath*
    MODAL-ASPECT: *Jada must have taken a bath*

    Intro Picture Choice (shown: deontic left, epistemic right)

11. INTRO: *Dan's father is on the phone with his grandma. Grandma hates Dan's long, messy hair*
    MODAL-ONLY: *Dan must get a haircut*
    MODAL-ASPECT: *Dan must have gotten a haircut*

    Intro Picture Choice (shown: deontic left, epistemic right)

12. INTRO: *Hansel and Gretel are in the witch's house; the witch is mean, especially to children!*
    MODAL-ONLY: *Hansel and Gretel must hide behind the curtains*
    MODAL-ASPECT: *Hansel and Gretel must have hidden behind the curtains*

    Intro　　　　　Picture Choice (shown: deontic left, epistemic right)

13. INTRO: *Michael is on his way to school, but it's raining outside!*
    MODAL-ONLY: *Michael must use an umbrella*
    MODAL-ASPECT: *Michael must have used an umbrella*

    Intro　　　　　Picture Choice (shown: deontic left, epistemic right)

14. INTRO: *Chris and Doggy are hungry; there's pizza for Chris and dogfood for Doggy.*
    MODAL-ONLY: *Doggy must eat his dogfood*
    MODAL-ASPECT: *Doggy must have eaten his dogfood*

    Intro　　　　　Picture Choice (shown: deontic left, epistemic right)

15. INTRO: *Ross sees a rabbit and a fox – the fox is hungry and likes to eat rabbits!*
    MODAL-ONLY: *The rabbit must jump the fence*
    MODAL-ASPECT: *The rabbit must have jumped the fence*

    Intro   Picture Choice (shown: deontic left, epistemic right)

16. INTRO: *Sarah was really naughty – she painted all over her wall!*
    MODAL-ONLY: *Sarah must clean the wall*
    MODAL-ASPECT: *Sarah must have cleaned the wall*

    Intro   Picture Choice (shown: deontic left, epistemic right)

Part II: **Lessons from case studies on underdescribed languages**

Isabella Coutinho Costa & Ana Lúcia Pessotto
6 On applying semantic fieldwork elicitation techniques to describe modality in Ye'kwana

Abstract: In the literature of the Cariban family so far, modal morphemes are not identified; however, all languages can use grammatical strategies to express possibility and necessity. Based on this assumption, we investigated modality in Ye'kwana, a language spoken on the Brazilian and Venezuelan border. Using the Kratzerian theoretical model and methodologies for conducting semantic fieldwork – based on elicitation and the modal questionnaire – we test deontic possibility vs. necessity interpretations and epistemic possibility vs. necessity. The results show that the suffix *-jhai* is used to convey an inference from the evidence available, and the suffix *-tai /-chai* is also found to occur in epistemic necessity contexts and may express possibility in epistemic contexts, but the data available are not sufficient to determine the modal force of these suffixes.

1 Introduction

This chapter aims to present the procedures and results of research identifying the grammatical categories responsible for expressing modality in Ye'kwana, a language of the Cariban family spoken in the extreme northwest of Roraima, Brazil. Our focus is to describe fieldwork accomplished following methodology for semantic fieldwork-based elicitation (Matthewson 2004; Vander Klok 2014), and to present the results we were able to gather from it. This is the first description of modality in a northern Cariban language, controlling the modal force and the modal flavor through providing different contexts, and following the Kratzerian approach to the semantics of modality in natural language (Kratzer 1981, 1991, 2012).

Acknowledgements: We want to thank the Ye'kwana consultants who kindly participated in our research and answered our questions.

Isabella Coutinho Costa, State University of Roraima, Rua Sete de Setembro, 231, Canarinho, Boa Vista -RR, Brasil, CEP 69.306-530, e-mail: isabella_coutinho@hotmail.com
Ana Lúcia Pessotto, Federal University of Santa Catarina, Campus Universitário Reitor João David Ferreira Lima Trindade, Florianópolis -SC, Brazil, CEP 88040-900, e-mail: anapessotto@gmail.com

https://doi.org/10.1515/9783110721478-007

According to Gildea (2012), Ye'kwana belongs to the Guyanese branch alongside the Tiryió and Wayana languages, as they share morphological and phonological features. In the literature of these languages, there is no evidence of specific grammatical strategies to denote modality. Tavares's (2005) analysis for Wayana and Meira's (1999) for Tiriyó describe mode only as a verbal inflection, but do not describe how modality works in the semantic domain.

In the next sections, the procedure of our research will be presented. Section 2 presents the Ye'kwana language and we highlight important issues concerning the fieldwork methodology used to work with Amerindian underdescribed languages, explaining why we chose the approach provided by Matthewson (2004) to conduct our semantic research. Section 3 discusses the theoretical framework used to explain the modality in Ye'kwana. Section 4 presents the step-by-step methodological procedures we conducted to elicit modal morphemes in Ye'kwana. We argue here that the modal *-jhai* may have an epistemic or deontic interpretation, and the suffix *-tai /-chai* can occur in epistemic necessity contexts and may express possibility in epistemic or deontic contexts, but the data available are not sufficient to determine the force of the modals. The last section presents our final remarks about fieldwork on semantics in an Amerindian underdescribed language.

2 Studies on the Ye'kwana language: Some considerations about the fieldwork methodology

The Ye'kwana live on the border of Brazil and Venezuela. In Brazil they live in the Roraima State, distributed in three villages, where there are almost 800 people (Costa 2018, 2019). In Venezuela, where they are almost 7,000 people, they mainly live in the Amazonas and Bolívar States (cf. Cáceres 2011). In Brazil, where this research was conducted, all children and most women are monolingual in Ye'kwana, while most men, especially adults, are bilingual in Portuguese and Ye'kwana, and some also speak Spanish.

The bilingual Ye'kwanas learn Portuguese from the age of 16, when they finish elementary school in the villages and go to high school in public schools in Boa Vista, a city in Roraima, Brazil. In general, women end up staying in the villages, taking care of the field and helping families, while men go to the city to study. In recent years, more and more women have been able to attend not only high school, but also complete graduate and postgraduate studies.

There are several grammatical descriptions of the Ye'kwana, such as Hall's (1988) pioneering dissertation, which presents the first analyzed data of the language based on translations of narratives and elicitations. Years later, the contributions of Chavier (2008) and Cáceres (2007, 2011) were put forth, which present typological-comparative descriptions of the language without focusing on its semantics. Costa's (2013) work on quantification showed that, in order to deepen the discussion, other methodological approaches were needed beyond elicitation. Later, Costa (2018) performed the first controlled judgment tasks, with an emphasis on quantification and on the acquisition of the interpretation of quantifiers. Costa (2018, 2020) describes a series of tasks carried out to access the consultants' interpretation of the quantifiers, bare nouns, constructions with numerals, and comparative sentences. Some of the tasks were a production task (Lima 2014) and a comprehension task, including "act out" and quantity judgment tasks (Barner and Snedeker 2005), a truth-value judgment task (Crain and Mckee 1985; Gordon 1996), and grammatical judgment tasks (Matthewson 2004). There is no reference to modality studies in these works.

According to Matthewson (2004), the data elicited using semantic fieldwork techniques assumes that the researcher already has knowledge about grammatical constructions in the language studied. Therefore, the description of the data elicited using semantic fieldwork methods is consistent with the analysis of narratives and other language data. As semantic data cannot be observed solely through examining narratives and language corpora, fieldwork using a specific methodology is necessary, as Costa (2018: 27) reminds us, due to the nuances in the meaning of grammatical structures that can only be accessed through the intuition of native speakers. Furthermore, narrative analysis may not provide negative evidence of the use of the phenomenon under investigation.

Thus, as we already have good prior knowledge of the phonology, morphology, and syntax of the language, we prepared an elicitation questionnaire based on the modal questionnaire from Vander Klok (2014) and used the elicitation methods described in Matthewson (2004). The contexts were provided to support the use of modal morphemes, and this method was crucial to transport the consultant to language usage that is as real as possible.

Semantic elicitation in fieldwork does not involve a direct question about the meaning of the sentence to be tested. The researcher must obtain indirect clues to truth and felicity conditions, through the construction of contexts that favor or disadvantage a target linguistic form, according to the researcher's hypothesis. Rather than asking a direct and inductive question, Matthewson's (2004) proposal is that the speaker's semantic judgment is accessed by presenting contexts and requesting either the translation of an utterance presented in the contact language or a judgment concerning whether an utterance in the target language is appropriate for the context. The contact language is a language spoken by both the consultant and the researcher. The context against which the language will be elicited can be presented in different ways, such as orally, with texts, or with drawings.

Following Matthewson (2004: 339), a judgment is something that the native speaker is qualified to perform due to their knowledge of the language: we accept a judgment as part of the competence of the native speaker. According to Matthewson (2004), there are three types of judgment: grammaticality, truth, and felicity values of use. A grammaticality judgment, although not the focus of this elicitation, is reflected in the translation and context manipulation, while truth and felicity judgments are both related to the domain of the investigation of meaning.

According to Matthewson (2004) the two major questions that must be answered with semantic fieldwork are: (i) what are the truth conditions of the sentence (how the world has to be for the sentence to be true; this is the meaning essential to the sentence, the core of the speaker's knowledge of its meaning)? and (ii) what are the felicity conditions of the sentence (this goes beyond the conditions of truth, involving the conditions in which the sentence is appropriate; that is, the context)?

The question about truth and felicity conditions cannot be a direct question or induce the speaker to make a conscious analysis of their language. According to Matthewson (2004), native speakers without formal training in linguistics are not qualified to make a conscious analysis since the relevant rules that govern language cannot be consciously accessed without instruction in linguistic analysis. As an example, they would not know how to distinguish a cancellable implicature in a judgment of truth conditions, or to identify an assumption. Assuming this perspective, the aim of the empirical part of this work was to collect the intuitive judgments of native speakers without formal knowledge or training in linguistics.

The manipulation of context allows the researcher to collect negative evidence, a fundamental factor for language description. Since the speaker can reject sentences that do not fit a particular context, an important part of the work of the linguist is to determine the reasons that lead the speaker to reject a sentence, and with that, understand and better describe its truth and felicity conditions. For this reason, the empirical aim of this work was to focus on judgments of utterances presented within contexts appropriate to spontaneous everyday spoken language.

In addition to examining how to collect the speaker's judgment (through the presentation of contexts), Matthewson (2004) discusses how these contexts should be presented. According to her, it is important to use a contact language different from the object language. The methodology presented in Matthewson (2004) was developed to describe indigenous languages whose informants are mostly bilingual English-object language speakers, with the shared language of the researcher and informants being English, which is then used as the contact language. When presenting the methodology, Matthewson assumes that the researcher is not a native speaker of the object language because it is this situation that offers the greatest challenge. The disadvantage of this approach is that the consultant must be fluent in the contact language used by the researcher. Another criticism of this method is that it is hard to make sure which level of bilingualism is enough to guarantee that the consultant will understand the context to give an appropriate response. Also, the context presented to the consultants must reflect their cultural knowledge, therefore it is important to adapt the contexts so that they fit the cultural reality of the consultants.

This methodology fits the circumstances in which we carried out our work since we were able to use Brazilian Portuguese as the contact language and to consult bilingual Ye'kwana-Brazilian Portuguese consultants. As we explained above, the Ye'kwana start learning Brazilian Portuguese by the age of 16, and some of them work or study in Boa Vista, Brazil. So, we managed to consult with these people who live in the city to guarantee that they were fluent enough to understand the contexts. According to Matthewson (2004: 379), it is not possible to obtain all information about the language without using a contact language. Thus, even when using images to provide contexts, it is also important to use explicit questions developed to elicit judgments.

In the next section, we will present the formal theoretical framework on which we rely to deal with modals in this description of Ye'kwana, and how our work approached them. Formalizations will only be presented as a matter of completeness since proposing formal analyses of the morphemes investigated here is not within the scope of this text.

3 Theoretical background: A formal semantics perspective for modality in natural languages

Modality, as understood here, concerns the category of expressions in a language responsible for conveying possibility or necessity (Kratzer 1981, 1991, 2012; von Fintel 2006). Moreover, modal expressions convey different types of possibility and necessity, depending on the context in which they are expressed. In this theoretical model for natural language modality, Kratzer (1981, 1991, 2012) assumes that part of the interpretation of modals is context-dependent; she seeks to formalize the contribution of contextual information in the logical form of modal morphemes.

The context is defined as a conversational background, where a set of premises (propositions) is shared by the speakers, and accessed according to the interpretation that is intended to the modal sentence. For this reason, the semantic analysis of modal sentences requires a method of data collection and analysis that establishes the context of use, since the context, according to the Kratzerian model, makes up part of the modal meaning. The modal is thus treated structurally as a two-place predicate, which takes as arguments a proposition (the embedded proposition) and a modal constraint (a set of premises provided by the context, defined as functions that map possible worlds to sets of propositions).

There are two conversational backgrounds involved in modal interpretation: the modal base, which is a function of worlds to a set of worlds resulting in a set of propositions that will determine what kind of modality is conveyed; and the ordering source, which is a set of propositions that orders the worlds of the modal base according to a given ideal parameter.

According to Kratzer (1991, 2012), there are two types of modal bases: epistemic and circumstantial, where the latter corresponds to root modality. The difference between them lies in the type of facts on which they rely. For Kratzer (2012), an epistemic modal base returns propositions that constitute "evidence of things" in the world: "everything that exists in the world including individuals, eventualities, and the world itself should, in principle, qualify as potential evidence of things in that world" (Kratzer 2012: 33), "implying or suggesting the existence of other facts in the past, present or future" (Kratzer 2012: 54). On the other hand, root modals are typically future-oriented, as they are used to talk about the propensities and potentials of people, things, and places, given the circumstances of the moment. Thus, a root modal base returns propositions related to properties or circumstances inherent to individuals, things, or places.

The "circumstances" that make up a root modal base are information that can help us to predict how things are or will be. We can then say that root modality is *prospective*. The "evidence of things" in the world, to which the epistemic basis is sensitive, is not defined in detail by Kratzer (2012). As opposed to the "circumstances" of the root base, we can understand that the "evidence of things in the world" are facts that can no longer interfere in the future of events, but rather attest to inferences about what is already established in the world.

Understanding the difference in the nature of these facts is crucial, as it will determine different truth values for each interpretation. However, as Kratzer (2012: 50) puts it, the difference between the facts that make up epistemic and root bases are difficult to characterize in formal terms. Anything that exists in the world can be evidence of things in the world used in the interpretation of an epistemic modal. In this way, could not the local circumstances (triggered by root modal bases) also constitute evidence of things in the world?

In order to simplify this characterization, which is relevant for the present work, we assume Pessotto's (2015) interpretation on the matter, which she presents in her analysis of the Brazilian Portuguese modal system. Pessotto groups under the term "evidence" any observable fact in the world, including local circumstances that are composed of root bases, and which we can call *circumstantial evidence*, and the facts that represent evidence of things themselves, which are recruited by epistemic modal bases, which we can call *epistemic evidence*. On this basis, from now on, we will use the (non-standard) terms "evidential" and "non-evidential" to classify types of contexts that we want to oppose, as defined below:

(I) Evidential context: An evidential context is one that projects a realistic, epistemic, or root modal base, ordered by a stereotypical ordering source (the ordering based on the expected course of the events according to what we can observe from the context).

(II) Non-evidential context: A non-evidential context is one that projects a root modal base ordered by ordering sources that do not require normality, such as deontic, teleological, and bouletic.

The modal interpreted based on an evidential context conveys a notion of probability (epistemic or root). We emphasize that here we understand evidential not as an element of the language that identifies the type of evidence, as occurs in many languages that mark evidentiality – inferential, reportative, and experiential, among others. Rather, we use the term evidential to indicate that the conversational background is composed of circumstantial (observable in the world) or epistemic (from general knowledge) evidence, without determining whether this evidence is obtained through experience, hearing, historical/official documents, or another source.

From the concepts of a modal base and an ordering source, Kratzer (1991, 2012) constructs the definitions of necessity, possibility, and "comparative possibility", which are presented below for a better understanding of the theoretical approach.

(i) Necessity: A proposition p is a necessity in a world w with respect to a modal base f and an ordering source g if, and only if, the following condition is satisfied: for every $u \in \cap f(w)$ there is a world $v \in \cap f(w)$ such that $v \leq_{g(w)} u$ and for all $z \in \cap f(w)$: if $z \leq_{g(w)} v$, then $z \in p$ (Kratzer 1991: 644).

The definition of necessity tells us that a proposition p is a necessity if, for each world u that belongs to the modal base: if there is a world v, also belonging to the modal base, such that v is better ordered than u, and for the world z that also belongs to the modal base, if z is better ordered than v, z belongs to p (p is true in z). That is, in all possible worlds restricted by the modal base, there is no better alternative to p; so, p is necessary.

(ii) Possibility: A proposition p is a possibility in a world w with respect to a modal base f and an ordering source g if, and only if, ¬p is not a necessity in w with respect to f and g (Kratzer 1991: 644).

The definition of possibility tells us that a proposition p is possible in a world w only if its negation ¬p is not a necessity in w. In other words, there is at least one world among worlds closest to the ideal defined by the modal base and ordering source where p is true.

Finally, the definition in (iii) below is one way to formulate the comparative possibility. We assume that this notion involves the idea of comparison and "probability".

(iii) Comparative possibility (one option among many that must be considered): A proposition p is at least as good a possibility as q in w with respect to [modal base] f and [ordering source] g if, and only if: ¬ ∃u (u ∈ ∩f(w) & u ∈ q − p & ∀v ((v ∈ ∩f(w) & v∈p-q) → u $<_{g(w)}$ v)) (Kratzer 2012: 41).

In other words, a proposition p is a better possibility than a proposition q in w with respect to f and g if, and only if, p is at least as good a possibility as q.

The ordering sources are responsible for setting modal gradation, which explains how in natural language we can convey and interpret not only the traditional dual possibility and necessity but also see situations as more or less possible or necessary than others. As a consequence, this perspective allows for the existence of modals without duals. Evidence for modals without duals is found in languages such as St'át'imcets (Rullmann, Matthewson and Davis 2008), Nez Perce (Deal 2011), Gitksan (Peterson 2012), and, in a way, in Brazilian Portuguese (Pessotto 2015, 2016).

This section presented a theoretical background on modality in general and on modality for our contact language – namely, Brazilian Portuguese – which we rely on to approach the semantics of modal expressions in Ye'kwana. With this background, we turn into a discussion of the elements that express evidential possibility and necessity in Ye'kwana and their truth and felicity conditions.

4 Context-based elicitations and felicity conditions to describe modality in Ye'kwana: The methodology

As argued in sections 3 and 4, any attempt of semantic description of a modal system must indisputably rely on methods that set a scenario, a state of things, against which the data will be interpreted. That is the reason why fieldwork methodology based on elicitation has been our first choice when starting to describe the semantics of a natural language modal system. In this section, along with the description of the methodology applied in our data collection, we will present how our work approached the elicitation step by step, wrapping up with the results we were able to gather by following this methodology.

As a first approach to elicit modality in Ye'kwana, we performed an elicitation session examining possibility and necessity expressions in evidential contexts only. We opted to restrict the elicitation to evidential contexts in order to avoid possible misunderstandings during the analysis. After showing the contexts to the consultants, they were asked to translate sentences from Brazilian Portuguese.

Since the language of the researchers is Brazilian Portuguese, and the second language of the consultants is also Brazilian Portuguese, the choice of sentences, contexts, and modals for the elicitation was based on the work of Pessotto (2015) on the Brazilian Portuguese modal verbs *pode* 'can/may/might', *deve* 'should/must', and *tem que* 'have to'. In her analysis, following the Kratzerian formal approach, Pessotto identifies *poder* 'can/may/might' as the prototypical possibility verb in Brazilian Portuguese (as defined in (ii) in section 3), *ter que* 'have to' as the expression of necessity (as defined in (i) in section 3), and *deve* 'should/must' as a modal without a dual (as defined in (iii) in section 3) that, according to the context, can sound stronger than a possibility and weaker than necessity. We drew on Pessotto's (2015) definitions for these modals, which were developed based on experimental work and analyzed within the Kratzerian theoretical framework.[1]

After the sentences were translated, we could understand some modal constructions in Ye'kwana. Feeling we were able to proceed with elicitation through acceptability judgments, our second step was, following Matthewson (2004), the construction of the contexts to be presented to the consultant. The context was presented first by the researchers, and then the consultant was asked to translate the target sentence.

The next step in semantic fieldwork is to know how to interpret the rejection or acceptance of the sentence in context. First, is the sentence rejected because it is false in the context or because it is infelicitous in the context? According to Matthewson (2004), after the rejection of the sentence, one possibility is to try to explain to the respondent the difference, in a simple way such as: does it seem like a lie, or does it just sound funny? We will show in the next section how the consultants behaved during the task, showing not only the translations to the sentences but their comments and reactions to the contexts.

---

1 "(a) $[[\text{pode-}p]]w,f,g = 1$ iff $\exists w''\ [w'' \in Og(w)(\cap f(w))$, e $p(w'') = 1$, and $g(w)$ = a set of evidence, or rules, or objectives, depending on the context]; (b) $[[\text{deve-}p]]w,f,g = 1$ iff, given p and q, p is a better possibility than q in w with respect to f and g, as defined. in (iii); (c) $[[\text{tem que-}p]]w,f,g = 1$ iff $\forall w''\ ((w'' \in Og(w)(\cap f(w)) \& g(w)$ = a set of rules, objectives, wishes or evidence, depending on the context) $\rightarrow p\ (w'') = 1$)" (Pessotto 2015: 129).

5 Preliminary data on the modality in Ye'kwana

According to the methodology presented in the last section, our first approach to elicit modality in Ye'kwana was an elicitation session including a translation task to examine possibility and necessity expressions only in evidential contexts. After presenting the context, the translated sentences obtained are presented below.[2,3]

(1) a. Context: Você vê muitas nuvens escuras no céu. Como você diz em Ye'kwana "Vai chover"?
'You see many dark clouds in the sky. How do you say in Ye'kwana "It will rain"?'
konoojo=je   ei-chai
rain=ATR   COP-FUT.IRR
'It will rain.'

b. Context: Você vê muitas nuvens escuras no céu. Como você diz em Ye'kwana "Deve chover"?
'You see many dark clouds in the sky. How do you say in Ye'kwana "It must rain"?'
konoojo=je   ei-jhai[4]
rain=ATR   COP-ABIL
'It can/must rain.'

c. Context: Você vê muitas nuvens escuras no céu. Como você diz em Ye'kwana "Tem que chover"?
'You see many dark clouds in the sky. How do you say in Ye'kwana "It has to rain"?'
konoojo=je   innha-tai[5]
rain=ATR   to.rain-FUT.IRR
'It has to rain.'

---

[2] The glosses used follow Cáceres (2011): ATR attributivizer; ABIL habilitative; COP copula; EXCL exclamative; FUT.IRR future irrealis; INT intensifier; NLZ nominalizer; PL plural; POSS possessive.
[3] The contexts were presented in Brazilian Portuguese to the consultants, no English examples were used. For the sake of general understanding, we provide here an approximate translation into English.
[4] The suffix *-jhai* /-haj/ does not have a palatalized allomorph.
[5] In Ye'kwana 't' /t/ is palatalized as [tʃ] after [j], therefore *-tai* is *-chai* in example 1.c (cf. Cáceres 2007; Costa 2018).

In example (1a) the suffix -*chai* in the copula brings the modal information that the rain will come, but in an uncertain future. In the example (1b) the copula appears, but this time the suffix -*jhai* is responsible for the modal information that there is a possibility for the rain to come. The example (1c) also includes the future irrealis suffix (see footnote 5 for further explanation) but now attached to the verb *innha* 'to rain', with a strength higher than that in the other two examples. From these sentences we can see that the copular constructions (copula or the verb plus future suffix -*tai*/-*chai* or the habilitative suffix -*jhai*) are responsible for conveying modality. However, we cannot predict the contexts in which they can be used.

Following the second step of the methodology, and after the preliminary knowledge about modals, we constructed culturally relevant contexts. The context was presented first, and then the consultant was asked to translate the target sentence from Brazilian Portuguese.

(2) a. Context: Você olha para o céu e vê nuvens escuras, há trovão e relâmpagos no céu. Como você diz em Ye'kwana "Vai chover"?
'You look at the sky and you see large storm clouds, there is thunder and lightning. How do you say in Ye'kwana: "It will rain"?'
konoojo=je   ei-chai
rain=ATR   COP-FUT.IRR
'It will rain.'

b. Context: Você olha para o céu e vê algumas nuvens escuras, mas não há vento. Como você diz em Ye'kwana "Deve chover"?
'You look at the sky and you see some dark clouds, but there is no wind. So, there is a chance of rain soon. How do you say in Ye'kwana: "It must rain"?'
konoojo=je   ei-jhai
rain=ATR   COP-ABIL
'It can/must rain.'

c. Context: Você olha para o céu e vê muitas nuvens escuras, e o vento está muito forte indicando que vai chover. Então você tem certeza de que vai chover em breve. Como você diz em Ye'kwana "Tem que chover"?
'You look at the sky and you see a lot of storm clouds and a strong wind typical of rain. So, you are pretty sure it will rain soon. How do you say in Ye'kwana: "It has to rain"?'
konoojo=je   innha-tai
rain=ATR   to.rain-FUT.IRR
'It has to rain.'

The suffix *-tai* (*-chai*) is used in (2a) and (2c). The consultant explained that the sentence in context (2a) is used to explain the rain was coming, and in context (2c) he said he was pretty sure that it would rain; he used the verb *innha* 'to rain' to emphasize this certainty. As he was not so sure of the context (2b), he used the copula construction with the habilitative suffix *-jhai*. Let us see other contexts using the verb *innha* 'to rain'.

(3)   a.   Context: Você está dentro de casa e ouve o barulho de trovões. Como você diz em Ye'kwana "Vai chover"?
'You are inside the house and you hear thunderstorms. How do you say in Ye'kwana "It will rain"?'
konoojo=je   ei-chai
rain=ATR   COP-FUT.IRR
'It will rain.'

     b.   Context: Você está dentro de casa e ouve o barulho de trovões e você tem certeza de que vai chover. Como você diz em Ye'kwana "Deve chover"?
'You are inside the house and you hear thunderstorms and you are pretty sure it will rain. How do you say in Ye'kwana "It must rain"?'
konoojo=je   innha-tai
rain=ATR   to.rain-FUT.IRR
'It can/must rain.'

The consultants explained that there is no possibility of guessing in contexts (3a) or (3b) because if they heard the thunderstorms, it meant it would rain. They also explained that *-tai* expresses certainty, even when there is no visual evidence.

Now that we gained a more consistent knowledge of the modality in Ye'kwana, we were able to understand how to interpret the rejection or acceptance of the sentence in context. We continued presenting the contexts and asking for translations, but we were aware that the comments that the consultants made were as important as the translation itself because they give clues to the reasons leading to the rejection or acceptance of a given sentence, as we can see below.

(4)   a.   Context: Hoje está um dia bonito e ensolarado, não há nuvens no céu e subtamente começa a ventar. Você pode dizer em Ye'kwana "*konoojoje eichai*"?
'Today is a sunny and beautiful day, there are no clouds or thunder and it suddenly it starts to get windy. Can you say in Ye'kwana "*konoojoje eichai*"?'

> # *konoojo=je   ei-chai*
> rain=ATR   COP-FUT.IRR
> ('It will rain.')
> Consultant's answer: "No. This sentence is good, but it is weird in this context because if it is sunny and blowing that does not necessarily mean it will rain."

b. Context: Hoje está um dia bonito e ensolarado, não há nuvens no céu e subtamente começa a ventar. Você pode dizer em Ye'kwana *"konoojoje eijhai"*?
'Today is a sunny and beautiful day, there are no clouds or thunder and suddenly it starts to get windy. Can you say in Ye'kwana in Ye'kwana *"konoojoje eijhai"*?'
konoojo=je   ei-jhai
rain=ATR   COP-ABIL
'It can/must rain.'
Consultant's answer: "This sentence is good in this context, as long as there is a possibility it is going to rain."

c. Context: Hoje está um dia bonito e ensolarado, e você está na floresta caçando. Você pode dizer em Ye'kwana *"konoojoje innhatai"*?
'Today is a sunny and bright day, and you are in the forest for hunting. Can you say in Ye'kwana *"konoojoje innhatai"*?'
> # *konoojo=je   innha-tai*
> rain=ATR   to.rain-ABIL
> ('It can/must rain.')
> Consultant's answer: "No. This sentence is good, but it is not true in this context because it does not describe what is really happening."

d. Context: Hoje o dia está nublado e está ventando, e você ouve trovões. Você pode dizer em Ye'kwana *"konoojoje eijhai"*?
'Today is a windy and cloudy day, and you hear thunderstorms. Can you say in Ye'kwana *"konoojoje eijhai"*?'
> # *konoojo=je   ei-jhai*
> rain=ATR   COP-ABIL
> 'It can/must rain.'
> Consultant's answer: "This sentence is good, but if you are sure it will rain, you should not say that."

The consultant rejected both contexts (4a) and (4b) because in the scenarios presented there was no clear evidence that it would rain. Another clue to indicate whether the speaker rejects the sentence for falsehood or felicity is that the true value judgments are more categorical for falsehoods (the sentence is good in the context or not). We perceived that sentence (4a) was rejected because it did not fit the context, but sentence (4b) was completely weird for the consultant, while (4d) shows that the consultant agreed with the sentence, but he would not use it. When it comes to felicity judgments, the contexts are more malleable and open to the speaker's comment (for example: "I understand what you mean, but I wouldn't say it like that").

From the data shown above, it can be observed that -*jhai* and -*tai* (-*chai*) can both be used in evidential contexts (inference from evidence); however, they differ in strength: -*jhai* can express that an event is possible/probable (in the words of the consultant, "divination"), but not "certain". On the other hand, -*tai* (-*chai*) is used to express certainty about what will happen. Consultants were unable to explain the difference between p and -*tai*-p. The differences found were morphosyntactic. These observations closed our first elicitation session.

Later, we were able to conduct another elicitation session. This time, we elicited possibility and necessity sentences both in evidential and non-evidential contexts (as defined in I and II). Still following the elicitation method described in Matthewson (2004), in this second elicitation we used the Modal Questionnaire for cross-linguistic use (Vander Klok 2014), after the translation of those contexts into Brazilian Portuguese with appropriate adaptations for the Ye'kwana cultural contexts. See Vander Klok (this volume) for a revised version of this modal questionnaire.

We were able to consult individually 4 bilingual Brazilian Portuguese-Ye'kwana speakers and test 6 non-evidential deontic contexts, 3 of permission (possibility) and 3 of obligation (necessity), as well as 6 evidential contexts, 3 conveying epistemic possibility, 3 conveying epistemic necessity. Again, the contexts and the questions were presented in Portuguese, our contact language; here they will be translated into English for convenience. For the sake of space, and since the results were consistent throughout the deontic contexts we elicited, we present below one sample of each target (namely, deontic possibility and deontic necessity):

(5) Deontic possibility context: According to the rules, hunting is only for children over 15 years old. Joãozinho is 12 years old, so he can't go hunting, but his brother Jonas can because he is 17 years old. How can I say in Ye'kwana "Jonas can go hunting"?

Jona maane eseeönge ta-jhai na
Jonas EXCL-INT hunting to.go-ABIL 3.COP
'Jonas can go hunting.'

(6) Deontic necessity context: In our culture, elders are very wise, so the parents of the children teach children to respect their elders. It is mandatory for children to respect their elders. How can I say in Ye'kwana: "The children must respect the elderly"?
Incho-komo   adekwe   mudeeshi'chä   y-ei-chö   koomo   tujuune   na
old-PL   order   child   3-COP-NLZ PL   MODAL   3.COP
'The elders speak and children must obey.'
Literally: 'Children have to be respectful to the elderly.'

As a preliminary observation, in deontic contexts (expressing permission or obligation), *-jhai* and *tujunne* are recurrent, while in contexts like (5), conveying permission, *-jhai* arises and in contexts like (6), conveying obligation, *tujunne* appears. Below we have some samples of the epistemic contexts elicited in this second round, for which the results were not as categorical as for deontic contexts.

(7) Epistemic possibility context: Maria is looking for her necklace. She's not sure if she lost the necklace when she went fishing or if she lent the necklace to Juliana. She looked for the necklace in her house and didn't find it there. She went to the river and didn't find the necklace there either. She looked inside the boat and didn't find it. Maria thought: The necklace might be with Juliana. How can I say in Ye'kwana: "The necklace might be with Juliana"?
Juliana   wää-ne   da'na-i   womo-du
Juliana   COP-INT   3.COP-MODAL   necklace-POSS
'The necklace might be with Juliana.'
Literally: 'Juliana certainly has my necklace.'

(8) Epistemic possibility context: João lives in Boa Vista. João goes to work by bicycle every day. He is not usually late, but today he is late and it is raining. João's colleagues then say: João might be at home because of the rain. How can I say in Ye'kwana: "João might be at home because of the rain"?
Konoojo-je   y-ei = jäkä   João   t-äsa-wä   ei-jhai   naa-de
rain-ATT   3s-COP=why   João   3-house-COP   COP-ABIL   3.COP-CONFIRM
'João might be at home because of the rain.'
Literally: 'The rain is why João must be in his own home.'

(9) Epistemic necessity context: João is a hardworking and studious boy. He's always at home, at work, or at school. Now it is not the time for work nor school. So, João must be at home. How can I say in Ye'kwana: "João must be at home"?

T-äsa-wä	ne	João	ei-jhai	naa-de
3-house-COP	INT	João	COP-ABIL	3.COP-CONFIRM

'João has to be at home.'
Literally: 'Certainly João should be at home.'

From the results above, we can observe that both *da'na-i* and *-jhai* occur in evidential contexts. The elicitation made so far was not enough to specify the modal force conveyed by each of them, whether necessity or possibility and in the future, we plan to conduct entailment tests to determine this. However, we are able to observe that both *da'na-i* and *-jhai* can convey epistemic inference, i.e., inference based on evidence, or what is known about the circumstances. We also observed something unexpected: in all epistemic contexts tested, the intensifier *-ne* occurs. We were not able to test for the semantic contribution of *-ne* in these contexts, but our hypothesis is that, associated with the modal, *-ne* plays a role in the strength of the assertion.

6 Final remarks

What we learn, we learn from experience, be it a personal experience, or the experience transmitted by others who preceded us. Nowadays, thanks to the groundwork provided by works such as Matthewson's, which we follow here, we have learned that semantic fieldwork involves subtleties that are difficult to categorically grasp, and impossible to understand or map without providing contexts during data collection. In order to get as close as possible to the precision required by a scientifically guided linguistic description, a well-described, previously tested, and precisely followed methodology is what leads us to the neatest results.

In this work, our aim was to show what kind of data we were able to collect on the semantics of modality in Ye'kwana using the semantic fieldwork methodology of elicitation. We showed that the suffix *-jhai* is used in both epistemic and deontic contexts, and the suffix *-tai/-chai* was also found to occur in epistemic necessity contexts. In the future, we plan to conduct other tasks to investigate the modal force of these suffixes.

During our fieldwork, we experienced firsthand that fieldwork in semantics involves specific challenges, because semantic facts are subtle, highly dependent on the context, and almost never directly accessible by intuition (see also the discussion in Ferreira and Müller, this volume). We observed, in our experience with Ye'kwana, that greater control over data collection was necessary when it comes to semantic investigation, especially when it involves the investigation of modals, which adds a layer of context-dependency and increases the challenge of this work. For this reason, as we moved forward in stages of research, we have been developing more control and organization in the set of contexts to be tested. At first, we chose to test only evidential contexts, with sentences and contexts created by us, and embedded verbs that favored evidential reading. With the results obtained in this first stage, we had a sufficient basis to expand the field of investigation and include non-evidential contexts. Building on the results obtained in the first round of elicitation, we employed the contexts suggested and already tested by Vander Klok (2014; see also Vander Klok, this volume), culturally adapted to our consultants. Then, we were able to map the use of modal expressions in deontic non-evidential contexts, and we observed that the issue is a little more challenging when it comes to evidential contexts. Perhaps the secret here is to improve the methodology to more accurately capture the nuances of the evidential contexts? We leave that question open for future research.

As with each stage of research like this, along with the results obtained, more avenues open up to be investigated. At this point, as we discussed at the end of the last section, the elicitation conducted so far was not sufficient to determine the modal force conveyed by *da'na-i* and *-jhai*, whether it was necessity or possibility. Our next step would be to conduct entailment tests in order to figure that out. We also must test for the semantic contribution of the intensifier *ne* in these contexts, but our hypothesis is that associated with the modal, *ne* plays a role in the strength of the assertion. Only future work will tell. This highlights another important lesson from this experience, which is that elicitation work to describe a language is an ant's work and it requires perseverance: the whole picture—if we will even get there—is painted little by little, and our Ye'kwana modals semantic description is only in the beginning stages.

References

Barner, David & Jesse Snedeker. 2005. Quantity judgments and individuation: Evidence that mass nouns count. *Cognition* 97 (1). 41–66.

Cáceres, Natalia. 2007. *Introduction à la langue des Ye'kwana: Profil sociolinguistique et esquisse phonologique* [Introduction to the language of the Ye'kwana people: sociolinguistic profile and phonology sketch]. Lyon: Université Lyon 2 MA thesis.

Cáceres, Natalia. 2011. *Grammaire Fonctionnelle-Typologique du Ye'kwana: Langue caribe du Venezuela* [Typological-Functional Grammar of Ye'kwana: A Carib language from Venezuela]. Lyon: Université Lumière Lyon 2 dissertation.

Chavier, Mariela. 2008. *Aspectos tipológicos y culturales en la morfosintaxis del Ye'kwana.* [Typological and cultural aspects in the morphosyntax of Ye'kwana]. Mérida: Universidad de Los Andes dissertation.

Costa, Isabella. 2013. *O número em Ye'kwana: Uma perspectiva tipológica* [Number in Ye'kwana: A typological perspective]. Rio de Janeiro: Universidade Federal do Rio de Janeiro MA Thesis.

Costa, Isabella. 2018. *A quantificação em Ye'kwana: A distinção contável-massivo* [Quantification in Ye'kwana: The count-mass distinction]. Rio de Janeiro: Universidade Federal do Rio de Janeiro dissertation.

Costa, Isabella. 2019. *Produto 02: Diagnóstico Sociolinguístico do povo Ye'kwana* [Product 02: Sociolinguistic Diagnosis]. Subprojeto Ye'kwana. Rio de Janeiro: PRODOCLIN. UNESCO / Museu do Índio.

Crain, Stephen & Cecile Mckee. 1985. The acquisition of structural restrictions on anaphora. *North East Linguistics Society* 16. 94–110.

Deal, Amy Rose. 2011. *Topics in the Nez Perce verb*. Amherst, MA: University of Massachusetts Amherst dissertation.

von Fintel, Kai. 2006. Modality and language. In Donald Borchert (ed.), *Encyclopedia of Philosophy*. vol. 10, 20–27. Detroit: MacMillan Reference. http://mit.edu/fintel/fintel-.2006-modality.pdf. (accessed 10 December 2021).

Gildea, Spike. 1998. *On Reconstructing Grammar: Comparative Cariban Morphosyntax*. Oxford: Oxford University Press.

Gildea, Spike. 2012. Linguistic studies in the Cariban family. In Lyle Campbell & Verónica Grondona (eds.), *Handbook of South American Languages*, 441–494. Berlin: De Gruyter Mouton.

Gordon, Peter. 1996. The truth-value judgment task. In Dana McDaniel, Cecile McKee & Helen Cairns (eds.), *Methods for accessing children's syntax*, 211–232. Cambridge: MIT Press.

Hall, Katherine. 1988. *The morphosyntax of discourse in De'kuana Carib*. Volumes I and II. Washington: Washington University dissertation.

Kratzer, Angelika. 1981. The notional category of modality. In Hans Eikmeyer & Hannes Rieser (eds.), *Word, worlds, and contexts: New approaches to word semantics*, 38–74. Berlin: Walter de Gruyter.

Kratzer, Angelika. 1991. Modality. In Armin von Stechow & Dieter Wunderlich (eds). *Semantics: An international handbook of contemporary research*. Berlin & New York: Walter de Gruyter.

Kratzer, Angelika. 2012. *Modals and conditionals*. New York: Oxford University Press.

Lima, Suzi. 2014. *The grammar of individuating and counting*. Amherst, MA: University of Massachusetts Amherst dissertation.

Matthewson, Lisa. 2004. On the methodology of semantic fieldwork. *International Journal of American Linguistics* 70 (4). 369–415.

Meira, Sergio. 1999. *A grammar of Tiriyó*. Houston, TX: Rice University dissertation.

Pessotto, Ana Lúcia. 2015. *Força e evidência: uma análise teórico-experimental da semântica de 'pode', 'deve' e 'tem que'* [Force and evidence: An experimental-theoretical analysis of the semantics of *pode*, *deve* and *tem que*]. Florianópolis: Universidade Federal de Santa Catarina dissertation.

Pessotto, Ana Lúcia. 2016. An experimental study on the meanings of Brazilian Portuguese modals *pode*, *deve* and *tem que*. In Thuy Bui & Rudmila-Rodica Ivan (eds.), *Proceedings of the 9th conference on the Semantics of Under-Represented Languages in the Americas*, 97–112. (SULA 9). Amherst, MA: GLSA Publications.

Peterson, Tyler. 2012. The role of the ordering source in Gitksan modals. In Elizabeth Bogal-Allbritten (ed.), *Proceedings of the 6th conference on the Semantics of Under-Represented Languages in the Americas*, 171–192. (SULA 6). Amherst, MA: GLSA Publications.

Rullmann, Hotze, Lisa Matthewson & Henry Davis. 2008. Modals as distributive indefinites. *Natural Language Semantics* 16. 317–357.

Tavares, Petronila da Silva. 2005. *A Grammar of Wayana*. Houston, TX: Rice University dissertation.

Vander Klok, Jozina. 2014. *Questionnaire on modality for cross-linguistic use*. https://www.eva.mpg.de/lingua/tools-at-lingboard/pdf/Modal_Questionnaire_CrossLing JVK.pdf (accessed 9 December 2021).

Sihwei Chen
7 Modality in elicited data and spontaneous texts: A case study of Atayal

Abstract: This paper argues that contextual elicitation is superior to analyzing transcriptions of naturally produced speech to identify the differences on lexical interpretations of modals, with a focus on Atayal (an Austronesian language spoken in Taiwan). I show that while spontaneous texts can be useful for discovering interesting phenomena of modals, an examination of texts does not draw equally adequate evidence for gathering a complete picture of modals' meaning. The investigation based on contextual elicitation uncovers that Atayal displays a set of modals that differ in terms of both modal strength and flavor, and has a paradigmatic gap in epistemic necessity modality. The same results are only partially confirmed by the examination of two sets of narrative texts. For one thing, the texts offer only positive evidence, with infelicitous uses of the modals being unattested, and direct elicitation must be used to determine whether lacking a particular interpretation is due to the modal being unusable, or whether it is simply an accidental gap. For another, most of the modal contexts in the texts under close scrutiny are either ambiguous or insufficient to decide the modals' meaning, despite the known fact that texts have rich discourse contexts. Moreover, the opposite conclusion may have been made as a result of a reliance on translation. Based on the methodological comparison, I suggest that elicitation with controlled contexts constitute the majority of fieldwork for the purpose of semantic analyses.

1 Introduction

Modal elements are human expressions that talk about possible ways in which our world could develop, based on our knowledge, rules, or our individual desires

---

Acknowledgments: This research is partially supported by Ministry of Science and Technology, Taiwan, under Grant no. MOST 108-2410-H-001-005. Thank you to Jozina Vander Klok for the invitation. The chapter benefited greatly by the reviewers' comments and the editors' help. Any remaining errors are my own.

Sihwei Chen, Institute of Linguistics, Academia Sinica, No. 128, Section 2, Academia Road, Nangang District, Taipei City 115201, Taiwan, e-mail: sihweichen@gate.sinica.edu.tw

https://doi.org/10.1515/9783110721478-008

and goals. This chapter addresses the advantages and disadvantages of employing two types of methods in studying modality – conducting direct elicitation with designed, controlled contexts, and observing modal utterances in written transcriptions of spontaneously produced oral narratives. Through an investigation of Atayal modality, I discuss the extent to which the results based on elicitation can also be validly concluded from analyzing transcriptions of naturally produced speech, and I argue that the analysis of spontaneeeous speech does not provide as full a picture as working with language data that has been elicited in controlled contexts.

Atayal (ISO code: tay) is an Austronesian family of languages that has been considered to belong to one of the primary subgroups of Austronesian (Blust 1999, among others), and it is often referred to as a Formosan language. Atayal is spoken in the northern and northeastern mountains of Taiwan, primarily in New Taipei City, Yilan, Taoyuan, Hsinchu, Miaoli, Taichung, and Nantou County.

Atayal features a typologically unique modal system: despite the fact that all the different types of modality are being grammaticalized, there is a paradigmatic gap in epistemic necessity. This modal system is based on uncovering the modals' lexical meaning, in terms of two typologically variable parameters—modal strength and flavor. The aim of my fieldwork was to seek empirically testable data, with the specific objective of testing whether the target modal in Atayal encodes a certain modal strength and flavor. I consider felicity judgments of speakers against a context (i.e., whether the speaker would say an utterance in a given context) to be mandatory for gathering such data (Matthewson 2004).

While oral narratives are an excellent tool to explore relevant phenomena and to confirm positive evidence for a hypothesis, it has been noted that spontaneous speech does not contain negative data (e.g., Matthewson 2004; Burton and Matthewson 2015). It can be imagined that infelicitous modal utterances are not available in the transcriptions of oral narratives to be examined in this study; by contrast, infelicity judgments for modal utterances can be obtained through controlled elicitation. Although this difference between the two methods is not a new point, a comparison of applying the two methods in the analysis of Atayal modality nicely illustrates how the need for negative data is not met in spontaneous speech. Firstly, infelicity judgments obtained in contextual elicitation, which are required to verify the possible hypotheses, are not attested in any of the written narratives. Secondly, a systematic examination of modal occurrences and their surrounding discourse in the oral narratives shows that non-attestation of a certain modal use may either result from infelicity *or* probability.

Other issues which the comparison between the two methods touches upon are the availability of context and the interference of translation. Unlike what one may assume, while spontaneous speech is embedded in a discourse context (such that it has been considered to contain rich contextual clues), it often lacks the precise context that is needed for testing a modal's meaning. This is in essence a variant of the decontextualized problem which has been criticized for elicitation sessions with isolated language utterances and translations (e.g., Mosel 2012: 84). In this regard, contextual elicitation is superior to spontaneous speech. The examination of the oral narratives also reveals that even with rich discourse, the reading of a modal sentence can often be ambiguous and heavily relies on translation. Based on these findings, I conclude that, in comparison to spontaneously produced text data, contextual elicitation should be prioritized in data collection.

The remainder of this chapter is organized as follows. Section 2 presents the theoretical framework within which this study is situated, background on the Atayal language, and previous descriptions of Atayal modals. Section 3 details both methods used to investigate Atayal modality. Section 4 discusses the findings from elicitation, which were systematically searched for in the text materials, as presented in section 5. Section 6 compares the methodologies and section 7 concludes.

2 Theoretical and language background

2.1 Modality and possible worlds

I follow the standard approach in modal logic, whereby modals denote quantifiers over possible worlds and possibility and necessity modals correspond to existential and universal quantifiers, respectively.[1] Modals acquire different flavors depending on the context in which they are uttered. For example, *have to* in (1) is interpreted as epistemic, deontic, bouletic, teleological, or pure circumstantial, when it quantifies over a set of worlds in which (1a) what is known or believed, (1b) a body of law or principles, (1c) the hearer's desires, (1d) the hearer's goals, or (1e) the relevant circumstances in the actual world is or are true.

(1) a. *It **has to** be raining.* [after observing people coming inside with wet umbrellas; epistemic]
 b. *Visitors **have to** leave by six pm.* [hospital regulations; deontic]
 c. *You **have to** see this movie. It's so good!* [bouletic]
 d. *To get home in time, you **have to** take a taxi.* [teleological]
 e. *I **have to** sneeze.* [given the current state of my nose; pure circumstantial] (adapted from von Fintel 2006 [2005]: 21)

---

[1] Modal strength can be ambiguous between universal or existential (see e.g., Rullmann, Matthewson, and Davis 2008) or be gradable (see e.g., Kratzer 2012).

According to Kratzer's (1981, 1991, 2012) theory, context determines which subset of possible worlds the modals quantify over; the decisive elements in the context are called conversational backgrounds. Conversational backgrounds are further comprised of a modal base and an ordering source. Two main types of modal bases are epistemic and circumstantial modal bases, the former concerning the speaker's available evidence, and the latter concerning relevant facts about the circumstances. The ordering source typically involves normative standards such as ideals or norms. A modal claim is then defined as asserting that, given certain circumstances or facts in the actual world, the relevant proposition is true in at least one or every possible world. For instance, (1d) asserts that every possible world is where your goal to get home in time is fulfilled and where you take a taxi.

The two parameters of modal meanings – quantificational strength and conversational background – have proved useful in uncovering language variation (see e.g., Matthewson 2016). Modals in other languages may lexicalize modal meaning differently from English (e.g., Rullmann, Matthewson, and Davis 2008; Peterson 2010; Deal 2011). For example, in direct opposition to English modals, all St'át'imcets modals exhibit quantificational variability between necessity and possibility while being restricted to a certain flavor of modality (Rullmann, Matthewson, and Davis 2008). On the other hand, there are languages whose modals are fully specified for both parameters (e.g., Paciran Javanese, Vander Klok 2013; Mandarin, Chen 2013). Samples (2)–(3) provide examples of deontic modality from St'át'imcets and Mandarin, respectively; the St'át'imcets modal *ka* allows for a possibility or necessity reading, whereas the Mandarin *bìxū* and *kěyǐ* have only one of the readings.[2] The study of these variations has driven much of the theoretical work on analyzing modality. This chapter will add Atayal to the empirical picture based on data from elicitation and textual observation.

---

[2] Abbreviations: 1,2,3 first, second and third person; ABIL ability modality; ABS absolutive; ACC accusative; AV actor voice; CAUS causative; CIRC circumstantial modality; CF counterfactual; CONJ conjunction; COS change of state; CV circumstantial voice; DEON deontic modality; DEP dependent mood; DET determiner; DIR directive transitivizer; DIST distal; E.PST existential past; EMPH emphatic; EPIST epistemic modality; ERG ergative; EXCL exclusive; FILL filler; FUT future; GEN genitive; INCL inclusive; LNK linker; LOC locative; LV locative voice; N neutral; NEC necessity; NEG negative; NMLZ nominalizer; OBL oblique; PFV perfective; PL plural; POS possibility; POSS possessive; PRF perfect; PROG progressive; PROX proximal; PRT particle; PV patient voice; REL relativizer; REP reportative; SG singular; SUBJ indicative subject; TOP topic; VBZR verbalizer.

(2) lán-lhkacw   **ka**   áts'x-en   ti   kwtámts-sw-a.
    already-2SG.SUBJ DEON see-DIR   DET   husband-2SG.POSS-DET
    'You {must/can/may} see your husband now.'
    (St'át'imcets, Rullmann, Matthewson, and Davis 2008: 328)

(3) a. Context: My meeting with the student isn't done but he has to attend a class.
       wǒ   **bìxū/*kěyǐ**   rang   tā   líkāi.
       I   CIRC.NEC/CIRC.POS let   he   leave
       'I have to let him go.'
       (Chen 2013: 16)

    b. Context: Only family members are allowed to enter the patient's room during visiting hours, but you're exceptional since you are a really close friend.
       nǐ   ***bìxū/kěyǐ**   jìnlái.
       you   CIRC.NEC/CIRC.POS come.in
       'You may come in.'
       (Chen 2013: 16–17)

2.2 The Atayal language

Atayal is an Austronesian language that is spoken in the northern and northeastern mountains of Taiwan. Most Atayal people are bilingual, speaking Atayal as well as being fluent in Mandarin Chinese (and/or Hokkien, Hakka, Japanese, or other Formosan languages). The size of the Atayal ethnic population is estimated at 93,043 as of April 2021,[3] but fluent speakers are usually over the age of 60. It is comprised of two main dialects, Squliq and C'uli'; the former has a larger number of speakers and has been considered to be less diverse, but each of these dialect groups has distinct dialectal variation within it. My data in this paper are based on the Squliq dialects spoken in Hsinchu and Yilan County and New Taipei City (see section 3 for further information).

Atayal is a predominately predicate-initial language, with a so-called subject/pivot that agrees with voice on the verb in the sentence-final position, as in (4). Voice is a morphological marking that (broadly) indicates the thematic role of

---

[3] The number is based on the census of the Council of Indigenous People, Executive Yuan, Taiwan.

the subject/pivot, and as typical of other western Austronesian languages, Atayal distinguishes between four voices: actor voice, patient voice, locative voice, and circumstantial voice. For example, (4a) is in the actor voice, with the agent being the subject, while (4b) is in the locative voice, whose subject is the location (i.e., the container).[4] Note that the form of these voices further varies depending on whether the sentence is indicative, dependent (i.e., a term unifying imperative, negative, and some specific sentences), or hortative, but the mood distinction is not relevant to my analysis of modals.

(4) a. cyux   h<m>zi'   ayang   sa   bungkung   qu   Temu'.
       PROG.DIST pour<AV>   soup   LOC   bowl(Taiwanese) ABS   Temu'
       'Temu' is pouring soup into the bowl.'

   b. cyux   hzy-an   ayang   ni   Maya'   qu   bungkung.
      PROG.DIST pour-LV   soup   ERG   Maya'   ABS   bowl(Taiwanese)
      'Maya' has poured soup into the bowl.'

There are quite a few reference grammars, such as Rau (1992) and L. Huang (1993, 1995, 2000a), and descriptive works on different aspects of the grammar, just to name a few: Li (1980, 1982, 1995), L. Huang (1994, 2000b, 2008), and J. Huang (2006, 2015). A recent pedagogical grammar is L. Huang and Wu (2016), and Egerod (1999 [1980]) has been a useful dictionary. I discuss works relating to modality in the next subsection.

2.3 Prior studies on Atayal modality

Previous research on the morphosyntax of modal constructions in the Squliq dialects of Atayal has identified several modal elements (Hsiao 2004; Chen 2014; Pitay 2014): *ki'a* and *hazi'* are epistemic possibility modals, *si ki* and *nway* are deontic modals, with necessity and possibility strength, respectively, and *baq* and *thuyay* are ability modals concerning mental and physical ability, respectively.[5] However, these lexical specifications have been made solely based on direct

---

[4] As shown by my glosses of Squliq Atayal, I use an ergative-absolutive analysis of the case and voice agreement. This, however, is orthogonal to my investigation of modality.
[5] The modal *thuyay* is also pronounced as *thuzyay* in my elicited data, which will be transcribed as was pronounced.

translations (by authors or consultants) without showing evidence that can conclusively falsify other possibilities; for example, how can one be confident of whether *ki'a* and *hazi'* are possibility modals? Many empirical questions also remain: are there any semantic differences between *ki'a* and *hazi'*? Is it an accidental gap in the study or a characteristic of Atayal modality that there are no modals in the realm of epistemic necessity? Do *si ki* and *nway* express subtypes of circumstantial modality other than deontic, e.g., bouletic, teleological, etc.?

Most of the modals in Squliq Atayal have a cognate in the dialects of Mayrinax (also called Matu'uwal), in the presence of a linker between the modal and the embedded verb. The modal *ki'i i* is argued to encode an evidential component (i.e., kinds of information source for evidence) – it involves "reasoning from knowledge" (Cheng 2013: 91) (rather than, e.g., indirect inference from observable evidence). In (5), for example, *ki'i i* is used when the speaker infers the truth of Payan's stealing chickens in the past based on his past actions. However, crucially for this claim, it is not shown that the modal is *only* compatible with evidence of pure reasoning.

(5) **ki'i**   *i*   q\<um\>\<in\>uliq   su   waylung   i   Payan.
probably LNK \<AV\>\<E.PST\>steal ACC chicken N Payan
'Payan probably stole chickens (since he has a bad reputation for stealing things).'
(Mayrinax Atayal, Cheng 2013: 92; morpheme glosses modified)

Drawing on data from the Squliq dialects, my earlier investigation has shown that contextually elicited data and storyboards uncover the finer semantic distinctions between modals (Chen 2018). The findings will be reviewed in section 4 and form the basis of the comparison with a study of spontaneously produced narratives in section 5.

3 Methodology

I employed two methods to study the semantics of Atayal modals; I discuss them in the order they were used. The first one is direct elicitation with designed, controlled contexts, following the techniques of Matthewson (2004). In elicitation sessions, I constructed a range of hypothetical contexts and asked each consultant (i) to provide judgments on the truth/felicity of an Atayal sentences in a context (i.e., whether the constructed Atayal sentence is true and appropriate there) and/or (ii) to provide an Atayal sentence for a context. In addition, I took note of each consultant's comment about their reasons for rejecting a sentence. I mostly presented these controlled contexts verbally. The primary speaker I consulted is a male born in 1949 from Wufeng, Hsinchu County (Taoshan Village); I also consulted another male speaker born in 1954 from the same village and a male speaker born in the same year from the north of Datong, in Yilan County (Songluo Village). These speakers are all above the age of 65 and very fluent in Atayal.

An extended form of contextual elicitation is targeted construction storyboards (see Burton and Matthewson 2015). Just like single contexts that are presented as stimuli to speakers, targeted construction storyboards contain discourse contexts designed to prompt a particular linguistic form, with the advantages of allowing the speaker to spontaneously produce an original text (as the contexts are connected into a story). My aim in this chapter is not to contrast storyboards with direct elicitation; instead, it is to compare the results of contextual elicitation and storyboards with those of textual observation.

Throughout my elicitation, Mandarin Chinese was used as an intermediate language in presenting contexts and storyboards to the consultants. The reason is practical: Mandarin is the official and prevalent language of the community and is spoken fluently by native speaker consultants.

The second method I used involved a thorough analysis of modal sentences in natural texts. I looked at two collections of narratives which were transcribed and translated from oral storytelling. The first one is from Yuqih and Yupas (1991), which compiles 20 myths and legends by seven speakers, and the other is nine folktales and real-life stories by eight speakers attached to Rau's (1992) dissertation.[6] Together they comprise a small 12,529-word corpus, which is, however, sufficiently illustrative for my exploratory purpose. Both sets of texts were recorded over a similar time period (1986–1987 and 1989–1990) and both are in Squliq Atayal.

The two text collections differ in several ways: size, sub-dialectal variation, age range of speakers, and language of translation used. As Table 1 shows, the text collection in Yuqih and Yupas (1991) is much larger than the one in Rau (1992) in terms of total words (around two-and-a-half times). Moreover, while the average length of the texts in the two collections is similar (443 and 407 words), the length deviation in Rau is more significant: there are three very long stories and six very short tales. The texts were also collected in different dialect regions: most stories in Yuqih and Yupas were collected in Wufeng Township and the rest were from

---

[6] Rau's textual data contain conversations, but I only include narratives for the sake of controlling genres.

Jianshi Township (both in Hsinchu County); Rau's texts come exclusively from speakers in the Wulai District (New Taipei City). Moreover, the speakers interviewed in Yuqih and Yupas were older than those in Rau. Perhaps the most salient difference is the language of translation used: Mandarin in Yuqih and Yupas and English in Rau; note that due to this difference, the examples extracted from Yuqih and Yupas (presented in section 5) are translated into English.

Table 1: Differences between the two text collections.

	word count (total: 12,529)	length of texts				dialect regions	years of birth	language of translation
		max	min	med	avg			
Yuqih & Yupas (1991)	8866 (71%)	946	289	392	443	Wufeng; Jianshi	1893–1933	Mandarin (by native speakers)
Rau (1992)	3663 (29%)	1405	45	145	407	Wulai	1915–1952	English (by a linguist)

Compared to the three speakers I interviewed in elicitation (one was born in 1949 and the others in 1954), the speakers interviewed in the two sets of oral narratives were significantly older. However, both textual and elicited data were collected in the same dialect, and at least the majority of the textual data (from Yuqih and Yupas 1991) uses Mandarin Chinese as the contact language, as does my elicited data. I will argue that the role of translation is crucial to the understanding of the texts and that, as a result, textual observation and elicitation *without contexts* are subject to very similar methodological issues.

Since the data I present in this chapter are solely based on Squliq dialects, henceforth Atayal refers to Squliq Atayal, unless otherwise indicated.

4 Atayal modality based on contextual elicitation

This section outlines two significant features of Atayal modality on the basis of my earlier findings in controlled elicitation: firstly, each modal is fully specified for flavor of modality (section 4.1) as well as quantificational strength (section 4.2), and secondly, despite possessing an array of modal elements, Atayal lacks direct equivalents of epistemic necessity modals (section 4.2). Most of the data presented here is found in Chen (2018).

4.1 Lexically encoded modal flavor

As noted in section 2.3, *ki'a* and *hazi'* have been recognized as epistemic modals. The modal *ki'a* is an auxiliary restricted to the sentence-initial position, and the modal *hazi'* is an adverb freely distributed in the sentence.[7] Both modals are accepted in epistemic (possibility) contexts; this is shown by (6), where there are many other possible reasons why Tali' changed his facial expression, either *ki'a* or *hazi'* alone or their co-occurrence is accepted.[8]

(6) Constructed context (epistemic): You met Tali' this morning and he was in a good mood, but when you see him again, he looks sad. You think:

    a. **ki'a=naha'** k<in>s'ang la.
        EPIST.POS=3PL.ERG scold<E.PST.PV> COS
        'He might have been scolded.'

    b. k<in>s'ang=naha' **hazi'** la.
        scold<E.PST.PV>=3PL.ERG EPIST.POS COS
        'He might have been scolded.'

    c. **ki'a=naha'** k<in>s'ang **hazi'** la.
        EPIST.POS=3PL.ERG scold<E.PST.PV> EPIST.POS COS
        'He might have been scolded.'

Moreover, both modals *only* allow epistemic uses: each of the contexts in (7)–(10) targets a subtype of circumstantial modality, *deontic, teleological, bouletic,* and *pure circumstantial*, and the modals are all infelicitous. Evidence for the modals being exclusively existential will be presented in the next subsection.

(7) Constructed context (deontic): My child asks my permission to go out. I say:

    a. **nway=su'** m-usa' g<m>naw.
        DEON.POS=2SG.ABS AV-go play<AV>
        'You can go to play.'

    b. # {**ki'a=su'** m-usa'/**hazi'** m-usa'=su'} g<m>naw.
        EPIST.POS=2SG.ABS AV-go AV-go=2SG.ABS play<AV>
        You might go to play.'

---

[7] See Chen (2014, 2018) for morphosyntactic differences in other modals.
[8] Unless otherwise stated, examples with no storyboard source come from contextual elicitation where the context was constructed and presented to the consultant orally (labelled as 'constructed context') or suggested by the consultant (labelled as 'volunteered context').

(8) Constructed context (teleological): Someone asks me about the direction to the tribe in the mountain. I answer:
    a.   *musa'*   **blaq**   *pwah*   *sa*   *tuqi*   *qani.*
        FUT   CIRC.POS   pass.AV   LOC   road   this
        'You can take this road.'

    b. #   *{ki'a/hazi'}*   *pwah*   *sa*   *tuqi*   *qani.*
        EPIST.POS   pass.AV   LOC   road   this
        'You might take this road.'

(9) Volunteered context (boulettic): Tomorrow is Saturday. I tell my kid, "If you like, you can sleep more and get up late."
    a.   *ana=su'*   *m-qsuqi*   *cikay*   *sasan*   *ga*   **blaq.**
        even=2SG.ABS   AV-late   a.bit   morning   TOP   CIRC.POS
        'You can be a bit late tomorrow morning.'

    b. #   *{ki'a/hazi'}*   *m-qsuqi*   *cikay*   *sasan.*
        EPIST.POS   AV-late   a.bit   morning
        'You might be a bit late tomorrow morning.'

(10) Constructed context (pure circumstantial): I acquire a new piece of land. I don't know if there are persimmons growing there but the soil and climate are very much like my old land at home, where persimmons prosper everywhere. (adapted from Kratzer 1991: 646)
    a.   *musa'*   **blaq**   *pmhy-an*   *qapu'*   *sqani.*
        FUT   CIRC.POS   plant-LV   persimmon   here
        'Persimmons can be planted here.'

    b. #   *{ki'a/hazi'}*   *pmhy-an*   *qapu'*   *sqani.*
        EPIST.POS   plant-LV   persimmon   here
        'Persimmons might be planted here.'

Unlike what has been claimed in the literature (e.g., Pitay 2014: 21), I argue that *ki'a* and *hazi'* do not distinguish between the three common subtypes of indirect evidentials – namely, inference from mental reasoning (including the speaker's intuition, experience or mental construct), results of causing events, and a report of some other person (see e.g., Willett 1988). Firstly, the context in (11) does not indicate any perceived results of the past stealing event (that is, the speaker utters the assertion only based on his reasoning), and both *ki'a* and *hazi'* are good (see also the examples in (33)–(34) taken from texts).

(11) Constructed context: I arrive home and find that the chicken I bought is gone. There's no one else in my house. I wonder, "Where is the chicken I bought? . . ."
{**ki'a**=nha wal /**hazi'** wal=nha}
EPIST.POS=3PL.ERG PFV.PRF EPIST.POS PFV.PRF=3PL.ERG
qriq-un la.
steal-PV COS
'It might have been stolen (by people/others).'

Secondly, both modals are felicitous in (12), where the speaker infers that their school's team won, based on seeing the team members' happy face (as a result of the winning event). See Chen (2018: 359–360) for *ki'a* and *hazi'* being compatible with other indirect sensory observations.

(12) Constructed context: Our school team comes back from a competition. Everyone looks happy.
{**ki'a/hazi'**} laha' wal l<m>aqux.
EPIST.POS 3PL.N PFV.PRF win<AV>
'They might have won (lit. who has won might be them).'

Lastly, neither of the two modals encode that their embedded proposition is acquired by means of a report. Such information is conveyed by the final particle *maha/mha/ma* 'hearsay, it is said, reportedly', and it appears that the source of a report could be from any person other than the speaker him/herself (L. Huang 2008: 33–34).[9] These modals are not restricted to cases where the inference is based on non-reportative uses either; if that were the case, they would still have a certain restriction on evidence source. Instead, both modals can co-occur with the hearsay marker; see the examples in (40)–(41), given in section 5.1. Summarizing thus far, *ki'a* and *hazi'* are both epistemic possibility modals that do not distinguish major subtypes of indirect evidentiality.[10] Note that this conclusion does not rule out other possibilities in which these epistemic modals relate an evidential component, such as whether they are indirect or direct evidentials. Evidentiality in Atayal is an area that requires further research.

---

9 According to L. Huang (2008), *maha/mha/ma* is an evidential marker grammaticalized from a saying verb through a stage of being a quotative marker and a complementizer. These uses are still attested synchronically.
10 I argue elsewhere that *ki'a* and *hazi'* differ in their degree of possibility strength (Chen 2018).

I now turn to non-epistemic modality. The modal *si ki* is a general necessity modal, one that is compatible with a range of circumstantial modality, such as deontic, teleological, bouletic, and pure circumstantial; some examples are given in (13)–(15). The elicited data reveal that the necessity modal *si ki* is not restricted to a deontic meaning as its Mandarin translation may imply, but rather it is a general circumstantial modal. Evidence for the necessity strength of *si ki* will be discussed in section 4.2.

(13) Context (deontic): Mary's mother says she can't go out to play until she has done her three chores. At 1 pm her friends come over to ask if she can come out to play. Mary says, "I can't, . . ." (elicited based on 'Chore girl', TFS Working Group 2011a).
si ki   suq-un=maku'   q<m>wax   a   pyatu'   ha.
CIRC.NEC   finish-PV=1SG.ERG   wash<AV>   FIL   dishes   first
'I have to wash dishes first.'

(14) Constructed context (teleological): There's only one road to that tribe.
m-usa'=su'   m-ita'   qalang   qasa   ga,   **si ki**
AV-go=2SG.ABS   AV-see   tribe   that   TOP   CIRC.NEC
pwah   tuqi   s-qani
pass.AV   road   LOC-this
'If you're going to visit that tribe, you must go this way.'

(15) Constructed context (pure circumstantial): It's usually very hard to not sneeze if you get pepper into your nose. (adapted from Matthewson 2013: 383)
si   sbu'   nguhuw   c<in>'qw-an   na
PRT   shoot.AV.DEP   nose   choke<E.PST>-LV   GEN
lacyaw   meluh   lga,   **si ki**   si   t'asi.
pepper(Mandarin)   spicy   COS.TOP   CIRC.NEC   PRT   sneeze. AV.DEP
'When people's nose is assailed by hot pepper, they have to sneeze.'

The modal *nway*, often glossed as a deontic possibility modal, is in complementary distribution with the modal *blaq*, which is compatible with many subtypes of circumstantial modality except for deontic modality; this is demonstrated by the contrast between (16) vs. (17) and (18) (compare (10)). Note that the context of (17) seems to favor a deontic interpretation (i.e., it describes a mother's permission), but as shown by the minimally different contexts the consultant volunteered for the two modals (i.e., a child's wish vs. a boss's permission), it is clearly intended as bouletic modality. The strength of the modals will be discussed in the next subsection.

(16) Volunteered context (deontic): Your farm has a giant hornet hive in it, and your neighbor is concerned and asks you if he can burn it. You say to him:
ana=su'   *m-usa'*   *l<m>awm*   *tryung*   *ga*
even=2SG.ABS   AV-go   burn<AV>   hornet.chrysalis   TOP
{***nway***   / # ***blaq***}.
DEON.POS / CIRC.POS
'You can burn hornet chrysalises.'
Comment for *blaq*: "Not permission. It could be that the weather is good."

(17) Volunteered context (bouletic) (the same as for (9)): Tomorrow is Saturday. I tell my kid, "If you like, you can sleep more and get up late."
ana=su'   *m-qsuqi*   *cikay*   *sasan*   *ga*   {#***nway***   /***blaq***}.
even=2SG.ABS   AV-late   a.bit   morning   TOP   DEON.POS /CIRC.POS
'You can be late tomorrow morning.'
Comment for *nway*: "That's what your boss would say to you, e.g., if you worked overtime."

(18) Constructed context (pure circumstantial) (the same as for (10)): I acquire a new piece of land. I don't know if there are persimmons growing there but the soil and climate are very much like my old land at home, where persimmons prosper everywhere. (adapted from Kratzer 1991: 646)
#   ***nway**=su'*   *pmhy-an*   *qapu'*   *qu*   *qmayah*   *qani.*
DEON.POS=2SG.ABS   plant-LV   persimmon   ABS   land   this
'You can plant persimmons on this land.'
Comment: "It means that 'I allow you to plant persimmons here'."

Atayal also possesses two ability modals that have been argued to differ in concerning mental and physical properties of the subject (Pitay 2014: 57–58). For instance, (19) shows that in contrast to *baq*, *thuyay* is incompatible with events involving the intellect and skills of the subject, whereas the context in (20) cares about the size of the rock and the condition of Tali's muscles, where *thuzyay* rather than *baq* is judged felicitous.

(19) Constructed context: Only few Atayal can play the traditional mouth harp. You can do that.
{***baq*** / # ***thuzyay***}=saku' tlubuw.
ABIL.AV=1SG.ABS play.AV
'I can play the mouth harp.'
Comments for *thuzyay*: "You are old, but you are able to play the mouth harp."; "You know how to play, but you were sick and could not play."

(20) Constructed context: You are talking about who can lift that big rock. You know Tali' has big muscles.
musa'=nya' {# ***baq-un*** / ***thyay-un***} l<m>ayliq.
FUT=3SG.ERG ABIL-PV lift<AV>
'He is able to lift that rock.'
Comments for *baqun*: "Lifting a rock doesn't need any skills."; "An excavator can lift a rock."

Nevertheless, unlike ability modals in other languages (e.g., German *kennen* and *können*, de Haan (2006: 61)), the Atayal ability modals have uses that extend beyond internal enabling conditions in the agent; this has not been documented in the literature. The contexts in (21)–(22) do not concern the mind or body of the addressee but rather (different) circumstances that allow the event of getting up and playing outside to happen:[11]

(21) Constructed context: You worked overtime last night. Your mother knocks on your door the next day:
{***p-qbaq*** / # ***p-thuyay***}=su' m-tuliq?
FUT.AV-ABIL=2SG.ABS AV-get.up
'Can you get up?'

---

11 Interestingly, the context of (22) was originally designed for a deontic interpretation (i.e., as the mother's permission to Mary), but the consultant seems to perceive the context, through his spontaneously re-telling of the story, as a circumstantial condition – namely, Mary's fulfilling all her chores, instead of as a permission. While I didn't have a chance to check whether the deontic modal *nway* is felicitous in this context, in a similar context with a permission but without a circumstantial condition as built in the story, in (i), *nway* is felicitous and *thuzyay* is not.

(i) Volunteered context: I allow you to pass through my land (as it is a faster route for you) and you want to confirm my intention:
{***nway*** / # ***thuyay***}=saku' m-wah s-qani maha=su'?
DEON.POS / ABIL.AV=1SG.ABS AV-come LOC-here say=2SG.ABS
'Did you say I can go from here?'

(22) Context: Mary can't go out to play until she has done her three chores. She finishes the chores. Her mother says: (elicited based on 'Chore girl', TFS Working Group 2011a).
musa'=su'   **thuzyay**   m-usa'   g<m>naw   la.
FUT=2SG.ABS   ABIL.AV   AV-go   <AV>play   COS
'You can go to play now.'

Moreover, these modals are found to be interchangeable in the scope of negation; for example, they are both accepted in (23), where the context has to do with the absence of a physical condition of the subject.

(23) Context: Mary finally finishes all of her chores. Her friends come to ask her out. But she says, "I broke my leg so ..." (elicited based on 'Chore girl', TFS Working Group 2011a)
iyat=saku'   {*qbaq*   /*p-thuzyay*}   m-usa'   g<m>naw   la.
NEG=1SG.ABS   ABIL.AV   /FUT.AV-ABIL   AV-go   play<AV>   COS
'I can't go to play now.'

To sum up, the elicited data demonstrate that all the modals in Atayal lexically distinguish between epistemic and circumstantial modal flavor and between necessity and possibility. The proposed modality system is sketched in Table 2.[12]

Table 2: An overview of Atayal modality system.

flavor / strength	epistemic	circumstantial		
		deontic	teleological	bouletic	empty
necessity	–		si ki		
possibility	ki'a; hazi'	nway		blaq	

4.2 Lack of epistemic necessity modals

Different kinds of evidence suggest that there are no modal elements in the realm of epistemic necessity. Firstly, the epistemic modals *ki'a* and *hazi'* are not offered in contexts of epistemic necessity; instead, a non-modal assertion is volunteered, as in (24) and (25a) (with the emphatic adverb *balay* 'really, truly') (see also (26),

---

[12] This table does not include two ability modals because the strength of ability modality is a complicated issue (see e.g., Xie 2012), which I will not pursue here.

(27a), and (28a) below). In other cases, the periphrastic phrase *si baqi sa* 'it is known that, it is for sure that' is used, as in (25b), but unlike a modal expression, this phrase is composed of a factive verb, which presupposes the truth of the embedded complement.

(24) Constructed context: You just arrive home and find that the chicken you had cooked before is gone. As far as you know, only Tali' has been at home, so you think, "Tali' must have taken it."
 wal gal-un ni Tali'.
 PFV.PRF take-PV ERG Tali'
 'Tali' took it.'
 Volunteered Mandarin translation: *Kěndìng shì Tali' tōu de.* 'It *must* be Tali' who took it.' [emphasis mine]

(25) Constructed context: You know that if Temu' is at home, his light is always on, and if he's out the light is off. You see the light on tonight, so "Temu' must be home."
 a. cyux m-aki' ngasal balay Temu' hya'.
  PROG.DIST AV-exist house truly Temu' EMP
  'Temu' is truly at home.'
 b. **si baq-i sa** cyux m-aki' ngasal
  PRT know-PV.DEP LOC PROG.DIST AV-exist house
  Temu' hya'.
  Temu' EMP
  'It is known that Temu' is at home.'

A relevant observation is that when the speakers translate these Atayal response utterances back into Mandarin, they use a Mandarin necessity modal, and this saliently contrasts with a weaker translation they offer in the presence of *ki'a* or *hazi'* (with a Mandarin possibility modal); for example, compare the translation in (24) and the comment in (28b).

Most importantly, *ki'a* and *hazi'* are judged infelicitous in necessity contexts. The context for (26) is extracted from the storyboard 'On the Lam', in which the policeman's inference entails the truth of the proposition, given that behind the curtain is the only possible hiding place in the cabin. Against this context, one speaker firmly rejected the modal *ki'a*, as in (26a); the other speaker first offered the modal *hazi'* when he told the story, but upon reviewing the story, he suggested retracting *hazi'*, and hence *hazi'* is also marked as infelicitous in (26b). A possible explanation for *hazi'* being produced in this story is that the speaker might have narrated the story by considering the ending of the story that the protagonists actually jump outside the cabin – hence behind the curtain is no longer a necessity context (see Kolagar and Vander Klok, this volume).

(26) Context: The police follow Tali' and Rimuy to the cottage. There are only three possible hiding places in the cabin. The policeman says, "They can't be hiding in the box because it's too small. And they can't be hiding under the bed because it's too low. They must be behind that curtain." (elicited based on 'On the Lam', TFS Working Group 2011b)

    a. *(# **ki'a**)*   *cyux*   *tlqing*   *suruw*   *na*   *pala*
        EPIST.POS   PROG.DIST   hide.AV   back   GEN   cloth
        qniway   *tubung*
        cover   window
        'They are hiding behind the curtain.'

    b. *(# **hazi'**)*   *cyux*   *tlqing*   *suruw*   *na*   *katen.*
        EPIST.POS   PROG.PROX   hide.AV   back   GEN   curtain
        'They are hiding behind the curtain.'

Similarly, the contexts in (27) and (28) are all set for epistemic necessity, and the presence of *ki'a* and *hazi'* either results in direct rejection, or a comment that they are equivalent to a weak modal (in Mandarin).

(27) Constructed context: Your neighbor kid played the whole day without doing his homework. Now he is trying to catch up, but you know his mom is coming back, and she's very strict . . .

    a. *musa'*   *ks'ang-un*   *ni*   *yaya'=nya'*   *la.*
        FUT   scold-PV   ERG   mother=3SG.GEN   COS
        'He will be scolded by his mother.'

    b. {# ***ki'a***   *musa'*   / # *musa'*   ***hazi'***}   *ks'ang-un*   *ni*
        EPIST.POS   FUT   FUT   EPIST.POS   scold-PV   ERG
        yaya'=nya'   *la.*
        mother=3SG.GEN   COS
        'He might be scolded by his mother.'
        Comment: "That means that (if he does something) he *might* be scolded by his mom." [emphasis mine]

(28) Constructed context: You have a persimmon farm and you know in one more month your persimmons will be able to be harvested.
    a.   *atu'*   *qutux*   *byacing*   *lga,*   *p-huqil*   *qu*
        area   one   month   COS.TOP   FUT.AV-die   ABS
        qapu'   *la.*
        persimmon   COS
        'After one month, the persimmons will be ripe.'
        Comment: "You are very sure. How do you know? It's you who planted them and have been taking care of them."
    b. # *atu'*   *qutux*   *byacing*   *lga,*   { ***ki'a*** / ***hazi'*** }   *musa'*
        area   one   month   COS.TOP   EPIST.POS   FUT
        m-huqil   *qu*   *qapu'*   *la.*
        AV-die   ABS   persimmon   COS
        'After one month, the persimmons might be ripe.'
        Comment: "*hazi'* and *ki'a* say that they *might* be ripe after one month." [emphasis mine]

Ideally, to show that *ki'a* and *hazi'* are genuinely non-necessity modals is to show that they are unambiguous possibility modals in downward-entailing contexts (see Deal 2011), but unfortunately, the two modals do not (syntactically or semantically) fall under the scope of sentential negations and other tests are not available for now. To express epistemic impossibility, the speaker simply removes the modal:

(29) Constructed context (continued from (24)): You tell Temu' your reasoning but Temu' thinks Tali' is not the person who would do this: "It can't be Tali'."
    iyat   (*hazi /**ki'a*)   *Tali'*   *wal*   *m-agal.*
    NEG   EPIST.POS   Tali'   PFV.PRF   AV-take
    'It's not Tali' who took it.'

Consider now whether the other modals allow epistemic necessity uses. While the circumstantial modal *si ki* is demonstrated to be a necessity modal, as shown by the fact that conjoining two *si ki* claims results in a contradiction, as in (30) (assuming leaving is synonymous with not staying), it does not allow an epistemic flavor, as in (31).[13]

---

[13] *Si ki* is future-oriented and does not 'scope over'; see Chen et al. (2017).

(30) # **si ki**   m-aki'   kya'   ga,   **si ki**   pyar-an   uzi.
     CIRC.NEC AV-live there TOP   CIRC.NEC escape-LV also
     'You must stay here, but you must also leave.'
     Comment: "Do you think this makes sense?"

(31) Constructed context: Last week a few people forgot to bring their own chopsticks for lunch and were punished, so I think no one will forget to bring them this time:
     {# **si ki** / musa'} m-aras   nanak   q~qway   kwara'=naha'
     CIRC.NEC   FUT   AV-bring self   PL~chopsticks all=3PL.GEN
     mnxal   qani.
     one.time   this
     'Everyone will bring their own chopsticks.'

The circumstantial modals *nway* and *blaq* are never volunteered in contexts of necessity. In contrast to *si ki*, when employing the conjunction test, the propositions '*nway* φ and *nway* ¬φ' and '*blaq* φ and *blaq* ¬φ' are both felicitous, as shown in (32). Hence, these modals can be demonstrated to be possibility modals.

(32) a. **nway**=su'   m-aki   kya'   uzi   ga,
        DEON.POS=2SG.ABS   AV-live   there   also TOP
        nway=su'   pyar-an   uzi.
        DEON.POS=2SG.ABS   escape-LV also
        'You can stay here, but you can also leave.'

     b. **blaq**   m-aki   kya'   uzi   ga,   **blaq**   pyaran   uzi.
        CIRC.POS   AV-live there also TOP   CIRC.POS   escape-LV also
        'You can stay here, but you can also leave.'

I conclude that Atayal lacks an epistemic necessity modal, and its two epistemic possibility modals *ki'a* and *hazi'* do not strengthen to fill this gap (that is, they are unambiguous possibility modals); neither do the other modals cross-cut epistemic uses (that is, *si ki*, *nway*, and *blaq* are all circumstantial modals).[14,15] Another lan-

---

[14] However, I suggest that plain non-modal utterances can form a strong scalemate with *ki'a* and *hazi'* on a Horn-scale. I analyze these epistemic modals as possibility modals with a scalar implicature – they mean 'possible and not necessary' – based on the fact that they do not express universal readings in non-downward entailing contexts.

[15] The lack of epistemic necessity modals seems to hold in Mayrinax Atayal as well (Cheng 2013: 99).

guage that lacks epistemic necessity modals is Tlingit, as reported by Cable (2017), but unlike Tlingit, which exhibits a paucity of grammaticalized modal expressions, Atayal possesses an array of modal auxiliaries and verbs, but just not for epistemic necessity. See also Deal (2011) on the lack of strength contrast in the realm of circumstantial modality in Nez Perce. The possibility of having a paradigmatic gap in modal systems, especially within the same flavor of modality, allows the picture of typological variation to be shaped. The finding of the Atayal modal system points to a hypothesis that modals without duals may stay weak and this opens many more possible ways in which modal systems can be organized in languages.

5 Atayal modality based on textual examination

The discussion in this section is based on an examination of 90 instances of seven modals in two corpora, Yupas and Yuqih (1991) and Rau (1992); the former contains 20 texts from Squliq dialects spoken in Hsinchu County, while the latter contains nine texts from Wulai Squliq (see section 3 for other details). Table 3 calculates the total number of instances of each modal in these two corpora, as well as the frequency of each modal over the 90 instances.[16] Note that the numbers of the modal occurrences in Yupas and Yuqih are much higher than those in Rau, as the overall size of Yupas and Yuqih is comparatively larger.

Table 3: Occurrences of seven modals in two corpora.

	ki'a 'EPIST. POS'	hazi' 'EPIST. POS'	si ki/si ga 'CIRC. NEC'	nway 'DEON.POS'	blaq 'CIRC.POS'	baq 'ABIL'	thuyay 'ABIL'
Yupas & Yuqih (1991)	30	13	8 (si ki)	2	0	9	14
Rau (1992)	0	4	5 (si ga)	0	0	2	3
total instance	30	17	13	2	0	11	17
frequency	33.3%	18.9%	14.4%	2.2%	0%	12.2%	18.9%

---

16 There are no instances of *ki'a* in the texts from Rau (1992), and *si ki* and *si ga* are only used in one of the texts; these are likely due to dialectal variation. The numbers given for *nway*, *blaq*, and *baq* have excluded clear non-modal uses, such as 'alright, no problem' for *nway*, 'good' and 'like' for *blaq*, and 'know' for *baq*; there are no modal uses of *blaq* in either corpus.

In this section, I focus on how the textual data inform us of the lexical specification of each modal and of the proposed absence of epistemic necessity modals. The context of the extracted data is directly taken from, or a summary of, the texts surrounding or developing up to the modal sentence, and is presented in a way for the reader to sufficiently understand the modal use.

I briefly discuss in section 6 other uses of the modals observed in the texts as well as other areas of modality that are worth further research. Section 6 also gives a thorough comparison of the results drawn from the textual data to those in contextual elicitation (section 4).

5.1 Epistemic modality

Evidence for the epistemic use of *ki'a* and *hazi'* in the two texts comes from contexts which imply that the speaker is making an inference in view of her/his knowledge or available evidence. Two examples are given here: in (33), the narrator explains why a woman acted in a greedy way; in (34), the narrator explains where the name *mksingut* comes from by what she/he heard about the height of the people.[17]

(33) Context: In old times, the Atayal people were sufficiently fed by cultivating a grain of millet in a year, and even wild animals would strive to sacrifice their tails to satisfy people's appetites. However, a lady was so greedy as to cut a big portion of a deer; maybe she covets meat very much. Since then, people had to hunt animals for food.

ki'a   *m-s-qawlu*   *iyal*   *lru*   *si=nya*
EPIST.POS   AV-VBZR-neck   very.much   COS.CONJ   PRT=3SG.ERG
qap-iy   *krahu*   *qu*   *papak*   *na*   *bqanux.*
cut.off-PV.DEP   big   ABS   ear   GEN   deer
'Maybe she covets meat very much, so she cuts off a big portion of the deer's ear.'
(Yuqih and Yupas 1991: 20)

---

[17] The modal *hazi'* is transcribed as *haziy* in Yupas and Yuqih (1991). I retain the original transcription when citing their examples but refer to the modal as *hazi'* in my discussion.

(34) Context: There was a special group of people, whom the Atayal call 'mksingut'. Where does this name come from? Maybe their height was very short, like a dwarf. When they stand up, their height would be like that of a *singut* 'pigeon pea'.

haziy	anan	na	rrawq	qu	in-rkyas-an=nha.
EPIST.POS	OBL		short.AV	ABS	E.PST-grow-LV=3PL.GEN

'Maybe their height was very short (like a dwarf).'
(Yuqih and Yupas 1991: 32)

Yet as illustrated in section 3.1, only data showing that *ki'a* and *hazi'* are incompatible with a subtype of circumstantial modality allow us to draw the definitive conclusion that they are unambiguous epistemic modals. Such collections of negative evidence are, however, not possible with natural texts. In the two texts examined, there are no occurrences of *ki'a* and *hazi'* statements with a deontic, bouletic, or teleological modality reading, but the non-occurrence does not entail that these modals cannot be used in a circumstantial context. (Conversely, a similar reasoning holds for the testing of non-epistemic modality of the remaining modals; see section 5.2.)

Regarding the strength of *ki'a* and *hazi'*, the textual data suggest the seemingly opposite result from what is concluded in section 4.2 (i.e., that they are unambiguously existential). However, I will argue that this result hinges on the translations provided with the texts, which may include target modal sentences, and thus are not adequate evidence for judging modal strength. The overall generalization can be stated as follows. There are a few instances of the modals being clearly interpreted as expressing a possibility claim with the discourse (19% for *ki'a* and 12.5% for *hazi'*; see Table 4 below); this is illustrated in (35)–(36). Many other instances receive a modal translation but the discourse in which they are situated is ambiguous – it can imply either a possibility or a non-modal interpretation (38.1% for *ki'a* and 31.3% for *hazi'*); this is illustrated in (37)–(38). In the remaining instances, they are understood as non-modalized claims without a clear modal context or translation (42.9% for *ki'a* and 56.2% for *hazi'*), as in (39)–(41).

In (35), as the story between the mother and daughter develops, the hunting team is approaching home, but the daughter cannot know their exact location. Similarly, in (36), the bear catching event is only inferred from the father's dream. In these two examples, discourse context plays a decisive role for the possibility strength of the modals, with the relevant sentence being translated with or without a possibility modal (in Mandarin): (35) has an existential modal, while (36) uses an attitude verb of an epistemic nature 'think'.

(35) Context: A daughter asks her mother for adornments to receive her father from head-hunting, but the mother keeps breaking her word even though the daughter has done the various chores that the mother has asked her to do. As the time of her father's return is approaching, the daughter says to the mother, "Please do not lie to me anymore and give me the adornments because..."
ki'a   nyux   zik   ngasal   qu   yaba'   la...
EPIST.POS PROG.PROX inside   house   ABS   father   COS
'Father might have been down the tribe...'
(Yuqih and Yupas 1991: 62)

(36) Context: Piray wants to bring his son to the mountain in order to train him not to be timid. He tells his son that he dreamed the night before that he had caught a bear:
haziy=maku'   cyux   triq-un   qu   qsinuw   bnkis   la...
EPIST.POS=1SG.ERG   PROG.DIST   steal-PV   ABS   wild   old   COS
'I think I have caught a wild bear...'
(Yuqih and Yupas 1991: 106)

By contrast, (37) and (38) contain a possibility modal in their original (Mandarin) translation but the discourse context does *not* favor a possibility or necessity interpretation. For instance, the reader may understand (37) in such a way that the hunting team walks exactly a whole day to get to the field, and in (38), it would make sense for the parrotbill to simply say that he should be the auger (without a possibility modal) after winning the competition.

(37) Context: A person named Yekliy runs very fast. One day he goes hunting with his tribe...
ki'a   qutux   ryax   pin-hkngy-an=nha   lga
EPIST.POS   one   day   NMLZ-walk-LV=3PL.ERG   COS.TOP
tehuk   squ   qzyunam...
arrive.AV   OBL   hunting.ground
'Their walking perhaps takes a whole day, and they arrive at the hunting ground.'
(Yuqih and Yupas 1991: 48)

(38) Context: In old days, the Atayal people are looking for an auger to judge good or bad things for them. When meeting by the river, they run into a crow and a siliq (i.e., parrotbill). The crow asks to compete with the siliq to be the Atayal auger. Surprisingly, the siliq easily beats the crow by lifting a giant stone and carrying it across the river. The siliq turns around and says to the Atayal people:

haziy	na	musa	kuzing	qu	gal-an=mamu
EPIST.POS	OBL	FUT	1SG.N	ABS	take-LV=2PL.ERG

squ	sspng-an	lwah ...
OBL	measure-LV	COS.PRT

'Maybe I ought to be your auger ...'
(Yuqih and Yupas 1991: 28)

There are also examples like (39)–(41), where neither the discourse context nor the translation provides a clue as to the strength of the modals: the contexts are all narrative and *ki'a* and *hazi'* are translated as a plain, non-modal claim.

(39) Context: Yekliy runs very fast. He volunteers to be a trumpeter for other hunters to locate prey. When the hunting stretches to the second ravine, he shouts and other hunters shout back ...

si	kta'	qu	b~bqanux	**ki'a**	m-nkux	lru
PRT	see.AV.DEP	ABS	PL~deer	EPIST.POS	AV-panic	COS.CONJ

wayal	memaw	m-bukut	m-gyay ...
PRF.PFV	so.that	AV-hump	AV-escape

'The deer get into a panic. They run away with a hump ...'
(Yuqih and Yupas 1991: 48)

(40) Context: (part of the contextual description in (39))

ki'a	qutux	uruw	qu	q<in>lup-an=nha	lmga ...
EPIST.POS	one	ravine	ABS	hunt<E.PST>-LV=3PL.ERG	COS.REP.TOP

'When the hunting stretches to the second ravine ...'
(Yuqih and Yupas 1991: 48)

(41) Context: One day, a giant stone cracks, and two men and a woman walk out of the stone. The world is full of cliffs and trees and the only living being is animals. One of the men feels it is meaningless to live in such a world and returns to the stone. After living in this world for a long time, the other man and the woman decide to find a way to give birth to their children.

bsyaq **haziy** mqyanux squ babaw cinbwanan qu r~rusa
long EPIST.POS live.AV OBL above world ABS PL-two
squliq qasa mga ...
people that REP.TOP
'After they live in this world for a long time, ...'
(Yuqih and Yupas 1991: 10)

Table 4 summarizes these three patterns numerically. I have excluded one instance where both modals co-occur, as in (42), for the reason that it is unclear whether the existential strength arises due to *ki'a* or *hazi*'; I have also excluded eight instances where *ki'a* modifies a *wh*-word and gives rise to a conjectural question (cf. Little, Matthewson, and Peterson 2010).[18] To illustrate, among the remaining 21 instances of *ki'a*, four of them can be classified as existential by their surrounding discourse context (as in (35)), eight of them by translation *alone* (as in (37)), and nine of them which lack either of the indications (as in (39) and (40)) are labeled as *non-modal*.

Table 4: Atayal epistemic modals in the texts.

	ki'a 'EPIST.POS'	*hazi*' 'EPIST.POS'
ki'a and *hazi* co-occur	1	1
conjectural question	8	0
w/ existential context	4 out of 21 (19%)	2 out of 16 (12.5%)
w/ existential translation	8 out of 21 (38.1%)	5 out of 16 (31.3%)
non-modal	9 out of 21 (42.9%)	9 out of 16 (56.2%)
total number	30	17

---

18 One example is given in (i); two other *wh*-words that occur with *ki'a* in the texts are *ki'a pira ryax* 'I wonder how many days' and *ki'a pira byacing* 'I wonder how many months'. This use is not found with *hazi*' in the texts.

(i) **ki'a mha nanu,** m-uwah sa qutux ryax qu sunu la.
    EPIST.POS how AV-come LOC one day ABS flood COS
    'Unknowingly (lit. I don't know how), the flood came one day.'
    (Yuqih and Yupas 1991: 15)

(42) Context: The world was originally a flat without any cliffs and valleys. One day, a big flood comes. The vast expanse of water forces people to go up to the top of the highest mountain. Considering that the flood signals God's word, they throw a bad person into the water, but the water does not fade. They wonder:

ki'a haziy nyux t'uqu nqu psqrg-an=ta
EPIST.POS PROG.PROX get.mad.AV OBL prank-LV=1PL.INCL
yaqih na squliq la?
bad.AV GEN person COS
'Maybe God is mad with us throwing Him a bad person?'
(Yuqih and Yupas 1991: 15)

What do the spontaneous textual data tell us about the strength of *ki'a* and *hazi'*? Data with an unambiguous discourse context, like (35) and (36), provide clear evidence that the modals *can* express possibility. We are then left with two hypotheses: either (i) these modals are possibility modals, or (ii) they are ambiguous and can indicate possibility or necessity (like e.g., St'át'imcets modals, Rullmann, Matthewson, and Davis 2008). One may suppose that the occurrences of *ki'a* and *hazi'* that are grouped under non-modals in Table 4, constituting nearly half or half the corpus data, encode necessity strength on the basis of the following reasoning: the contexts appear to call for a non-modal assertion (as in (39)–(41)), and the truth of a non-modal assertion entails that of a *must*-assertion (i.e., φ entails *must* φ) (see e.g., Kratzer 1981: 56–57).[19]

However, the understanding of the discourse contexts as non-modal assertions relies largely on the translations provided with the sentences containing *ki'a* and *hazi'*. For example, the context of (39) could have been understood as describing the reason why deer run away – that they are possibly scared by the hunters' shouts – had the translation contained a possibility modal. Such a reinterpretation can also apply to (40) and (41): it could have been the case that the narrator estimates when Yekliy shouts in (40) and how long the couple live alone in the world without other human beings in (41).[20] That means that the non-modal data are just like those with an existential translation alone (such as (37) and (38)) in lacking an unambiguous context for testing the strength of *ki'a* and *hazi'*. In other words, the majority of the textual data is insufficient for distinguishing between the different hypotheses.

A search of the necessity contexts in the texts also shows that there is a lack of evidence for knowing whether *ki'a* and *hazi'* express necessity. For example, (43)

---
[19] The entailment direction is not without debate (see e.g., von Fintel and Gillies 2010).
[20] Interestingly, a translation with an epistemic possibility modal would be more natural in these examples than one with a necessity modal.

and (44) are excerpts from a story in Yuqih and Yupas (1991) which details how the Atayal chief Buta defeats the enemy; in (43), the discourse in which Buta easily shoots the enemy chief's brother and then the enemy chief draws a reasonable conclusion as to why the enemy is frightened and runs away, whereas in (44), Buta is confident that all the Atayal tribe leaders will find the places he has captured, given that he has conquered the plains of the rivers from the north to the middle of Taiwan and has put a mark in those places. In both examples, neither of the modals *ki'a* and *hazi'* occurs, even though the Mandarin translations contain a necessity modal. However, we don't know whether the modals happen not to be used or they cannot express necessity. Note that the search process goes through the whole story of the narrative texts but does not merely depend on the translations of the texts.

(43) Context: In a fight with the Sinkhmayun people, the Atayal chief Buta shoots their chief, Obing Bilaq.[21] Having witnessed that their chief is killed in a blink of an eye, the rest of the Sinkhmayu people flee ...

...gi baq-un=nha mha ini tring-iy qu
because know-PV=1PL.ERG CMP NEG touch-PV.DEP ABS
mrhuw na Tayal ka lk-Buta qasa.
sage GEN Atayal REL former-Buta this

'... because they must know chief Buta's majesty (lit. that he is not touchable).'
(Yuqih and Yupas 1991: 90)

(44) Context (continued from (43)): The chief Buta leads the Atayal soldiers to defeat the Sinkhmayun people and conquer the plain areas of northern Taiwan. After the battle, Buta gathers all the leaders of the Atayal tribes and tells them, "Let's send our people to cultivate every place where the rivers run through ..."

musa=simu kya ga, k~kt-an=mamu qu
go.AV=2PL.ABS there TOP FUT~see-LV=2PL.ERG ABS
s<in>bil-an=maku phngu pneluq ru m-ucing
leave<E.PST>-LV=1SG.ERG tick arrow CONJ AV-follow
kya k<in>wag-an=mu.
there sweep<E.PST>-LV=1SG.ERG

'When you arrive there, you will definitely see the arrows and knives I have left, and you can find the places I captured.'
(Yuqih and Yupas 1991: 91)

---

21 Sinkhmayun refers to Ketagalan, which is one of tribes from the Plains.

Summarizing thus far, the examination of two spontaneously produced texts has shown that we do not draw equally clear evidence for each possible interpretation of modality. While the textual data are very useful for providing data for available interpretations, they only make a suggestion when it comes to interpretations that are unavailable with a modal, and due to a reliance on translation, they may lead to the opposite conclusion (as in the case of non-modal translations provided with *ki'a/hazi'* assertions). The results are recapitulated in Table 5, and compared with the results of the elicitation data.

Table 5: Modal meaning of *ki'a* and *hazi'* using the two types of methods.

		textual data	elicitation data
flavor	epistemic	✓ (attested)	✓ (judged to be acceptable)
	circumstantial	? (not attested)	✗ (judged to be unacceptable)
strength	existential	✓ (attested)	✓ (judged to be acceptable)
	universal	? (not attested)	✗ (judged to be unacceptable)

5.2 Non-ability circumstantial modality

None of the occurrences of the modal *si ki/si ga* has an epistemic interpretation in the two texts; however, as with the epistemic modals, the non-occurrence in the texts does not lead to the conclusion that these modals have no epistemic uses.[22] In contrast, there is abundant evidence for *si ki/si ga* expressing subtypes of circumstantial modality. For example, (45) is deontic, saying that according to Atayal ethics, a marriage is only allowed for relatives beyond three generations; the conditional clause in (46) expresses the goal-oriented modality of *si ki*. There are less clear contexts of pure circumstantial modality; for example, (47) may be understood as our having night guards in every possible world which is consistent with the current status of the tribe members' safety.[23]

---

22 *Si ki* is transcribed as *siki or si ki* in Yuqih and Yupas (1991) and *si ga* is transcribed as *siga'* in Rau (1992). I retain the original transcription but refer to them as *si ki and si ga* in my discussion.

23 *Si ki/si ga* appears to lose its modal meaning in (i), where it follows the semantically-bleached *wh*-word *nanu'* 'what' (L. Huang 2008: 39) and together they indicate that the events advance. (Rau (1992) transcribes a word-final [l] sound that is neutralized to an [n] sound as N.)

(45) Context: A couple of brothers and sisters once slept together and had serious consequences. Since then, it has been regarded as taboo for relatives within three generations to marry.

siki	*msncyugal*	*p-<in>shriq-an*	*nqu*
CIRC.NEC	three.generations	CAUS-<E.PST>leave-LV	OBL

pintze'an	*na*	*tayal*	*lga,*	*m-'agal*	*ru*	*m-squn*
blood.relation	GEN	Atayal	COS.TOP	AV-take	CONJ	AV-unite

aring	*kya*	*la.*
start	there	COS

'Since then, only if the relation between Atayal people is beyond three generations, they can marry.'
(Yuqih and Yupas 1991: 85)

(46) Context: A story about how people are judged to go to Heaven after their death.

mha ni	*m-usa*	*squ*	*'tuxan*	*mga,*	**siki**
if	AV-go	OBL	heaven	REP.TOP	CIRC.NEC

krayas=su	*squ*	*hongu*	*na*	*utux*	*ma.*
past.AV=2SG.ABS	OBL	bridge	GEN	God	REP

'To go to Heaven, you need to walk across God's bridge.'
(Yuqih and Yupas 1991: 24)

(47) Context: An Atayal tribe was attacked one night, and many people were killed. The tribe members gather and discuss solutions. One suggests that young people take turns to guard the village at night, but another person replies, "The enemy may kill the guards first before they invade the village ..."

...nanu	*ana*	*ga*	**si ki**	*syan=ta*	*qu*	*pr'ra*	*hiya!*
then	even	TOP	CIRC.NEC	put.LV=1PL.INCL	ABS	guard	EMPH

'...in spite of this reason, we need to have the guards.'
(Yuqih and Yupas 1991: 79)

(i) Context: A woman was felling a tree and a bear came and grabbed her ...

mita'	*squ*	*kneriN*	*mga,*	**nanu' siga',**	*p-sliq-an*	*nqu*
see.AV	OBL	woman	REP.TOP	what	CAUS-be.tore-LV	OBL

lukus	*kneriN*	*mga*	*lru,*	**nanu' siga',**	*bbwax*	*qu*
clothes	woman	REP.TOP	COS.CONJ	what	be.naked	ABS

kneriN	*uzi*	*lpi.*
woman	also	COS.PRT

'When he saw the woman, he tore her clothes. And the woman became naked.'
(Rau 1992: 198)

All the discourses in the texts in which *si ki/si ga* occurs have universal strength. Take (45)–(47), for example: each will be true in all possible worlds consistent with the Atayal people's ethics surrounding marriage, the goal of going to Heaven, and the circumstances of the tribe's safety, namely that that you marry relatives beyond three generations, you walk across God's bridge, and we have the guards at night. However, we do not have data to falsify the hypothesis that *si ki/si ga* are existential, presumably because *si ki/si ga* are purely necessity modals (see section 4.2) and such data are unavailable in spontaneous speech.

There are only two modal examples of *nway* in the texts (and only in Yupas and Yuqih (1991)), as given in (48)–(49), and no modal examples of *blaq* in either of the texts (see fn. 16 for their non-modal uses); the poverty of modal uses of *nway* and *blaq* may be overcome by including more genres of text. Both discourse contexts in (48) and (49) are clearly deontic, where the speaker asks for the approval of the addressee to take a break and to stay at the place of origin. Again, as expected, there are no data in the texts showing that *nway* is *only* deontic (compared to (17) and (18) above).

(48) Context: A group of Atayal people return from visiting their family. They walk in the snow for more than two days and finally see their village. A female elder suggests that everyone take a rest since they are almost home:
*aki=ta   minsuna   cikay   ha,   **nway** . . .*
CF=1PL.INCL   breathe.AV a.bit   first DEON.POS
'Shall we take a break?' (lit. 'We could take a break.')
(Yuqih and Yupas 1991: 42)

(49) Context (continued from (44)): The Atayal chief Buta tells the leaders of the Atayal tribes to go to the plains areas that he conquered to expand the Atayal territory, and suggests that he and other soldiers stay at the place of origin.
***nway**=sami   si   giba   squ   pinsbkan   na*
DEON.POS=1PL.EXCL.ABS   PRT   hug.AV.DEP OBL   origin.place   GEN
mrhuw=ta   tayal   sami   hiya   la.
sage=1PL.INCL   Atayal   1PL.EXCL.N   EMPH   COS
'Let us (lit. we can) stay at the place where our elders originated.'
(Yuqih and Yupas 1991: 91)

5.3 Ability modality

The ability modals *baq* and *thuyay* are found to be compatible not only with internal (intellectual vs. physical) properties of the subject but also with circumstances that can be managed (in different ways) by the subject for the event to happen:

(50) Context: The Hakka people plan to take revenge on the Atayal people. They persuade the Saisiyat people to invite the Atayal for dinner. The Hakka promise that they will supply the Saisiyat with farm tools in return.
teta=simu **baq** *m-qumah qmayah.*
so.that=2PL.ABS ABIL.AV AV-cultivate land
'So that you can cultivate lands (with sufficient tools).'
(Yuqih and Yupas 1991: 73)

(51) Context: A guy called Halus has a giant penis and likes to harass women. Even if the door is closed, Halus can insert his penis through the window.
***thyay-an**=nya m-usa m-rawiy qu kneril ma.*
ABIL-LV=3SG.ERG AV-go AV-nasty ABS woman REP
'He can still molest the women inside the house.'
(Yuqih and Yupas 1991: 36)

An instance of mental ability modal *baq* found in the scope of negation seems to denote physical ability (i.e., the hotness of the stone makes it untouchable; compare (23)).

(52) *memaw mtalah ka ini* **baq-iy** *t<m>ring*
so.that AV-red REL NEG ABIL-PV.DEP touch<AV>
kin-mkilux qu btunux qasa la.
NMLZ-hot ABS stone that COS
'The stone becomes red and hot to the extent that it cannot be touched.'
(Yuqih and Yupas 1991: 36)

Lastly, the texts do not offer evidence for verifying if the ability modals allow for non-ability circumstantial modality, the result of which has been shown to be negative in contextual elicitation (see Chen (2018: 395–397); see also fn. 11 for the lack of a deontic interpretation in *thuzyay*).

6 A methodological comparison

I have explicitly compared elicited and textual data in terms of what they tell us about the lexical meaning of modals in Atayal. The elicited data show clearly that each modal has a fixed flavor and strength, as the use of the modal in other contexts is infelicitous, such as: the rejection of *ki'a* and *hazi'* with a circumstantial flavor and a universal strength, the rejection of *si ki/si ga* with an epistemic flavor and an existential strength, and the rejection of *nway* and *blaq* with an epistemic flavor and a universal strength. Unsurprisingly, these infelicitous uses are not attested in the texts, given that they are not meanings available with the modals and unavailable meaning would not be spontaneously produced. The chance of finding negative evidence would not be increased by enlarging the size of a corpus.

By contrast, the textual data serve well in providing positive evidence for the opposite of the above: the epistemic and possibility use of *ki'a* and *hazi'*, the different circumstantial flavors and the necessity use of *si ki/si ga*, as well as the extended meaning of *baq* and *thuyay* and the compatibility between *ki'a* and *hazi'* and the hearsay marker. (Note that the instances of *nway* and *blaq* in the texts are not significant, see Table 3 and section 5.2.)

The contrast highlights an essential methodological difference in that only elicited data supply negative evidence, while both elicited and textual data are comparable in terms of finding positive evidence. The question arises whether negative evidence is required for the understanding of modality and even other aspects of a language. With the goal of conducting a scientific study (instead of describing a collection of language data), I agree with Davis, Gillon, and Matthewson (2014) that negative evidence is crucial for verifying a hypothesis or distinguishing between hypotheses (see also Krifka 2011: 247). To illustrate with what we have seen about Atayal modality, if non-attestation were taken as evidence of impossibility, *blaq* would have no modal uses (which is false, see (8)–(10)). If the size (and/or the type) of a corpus mattered for (non-)attestation, to what extent would it be sufficient to conclude that *ki'a* and *hazi'* have no circumstantial flavor?

Another methodological point that is made clear through comparing elicited and textual data is that while texts have been considered to have rich discourse contexts, the contexts are often insufficient to disambiguate meaning. This is best shown by the examination of the strength of *ki'a* and *hazi'* in the texts, in which the majority data under scrutiny turn out to lack an unambiguous context and are not applicable in deciding their strength (section 5.1). The difficulty does not arise with contextualized elicitation, as contexts are purposely designed and controlled.

Contextualized elicitation also has the advantage of avoiding translation interference, given that target utterances are asked to be judged against a context rather than merely being translated. Translation is known to be unreliable in understanding truth-conditional meaning (Matthewson 2004; see also Krifka 2011); we have seen that the translations of some examples do not seem to convey the real interpretation of some of the modals shown. However, the comprehension of texts themselves largely depends on translations, as long as the researcher is not a (native) speaker of the research language. For example, as discussed above, exploring the strength of *ki'a* and *hazi'* in the texts is not successful because the modal sentences lack a clear context, the result of which would be subject exclusively to how one interprets the translations. A variable that accentuates the problem is that these texts (and perhaps many others) are not translated by the narrators themselves but by someone else – native speakers in Yupas and Yuqih (1991) and a linguist in Rau (1992) (see section 3).

What has not been compared so far is the fact that the texts reveal quite a few examples of phenomena that go beyond the focus on the modals' lexical meaning (e.g., fn. 18; fn. 23), synchronic non-modal uses of the modals (e.g., fn. 16), collocations with the modals, such as *hazi' anan na* in (34), and frequent co-occurrences of *hazi'* with adjective predicates (e.g., *bsyaq* 'for a long time' in (41)), and modal doubling (e.g., *ki'a* and *hazi* in (42)). Textual materials are also excellent tools for surveying facts of which the investigator has previously been unaware or largely ignorant; see e.g., Chelliah (2001: 156–157). Two salient cases that belong to modality but have been understudied in the Atayal literature are futurity and counterfactuality, many examples of which emerge in the texts. While none of these abovementioned phenomena come to my attention solely through examining the texts, the attestation in the texts sparks a lot of great questions that deserve further research.

Table 6 summarizes the comparison. It shows that a search for negative evidence in naturally occurring utterances is impossible, and the goal of having unambiguous contexts and avoiding the interference of translation is only met by chance, whereas all these tasks are feasible with contextual elicitation. Yet looking into a collection of texts is a more efficient way of being exposed to a wider range of phenomena; see Chelliah (2001: 254); see also Chelliah and Reuse (2011: 423) for how texts can be used along with elicitation.

Table 6: A comparison between elicited and textual data.

	contextual elicitation	spontaneous speech
provide positive evidence	yes	yes
provide negative evidence	yes	no
provide unambiguous contexts	yes	by chance
avoid translation interference	yes	by chance
explore phenomena	inferior	better

7 Concluding remarks

In this chapter, I have drawn theoretical and methodological conclusions by comparing the findings of studies on Atayal modality that used two different methods of collecting data—conducting contextualized elicitation and observing naturally occurring utterances. The theoretical conclusions are that all the Atayal modals have fixed quantificational strength as well as an epistemic or (subtype of) circumstantial flavor, and that the whole modal system is not organized in a symmetrical manner, in the sense that a paradigmatic gap exists.

Methodologically, although both contextualized elicitation and textual observation provide positive evidence for the available meaning of the modals (e.g., the existential interpretation of *ki'a*; the circumstantial interpretation of *si ki*), only contextualized elicitation is able to obtain infelicity judgments against a context. My examination of two textual collections reveals that non-attestation is not equivalent to infelicity, and even when attested in texts, a modal utterance being supplied with an unambiguous context relies on chance. The methodological asymmetry is independent of the fact that the texts are useful for providing many instances of modals and for discovering interesting or previously unaware phenomena, which may not have been uncovered easily with targeted elicitation, and that they are embedded by naturally produced discourse.

These pros and cons suggest that contextualized elicitation should be given priority over corpus-based studies and constitute the majority of fieldwork *for the purpose of linguistic analyses*. With controlled contexts, direct elicitation need not be used merely at the beginning of an investigation or as a last resort in filling data gaps (a position that has been noted before in the literature, e.g., Dixon 2010: 323; 327; Mosel 2012: 85).

References

Blust, Robert. 1999. Subgrouping, circularity and extinction: Some issues in Austronesian comparative linguistics. In Elizabeth Zeitoun & Paul Jen-kuei Li (eds.), *Selected papers from the 8th International Conference on Austronesian Linguistics*, 31–94. Taipei: Academia Sinica.

Burton, Strang & Lisa Matthewson. 2015. Targeted construction storyboards in semantic fieldwork. In M. Ryan Bochnak & Lisa Matthewson (eds.), *Methodologies in semantic fieldwork*, 135–156. New York: Oxford University Press.

Cable, Seth. 2017. The expression of modality in Tlingit: A paucity of grammatical devices. *International Journal of American Linguistics* 83 (4). 619–678.

Chelliah, Shobhana L. & Willem J. De Reuse. 2011. *Handbook of descriptive linguistic fieldwork*. Heidelberg: Springer.

Chelliah, Shobhana L. 2001. The role of text collection and elicitation in linguistic fieldwork. In Paul Newman & Martha Ratliff (eds.), *Linguistic fieldwork*, 152–165. Cambridge: Cambridge University Press.

Chen, Sihwei. 2013. The temporal interpretation of modals in Mandarin Chinese. In Alexis Black & Meagan Louie (eds.), *UBC Working Papers in Linguistics* 34, 15–30. Vancouver, BC: University of British Columbia.

Chen, Sihwei. 2014. The syntactic categories of adverbials in Atayal. In Zoe Lam & Natalie Weber (eds.), *UBC Working Papers in Linguistics* 38, 1–26. Vancouver, BC: University of British Columbia.

Chen, Sihwei. 2018. *Finding semantic building blocks: Temporal and modal interpretation in Atayal*. Vancouver, BC: University of British Columbia dissertation.

Chen, Sihwei, Vera Hohaus, Rebecca Laturnus, Meagan Louie, Lisa Matthewson, Hotze Rullmann, Ori Simchen, Claire K. Turner & Jozina Vander Klok. 2017. Past possibility cross-linguistically: Evidence from 12 languages. In Ana Arregui, Maria-Luisa Rivero & Andrés Salanova (eds.), *Modality across syntactic categories*, 235–287. Oxford: Oxford University Press.

Cheng, Yi-Yang. 2013. *Modality in Mayrinax Atayal*. Taipei: National Taiwan University MA thesis.

Davis, Henry, Carrie Gillon & Lisa Matthewson. 2014. How to investigate linguistic diversity: Lessons from the Pacific Northwest. *Language* 90 (4). 180–226.

Deal, Amy Rose. 2011. Modals without scales. *Language* 87 (3). 559–585.

Dixon, R. M. W. 2010. *Basic linguistic theory. Volume 1: methodology*. Oxford: Oxford University Press.

Egerod, Søren Christian. 1999 [1980]. *Atayal-English dictionary*, 2nd edn. Copenhagen: The Royal Danish Academy of Sciences and Letters.

von Fintel, Kai. 2006 [2005]. Modality and language. In Donald M. Borchert (ed.), *Encyclopedia of philosophy*, 2nd edn., Vol. 10, 20–27. Detroit: MacMillan Reference USA.

von Fintel, Kai & Anthony S. Gillies. 2010. Must . . . stay . . . strong! *Natural Language Semantics* 18 (4). 351–83.

de Haan, Ferdinand. 006. Typological approach to modality. In William Frawley (ed.), *The expression of modality*, 27–71. Berlin: Mouton de Gruyter.

Hsiao, Stella I-ling. 2004. *Adverbials in Squliq Atayal*. Taipei: National Tsing Hua University MA thesis.

Huang, Hui-chuan J. 2006. Resolving vowel clusters: A comparison of Isbukun Bunun and Squliq Atayal. *Language and Linguistics* 7 (1). 1–26.

Huang, Hui-chuan J. 2015. Syllable types in Bunun, Saisiyat, and Atayal. In Elizabeth Zeitoun, Stacy F. Teng & Joy J. Wu, (eds.), *New advances in Formosan linguistics*, 47–74. Asia-Pacific Linguistics.

Huang, Lillian M. 1993. *A study of Atayal syntax*. Taipei: Crane Publishing Co., Ltd.

Huang, Lillian M. 1994. Ergativity in Atayal. *Oceanic Linguistics* 33 (1). 129–143.

Huang, Lillian M. 1995. *A study of Mayrinax syntax*. Taipei: Crane Publishing Co., Ltd.

Huang, Lillian M. 2000a. *Taiyayu cankao yufa* [A reference grammar of Atayal]. Taipei: Yuanliu.

Huang, Lillian M. 2000b. Verb classification in Mayrinax Atayal. *Oceanic Linguistics* 39 (2). 364–390.

Huang, Lillian M. 2008. Grammaticalization in Squliq Atayal. *Concentric: Studies in Linguistics* 2. 1–46.

Huang, Lillian M. & Xin-Sheng Wu. 2016. *Introduction to Atayal grammar*, 1st edn. Formosan Language Series 2. Taipei: Council of Indigenous Peoples.

Kratzer, Angelika. 1981. The notional category of modality. In Hans-Jurgen Eikmeyer & Hannes Rieser (eds.), *Words, worlds, and contexts: New approaches in word semantics*, 38–74. Berlin: Mouton de Gruyter.

Kratzer, Angelika. 1991. Modality. In Armin von Stechow & Dieter Wunderlich (eds.), *Semantics: An international handbook of contemporary research*, 639–650. Berlin: Mouton de Gruyter.

Kratzer, Angelika. 2012. *Modals and conditionals*. Oxford: Oxford University Press.

Krifka, Manfred. 2011. Varieties of semantic evidence. In Claudia Maienborn, Klaus von Heusinger & Paul Portner (eds.), *Semantics: An international handbook of natural language meaning*, Vol. 1, 242–267. Berlin: Mouton de Gruyter.

Li, Paul Jen-kuei. 1980. The phonological rules of Atayal dialects. *Bulletin of the Institute of History and Philology, Academia Sinica* 51 (2). 349–405.

Li, Paul Jen-kuei. 1982. Male and female forms of speech in the Atayalic group. *Bulletin of the Institute of History and Philology, Academia Sinica* 53 (2). 265–304.

Li, Paul Jen-kuei. 1995. The case-marking system in Mayrinax Atayal. *Bulletin of the Institute of History and Philology, Academia Sinica* 66 (1). 23–52.

Little, Patrick, Lisa Matthewson & Tyler Peterson. 2010. On the semantics of conjectural questions. In Tyler Peterson & Uli Sauerland (eds.), *Evidence from evidentials*, 89–104. Vancouver: University of British Columbia Working Papers in Linguistics.

Matthewson, Lisa. 2004. On the methodology of semantic fieldwork. *International Journal of American Linguistics* 70 (4). 369–415.

Matthewson, Lisa. 2013. Gitksan modals. *International Journal of American Linguistics* 79 (3). 349–394.

Matthewson, Lisa. 2016. Modality. In Aloni Maria & Paul Dekker (eds.), *The Cambridge handbook of formal semantics*, 525–59. Cambridge University Press.

Mosel, Ulrike. 2012. Morphosyntactic analysis in the field: A guide to the guides. In Nicholas Thieberger (ed.), *The Oxford handbook of linguistic fieldwork*, 72–89. (Oxford Handbooks in Linguistics). Oxford: Oxford University Press.

Peterson, Tyler. 2010. *Epistemic modality and evidentiality in Gitksan at the semantics-pragmatics interface*. Vancouver, BC: University of British Columbia dissertation.

Pitay, Kagaw. 2014. *Modal constructions in R'uyan Atayal: A view from cartographic approach*. Taipei: National Tsing Hua University MA thesis.

Rau, Der-hwa Victoria. 1992. *A grammar of Atayal*. Ithaca, NY: Cornell University dissertation.

Rullmann, Hotze, Lisa Matthewson & Henry Davis. 2008. Modals as distributive indefinites. *Natural Language Semantics* 16 (4). 317–357.

TFS Working Group. 2011a. Chore Girl. (Totem Field Storyboards.) http://www.totemfieldstoryboards.org (accessed 9 June 2018).

TFS Working Group. 2011b. On the Lam. (Totem Field Storyboards.) http://www.totemfieldstoryboards.org (accessed 9 June 2018).

Xie, Zhiguo. 2012. The modal uses of *de* and temporal shifting in Mandarin Chinese. *Journal of East Asian Linguistics* 21 (4). 387–420.

Vander Klok, Jozina. 2013. Pure possibility and pure necessity modals in Paciran Javanese. *Oceanic Linguistics* 52 (2). 341–374.

Willett, Thomas. 1988. A cross-linguistic survey of the grammaticalization of evidentiality. *Studies in Language* 12 (1). 51–97.

Yuqih, To'aw & Atung Yupas. 1991. *Pin'aras ke' na bnkis Tayal* [Selected Atayal legendary stories]. Taipei: Promotion Committee of Native Languages, Presbyterian Christian Church.

Ana Lívia Agostinho & Núbia Ferreira Rech
8 Lessons from the field: Irrealis mood in Lung'Ie

Abstract: This chapter is organized into two parts. In the first one, we discuss methodologies for studying modality of underdescribed and endangered languages, focusing on Lung'Ie, a Portuguese-lexifier creole language spoken in São Tomé and Príncipe, located in the Gulf of Guinea. Initially, we present the social historical context of the emergence of this language and some issues regarding fieldwork. Then, we present the methods employed in this work for the study on modality: (i) storyboards and (ii) traditional stories, discussing the benefits and the drawbacks of these methods. In the second part of the chapter, we discuss the use of *ka* and its relation to tense, mood, and aspect categories in Lung'Ie. From the analyzed data, we find that *ka* appears in prototypical irrealis contexts, such as counterfactual, conditional, and hypothetical constructions, as well as constructions in the future tense and in the habitual aspect; while constructions in the past or at the moment of utterance show restrictions on the occurrence of *ka*. Based on these data, we propose that *ka* is an irrealis marker in Lung'Ie. Finally, we present some issues that need to be further investigated within the TMA system of Lung'Ie.

1 Introduction

Creole languages are rarely covered in volumes on mood and modality. This is evident in recent publications such as *The Routledge handbook of modality* (Bueno and Shalkowski 2020), *Mood* (Portner 2018), *Modality across syntactic categories* (Arregui, Rivero and Salanova 2017), and *Modality* (Portner

---

Acknowledgments: We would like to thank the Brazilian National Council for Scientific and Technological Development – CNPq (grants #200519/2019-0 to Ana Lívia Agostinho and #424025/2016-7 to Núbia Ferreira Rech) and the Graduate Program in Linguistics from Universidade Federal de Santa Catarina for their financial support.

Ana Lívia Agostinho, Universidade Federal de Santa Catarina, Florianópolis, Brazil, e-mail: a.agostinho@ufsc.br, ORCID: https://orcid.org/0000-0002-2395-4961
Núbia Ferreira Rech, Universidade Federal de Santa Catarina, Florianópolis, Brazil, e-mail: nubiarech1971@gmail.com, ORCID: https://orcid.org/0000-0002-9278-2702

2009), among others, which do not mention any creole language; as well as *The Oxford handbook of modality and mood* (Nuyts and Auwera 2016) and *The expression of modality* (Klein and Levinson 2006), which allude to a single creole language.

Even in studies in the area of creolistics, "mood and modality remain the most neglected aspects of the study of creole TMA [tense – mood – aspect] systems" (Winford 2018: 203). Thus, we intend to contribute to the description and to a better understanding of the mood category in creole languages, focusing on Lung'Ie (ISO 639-3 code: pre), also known as Principense, an underdescribed and endangered creole language spoken in Príncipe Island, in São Tomé and Príncipe. This chapter has two objectives: (i) to discuss methodologies for collecting modality data in fieldwork with minority and underdescribed languages and (ii) to present a description and analysis of the functional item *ka* in Lung'Ie, based on its relationship with other categories that make up the TMA system.[1]

This chapter is organized into six sections. In section 2, we present the historical context of the emergence of Lung'Ie. In section 3, we present some of challenges we faced when studying modality in Lung'Ie. In section 4, we describe the methodology used for data collection. Section 5 details how the hypothesis we investigated in our research was constructed and verified, and section 6 presents our analysis. Finally, in section 7, we indicate some points that still need to be investigated with regard to the use of *ka* in Lung'Ie. We emphasize that the glosses and translations referring to the data of Agostinho (2009, 2010, 2015, 2016a) and Agostinho and Rech (2016) are ours. The glosses and translations of other authors were kept in their original versions.

2 Historical context

Lung'Ie [luŋgíɛ], literally 'language of Príncipe' or 'language of the Island', is a highly endangered Portuguese-lexifier creole language spoken in Príncipe Island, in São Tomé and Príncipe, a multilingual country located in the Gulf of Guinea. Its origin is linked to Portuguese exploration and the kidnapping and confinement of African populations from the 15th to the 19th century.

There are four autochthonous and genetically related creole languages in the Gulf of Guinea: Santome (or Forro) (ISO 639-3 code: cri), Angolar (aoa), Lung'Ie (pre), and Fa d'Ambô (fab) (Schuchardt 1889; Günther 1973; Ferraz 1979; Maurer

---

[1] See also Rech and Agostinho (in submission).

2009; Hagemeijer 2009; Agostinho 2015; Bandeira 2017). Currently, the first three are spoken in São Tomé and Príncipe, with the status of national languages; the latter is spoken on the islands of Annobón and Bioko, in Equatorial Guinea. The four languages, although related, are currently unintelligible to each other.

The islands of the Gulf of Guinea (Figure 1) were uninhabited before the arrival of the Portuguese in the late 15th century. According to Cardoso (2007), the islands of São Tomé and Príncipe were discovered by Portuguese navigators João de Santarém and Pedro Escobar, reaching São Tomé on December 21, 1470, and Príncipe on January 17, 1471.

Figure 1: The Gulf of Guinea.
Source: https://commons.wikimedia.org/wiki/File:Gulf_of_Guinea_(English).jpg

The occupation of São Tomé by the Portuguese, other Europeans, and enslaved people took place through an order of the Portuguese crown and began to be continuous in 1493 (Cardoso 2007). The island of São Tomé was the first to be populated, between the years 1480 and 1493. The islands of Príncipe and Annobón were populated by the Portuguese and enslaved Africans from São Tomé from 1500 and 1503, respectively. São Tomé Island was initially populated by enslaved people mainly from the Niger Delta, where Edoid languages are spoken, and later mainly from Congo and Angola (Caldeira 2008, 2013: 67–72; Seibert 2013: 66–67, 2014: 46), where languages of the Bantu group are spoken.

In this multilingual scenario, the Proto-Creole of the Gulf of Guinea (henceforth PGG) emerged from the contact between Portuguese and African populations during the 15th and 16th centuries in São Tomé (Bandeira 2017; Ferraz

1979; Hagemeijer 2011). After the formation of the PGG, from the beginning to the middle of the 16th century, the geographic separation of its speakers (cf. Bandeira 2017) contributed to the speciation that resulted in the four languages spoken today. In this sense, we consider that the enslaved people taken from São Tomé to Príncipe were already PGG speakers (Bandeira 2017).

Subsequently, a contingent of enslaved people from the Niger Delta region was directly relocated to Príncipe Island. At the same time, unlike São Tomé, Príncipe received a small number of prisoners from Bantu regions after the separation of PGG speakers (Hagemeijer 2011). Thus, the main African substrate of the PGG are the Niger Delta languages, particularly the Edoid languages, while the languages of the Bantu group played a secondary role (Hagemeijer 2011; see also Ladhams 2012; Agostinho, Araujo and Santos 2019).

3 Challenges for the study of modality in creole languages: The case of Lung'Ie

The Afro-Atlantic creoles are languages that emerged from the contact of typologically different languages in multilingual environments where there usually was a language from the politically and socially dominant group and several minority languages. Despite the fact that some creole languages have thousands of speakers, most still face a situation of minorization and are not, in general, used in basic education schools or media outlets.

Portuguese, which is the lexifier of PGG, has been the official language in São Tomé and Príncipe since 1975, the year of its independence, and is the mother tongue of most inhabitants. The 2011 census (INE 2012) states that around 98.4% of the population speak Portuguese. According to the 2011 census, 36.2% of the population speak Santome, 8.5% speak Kabuverdianu (a Portuguese-lexifier creole native to Cape Verde), 6.6% speak Angolar, and 1% Lung'Ie. The census does not provide data on bilingualism or multilingualism and does not define whether it is L1 or L2 (Araujo and Agostinho 2010).

Currently, the number of native speakers of Lung'Ie varies from 20 (Maurer 2009) to 200 (Agostinho 2015, 2016b), depending on the consideration of different levels of proficiency. Valkhoff (1966) mentioned having difficulty finding native speakers of the language as early as 1958. Günther (1973) points out that Lung'Ie already was in the process of extinction in the 70s, being replaced by Santome and Portuguese. According to Araujo and Agostinho (2010), media and schooling (post-independence phenomena) give Portuguese a prestige that cannot be rivaled, which implies a growing abandonment of the national languages. According to Agostinho, Bandeira, and Araujo (2016), in line with Crystal's (2000) typology, Lung'Ie can be categorized as a threatened language, due to the absence of children acquiring it as a first language; the attitude of the community, which has not for the most part sought to make regular use of Lung'Ie in all social circumstances; and, finally, the level of impact of other languages, especially Portuguese, the official language and most used in all social spheres, and Kabuverdianu, since there are many speakers descendent from the hired workers who arrived on the island at the end of the 19th and beginning of the 20th centuries. Currently, there are more native speakers of Kabuverdianu, including monolinguals, in Príncipe than native speakers of Lung'Ie (Agostinho 2015).

Regarding databases, there are the corpora of the *Centro de Linguística da Universidade de Lisboa*, available at http://alfclul.clul.ul.pt/CQPweb/, based on published texts and on fieldwork by several researchers. In addition, the Atlas of Pidgin and Creole Languages Structures, available at https://apics-online.info/, provides data and information on creole languages and other contact languages. These materials can be used as a guide for the study of modal items in Lung'Ie, but fieldwork was essential for advancing our studies on this topic. As the language does not have many native speakers, it is difficult to carry out fieldwork outside the community. According to Vaux et al. (2007: 5), fieldwork is obviously necessary for researchers who are not working with their mother tongue, as judgments on the grammaticality of data depend on the intuition of native speakers. The main benefit of conducting fieldwork is that it allows for varied data collection, the cross-checking of data with native speakers, and the possibility to document unique instances of language use and linguistic interaction with the speakers. Crystal (2000: 101) states that it is crucial for linguistic studies to rely on descriptions of minority languages – in this case, the creole languages of the Gulf of Guinea.

Currently, all Lung'Ie speakers are also Portuguese speakers, thus enabling Portuguese-speaking researchers to carry out fieldwork without needing a translator. A major challenge in the study of Lung'Ie and other endangered creole languages appears, however, to be the difficulty in finding native speakers. In addition, it is common to identify the influence of synchronous linguistic contact with Portuguese, the country's official language and a language that maintains the status of superstrate in the community to this day. It is possible to observe, for example, the influence of Portuguese in some synchronic phonological processes, such as syncope, depalatalization, and phonetic alternations (cf. Agostinho 2015). To avoid these hindrances, it is important to look for older speakers who have acquired Lung'Ie in childhood and who are still using this language in their family environment.

4 Research methodology

In this section, we detail the research methodology used in our study on modality in Lung'Ie, noting that it can be extended to the study of other undescribed creole languages with a low number of native speakers. We remark that two data collection methodologies were used at different times of the research:
i.   Specific storyboards for the understanding of modality
ii. Traditional oral narratives in the community

We detail, in section 4.1, how we applied the storyboards task to 4 (four) bilingual Lung'Ie-Portuguese participants, inhabitants of the island of Príncipe. In section 4.2, we present the methodology used to obtain traditional storytelling data through orality. Our data were transcribed according to the rules of the *Alfabeto Unificado para a Escrita das Línguas Nativas de São Tomé e Príncipe* (Unified Alphabet for Writing the Native Languages of São Tomé and Príncipe – ALUSTP, in Portuguese) (Pontífice et al. 2010) and the pedagogical method *Lung'Ie, lunge no: método para aprender lung'Ie* (Agostinho and Araujo 2021). The spelling of the data from other authors was left as in the original.

4.1 Storyboards

We chose to use storyboards since this resource employs visual language, thus reducing the interference of Portuguese (the researchers' language) in the collection of linguistic data, since the consultants, in our case, are Lung'Ie-Portuguese bilinguals. In our field trip, we used two storyboards: *Tom and Mittens* (TFS Working Group 2014) and *Chore Girl* (TFS Working Group 2011), the first for the detection of epistemic modality markers and the second for the detection of deontic modality markers (Agostinho and Rech 2016). The main criterion that guided our choice was that there were no elements in the plot of the storyboards that were foreign to the culture of the research participants' community, in our case, the inhabitants of Príncipe Island.

The images that make up the stories can be printed with or without the captions corresponding to the event illustrated in the image; the captions, if one chooses to print the image with them, are only available in English. We opted for the version without captions. After being printed, the images were pasted on cardboard, one for each frame. Before carrying out the fieldwork, we tested the activity, applying the experimental task to three students of the Portuguese Language course at the Universidade Federal de Santa Catarina, in Brazil.

During the fieldwork, the task was applied, separately, to four participants,[2] all Lung'Ie-Portuguese bilinguals. This was completed by the first author of this chapter. Before asking each of the participants to tell the story from the display of the images, all the images were shown in the correct sequence, so that they could understand the plot. The researcher then carried out a test round with some images to verify their comprehension of the activity and, immediately afterwards, she applied the task in its entirety, recording the narratives produced. For this kind of recording, we highlight the importance of using equipment[3] that ensures optimal sound quality, since tone may be relevant to the study of modality of the Gulf of Guinea languages, as argued by Hagemeijer (2011, 2013b) for Santome. In addition, a good audio recording is necessary to ensure the possibility of using the data in future studies in the field of phonetics and phonology, for example. Due to difficulties in conducting field research as well as the scarcity of data for research in creole languages, it is desirable that all collections carried out are properly recorded, translated, and glossed.

Even having selected stories that did not present cultural elements foreign to the participants, the task of telling stories from images produced unexpected data, such as the simple description of the images shown by the researcher, as illustrated in examples (1a) (Figure 2) and (1b) (Figure 3), taken from the story of participant SMN.[4]

(1) a. *Na nixi, no sa vê minu ugatu ũa ki minu mosu ũa.*
in here 1PL COP see child cat one with child boy one
'Here, we are seeing a kitten and a boy.' (Agostinho and Rech 2016)

b. *Dêpôji, na nixi bê no sa vê minu ugatu ũa suzu*
after in here also 1PL COP see child cat one dirty
kotokoto ki musuka na igbê sê sa zudya li, ê
IDEO with fly in body DEM COP hurt 3SG 3SG
suzu, ê sa suzu.
dirty 3SG COP dirty
'Then, here we are also seeing a very dirty kitten with flies on its body hurting it, it is dirty, it is dirty.' (Agostinho and Rech 2016)

---

2 Our consultants are identified in this chapter by the initials of their names. Three male consultants participated in this research: MS, SMN, and FP; and one female consultant: SGFP. All participants were over 50 years of age.
3 We used a Tascam DR-100 MK II recorder and a Shure WH20 microphone. The recordings were carried out on Príncipe Island in 2016.
4 The following abbreviations will be used in this chapter: 1,2,3 first, second and third person; COMPL complementizer; COP copula; COUNT counterfactual; DEM demonstrative; ENF emphatic; FUT future; HAB habitual; IDEO ideophone; INT interrogative; IRR irrealis; MOD modal; NEG negative; S subject; O direct object; PST past; PL plural; POSS possessive; PROG progressive; REL relative; SG singular; VAL validator. All glosses are from the original authors.

Figure 2: Slide 1 of *Tom and Mittens* by Matthew Rolka and Seth Cable (2014). Retrieved from http://totemfieldstoryboards.org/stories/tom_and_mittens/ on September 23, 2020.

Figure 3: Slide 2 of *Tom and Mittens* by Matthew Rolka and Seth Cable (2014). Retrieved from http://totemfieldstoryboards.org/stories/tom_and_mittens/ on September 23, 2020.

Considering that the researcher, before applying the task, showed all the images to each of the participants so that they could observe them in sequence and understand the plot of the visual narrative, it was not expected that a description of the images would be done in isolation, unrelated to the other events represented, such as the data illustrated above. We assume that these data resulted from the unfamiliarity of the participants with this type of task, as they are part of a culture in which traditional stories are passed on orally. Of the four research participants, three produced data similar to those illustrated in (1a) and (1b) at some point during the research.

In (2), we transcribe in full one of the stories in which the participant produced sentences with a narrative sequence (Agostinho and Rech 2016). These data correspond to the images of the *Tom and Mittens* storyboard (Rolka and Cable 2014), created for the detection of epistemic modality markers:

(2) a. *Mosu sê, mosu sê   ki   sa   nii, ê   txinha   ugatu*
       boy DEM   boy   DEM   REL COP here 3SG have.PST cat
    ŭa.
    one
    'This boy, this boy who is here, he had a cat.'

   b. *I   ugatu sê   tava   ki   igbê suzu, ê   tama*
      and cat   DEM   COP.PST REL body dirty 3SG taking
      banhu fa.
      bath   NEG
      'And this cat was dirty, he hadn't bathed.'

   c. *Mosu faa: "ugatu sê   **tê**   **di** tama banhu".*
      boy   say   cat   DEM   have   to   take bath
      'The boy said: "This cat has to take a bath."'

   d. *Depôji, ê   we buka ugatu pa   ê   da   ugatu banhu.*
      after   3SG go get   cat   to   3SG give cat   bath
      'Then he went to get the cat to bathe him.'

   e. *Ê   vê   ugatu fa.*
      3SG see cat   NEG
      'He didn't see the cat.'

   f. *Ê   lenta kaxi   pa   ê   we buka ugatu, ugatu xyê   na poto.*
      3SG enter house for 3SG go get   cat   cat   leave in door
      'He went into the house to look for the cat, the cat went out through the door.'

   g. *Ê   vya   lenta, pa   ê   kwê uê   pa   ê   buka ugatu, ê*
      3SG turn enter   to   3SG run eye to   3SG get   cat   3SG
      vê   têêxi bidan: bidan   ŭa   vêmê, bidan   ŭa
      see three container container one   red   container one
      amarelu i   bidan   ŭa   zulu.
      yellow   and container one   blue
      'He went back in to search, to look for the cat, he saw three containers: a red container, a yellow container and a blue container.'

   h. *Dêpôji, ê   fa a: "bon, avêzê ugatu sê   **ka** **po** sa*
      after   3SG say   well   maybe cat   DEM   IRR   can   COP
      na vêmê".
      in red
      'Then he said: "Well, maybe this cat could be in the red one."'

i. *Ê we vêmê sê, ê vê ugatu fa.*
   3SG go red DEM 3SG see cat NEG
   'He went to the red one and didn't see the cat.'

j. *Ê vya we kwê lala ê vê ugatu fa.*
   3SG turn go run there 3SG see cat NEG
   'He ran back there and didn't see the cat.'

k. *Ê we amarelu, pa ê kwê uê, ê vê ugatu fa.*
   3SG go yellow to 3SG run eye 3SG see cat NEG

l. *Ê vya we kwê ê vê ugatu fa.*
   3SG turn go run 3SG see cat NEG
   'He ran back again and didn't see the cat.'

m. *Dêpôji ê faa: "bon, kumi ugatu sê **ka po** sa nêli a"?*
   after 3SG say good where cat DEM IRR can COP in.3SG INT
   'Then he said: "Well, where can this cat be?"'

n. *Kwa ũa ki fika nii ê bidan zulu.*
   thing one REL stay here 3SG container blue
   'The one that is left here is the blue container.'

o. *Ugatu sê sa udentu bidan sê zulu.*
   cat DEM COP inside container DEM blue
   'This cat is inside this blue container.'

p. *Ora ê we ê vê ugatu na udentu bidan zulu*
   when 3SG go 3SG see cat in inside container blue
   i ê tama bidan sê vya ka kubi i ugatu
   and 3SG take container DEM turn face cover and cat
   tava udentu sê vya ê da ugatu banhu.
   COP.PST inside DEM turn 3SG give cat bath
   'When he went, he saw the cat inside the blue container, and he took that container and turned it upside down and the cat was inside it and he gave the cat a bath.'
   (Agostinho and Rech 2016)

Considering that the contexts presented in the *Tom and Mittens* storyboard (Rolka and Cable 2014) enable the production of items with variation in modal force, we were looking for expressions or grammatical strategies to express necessity and possibility. We found expressions of modality in (2c), (2h), and (2m), of the story transcribed above. The first modal item, *tê di* in (2c), can denote deontic necessity modality, while the last two in (2h) and (2m) can denote epistemic possibility modality. In the data from this story, as well as in the data from the other storyboards produced by the participants, we identified the presence of *ka* in sentences with the modals *po*, *podi* 'can', and *pudya* 'could, should', but not with the modal *tê di/tê ki* 'have to', as seen in (2c). This data drew our attention to this item (*ka*). We then proceeded to observe the use of *ka* in Lung'Ie data, consulting sentences and texts cited in the literature on this language (Günther 1973; Maurer 2009; Agostinho 2015).

Thus, we searched for systematicity in the use of *ka* in constructions with modal auxiliaries. The data we had access to, through consultation of Günther (1973), Maurer (2009), and Agostinho (2015), indicated that *ka* is used in modal contexts of possibility, but not necessity.

In the storyboard data, we observed that, in negative modal constructions, there was no occurrence of *ka*, as shown in examples (3a) and (3b) below:

(3) a. N   sa   po   xyê   fa   pokê   n   tê   xiivisu   di
       1SG COP   can   leave NEG   because 1SG have work   of
       fêzê.
       do
       'I can't leave because I have work to do.' (Agostinho and Rech 2016)

    b. N   ma   sa   podi   we   fô.
       1SG more   COP can   go   NEG.ENF
       'I can't go anymore.' (Agostinho and Rech 2016)

These data called our attention, in principle, for suggesting a restriction on the use of *ka* in modal constructions with a sentential negation operator (*fa*). According to Maurer (2009: 83–84), there is a relationship between *ka*, which appears in affirmative constructions, and *sa*, which takes place in negative constructions. Maurer (2009) does not explain how such forms would be related, whether or not they would be the same item with different phonological realizations.

Given this scenario, we directed our research to investigate the use of *ka* in modality contexts. Therefore, we needed to expand our query to language data that would allow the production of modal items, preferably in natural communication situations, which led us to use another data collection methodology: traditional storytelling in the community, that is, the production of oral narratives without the use of visual stimuli such as storyboards. In the next subsection, we detail the steps we followed to collect these data. Before, however, we present a table with the total number of words and modal items used by each participant (MS, SMN, FP, and SGFP) from the images of the storyboards corresponding to the *Tom and Mittens* (Rolka and Cable 2014) and *Chore Girl* (TFS Working Group 2011) stories.

Table 1: Occurrences of modal items by participants (MS, SMN, FP, and SGFP) in each of the storyboards (*Tom and Mittens* and *Chore Girl*).

	MS		SMN		FP		SGFP	
	words	modals	words	modals	words	modals	words	modals
Tom and Mittens	151	0	196	6	172	4	181	5
Chore Girl	252	7	338	10	372	8	227	4

It should be noted that, although there was low production of modal items, considering the total number of words used by the participants in each story, the storyboard *Chore Girl*, applied to the detection of deontic modal items, promoted the production of more modality data. This fact is possibly related to the length of the stories, since the images corresponding to the *Tom and Mittens* story were organized into 11 frames, while *Chore Girl* had 19 frames.

4.2 Traditional stories

The option to use stories of oral tradition in the community for the analysis of modality markers in Lung'Ie was motivated, in part, by the nature of the data generated with the application of the storyboards task, which, in some cases, corresponded to descriptions of the images presented, with no connection between the events that make up the narrative. In addition, the storyboard technique resulted in a low production of modal items in relation to the total number of words, as shown in Table 1 at the end of section 4.1. We assumed that telling traditional stories from the community would result in the production of more natural and spontaneous data, as this is a common practice among community members and because it constitutes a means to disseminate local culture; narrating such stories to a member outside the community, in this case the researchers, is an activity that makes sense to the language consultant. Besides, the traditional storytelling method guarantees that there will be no elements in the data that are foreign to the local culture since they correspond to the expression of the internal members of the community.

The traditional stories of São Tomé and Príncipe, *swa* in Lung'Ie, are characterized by the presence of fantastic elements and anthropomorphic figures, as

shown below. In this study, we used eight traditional stories for the analysis of modality in Lung'Ie, all part of Agostinho's corpus (2009, 2010, 2015, 2016a), collected during fieldwork on Príncipe Island over several years. They are:
1. *Sun arê tama poxta ki Têtuuga* 'The king made a bet with the Turtle', told by Cenoria Gomes Ventura Furtado Pernambuco (Agostinho 2010)
2. *Têtuuga ki Ôkê* 'The Turtle and the Monkey', told by Frutuoso dos Santos Luís Fernandes (Agostinho 2010; Agostinho and Araujo 2021: 191)
3. *Têtuuga ki mye sê* 'The Turtle and its wife', told by Salvador Manuel das Neves (Agostinho 2016a)
4. *Têtuuga ki Paage* 'The Turtle and the Parrot', told by José Ananias (Agostinho 2016a)
5. *Têtuuga ki Ôkê II* 'The Turtle and the Monkey', told by José Ananias (Agostinho 2016a)
6. *Sun arê ki Têtuuga* 'The King and the Turtle', told by José Ananias (Agostinho 2009)
7. *Kabê-gaani, Bweega-gaani, Ope-fina* 'Big Head, Big Belly, and Skinny Foot', told by Cesaltina dos Santos (Agostinho 2016a)
8. *Têtuuga ki bengela* 'The Turtle and the cane', told by Frutuoso dos Santos Luís Fernandes (Agostinho 2009)

Finally, we emphasize that the collection, documentation, and publication of data from traditional stories can also contribute to the preservation of oral and narrative literature (cf. Inegbeboh 2016) of languages in danger of extinction, such as Lung'Ie, in addition to being used for the analysis of linguistic phenomena beyond modality.

The collection of traditional stories can be performed in real storytelling situations or requested by the researcher. In general, it is important that the researcher talks to community members in order to verify which speakers participate in this practice. During the story, the researcher must behave like the audience, joining other members of the community who are participating in the activity when the practice is carried out in the presence of an audience. This insertion of the researcher among the other listeners contributes to a more natural dynamic, since telling a story only makes sense if there is a real interlocutor interested in the narrative (Bowern 2015: 134). In communities where the language is rarely spoken, as in the case of Lung'Ie, the practice of storytelling may not be recurrent. In these cases, it is common for the consultant to tell the story only to the researcher. This was the methodology adopted to obtain data from the traditional stories used in our research.

Ideally, the transcription and glossing of the stories should be done during fieldwork by the researcher with the collaboration and/or review of a native speaker. When the researcher does not have enough knowledge of the language to prepare the gloss and translate the data, this task can be performed by a member of the community collaborating in the project. In our case, the first author understands Lung'Ie, which allowed her to work on the construction of the glosses of the sentences of the narratives. After this step, it is important to check the information with a native speaker. If the researcher does not have previous knowledge of the language, an alternative is that the construction of the glosses and the translation are made from the information given by a native speaker; the researcher is responsible for recording this information, organizing it, and requesting a final review by a native speaker. The work of the consultant in the construction of the glosses, which requires linguistic knowledge, can be supervised by the researcher. During our field trip, we asked the same language consultants who carried out the storytelling activity for free translations to Portuguese. The Portuguese versions of the stories facilitated the work of transcription, elaboration of glosses, and translation of Lung'Ie data, which, in our case, was not done in its entirety during the field trip.

We believe that the importance of using traditional stories for the understanding of modality markers in the language lies in the fact that the produced text – as it results from an internal practice in the community and is, therefore, very natural to the speakers – presents features that are characteristic of the speech community under study, which would probably not arise in the application of tasks with the use of storyboards, for example.[5] In Lung'Ie, we found in the data some expressions characteristic of the community linked to the structure of a narrative. Example (4) shows typical ways to start (4a-c) and end (4e-g) a traditional story:

(4) a. *Anu   ki   neli. Mintxya maxi montxi dêkê vedadi.*
       year and ring   lie   more lot   than truth
       'A year and a ring. More is a lie than the truth.' (Agostinho 2016a)

   b. *Swa   ki   n   tê,   komesa to,   awa   pwê.*
      story   REL 1SG have   start   drip   water pour
      'The story I have started to drip, to pour water.' (Agostinho 2016a)

   c. *Abôdê. Ale. Tokito   peegu ki   matelu.*
      abôdê   ale   tap-tap   nail   and hammer
      '*Abôdê. Ale.* Tap-tap from a nail and a hammer.' (Agostinho 2014)

---

5 Longacre (1990: 1), for example, argues that "in some (perhaps all) languages, storyline clauses are the most typical and diagnostic of the word order typology itself (. . .). Thus, a language of VSO typology in narrative may be SVO in expository or descriptive discourse (. . .)".

e. *Kêtê   kêtê   ki   n   tê,   êli   n   paatxi   da   txi.*
    a.little a.little REL   1SG have   3SG   1SG share   give 2SG
    'What little I have I shared with you.' (Agostinho 2016a)
    Kêtê   kêtê   ki   n   tê,   êli   n   paatxi   da   ningê
    a.little a.little REL   1SG have   3SG   1SG share   give person
    tudu   pe.
    all   IDEO
    'What little I have I shared with you all.' (Agostinho 2009)

g. *Kêtê   kêtê   ki   n   tê,   n   tolo   da   ningê   tudu.*
    a.little a.little REL   1SG have   1SG divide   give people   all
    'What little I have, I shared with everyone.' (Agostinho 2014: 201)

In (4a), the expression *Anu ki neli* 'A year and a ring', which has the variants *Neli ki neli* and *Ani ki neli* (Maurer 2009: 188), is used when starting to tell a story, constituting a form of interaction with the audience, who responds *Mintxya maxi montxi dekê vedadi* 'More is a lie than the truth'. The expression in (4b) also indicates that the narrator has started to tell a traditional story or riddle. Example (4c) presents a formula where the narrator says *abôdê*, and the listeners respond *ale*. These expressions are only used in narrative contexts and they have no translation. The expressions in (4d-f) exemplify formulas to end a traditional story.

In addition to showing traditional storytelling formulas in the beginning and end of a narrative, these stories contain cultural elements that would not appear in data motivated by stimuli external to the Príncipe culture. An example would be the existence of the character *Têtuuga* – 'Turtle'. Many traditional stories of São Tomé and Príncipe present this character as an anthropomorphic figure who is always very smart and treacherous. In Agostinho (2016b), there is the following observation by one of the language consultants: *Têtuuga tê swa mutu* '[the] Turtle has many stories.' This character is also found in traditional stories from Nigeria and West Africa (cf. Inegbeboh 2016; Okeh 1995; Longacre 1990; Thomas 1913; Achebe 1958), some of which are also found in Príncipe.[6] This linguistic and cultural fact indicates the historical relationship of the languages of the Gulf of Guinea with the languages of Nigeria, since such stories were possibly brought by the enslaved people who were taken from the Niger Delta to São Tomé and Príncipe in the 16th and 17th centuries. In (5), we transcribed the opening part of

---

6 According to Inegbeboh (2016: 10), "(t)he character, tortoise, for example, dominates many folktales in Nigeria, Benin, Cameroon and countries in Central Africa. (...) The tortoise is intelligent, resourceful, but tricky and selfish." The same character features are found in the *Têtuuga* character in São Tomé and Príncipe.

the traditional story *Sun arê tama poxta ki Têtuuga* 'The king made a bet with the Turtle' (Agostinho 2010), in which the character *Têtuuga* plays a key role:

(5) a. *Sun   arê   tama   poxta   ki   têtuuga.*
       sir   king   take   bet   with   turtle
       'The king made a bet with the turtle.'

   b. *Têtuuga   faa   sun   arê   ya   ê   ka   gbô*
      turtle   say   sir   king   COMPL   3SG   IRR   defecate
      xi   pêêmê.
      without   squeeze
      'The turtle told the king that it would defecate without squeezing.'
      [...]

   c. *"E-e,   txi   sa   po   gbô   xi   pêêmê   fa".*
      no   2SG   COP   can   defecate   without   squeeze   NEG
      '"No, you can't defecate without squeezing."'

   d. *Dêpôji   ê   faa: "n   ka   pêêmê,   n   ka   gbô*
      then   3SG   say   1SG   IRR   squeeze   1SG   IRR   defecate
      xi   pêêmê".[1]
      without   squeeze
      'Then he said: "I will squeeze; I will defecate without squeezing."'
      (Agostinho 2010)

In the four opening sentences of the story, we observed three occurrences of the item *ka*. Differently from the storyboard data transcribed in (3), *ka* is shown here in sentences without the occurrence of a modal item. The data in (5c), in which a modal item of possibility (*po* 'can') is not preceded by *ka*, as in the occurrences of the story in (3) also caught our attention; it should be noted, however, that this sentence also differs from those in (3) due to the presence of the morpheme *fa*, which corresponds to the sentential negation operator in Lung'Ie. Finally, we observed that *ka* takes place between the subject and the lexical predicate. In Lung'Ie, this position is occupied by functional items indicating mood, modality, tense, and aspect, such as *po/podi* 'can', *pudya* 'could, should', *divya* 'should, could', and *tê ki/tê di* 'have to' (modal auxiliary verbs); *sa* and *tava* (non-past

---

[7] In this excerpt, the participant narrating the story initially produces the sentence *N ka pêêmê* (I will squeeze) and then corrects it for *N ka gbô xi pêêmê* (I will defecate without squeezing).

copula and past copula,[8] respectively).[9] For this reason, our hypothesis is that *ka* is associated with (one of) these notions. Considering that recent studies on creoles and African languages indicate that the same item can correspond to a particle indicating the notions of tense, mood, and aspect (cf. Holm 2004: 84, 183), we mapped the uses of *ka*, both in the storyboards and in the traditional stories, to identify whether this item is associated with one (or more than one) of these notions. Our analysis prioritized the data produced in traditional storytelling, as such situations are closer to a real communication context for the community under study. Furthermore, such stories are characterized by the alternation between direct and indirect discourses and located in a non-logical reality, in which Turtle dialogues with the king, for example. Such contexts are important for the production and understanding of features associated with notions of tense, mood, modality, and aspect.

In the next section, we show how our preliminary data analysis led us to construct the hypothesis to be investigated in our research and the steps we followed to verify it.

5 Construction and verification of the hypothesis

In this study, our focus was the description and analysis of modality in Lung'Ie in constructions with dynamic predicates, since stative verbs seem to behave differently in relation to the interaction with the categories of tense, mood, and aspect in Lung'Ie and in creole languages in general (cf. Maurer 2009: 71; Bickerton 1981: 58, 1984).[10] Winford (2018: 205) even observes that "[i]t has now been well established that the distinction between stative and nonstative or dynamic predicates is central to all creole TMA systems, although there are differences across creoles concerning which verbs are assigned to one or the other category".

Initially, our proposal was to observe the modal *po/podi* 'can', *pudya* 'could, should', *divya* 'should, could', and *tê ki/tê di* 'have to' in relation to the context and frequency of use and type of modality they may denote. A preliminary analysis of the data indicated that items with modal force of possibility, but not necessity,

---

8 Another form for the past copula is *era* (Maurer 2009: 101).
9 Daval-Markussen and Bakker (2017: 111) claim that "[i]n the Atlantic Creoles, verbs generally indicate tense and aspect not with inflections but rather with preverbal (in some cases postverbal) markers."
10 Bickerton (1981: 58; 1984) proposes that creole languages generally use morphologically unmarked verbs to convey the meaning of present tense, in stative verbs; and past tense, in action verbs.

could co-occur with *ka*. This data aroused our interest in the relationship between *ka* and modality, specifically modal force. The sentences in (6) are taken from the story *Têtuuga ki Ôkê*. In both occurrences, *ka* is followed by a modal item:

(6) a. *Dya ũa   têtuuga fala ôkê   ya   ê   ka*
       day one turtle   say   monkey COMPL 3SG IRR
       po   fêzê poxta ũa   kôli.
       can make bet   one with.3SG
       'One day, the turtle told the monkey that he could make a bet with him.' (Agostinho 2010; Agostinho and Araujo 2021: 191)

   b. *Têtuuga fala: "bon, ôzê   n   mêsê pya   xi txi ka*
       turtle   say   good today 1SG want see   if 2SG IRR
       po   gan mi".
       can win 1SG
       'The turtle said: "Well, today I want to see if you can beat me."'
       (Agostinho 2010; Agostinho and Araujo 2021: 191)

In the sentences of example (6), *ka* co-occurs with the auxiliary *po*, indicating symbolic modality ("suggestion") in (6a) and dynamic modality ("capacity") in (6b). The type of modality is different in each case, but the modal force (of possibility) is the same. We also find many examples where *ka* does not co-occur with a modal auxiliary. The sentences in (7) were both taken from traditional stories: (7a) is part of the story *Têtuuga ki Paage* 'The Turtle and the Parrot', in which the turtle and the parrot, his godmother, go to harvest fruits from a palm-oil tree and (7b) was taken from the story *Têtuuga ki mye sê* 'The Turtle and its wife', whose narrative is about a magic bag that grants wishes to the turtle:

(7) a. *Dêpoji ê   sama pêxi sê,   pêxi sê   bê   vika rompê, vika*
       after   3SG call fish DEM   fish DEM   also come a.lot, come
       lêlê   têtuuga. "Sun arê   manda pa n   faa owo."
       accompany   turtle   sir   king order to 1SG say 2PL
       [...] I   êli têtuuga faa ine: 'N   ka   wada owo
       [...] and 3SG turtle   say 3PL   1SG IRR wait 2PL
       amanhan   na ora'.
       tomorrow in hour
       'Then he called these fish, these fish also came in piles, they came to accompany the turtle. "The king sent me to tell you". [. . .] And he told them: "I'll wait for you tomorrow at eleven o'clock."' (Agostinho 2016a)

b. Ê   teega   e   ê   fala   e: "buseta   sê,   txi
   3SG.S   deliver   3SG.O   3SG.S   say   3SG.O   bag   DEM   2SG
   ka   we   kôli   txi   ka   xiga   kaxi,   txi   ka   pwê
   IRR   go   with.3SG   2SG   IRR   arrive   house   2SG   IRR   put
   buseta   sê."
   bag   DEM
   'He handed it over and told him: "This bag, you go with it, you are going to get home, you are going to wear this bag."' (Agostinho 2016a)

Examples such as (7a) and (7b) further show that *ka* is not dependent on the occurrence of a modal item in the structure, but, at the same time, it can figure in modal constructions, as in (6). In the examples without the occurrence of a modal item, *ka* is positioned between the subject and the verb of the sentence; on the other hand, with the occurrence of a modal item, *ka* is positioned between the subject and the modal auxiliary, which, in turn, precedes the lexical verb, as in (6a-b).

Considering the position in the sentence and the possibility of co-occurrence with modal items (*ka > modal auxiliary)*, we assumed that *ka* corresponds to a functional item connected to the TMA system. To test and refine this hypothesis, we then investigated the employment of *ka* in relation to tense, in subsection 5.1; mood, in 5.2; and aspect, in 5.3. The examples cited throughout this section are mostly drawn from traditional stories collected during Agostinho's fieldwork (2009, 2010, 2015, 2016a).

5.1 Tense

As mentioned, the traditional stories of São Tomé and Príncipe are marked by fantastic elements. In one of them, the story of a magic bag is told, which grants the character *Têtuuga* wishes. In (8), below, we transcribe a dialogue extracted from this story. As it corresponds to an excerpt of the narrative in which direct speech is used, the example contains verbal forms in different tenses.

(8) I   kuman   faa: "bon   n   ke   kaba   ki   xatxisi
    and   godmother   say   good   1SG   IRR.go   finish   with   annoyance
    sê.   N   ka   ranja   kwa   ũa   da   kompwe   me   pa
    DEM   1SG   IRR   find   thing   one   give   godfather   1SG.POSS   to
    ê   tê   manêra   ki   ê   ka   vika   xatxya   ma   fa
    3SG   have   way   with 3SG   IRR   come   upset   more   NEG

ki	ine	ka	vêvê	maxi	alegi	pôkê	ine	mosu	vya
with	3PL	IRR	live	more	happy	because	3PL	boy	turn

gaani	gaani	za	i	ine	sa	vêvê	sempi	na	mizerya".
big	big	already	and	3PL	COP	live	always	in	misery

'And the godmother said: "Well, I'm going to put an end to this annoyance. I'm going to find something for the godfather so that he has a way that, if he doesn't get upset anymore, they're going to live happier, because their children are already grown up, and they're always living in misery.'"
(Agostinho 2016a)

The first sentence, which corresponds to the narrator's speech, describes the event in the past tense. In Lung'Ie, the past is not morphologically marked in dynamic verbs (cf. Maurer 2009: 72). Marking the past occurs through the absence of a preverbal marker. The first two occurrences of *ka* in (8) are in sentences whose events are future-oriented: *bon n ke kaba ki xatxisi sê* 'well, I'm going to put an end to this annoyance' – where *ke* is a contraction of *ka* and *we* 'go', after undergoing an external sandhi process – and *N ka ranja kwa ũa da kompwe me* 'I'm going to find something for the godfather', both describing events that reveal an imprecise planning from the godmother to help the godfather. In the other two occurrences of *ka* in the sequence, the speaker makes assumptions regarding the future psychological state of *kompwe*, if her planning works out: *ki ê ka vika xatxya ma fa ki ine ka vêvê maxi alegi* 'that, if he doesn't get upset anymore, they're going to live happier'. Note that the eventualities described in these sentences are linked, so the psychological state described in the second is dependent on the one described in the first. It is important to note that all sentences in excerpt (8) in which *ka* is used have in common a temporal orientation towards the future and a certain degree of uncertainty, since they describe plans and states resulting from these plans, if successful.

Example (9) was also taken from a traditional story, which relates a bet made between the famous character *Têtuuga* and *Ôkê* 'monkey':

(9)
Ine	pwê	poxta	di	kwê,	ningê	ka	kwê	maxi	ki	ôtô.
3PL	put	bet	of	run	who	IRR	run	more	REL	other

'They made a bet on running, who will outrun the other.' (Agostinho 2016a)

The excerpt transcribed in (9) corresponds to the narrator's speech. In the first sentence, the event is located in the past, as can be seen from the use of the verb without any pre-verbal marker. Note that, in this first sentence, *ka* is not used. The second sentence, where *ka* is used, describes a future event in relation to the betting event. These data allow us to assume that the use of *ka* is linked to an event marked as future in relation to another event and/or uncertain as to who will be the winner of the bet.

In (10), we transcribe another example of data extracted from traditional stories. In this story, there is a dialogue between *Têtuuga* and his godmother about the magic bag that grants wishes. In this context, the godmother gives the bag to *Têtuuga* and says (10):

(10) Kwa   kwa   txi   ka   pidi, buseta sê   ka   da   txi.
     thing thing 2SG   IRR   ask   bag   DEM   IRR   give 2SG
     'Anything you ask for, this bag will give you.' (Agostinho 2016a)

In (10) there are two occurrences of *ka*, one in each clause. In this example, similarly to that in (9), there is also an ordering of the events. Although both are located in a future time in relation to the moment of the utterance, the second is dependent on the occurrence of the first, which, in turn, is dependent on an action by the interlocutor. From the data considered so far, *ka* seems to be associated with future and/or uncertain events. In addition to the corpus used in this work, we found 106 sentences in the future tense in the data from Agostinho (2015) and Maurer (2009). All these data contain *ka* or some form with *ka*, such as *ke* (contraction of *ka* and *we* 'go'), *keka* (contraction of *ka* and *vika* 'come' (Maurer 2009: 36)), or the phonetic variant *ga*.

The following examples are quite interesting because, although Lung'Ie does not have a past morphology for action verbs, there are clear indications that the described events occurred at a time prior to the utterance. Both examples were taken from the story *Têtuuga ki mye sê* 'The Turtle and its wife'. The excerpt transcribed in (11) reports the part in which *Têtuuga* sleeps for a few hours and example (12) was transcribed from an excerpt in which the narrator talks about João and Antônio, sons of *Têtuuga*.

(11) Ê   we   ukantu ũa   diimi ki   sê   a   vontadi
     2SG   go   corner one   sleep with 3SG.POSS   at   will
     dina   mêy-dya ten   kwaji   têêxi   ora.
     from   noon   to   almost   three   hour
     'He went to a corner and slept freely from noon until three o'clock.'
     (Agostinho 2016a)

(12) I   ine   minu   sa   kêêsê.   Mene   vya   gaani   za. [...]
    and   3PL   child   COP   grow.up Manuel turn   big   already
    Zwan   bê   vya   gaani za.   I   ixila Tooni   bê
    João   also turn   big   already and   DEM   Antônio also
    kêêsê   za.
    grow.up   already
    'And their children are growing up. Manuel has become an adult already. [...] João has also become an adult already. And that one, Antônio, has also grown up already.' (Agostinho 2016a)

In (11), two events in the past are described, the first being prior to the second. The phrase *dina mêy-dya ten kwaji têêxi ora* 'from noon until three o'clock' indicates that both events were concluded at a time before the utterance. The first sentence of example (12) describes an ongoing process, with the use of the non-past copula (*sa*) followed by a lexical verb (*kêêsê*). In the other sentences of this example the adverb *za* 'already' is used, indicating that the events described occurred in a time before the moment of the utterance. Example (11) and the sentences with the use of the adverb *za* 'already' in (12), as well as the first sentences of examples (8) and (9), are important because they suggest that the item *ka* is not compatible with past tense if it corresponds to a specific event, as in the cases cited here. In the next subsection, we investigate *ka* in contexts described in the linguistic literature as prototypically irrealis and realis, respectively, in order to verify whether this item corresponds to the functional category of mood in Lung'Ie.

5.2 Mood: Irrealis and realis

The irrealis mood is used in constructions that express actions or states that speakers portray in a structural way in the sphere of thought, such as plans, goals, dreams or hypothetical events. According to Bickerton (1975: 42), "[i]rrealis mood refers to 'unreal time'— that is, futures and conditionals, subjunctives, and so forth. 'Irrealis system' includes 'all states and actions which have not actually occurred'". Due to these characteristics, counterfactual, hypothetical, and conditional contexts are marked as irrealis across many languages. The realis mood, on the other hand, is related to factual situations. When speakers mark a context as realis, they are presenting the information as a fact, not as a possibility. This mood is associated with eventualities that are taking place at the time of the utterance or that are located in the past. However, other contexts can be marked as realis or irrealis depending on the language. They are: future tense, habitual aspect, imperative, contexts of obligation, negation, and interrogation (cf. Mithun 1995; Elliott 2000).

5.2.1 Prototypical irrealis contexts

Considering that hypothetical, conditional, and counterfactual constructions are more closely related to the domain of thought than of reality, they are expected to be prototypical irrealis contexts in languages in general. For this reason, we will start the analysis of irrealis marking in Lung'Ie from these contexts.

The example below illustrates a hypothetical construction. The quoted passage was taken from the *Têtuuga ki Paage* story 'The Turtle and the Parrot', from a context in which the turtle and the parrot are taking advantage of the low tide to go to a palm-oil tree to pick its fruits. The tide starts to rise, and the parrot, the turtle's godmother, warns that the fish will start throwing themselves at them if they stay there. The turtle, concerned with eating as much fruit as possible, does not leave in time. The parrot, however, flies away. Let us see the example:

(13) "Sun   ka   po   we   di   ope,   vya   vika   di   ope.   Xi
     sir   IRR   can   go   of   foot   turn   come   of   foot   if
     umwe   xya, ê   ka   da   fofo." Bon, têtuuga [...] tendê
     sea   fill 3SG   IRR   give weapon good   turtle   hear
     kwa   kumandê sê   faa.   "N   ka   we,   n   ka   we."
     thing godmother 3SG.POSS   say   1SG   IRR   go   1SG IRR   go
     "'You can go on foot and come back on foot. If the sea rises, they will throw themselves." Well, the turtle heard what his godmother said. "I'm already going, I'm already going."' (Agostinho 2016a)

In (13), there are several occurrences of the functional item *ka*. In the first occurrence this item appears in a modal context, as it accompanies a modal auxiliary (*po* 'can'). In the last two occurrences *ka* is used in future tense contexts. The occurrence we want to highlight here is the second one, because *ka* appears in a hypothetical construction, which corresponds to a prototypical irrealis context, along with conditionals and counterfactuals (cf. Mithun 1995): *Xi umwe xya, ê ka da fofo* 'If the sea rises, they will throw themselves', in which the parrot (female) assumes that the fish will throw themselves at them if the tide rises. It should be noted that, in Lung'Ie, *xi* 'if' is only used in hypothetical, conditional, and counterfactual contexts; therefore, if *ka* matches an irrealis marker, as we are supposing, its occurrence is expected in all contexts with *xi* 'if', but not the other way around.

In (14), we present another example of a hypothetical context. This one is taken from the story *Kabê-gaani, Bweega-gaani, Ope-fina* 'Big-head, Big-belly, and Skinny-foot', about three brothers with different physical characteristics who discuss which would be the most suitable to climb up a jackfruit tree to pick a ripe fruit.

(14) *Kabê-gaani faa: "xi n subi li kabê me ka*
head=big say if 1SG go.up 3SG head 1SG.POSS IRR
pega, ê sa da pa n subi fa." [...]
twine 3SG COP give to 1SG go.up NEG
Ope-fina faa: "xi n subi ope me ka keba,
foot=skinny say if 1SG go.up foot 1SG.POSS IRR break
ê sa da pa n subi fa." [...]
3SG COP give to 1SG go.up NEG
Bweega-gaani faa: "xi n ka subi, xi n subi,
belly=big say if 1SG IRR go.up if 1SG go.up
bweega me ka po va."
belly 1SG.POSS IRR can split
'The big-head said: "If I go up, my head will twine, I can't go up." [...] The skinny-foot said: "If I go up, my foot will break, I can't go up." [...] The big-belly said: "If I go up, if I go up, my belly can split."' (Agostinho 2016a)

In this context, the three brothers' speeches present assumptions about what could happen to each of them if they climbed the jackfruit tree. The eventualities described are clearly hypothetical, considering that they are presented as consequences of an equally hypothetical event (*xi n (ka) subi* 'if I go up'). Note that *ka* commonly appears in the second sentence of this construction, perhaps because the first sentence already displays a hypothetical context marker: *Xi*. It is noteworthy that, in the speech of brother *Bweega-gaani*, the sentence initiated by *Xi* is repeated, being pronounced first with *ka* and then without *ka*. This fact may indicate two possible forms in the language, or else a correction by the speaker, who inserted *ka* in a context where it would not normally occur.

The following examples, transcribed from Maurer (2009), illustrate counterfactual and conditional contexts, respectively:

(15) *Xi ôzê n ka tava tê dyô, n ka tava kopa*
if today 1SG COUNT MOD have money 1SG MOD PST buy
kaxi ũa.
house one
'If today I had had money, I would have bought a house.' (Maurer 2009: 89)

(16) Xi ê   sa   ladran, n   ka   fala kôli   fa.
     if 3SG COP thief   1SG FUT speak with.3SG NEG
     'If he were a thief, I wouldn't speak to him.' (Maurer 2009: 99)

According to the glosses of the examples above, it is evident that Maurer associates the item *ka* with various functions in the language. In (15), the first occurrence of *ka* is identified as a counterfactuality marker and the second occurrence is associated with a modal marker; still, in (16) *ka* is identified as a future tense marker. Example (15) corresponds to a counterfactual context, as it describes an event that did not happen (*buying the house*), but which could have happened if a condition were met (*having money today*). Considering what is stated in the literature on irrealis marking and counterfactual contexts, both occurrences of *ka* in (15) seem to be marking the counterfactual context as irrealis in Lung'Ie, just as counterfactual contexts receive irrealis marking in languages which feature grammatical markers to make the opposition realis/irrealis.

Example (16) corresponds to a conditional context, which is also marked as irrealis in languages that exhibit such marking. In Maurer's gloss, *ka* is associated with a future tense marker. The classification of *ka* as a marker of the irrealis mood accounts for both conditional and future contexts, since in both cases there is no certainty about the occurrence of the event '*I wouldn't speak to him*', as it is conditioned to a situation described in the previous sentence (*if he were a thief*), about which doubts are cast. The occurrence or not of the event described in the sentence with *ka* depends on the fact described in the first one. Therefore, it is a probable event, but not a certain one; thus, it is possible to associate *ka* with irrealis mood marking in this case as well. It is important to mention that, in addition to considering the occurrences of these data in traditional stories, we searched for hypothetical, conditional, and counterfactual constructions in the literature on Lung'Ie, more specifically in Agostinho (2015) and Maurer (2009). Initially, we searched for *xi* 'if', which is present in these constructions; secondly, we considered information from the context to verify whether, in fact, they were hypothetical, conditional, and counterfactual constructions. What was interesting in this search was the occurrence of the item *ka* in all 37 constructions that we located.

5.2.2 Prototypical realis contexts

According to Mithun (1995), prototypical realis contexts are those that describe situations that have occurred in the past or at the time of speech. Examples (17) and (18) below respectively illustrate each of these uses.

(17) "Txi kume za?" "Ozê n pasa mali mutu n maxi kume
2SG eat now today 1SG feel sick very 1SG more eat
fa. [...] n nda mutu, n keba umatu mutu."
NEG 1SG walk very 1SG break bush very
'"Have you eaten already?" "Today I felt really sick, I still haven't eaten. I walked a lot, I cut a lot of bush."' (Agostinho 2009)

(18) A: "Sabiina, kwa txi sa fêzê wo sê a?"
Sabrina thing 2SG COP do moment DEM INT
'"Sabrina, what are you doing now?"'

B: "Ami a? N sa kuxi."
1SG INT 1SG COP cooking
'"Me? I'm cooking."'

A: "Kwa txi sa kuxi a?"
thing 2SG COP cook INT
'"What are you cooking?"'

B: "N sa kuxi kumê Baji."
1SG COP cook food Brazil
'"I am cooking Brazilian food."'
(Modified from Agostinho 2015: 203)

The events described in (17), from the story *Têtuuga ki bengela* 'The turtle and the cane', occur in a time prior to the utterance time. This information is evident in the use of the adverb *za* 'already' in *Txi kume za?* 'Have you eaten already?', as the turtle's wife asks him when he gets home, after having spent the day in the fields. The turtle's response reports a sequence of events that took place throughout the day, all prior, thus, to the moment of speech. Note that in none of the sentences in this example the item *ka* is used. The sentences of example (18), in turn, refer to the moment of speech. Interlocutor A asks questions about what interlocutor B is doing at the moment of speech, a time marked by the presence of the adverb *wo sê* 'now'. Note that the sentences in this example are constructed from dynamic verbs and that in none of them the *ka* particle is used. Examples (17) and (18) correspond to typical realis contexts since they describe events about whose occurrence there is no doubt or because they have occurred already, as is the case of (17), or because they occur parallel to the moment of speech, as in (18). If, as we are pointing out, *ka* was an irrealis indicator in Lung'Ie, then its non-occurrence in past constructions, as in (17), or simultaneous to the moment of speech, as in (18), was already expected.

As we have shown throughout this subsection, *ka* figures in hypothetical, conditional, and counterfactual contexts, indicated in the literature as prototypical irrealis, since they are marked as irrealis in all languages that exhibit this marking. Nevertheless, in prototypical realis contexts that describe specific events in the past or simultaneous to the time of speaking we found no instances of *ka*. In the next subsection, we investigate the use of *ka* in aspectual constructions.

5.3 Aspect

Comrie (1976) subdivides grammatical aspect into two categories: the perfective aspect and the imperfective aspect. To account for other aspectual distinctions, the author subdivides the imperfective aspect into habitual and continuous, the latter being further subdivided into progressive and non-progressive. The habitual aspect represents a "situation characteristic of an extended period of time, so extended that the situation is viewed, as a characteristic feature of a whole period" (Comrie 1976: 27). This aspectual notion refers to situations that occur during a period presented as being unlimited, describing an event that is characteristic of that period of time. In our data, this notion was identified in constructions with *ka* followed by a dynamic verb, as in *N goxta di palapala montxi fa, maji n ka kume li* 'I don't like *palapala* very much, but I eat it' (Agostinho 2015: 217). The continuous imperfective aspect, on the other hand, describes an event that is in progress during a certain period of time and can be characterized as progressive or non-progressive. According to Mair (2012), "while the progressive is usually reserved for dynamic verbs and predicates, non-progressive continuous aspectuality additionally covers stative predicates" (Mair 2012: 4). For this study, which aims to investigate the use of *ka* with dynamic verbs, the continuous-progressive aspect will be considered in parallel to the habitual one. The continuous-progressive aspect "narrows attention to the temporal space around the time of reference or speaking" (Nurse et al. 2016: 27). In Lung'Ie, this aspectual notion is constructed by employing the copula *sa* (non-past) followed by a dynamic verb, as in *N sa kume doxi wo sê* 'I'm eating sweets now' (Agostinho 2009: 43).

Example (19), from the story *Têtuuga ki mye sê* 'The Turtle and his wife', below, corresponds to a habitual construction, in which the narrator is telling about the day-to-day life of the turtle and his wife.

(19) Ê   ka   rêgê   pemya   ê   ka   we   umatu, ê   ka
    3SG   IRR   get.up   morning 3SG   IRR   go   bush   3SG IRR
    ranja kwalke coisa¹¹ ê   ka   daka. Mye   bê   ka
    get   any   thing   3SG IRR bring women too IRR
    ranja kwalke kwa   na   kaxi.
    get   any   thing in   house
    'He gets up in the morning, he goes to the fields, he gets anything, he brings it. The wife also gets something in the house.' (Agostinho 2016a)

In this example, it is possible to observe that no specific event is being described. Instead, we have the description of customary events, in which a specific time of occurrence is not identified. In (19), routine actions are related, describing *Têtuuga*'s day-to-day life: he gets up in the morning, goes to the farm, finds something to eat and take home. Another routine event is also described: Turtle's wife usually gets something for the family to eat. Note that, in (19), the *ka* particle is used before all the verbs: *rêgê* 'get up', *we* 'go', *ranja* 'get', and *daka* 'bring'.

Examples (20) and (21) below, transcribed from Maurer (2009), show *ka* in sentences also associated with the habitual aspect but, unlike (19), the events described in (20) and (21) no longer occur.

(20) *Dya tudu pe   n   tava ka   rêgê   na xink'ora   di*
     day all   IDEO   1SG PST   HAB get.up   at five.o'clock   of
     pemyan.¹²
     morning
     'I used to get up at five o'clock in the morning every day.' (Maurer 2009: 87)

(21) *Ine   na   tava ka   kume kani pôkô¹³ dyêxi   tudu pe.*
     3PL   VAL PST   HAB eat   meat pig   day.DEM   all   IDEO
     'They really used to eat pork every day.' (Maurer 2009: 67)

The marker of the past (*tava*) locates the habitual events described in (20) and (21) in a time prior to the moment of the utterance. These examples are important because they reveal that *ka* is not incompatible with past tense, as we might assume from the data presented in subsection 5.1. If the event is described as habitual, *ka* appears in past constructions.

---

11 The consultant uses the Portuguese word *coisa* 'thing' and not *kwa* in Lung'Ie.
12 Varies with *pemya* (cf. Agostinho and Araujo 2021). The nasal onset triggers the progressive nasalization (Agostinho 2016b).
13 *Kaani pôôkô* in Agostinho and Araujo (2021).

In example (22), below, there is also the occurrence of the functional items *tava* and *ka*, but, in this case, there is no description of a habitual event in the past.[14] It is a prototypical irrealis context, as it describes a counterfactual situation whose event, which could have been ongoing at the time of the utterance, has not been initiated.

(22)   *Xi   non*[15] *ka   tava   sa   xivi*[16] *wosê,*[17] *non   ka*
       if   1PL   COUNT   PST   PROG   work   now   1PL   COUNT
       tava   tê   dyô.
       MOD   have   money
       'If we were working now, we would have money.' (Maurer 2009: 90)

Example (22) indicates a progressive interpretation, but not a habitual one. The presence of the adverb *wosê* 'now' determines the time (simultaneous with the moment of the utterance) in which the event *sa xivi* 'to be working' should be in progress for the state *tê dyô* 'to have money' to be true. In (22), *tava* does not correspond to a past tense marker, unlike in (20) and (21). Evidence thereof is that this marking would be incompatible with the one indicated by the adverb *wosê*.

In the following example, also transcribed from Maurer (2009), the sequence *ka > tava* appears in a counterfactual context with the occurrence of an adverb indicating future tense:

(23)   *Xi   amanhan   non   ka   tava   xivi,   non   ka   tava*
       if   tomorrow   1PL   COUNT   MOD   work   1PL   COUNT   MOD
       tê   dyô,   maji   xivisu   tê   fa.
       have   money   but   work   there.be   NEG
       'If tomorrow we worked, we would get money, but there is no work.'
       (Maurer 2009: 89)

In (23), similarly to (22), *tava* occurs after *ka* in a sentence whose event is not located in the past, as evidenced by the presence of the adverb *amanhan* 'tomorrow'. The counterfactual reading is generated because the event *xivi* 'worked' is not likely to happen, not because it is located in the past, as is common in coun-

---

14 Maurer (2009: 90) argues that *ka tava sa* occurs only in counterfactual conditional clauses and is synonymous with *ka tava*.
15 Varies with *no* (cf. Agostinho and Araujo 2021). The nasal onset triggers the progressive nasalization (Agostinho 2016b).
16 *Xiivi* and *xiivisu* in Agostinho and Araujo (2021).
17 *Wo sê* in Agostinho and Araujo (2021).

terfactual constructions, but because there is no work, information given in the sentence *maji xivisu tê fa* 'but there is no work', which integrates the construction.

Regarding example (23), Maurer (2009: 90) notes that "[t]he fact that counterfactuality can be expressed by *ka* alone and that *tava* co-occurs with time adverbs like *ôzê* 'today' and *amanhan* 'tomorrow' shows that in this context, the past marker *tava* does not exert a temporal function; it metaphorically reinforces the counterfactuality already expressed by *ka*".[18]

We are assuming that the interpretation associated with *tava* – as past tense or not – is directly related to this ordering and is a consequence of the position of the functional head to which *tava* corresponds in the sentence structure and the way this head relates to the other functional categories that integrate the Lung'Ie TMA system. In (24), we present part of the hierarchy of functional heads proposed by Cinque (1999) for the categories of mood, modality, tense, and aspect in natural languages:

(24) Functional Projections Hierarchy:
Moodspeech act > Moodevaluative > Moodevidential > Modepistemic > **T(Past)** > T(Future) > **Mood(irrealis)** > Modnecessity > Modpossibility > **Asphabitual** > Asprepetitive(I) > Aspfrequentative(I) > Modvolitional > . . . > Aspperfect > Aspretrospective > Aspproximative > AspPdurative > **AspPprogressive** > AspPprospective > . . . > > ModPobligation > ModPability > AspPfrustrative/success > ModPpermission > AspPconative > AspPcompletive (I) > VoiceP. . .
(Cinque 1999: 106, our emphasis)

The sequence *tava > ka,* in (20) and (21), generates an interpretation of the habitual past, with the item *tava* being interpreted in the category T(Past) and *ka* in the Mood(irrealis) category. Note that the interpretation associated with the sequence *tava > ka* is in accordance with the ordering of the functional heads to which they correspond in the hierarchy proposed by Cinque: T(Past) > . . . > Mood(irrealis). Examples (22) and (23), in turn, show that *tava* cannot be associated with the notion of past time in the sequence *ka tava (sa)*. If *ka*, as we have

---

18 Even so, Maurer glosses *tava* as past tense in (22). In (23), on the other hand, *tava* is glossed as modal. Furthermore, the author presents the same example without *tava* as a synonym for (23):

(i) *Xi amanhan no ka xivi, non ka tê dyô, maji xivisu tê fa.*
'If tomorrow we worked, we would get money, but there is no work.' (Maurer 2009: 90)

While the counterfactual reading is given by *ka* in both, Maurer's translation in (23) does not seem to grasp any meaning behind *tava*.

been arguing, corresponds to irrealis marking, then it was already expected that *tava* in the sequence *ka > tava* would not generate a past tense interpretation, otherwise it would violate the hierarchy transcribed in (24). The Lung'Ie data thus provides further evidence that the ordering proposed by Cinque is part of Universal Grammar (UG).

On the other hand, sentences in which the event is marked with a progressive aspect, as in (25) and (26), do not appear with *ka*:

(25) Ine   tava sa   kirya minu   sê   pobêmentê.
     3SG   PST   COP raise child 3PL.POSS poorly
     'They were raising their children poorly.' (Agostinho 2016a)

(26) Ningê   tudu pe   ki   sa   pasa subi   sa   faa: "eeee."
     person   all   IDEO REL COP pass go.up COP say   INTERJ
     'Everyone who is going up is saying: "Eeee."' (Agostinho 2009)

Example (25) corresponds to a passage in the story *Têtuuga ki mye sê* 'The turtle and his wife' in which the narrator describes how they were raising their children. The use of the copula *sa* followed by a dynamic verb marks the past event as progressive.[19] The sequence of functional items in this example is also in accordance with the hierarchy proposed by Cinque, since *tava* corresponds to the marker of the past and *sa* to the marker of the progressive aspect: T(Past) > . . . >AspPprogressive (see the ordering of the functional heads in (24)). In (26), the narrator describes two actions (*pasa subi* 'go up' and *faa* 'speak'), which occur at a time simultaneous to the moment of the utterance. In this construction, *sa* is also forming a sequence with dynamic verbs, corresponding to the head which indicates the progressive aspect (AspPprogressive). In examples (25) and (26), which correspond to prototypical realis contexts (see subsection 5.2.2), *ka* does not occur. An example from Maurer (2009) reveals, however, that *ka* is not incompatible with the progressive aspect if the event is located in the future:

---

19 Sentences with *tava* and dynamic verbs without the use of *sa* do not express a progressive aspect. In the example below, *tava* is configured as a Past Perfect Simple construction, as already pointed out by Maurer (2009: 87):

(i) Ora   xiga   na   lala   na   maaka ki   ine   tava konvesa, ê
    hour   arrive   in   there in   mark   REL 3PL   PST   talk   3SG
    vê   têtuuga tusandu sa   wada li
    see   turtle   siting   COP wait 3SG
    'When he reached the mark they had agreed to, he saw the turtle sitting there waiting for him.' (Agostinho 2015: 339)

(27) Ora   txi   ka   xiga   amanhan,   no   ka   sa   kume.
     hour 2SG   FUT   arrive tomorrow   1PL   FUT PROG   eat
     'When you arrive tomorrow, we'll be eating.' (Maurer 2009: 88)

The progressive aspect is marked by the use of the copula *sa* followed by the dynamic verb, indicating that this event will be in progress in the future when another event, also future, as indicated by the use of the adverb *amanhan* 'tomorrow' in the first sentence, will occur. In subsection 5.1, we showed that item *ka* appears in constructions in the future. Example (27) reveals that this use does not depend on the progressive aspect marking, since, in the sentence ... *no ka sa kume* 'we'll be eating', there is a combination of *ka* with future tense and progressive aspect. Hence, *ka* seems to offer no restriction on the progressive aspect if it is associated with an irrealis context, as seems to be the case with future-tense constructions in Lung'Ie.

Examples (28) and (29) provide further evidence that the item *ka* is not incompatible with the continuous-progressive aspect in irrealis contexts, such as in the case of hypothetical and counterfactual constructions:

(28) Wo   sê   n   pixiza kwê   pwê   we   kaxi   pa   we   kuxi
     moment   DEM   1SG   need   run   put   go   house   for   go   cook
     da   mana   me.   Xi   n   ka   sa   kuxi   wo   sê,
     give   sister   1SG.POSS   if   1SG   IRR   COP   cook   moment DEM
     no   ka   tê   kumê   za.
     1PL   IRR   have   food   already
     'Now I need to run home to cook for my sister. If I were cooking now, we would already have food.' (Agostinho 2015: 261)

(29) Ontxi,   ora   txi   xiga,   xi   no   ka   tava   as   xivi,
     yesterday   hour   2SG   arrive   if   1PL   COUNT MOD   PROG work
     no   ka   tava   vê   txi   fa.
     1PL   MOD   PST   see   2SG   NEG
     'Yesterday, when you came, if we had been working, we wouldn't have seen you.' (Maurer 2009: 90)

In the sentence *Xi n ka sa kuxi wo sê* 'If I were cooking now', in example (28), *ka* combines with the progressive aspect (*ka* > *sa kuxi*) and with the adverb indicating present tense (*wo sê*). This data indicates that prototypically irrealis contexts, such as the hypothetical context, are marked with *ka* regardless of the combinations with tense and aspect categories. In the sentence ... *xi no ka tava sa xivi* 'if we had been working', from example (29), *ka* precedes the functional item *tava* and then the form of the progressive (*sa xivi*) occurs, resulting in the following ordering: *ka* > *tava* > *sa* > dynamic verb. Example (29) also corresponds to a prototypical irrealis context: the counterfactual. Thus, *ka* is indicating irrealis mood; *tava*, in this position, does not correspond to the marker of the past (see discussion of examples (22) and (23) above); *sa* followed by a dynamic verb is marking the progressive aspect. In both (28) and (29), the functional items seem to follow the ordering proposed by Cinque's hierarchy: Mood(irrealis) > ... > ... > ... > AspPprogressive. Until this moment of the research, we did not know the precise interpretation position of the functional item *tava* when it appears after *ka,* but we found clear evidence that it does not correspond to the T(past) head. Considering the sequence *ka* > *tava* > *sa,* it is expected that *tava* corresponds to a head located, in the hierarchy in (24), between Mood(irrealis) and AspProgressive.

The absence of *ka* in the sentences in (25) and (26) and its occurrence in the sentences of the examples (27)–(29) suggest that *ka* only combines with the progressive aspect in irrealis contexts, such as future tense constructions, as in (27), and hypothetical, conditional, or counterfactual constructions, as in (28) and (29). The relationship of *ka* with tense (future and past) was shown in subsection 5.1.

6 *Ka*: Irrealis marking in Lung'Ie

In section 5, we investigated how *ka* relates to the categories of tense, mood, and aspect, seeking to understand what determines or constrains its use in Lung'Ie. In relation to tense, the data indicate that *ka* appears in constructions in the future but does not seem to be compatible with events described in the past or simultaneous to the moment of speech. The occurrence of *ka* in constructions in the past seems to be licensed if the event is described as habitual, as in examples (20) and (21) of subsection 5.3. When analyzing the use of *ka* in relation to the aspect category – habitual and continuous – we found that this item occurs in habitual constructions; its occurrence together with the progressive continuous aspect is only licensed in future contexts, as in (27), or hypothetical, conditional, or counterfactual ones, as in (28) and (29). Analysis of the contexts in which *ka* may or may not figure led us to consider it as a possible irrealis marker in Lung'Ie. To test this hypothesis, we analyzed the distribution of *ka* in contexts presented by the linguistic literature as being typically irrealis and typically realis. We identified that the item *ka* was used in all the constructions that characterize irrealis contexts – counterfactual, hypothetical, and conditional – but did not figure in realis contexts – *non-habitual* events described in the past or at a time simultaneous to the moment of the utterance.

In addition to the contexts presented as prototypical irrealis and realis, the literature on mood treats modal, imperative, interrogative, aspectual, and future tense constructions as contexts that can be marked as irrealis or realis, depending on grammatical factors – such as being or not being a finite sentence – diachronic factors, or even cultural ones that interfere with the speaker's expectation regarding the occurrence of the event (cf. Mithun 1995, 1999; Elliott 2000; de Haan 2006, 2012). Our analysis of Lung'Ie indicated that *ka* figures in constructions in the future tense, signaling that, in Lung'Ie, the future is marked as irrealis. De Haan (2006: 41) holds that it "can be argued that future is a prototypical irrealis category because it refers to events that have not yet happened and are therefore unreal. [. . .] However, in others [languages] it is treated as a realis category". Thus, Lung'Ie would be another example of a language, such as Amele and Muyuw (cf. de Haan 2006: 41), in which the future is marked as irrealis. In addition to the contexts discussed in this chapter, we analyzed negative and imperative constructions. We did not find occurrences of *ka* in them, leading us to assume that such constructions are characterized as realis contexts in Lung'Ie. The occurrences of *ka* with negation were restricted to hypothetical, conditional, and counterfactual contexts, indicating that they prevail over negation for the marking of mood in a sentence.[20]

De Haan (2012: 121) observes that "[h]abitual aspect is perhaps a strange category to discuss in a section about realis and irrealis. As this category denotes that an action is or was done habitually, there would seem to be little doubt that such actions are real and any marker of habitual aspect would fall into the realis camp. Nevertheless, there are languages in which habitual aspect is marked either identical to other irrealis categories or has a separate irrealis morpheme attached". For Elliott (2000: 79), one potential explanation for this is that the non-specific character of the events being addressed leads to the use of irrealis, because no specific realized event is being mentioned. Along the same lines, Payne (2007: 245) states that because habitual aspect defines a type of event that is instantiated from time to time by actual events, it is less realis than perfective aspect clauses. Thus, the occurrence of *ka* in habitual constructions is not necessarily a counter-argument for the analysis we are proposing for Lung'Ie since habitual constructions could correspond to irrealis contexts in this language.

As we have shown throughout section 5, *ka* does not figure in constructions that describe events in the past or simultaneous to the moment of speech, unless such events are narrated as habitual. This allows us to infer that it is the habitual

---

[20] For more details on the analysis of negative and imperative contexts in Lung'Ie, see Rech and Agostinho *(in submission)*.

aspect that is determining the occurrence of *ka*, either because this notion corresponds to an irrealis context in Lung'Ie, or because *ka* indicates habitual aspect as well as irrealis mood. According to de Haan (2012: 122), "if a language has separate (...) constructions for past and present habituals, it can choose whether to mark one or both of them as realis or irrealis". In principle, we are assuming that *ka* uniquely corresponds to an irrealis mood marker, and that constructions in the habitual aspect exhibit *ka* because they correspond to an irrealis context in Lung'Ie. We observe, however, that this point requires a more accurate investigation of the relationships between the functional items that make up the TMA system in Lung'Ie, analyzing constructions in which these items co-occur in the same sentence.

Lung'Ie would not be the only creole language to equate notions of future and habitual with irrealis. According to Winford (2018: 203) "[c]reolists have generally interpreted irrealis (...) as a cover term for future, conditional, and subjunctive meanings. Creoles generally employ future markers in conditional clauses to express hypothetical or counterfactual notions that are associated with conditional or subjunctive mood in other languages". Taylor (1971, 1977) even proposes to group the Atlantic Creoles not only based on similarities in their lexicon but also based on their syntax. His main criterion is how the habitual aspect marking occurs. The author cites, for example, creole languages in which the habitual aspect is indicated by the same future or irrealis marker, such as Kabuverdianu and Negerhollands, as well as Santome (which is genetically related to Lung'Ie).

Our objective in this research was not to investigate the relationships between all the functional items that make up the Lung'Ie TMA system. We note, however, that our findings fit the model of Bickerton (1981: 58; 1984), who argues that the prototypical TMA system of creole languages is formed by three categories[21]: past tense, irrealis mood, and non-punctual aspect; which, in Lung'Ie, would be respectively marked by: Ø/*tava*, *ka*, and *sa*.

Rech and Agostinho (in submission) note that the item *ka* occurs in similar contexts in the languages of the Gulf of Guinea genetically related to Lung'Ie (Santome, Angolar, and Fa d'Ambô) (cf. Ferraz 1979; Muysken 1981; Singler 1990; Bakker et al. 1994; Hagemeijer 2007, 2013a, 2013b; Post 2013; Bandeira 2017; among others), appearing in conditional, counterfactual, future, and habitual aspect constructions. Hagemeijer (2007, 2013a) argues that Santome's *ka* corresponds to two distinct items with different tone patterns: (i) a future and habit-

---

21 Voorhoeve (1957) and Bickerton (1975, 1981) claim that the prototypical order of pre-verbal functional items in creole languages is TMA.

ual/generic function, and (ii) a mood (hypothetical) function.[22] This analysis was based on the syntactic distribution of *ka* in relation to the copula (*sa* ~ *tava*) and on the tonal marking of *ka*, which, according to the author, presents two distinct tonal patterns. However, this is not supported by a phonological analysis. In Lung'Ie, *ka* is not associated with more than one phonological tone pattern, according to the study by Rech and Agostinho (in submission). Maurer (2009: 25) also does not assume two phonological tonal patterns for *ka*, citing only a phonetic variation resulting from the pitch of the subsequent verb.

In the literature on Lung'Ie, *ka* is associated with more than one function. For Günther (1973), *ka* corresponds to a marker of habitual aspect, future tense and generic reference. Maurer (1997, 2009) associates *ka* with various functions, such as marking the habitual present, habitual past, future, modality, counterfactuality, imperfective aspect, and generic reference, among others. Contrary to the work of these authors, we propose that item *ka* performs a single function in Lung'Ie: that of marking a context as being irrealis. Our proposal is that mood marking in Lung'Ie is performed by the opposition between realis – unmarked form in the language – and irrealis, marked by the occurrence of *ka* in hypothetical, conditional, counterfactual, future, and habitual contexts. The linguistic literature on mood present languages that exhibit different morphemes marking mood for realis and irrealis such as Central Pomo (see Mithun 1995: 370–372). Sometimes, however, only one member of this opposition displays explicit marking; in these cases, the commonly marked member is irrealis (cf. Elliott 2000: 57). This is the case for languages such as Jamul Diegueño (see Mithun 1999: 179) and Paresi (see Rech and Brandão 2018: 2823; Rech, Brandão and Wit 2018: 15); this also seems to be the case for Lung'Ie.

7 Conclusion

Regarding the methodology for collecting data for the study of modality in endangered languages, we discussed the use of traditional stories collected in fieldwork. This was the method used in our research, which allowed us to obtain natural data without the need to adapt external material to the community's culture. We also emphasized that the collection of these stories contributes to the documen-

---

[22] In Hagemeijer (2013a), the author considers the markers *ká tava* and *ká tava ka* as irrealis mood. However, in Hagemeijer (2011, 2013b), the author considers *ká* as an irrealis marker by itself. In Lung'Ie, the sequence *ka tava ka is not attested (cf. Günther 1973; Maurer 1997, 2009: 140; Agostinho 2009, 2010, 2015, 2016a; Agostinho and Rech 2016).

tation of oral literature in languages that are poorly described and in danger of extinction, as is the case with Lung'Ie. At the same time, this type of material may come to be used by researchers from other areas of linguistics and by members of the community itself (linguists or not) and may thus constitute a source of consultation for linguistic conservation and revitalization projects as well as support future educational projects.[23]

It is important to state that many issues have only been suggested in this chapter, which points to future research on how *ka* relates to other categories of the TMA system in Lung'Ie and the other creole languages of the Gulf of Guinea.[24] We point out, throughout the chapter, that this functional item has a close relationship with the modality category, more specifically with the expression of possibility, as it *co-occurs* with the modal auxiliary *po/podi* 'can', but not with *tê di/tê ki* 'have to', which corresponds to a strong necessity modal. This finding was made from the consultation of data from traditional stories from fieldwork research by Agostinho (2009, 2010, 2015, 2016a) and Agostinho and Rech (2016) in addition to data from the works of Günther (1973) and Maurer (2009). This point needs to be carefully investigated to understand if there is, in fact, a restriction on the use of *ka* in constructions with necessity modals. If *ka* corresponds to irrealis marking in Lung'Ie, as we are proposing, such a restriction would be expected, since the force of necessity, linked to *tê di/tê ki* 'have to', indicates that the proposition on which the modal item operates is necessarily true (realis) in all the worlds of evaluation considered.

An important next step would be to investigate the scope relationships that are established between the categories that make up the TMA system. An accurate analysis of constructions with the co-occurrence of more than one functional head will contribute to a better understanding of sequences such as *ka > tava; tava > ka;* and *ka > tava > sa*, which figured in our data. Winford (2018: 206) notes that studies testing whether TMA systems of creole languages conform to Cinque's (1999) hierarchy reveal that the combinatorial possibilities of TMA morphemes are quite complex (see van de Vate (2011) and Durrleman (2000)). Considering that such studies have not been replicated in other creole languages (cf. Winford 2018: 205), this author states that there is still no basis for establishing a comparison between the ordering of the functional heads in these languages.

---

[23] For more information on educational projects involving Lung'Ie, see Agostinho (2015); Agostinho, Bandeira, and Araujo (2016); and Agostinho and Araujo (2021).

[24] Rech and Agostinho (in submission) proposed that *ka* was already present in the Proto-Creole of the Gulf of Guinea, as it occurs in Santome, Angolar, and Fa d'Ambô in contexts similar to those of Lung'Ie. Therefore, we consider it interesting to carry out comparative studies on irrealis mood marking between Lung'Ie and the other creole languages of the Gulf of Guinea.

In this vein, we believe it is important to continue the study of the categories that make up the TMA system of Lung'Ie, adopting the assumptions of cartographic syntax (Cinque 1999, 2006), to map the positions in which each functional item is interpreted in the structure as well as to verify the explanatory power of the hierarchy of functional heads across languages.

References

Achebe, Chinua. 1958. *Things fall apart*. London: Heinemann.
Agostinho, Ana Lívia. 2009. *Fieldnotes and data collection – São Tomé and Príncipe*. Manuscript.
Agostinho, Ana Lívia. 2010. *Fieldnotes and data collection – São Tomé and Príncipe*. Manuscript.
Agostinho, Ana Lívia. 2015. *Fonologia e método pedagógico do lung'Ie* [Phonology and pedagogical method of Lung'Ie]. São Paulo: University of São Paulo dissertation.
Agostinho, Ana Lívia. 2016a. *Fieldnotes and data collection: São Tomé and Príncipe*. Manuscript.
Agostinho, Ana Lívia. 2016b. *Fonologia do lung'Ie* [The phonology of Lung'Ie]. München: Lincom.
Agostinho, Ana Lívia, Gabriel Antunes de Araujo & Eduardo Ferreira dos Santos. 2019. Interrogative particle and phrasal pitch-accent in polar questions in Fa d'Ambô. *Boletim do Museu Paraense Emílio Goeldi Ciências Humanas* 14 (3). 1–16.
Agostinho, Ana Lívia & Gabriel Antunes de Araujo. 2021. *Lung'Ie, lunge no: Método para aprender lung'Ie* [Lung'Ie, our language: A method to learn Lung'Ie]. São Paulo: FFLCH/USP.
Agostinho, Ana Lívia, Manuele Bandeira & Gabriel Antunes de Araujo. 2016. O lung'Ie na educação escolar de São Tomé e Príncipe [Lung'Ie in the educational system of São Tomé and Príncipe]. *Trabalhos em Linguística Aplicada* 55 (3). 591–618.
Agostinho, Ana Lívia & Núbia Ferreira Rech. 2016. *Fieldnotes and data collection – São Tomé and Príncipe*. Manuscript.
Araujo, Gabriel Antunes de & Ana Lívia Agostinho. 2010. Padronização das línguas nacionais de São Tomé e Príncipe [Standardization of the national languages of São Tomé and Príncipe]. *Língua e Instrumentos Linguísticos* 26. 49–81.
Arregui, Ana, Maria Luisa Rivero & Andres Salanova (eds.). 2017. *Modality across syntactic categories*. Oxford: Oxford University Press.
Bakker, Peter, Marike Post & Hein van der Voort. 1994. TMA particles and auxiliaries. In Jacques Arends, Pieter Muysken & Norval Smith (eds.), *Pidgins and creoles: An introduction*, 247–258. Amsterdam: John Benjamins.
Bandeira, Manuele. 2017. *Reconstrução fonológica e lexical do Protocrioulo do Golfo da Guiné* [Phonological and lexical reconstruction of Proto-Creole from the Gulf of Guinea]. São Paulo: Universidade de São Paulo dissertation.
Bickerton, Derek. 1975. *Dynamics of a creole system*. Cambridge: Cambridge University Press.
Bickerton, Derek. 1981. *Roots of language*. Ann Arbor: Karoma Press.
Bickerton, Derek. 1984. The language bioprogram hypothesis. *Behavioral and Brain Sciences* 7 (2). 173–188.
Bowern, Claire. 2015. *Linguistics fieldwork: A practical guide*. Hampshire: Palgrave Macmillan.
Bueno, Otávio & Scott A. Shalkowski (eds.). 2020. *The Routledge handbook of modality*. London: Routledge.

Caldeira, Arlindo Manuel. 2008. Tráfico de escravos e conflitualidade. O arquipélago de São Tomé e Príncipe e o Reino do Congo durante o século XVI [Slave trade and conflict. The archipelago of São Tomé and Príncipe and the Kingdom of Congo during the 16th century]. *Revista Ciências e Letras* 44. 55–76.
Caldeira, Arlindo Manuel. 2013. *Escravos e traficantes no império português* [Slaves and traders in the Portuguese empire]. Lisboa: Esfera do Livro.
Cardoso, Manuela. 2007. *Cabo Verde e S. Tomé e Príncipe* [Cape Verde and S. Tomé and Príncipe]. Porto: IPAD.
Cinque, Guglielmo. 1999. *Adverbs and functional heads: A cross-linguistic perspective.* New York: Oxford University Press.
Cinque, Guglielmo. 2006. *Restructuring and functional heads: The cartography of syntactic structures.* New York: Oxford University Press.
Comrie, Bernard. 1976. *Aspect.* Cambridge: Cambridge University Press.
Crystal, David. 2000. *Language death.* Cambridge: Cambridge University Press.
Daval-Markussen, Aymeric & Peter Bakker. 2017. Creole typology II. In Peter Bakker, Finn Borchsenius, Carsten Levisen & Eeva Sippola (eds.), *Creole studies – Phylogenetic Approaches*, 103–140. Amsterdam & Philadelphia: John Benjamins.
de Haan, Ferdinand. 2006. Typological approaches to modality. In William Frawley (ed.), *The Expression of Modality*, 27–69. Berlin: Mouton de Gruyter.
de Haan, Ferdinand. 2012. Irrealis: fact or fiction? *Language Sciences* 34 (2). 107–130.
Durrleman, Stephanie. 2000. The architecture of the clause in Jamaican creole. *Generative Grammar in Geneva* 1. 189–240.
Elliott, Jennifer R. 2000. Realis and irrealis: Forms of grammaticalisation of reality. *Linguistic Typology* 5. 55–90.
Ferraz, Luiz Ivens. 1979. *The creole of São Tomé.* Johannesburg: Witwatersrand University Press.
Günther, Wilfried. 1973. *Das portugiesische Kreolisch der Ilha do Príncipe* [The Portuguese Creole of Príncipe Island]. Marburg an der Lahn: Im Selbstverlag.
Hagemeijer, Tjerk. 2007. *Clause structure in Santome.* Lisboa: Universidade de Lisboa dissertation.
Hagemeijer, Tjerk. 2011. The Gulf of Guinea creoles: genetic and typological relations. *Journal of Pidgin and Creole Languages* 26 (1). 111–154.
Hagemeijer, Tjerk. 2013a. Santome. In Susanne Maria Michaelis, Philippe Maurer, Martin Haspelmath & Magnus Huber (eds.), *Atlas of pidgin and creole language structures online*, Leipzig, Max Planck Institute for Evolutionary Anthropology, https://apics-online.info/.
Hagemeijer, Tjerk. 2013b. The Gulf of Guinea creoles: Genetic and typological relations. In Parth Bhatt & Tonjes Veenstra (eds.), *Creole languages and linguistic typology*, 163–206. Amsterdam & Philadelphia: John Benjamins.
Holm, John. 2004. *An introduction to pidgins and creoles.* Cambridge: Cambridge University Press.
INE. 2012. *População segundo línguas faladas* [Population according to languages spoken], RGPH 2012. São Tomé: Instituto Nacional de Estatística.
Inegbeboh, Bridget O. 2016. *"Okha": Folktale tradition of the Esan people and African oral literature.* Paper presented at the Inaugural Lectures of Samuel Adegboyega University, 16 May.
Frawley, William (ed.). 2006. *The expression of modality.* Berlin: Mouton de Gruyter.
Ladhams, John. 2012. Article agglutination and the African contribution to the Portuguese-based creoles. In Angela Bartens & Philip Baker (eds.), *Black through white. African words and calques which survived slavery and creoles and transplanted European languages*, 31–50. London: Battlebridge Publications.

Longacre, Robert E. 1990. *Storyline concerns and word order typology in East and West Africa*. Los Angeles: University of California, Los Angeles.
Mair, Christian. 2012. Progressive and continuous aspect. In Robert I. Binnick (ed.), *The Oxford handbook of tense and aspect*. Published online, https://www.oxfordhandbooks.com/view/10.1093/oxfordhb/9780195381979.001.0001/oxfordhb-9780195381979-e-28.
Maurer, Philippe. 1997. Tense-aspect-mood in Lung'Ie. In Arthur K. Spears & Donald Winford (eds.), *The structure and status of pidgins and creoles*, 415–435. Amsterdam: Benjamins.
Maurer, Philippe. 2009. *Principense (Lung'Ie)*. London: Battlebridge Publications.
Mithun, Marianne. 1995. On the relativity of irrealis. In Joan Bybee & Suzanne Fleischman (eds.), *Modality in Grammar and Discourse*, 367–388. Amsterdam: John Benjamins.
Mithun, Marianne. 1999. *The languages of native North America*. New York: Cambridge University Press.
Muysken, Peter. 1981. Creole tense/mood/aspect systems: The unmarked case? In Peter Muysken (ed.), *Generative studies on creole languages*, 181–199. Dordrecht: Foris.
Nurse, Derek, Sarah Rose & John Hewson. 2016. *Tense and aspect in Niger-Congo*. Tervuren: Royal Museum for Central Africa.
Nuyts, Jan & Johan van der Auwera (eds.). 2016. *The Oxford handbook of modality and mood*. Oxford: Oxford University Press.
Okeh, Peter I. 1995. Nigeria language arts in the Delphic games. *Proceedings of the Workshop on the Nigerian Delphic Games*. Lagos.
Payne, Thomas E. 2007. *Describing morphosyntax: A guide for field linguists*. Cambridge: Cambridge University Press.
Pontífice, João, Caustrino Alcântara, Beatriz de Castro Afonso, Tjerk Hagemeijer & Philippe Maurer. 2010. *Alfabeto unificado para a escrita das línguas nativas de S. Tomé e Príncipe (ALUSTP)* [Unified alphabet for writing the native languages of S. Tomé and Príncipe (ALUSTP)]. Manuscript.
Portner, Paul. 2009. *Modality*. Oxford: Oxford University Press.
Portner, Paul. 2018. *Mood*. Oxford: Oxford University Press.
Post, Marike. 2013. Fa d'Ambô. In Susanne Maria Michaelis, Philippe Maurer, Martin Haspelmath & Magnus Huber (eds.), *Atlas of pidgin and creole language structures online*, Leipzig, Max Planck Institute for Evolutionary Anthropology, https://apics-online.info/.
Rech, Núbia Ferreira & Ana Lívia Agostinho. In submission. *Irrealis mood in Lung'Ie: Ka*.
Rech, Núbia Ferreira & Ana Paula Brandão. 2018. A marcação de modalidade deôntica no Paresi [Marking of deontic modality in Paresi]. *Fórum Linguístico* 15 (1). 2816–2827.
Rech, Núbia Ferreira, Ana Paula Brandão & Marina de Wit. 2018. The relationship between irrealis mood and deontic modality in Paresi (Arawak). *Liames – Línguas Indígenas Americanas* 18 (2). 229–252.
Rolka, Matthew and Seth Cable. 2014. Tom and mittens. Totem Field Storyboards. URL http://www.totemfieldstoryboards.org/stories/tom_and_mittens/ (accessed 23 September 2020).
Schuchardt, Hugo. 1889. Beiträge zur Kenntnis des kreolischen Romanisch IV. Zum Negerportugiesischen der Ilha do Principe [Contributions to the knowledge of Romance Creole IV. On the Negro-Portuguese of the Príncipe Island]. *Zeitschrift für Romanische Philologie* 13. 461–475.
Seibert, Gerhard. 2013. São Tomé and Príncipe: The first plantation economy in the tropics. In Robin Law, Suzanne Schwarz & Silke Strickrodt (eds.), *Commercial agriculture, the slave trade and slavery in Atlantic Africa*, 54–78. Suffolk: Boydell & Brewer.

Seibert, Gerhard. 2014. Crioulização em Cabo Verde e São Tomé e Príncipe: Divergências Históricas e Identitárias [Creolization in Cape Verde and São Tomé and Príncipe: Historical and Identity Divergences]. *Afro-Ásia* 49. 41–70.
Singler, John Victor (ed.). 1990. *Pidgin and creole tense/mood/aspect systems*. Amsterdam & Philadelphia: John Benjamins.
Taylor, Douglas. 1971. Grammatical and lexical affinities of creoles. In Dell Hymes (ed.), *Pidiginization and creolization of languages*, 293–296. Cambridge: Cambridge University Press.
Taylor, Douglas. 1977. *Languages of the West Indies*. Baltimore: Johns Hopkins University Press.
TFS Working Group. 2011. Chore girl. Totem Field Storyboards. URL http://www.totemfieldstoryboards.org/stories/chore_girl/ (accessed 23 September 2020).
Thomas, N. W. 1920. Thirty-two folk-tales of the Edo-speaking peoples of Nigeria. *Folklore* 31 (3). 210–230.
Valkhoff, Marius F. 1966. *Studies in Portuguese and Creole*. Johannesburg: Witwatersrand University Press.
van de Vate, Marleen Susanne. 2011. *Tense, aspect and modality in a radical creole: The case of Saamáka*. Tromsø, Norway: University of Tromsø dissertation.
Vaux, Bert, Justin Cooper & Emily Tucker. 2007. *Linguistic field methods*. Oregon: Wipf & Stock.
Voorhoeve, Jan. 1957. The verbal system of Sranan. *Lingua* 6. 374–396.
Winford, Donald. 2018. Creole tense-mood-aspect systems. *Annual Review of Linguistics* 4 (1). 193–212.

Marianne Huijsmans
9 Analyzing ʔayʔaǰuθəm evidentials: Evidence for epistemic modality

Abstract: This chapter provides an analysis of two evidential clitics in ʔayʔaǰuθəm (Comox-Sliammon), a Central Salish language. These evidentials, an inferential and reportative, are argued to be strong epistemic modals, supporting claims that evidentials and epistemic modals are overlapping categories. Because the commonly used diagnostics for distinguishing between modal and nonmodal evidentials have all been criticized, a major focus of this chapter is identifying which diagnostics actually probe this distinction and how they can be implemented in fieldwork contexts.

1 Introduction

In this chapter, I argue that two evidential clitics in ʔayʔaǰuθəm, a Central Salish language, are epistemic modals. Both of these evidentials, an inferential clitic č̓ɛ and a reportative clitic k̓ʷa, contribute a strong modal claim to the at-issue content of the clause and an evidential presupposition. ʔayʔaǰuθəm evidentials thus provide counterevidence to the claim that evidentiality and epistemic modality are non-overlapping categories (De Haan 1999; Aikhenvald 2004); instead, these evidentials provide additional evidence that at least some evidentials are epistemic modals (Matthewson, Rullmann and Davis 2007; Peterson 2010; Tan Almazán 2019, among others; see Matthewson 2012 for arguments that all evidentials are epistemic modals). Since the commonly used diagnostics for distinguishing between modal and nonmodal evidentials have all been criticized

---

Acknowledgements: I want to thank my consultants for sharing their language with me so patiently and generously; without their heroic dedication to their language, this work would not be possible. In particular, I would like to thank Elsie Paul, Freddie Louie, Betty Wilson, and Joanne Francis for their contributions to this chapter: čɛčɛhatanapɛč! I would also like to thank Lisa Matthewson, Henry Davis, Gunnar Hansson, and two anonymous reviewers for their very helpful feedback, as well as Daniel Reisinger with whom I discussed many of these topics. Finally, I am grateful for support for this research through a SSHRC Insight grant (#435-2016-1694) to Henry Davis and a Jacobs Research Funds grant. All errors are my own.

Marianne Huijsmans, University of British Columbia, Department of Linguistics, 2613 West Mall, Vancouver, BC V6T 1Z4, e-mail: marianne.huijsmans@ubc.ca

https://doi.org/10.1515/9783110721478-010

(e.g., Korotkova 2016), a major focus of this chapter is identifying which diagnostics can be used to argue for a modal (or nonmodal) analysis and how they can be implemented in a fieldwork situation.

ʔayʔajuθəm is the northernmost of the chain of languages making up the Central Salish branch of the Salish language family. The language is traditionally spoken in the Tla'amin, Homalco, Klahoose, and Kómoks First Nations, along the northern part of the Georgia Straight in British Columbia. According to the 2018 First Peoples' Cultural Council report, there are approximately 47 first language speakers remaining. Determined efforts are underway within the four communities to document and transmit the language to future generations.

Reisinger (2018) provides an overview of elements suspected to be modal in ʔayʔajuθəm, including the two evidentials discussed here. While he provides much interesting documentation, however, he assumes, rather than establishes, the modality of these evidentials. My goal in this paper is to provide empirical support for the claim that these elements are epistemic modals. All data in this chapter comes from original fieldwork using methodologies advocated in, for example, Matthewson (2004) and Bochnak and Matthewson (2015).

The two evidential particles discussed in this paper are second-position clitics. The inferential clitic če indicates that the speaker is making an inference in uttering the prejacent, while the reportative clitic k̓ʷa indicates that the speaker heard the prejacent from a third party. These clitics are members of a large set of clitics that appear in a fixed order following the initial prosodic word in the clause (see Watanabe (2003: 509–531) for the most extensive previous description of the ʔayʔajuθəm second-position clitic system). The clitic string includes indicators of force, evidentiality, and temporal reference, as well as subject agreement clitics and discourse particles.[1] Table 1 shows the inventory of clitics arranged according

---

[1] The glosses used in this paper are as follows: 1,2,3 first, second and third person; ACT.INTR active intransitive; CAUS causative; CHAR characteristic reduplication; CL.DEM clausal demonstrative; CNJ conjunctive; COMP complementizer; CONJ conjunction; COP copula; CTR control transitivizer; DEM demonstrative; DET determiner; DPRT discourse particle; EPST epistemic uncertainty; ERG ergative; EXCL exclusive; EXCLAM exclamative; FUT future; IND indicative; INFER inferential; INT intensifier; IRR irrealis; MD middle; NCTR non-control transitivizer; NEG negative; NMLZ nominalizer; OBJ object; OBL oblique; PASS passive; PL plural; POSS possessive; PRF perfect; PROG progressive; PRT particle; PST past; Q question particle; REFL reflexive; REL relative; REP reportative; RPT reportative; SBJ subject; SG singular; STAT stative; SUBJ subjunctive. A hyphen (-) is used to represent morpheme boundaries within words, an equals sign (=) is used to represent clitic boundaries, and a plus sign (+) is used where two co-occurring morphemes fuse in a way that is not predictable from the phonology. 'vf' (volunteered form) following an example indicates that the form was volunteered by the consultant. 'sf' (suggested form) following an example indicates that the researcher constructed the example and then asked if it was grammatical and/or appropriate in a given context.

Table 1: ʔayʔaǰuθəm 2PCs and ordering.

Force	Subject		Evid		Fut		ClDem		Other	
a	č (čan)	'1SG.SBJ'	ča	'INFER'	səm/saʔ	'FUT'	kʷi	'CL.DEM'	ga	'DPRT'
ala 'EXCLAM'	čxʷ (čaxʷ)	'2SG.SBJ'	k̓ʷa	'RPT'			kʷa	'CL.DEM'	ʔut	'EXCL'
	št (čat)	'1PL.SBJ'					ti	'CL.DEM'	hiyt	'DPRT'
	čap	'2PL.SBJ'					ta	'CL.DEM'	χʷuʔt	'DPRT'
									qəɬ	'IRR'

to their position in the clitic string; the clitics are represented in their underlying forms (but note that I will be using the orthographic forms to represent the evidential clitics in the text throughout the chapter).[2]

As can be seen from the table above (see also (1a) and (1b) below), čɛ and k̓ʷa both occur following the question clitic and preceding the future clitic.[3]

(1) a. Context: It's very cloudy out.
  čɬa čɛ səm.
  čəɬ=a=čɛ=səm
  rain=Q=INFER=FUT
  'I wonder if it will rain.'   vf

 b. Context: I missed the news, but I know that you listened to the news.
  čɬa k̓ʷa səm   snat?
  čəɬ=a=k̓ʷa=səm   snat
  rain=Q=RPT=FUT tonight
  'Is it going to rain tonight (according to the report)?'   vf

The inferential and reportative clitics cannot co-occur (2a–b), cf. (2c–d), suggesting that they occupy the same syntactic position.[4] I assume that this is a head in the upper part of the clause between TP and CP.

---

[2] Watanabe (2003) includes several additional clitics which I take to be contractions of the clitics listed here. I also only include indicative subject agreement in the table, but there are subjunctive and possessive subject clitics that occupy the same position and occur in embedded clauses.
[3] Each example in this paper is represented both in the ʔayʔajuθəm orthography (the first line under the context) and in a roughly phonemic representation with morpheme breaks (the line following the orthographic representation).
[4] An anonymous reviewer asks if the restrictions on co-occurrence could be semantic as well as syntactic. One can imagine a situation where the speaker has reported evidence that p, but due to conflicting evidence or a conflicting report must take additional knowledge into account to infer whether p is true. This would seem to be a case where semantically both evidentials would be licensed. Even in such cases, however, co-occurrence is impossible. I therefore take this restriction to be syntactic rather than semantic in nature.
 (i) Context: There's a dispute about whether Freddie is home or in Vancouver. My sister said she saw Freddie at the store, but my brother insists that he is still in Vancouver. I trust my sister in these things more than my brother, so when discussing later with you, I say:

  *čɛ k̓ʷak̓ʷa   qʷol   hɛwt   Freddie.
  ča=k̓ʷa=k̓ʷa   qʷəl   hiwt   Freddie
  INFER=RPT=CL.DEM   come   get.home Freddie
  'Freddie must be home.'

(2) a. * ho čɛ k̓ʷa səm.
   hu=ča=k̓ʷa=səm
   ho=INFER=RPT=FUT
   Intended: 'I'm guessing they said he would go.'   sf

   b. * ho k̓ʷa čɛ səm.
   * hu=k̓ʷa=ča=səm
   ho=RPT=INFER=FUT
   Intended: 'They said they thought he would go.'   sf

   c. ho k̓ʷa səm.
   hu=k̓ʷa=səm
   go=RPT=FUT
   'They say he'll go.'   sf

   d. ho čɛ səm.
   hu=ča=səm
   go=INFER=FUT
   'I guess he'll go.'   sf

Evidential marking does not appear in every clause in ʔayʔaǰuθəm. čɛ and k̓ʷa occur frequently, however, and are preferred where the context supports their use. Unmarked clauses are usually interpreted as based on direct evidence, but this does not seem to be obligatorily the case. I therefore do not propose a null direct evidential in the paradigm. The quasi-obligariness is consistent with an analysis where absence of čɛ and k̓ʷa implies (through a quantity implicature, e.g., Grice 1989), rather than encodes, direct evidence.[5]

For the semantic contribution of čɛ and k̓ʷa, I adopt von Fintel and Gillies' (2010) approach to epistemic modals. von Fintel and Gillies argue that all epistemic modals are evidentials which signal that the speaker bases the prejacent on inference rather than direct evidence. This is captured through a presupposition that the speaker's direct information does not settle whether the prejacent

---

[5] According to Aikhenvald (2007) only obligatory markers of evidence source can be classified as evidentials – that is, only languages where evidentiality is obligatorily marked in every clause can be said to have evidentials. Most classifications are less stringent, however. Brugman and Macaulay (2015), for instance, argue that evidentials are morphemes that mark source of evidence for the embedded proposition and are members in grammatical systems. Insofar as the ʔayʔaǰuθəm evidential clitics form a closed 'grammatical system', these clitics are straightforwardly classified as evidentials.

is true.[6] I adopt their denotation for English *must* to capture the meaning of the inferential *čɛ*. The reportative *kʷa* requires some additional content for which I follow Matthewson's (2010) adaption of von Fintel and Gillies' proposal for the St'át'imcets reportative *ku7*. She proposes that the reportative carries an additional presupposition that the prejacent is known through a report. She also proposes that the reportative requires a differentiation between the speaker's direct sensory information and general knowledge. The inferential cannot be used with a prejacent that is general knowledge, since general knowledge counts as direct information (cf. English # *The earth must be round*.). In contrast, the reportative is compatible with the prejacent being general knowledge learnt through report. Matthewson therefore proposes that the reportative's presupposition concerning the speaker's absence of direct information settling whether the prejacent is true only makes reference to the speaker's direct *sensory* information.

The remainder of this paper is organized as follows. Section 2 provides background on modal and non-modal approaches to evidentials. In section 3, I identify diagnostics for distinguishing between modal and nonmodal evidentials and discuss the results of implementing these diagnostics for the inferential and reportative evidentials in ʔayʔaǰuθəm. In section 4, I discuss the use of these evidentials in questions and address potential counter-evidence for a modal analysis. Finally, in section 5, I propose a formal analysis of the two evidentials adopting von Fintel and Gillies' (2010) framework for epistemic modals.

2 Modality and evidentiality

There is an obvious link between indirect evidentiality and epistemic modality; both indicate that the speaker infers the truth of the prejacent from indirect information. The presence of this link has generated debate about the relationship between evidentials and epistemic modals, at least since Izvorksi's (1997) seminal modal analysis of the Bulgarian perfect of evidentiality. Evidentials emerged as a prominent topic in linguistics in the 1980's and 1990's in part through typological studies such as Willett (1998) and De Haan (1999). De Haan (1999) and later Aikhenvald (2004) argued that evidentials are a distinct category from epistemic modals and that the two categories do not overlap. In the formal semantics litera-

---

[6] By presupposition here, I am referring to a non-cancellable, non-at-issue contribution that projects. I am not claiming that modals in ʔayʔaǰuθəm involve Common Ground restrictions. Salish languages are known for not placing restrictions on the Common Ground (Matthewson 1998, 2005; Gillon 2006; Huijsmans et al. 2018).

ture, Izvorski (1997), followed by others such as Garrett (2001), Faller (2002), and Matthewson, Rullmann and Davis (2007), proposed that at least some evidentials are best analyzed as epistemic modals. Matthewson (2012) takes the strong position that all evidentials are epistemic modals and vice versa, while von Fintel and Gillies (2010) and Kratzer (2012) take the slightly weaker position that epistemic modals are evidentials (but evidentials need not be epistemic modals).

Faller's (2002) dissertation emerges as an important contribution to this discussion because she develops a nonmodal formal model for analyzing evidentials (see also Garrett 2001), proposing that they can be illocutionary operators, rather than epistemic modals. She argues that modal and non-modal evidentials co-exist in the same paradigm in Cuzco Quechua (see also Garrett (2001) for Tibetan and Peterson (2010) for Gitksan): she analyzes the conjectural evidential as having an epistemic modal component, but the reportative and direct evidentials as nonmodal evidentials. She proposes that all three of these evidentials in Cuzco Quechua are illocutionary operators that modify the sincerity conditions and/or illocutionary force of the speech act. Murray (2010) later also develops a nonmodal analysis of the evidentials in Cheyenne; she proposes that the evidentials contribute not-at-issue content concerning the source of evidence, and an illocutionary relation concerning how/whether to update the common ground with the scope proposition.

Empirically, the modal and nonmodal approaches make different predictions. In the modal approach, the speaker is committed to a modal claim concerning the prejacent: that it is possibly or necessarily true. Modal evidentials are therefore predicted to alter the at-issue content and truth conditions of the proposition. Illocutionary evidentials, on the other hand, make no at-issue contribution and do not alter the truth conditions. They can, however, change the illocutionary force of the speech act. Below, I briefly present an analysis under each approach to illustrate the key aspects of the different analyses before identifying diagnostics that can distinguish between them.

2.1 A modal analysis of evidentials

Izvorski (1997), discussing the Bulgarian perfect of evidentiality, provides the first modal analysis of an evidential. The Bulgarian perfect of evidentiality is used when the speaker has indirect evidence for the prejacent, and is infelicitous where the speaker has direct evidence. It is therefore infelicitous with following assertions to the effect that the speaker has prior direct information that the prejacent is true (3).[7]

(3) *Maria celunala Ivan.*
 Maria kiss-PE Ivan
 'Maria apparently kissed Ivan.'
 #(Actually) I witnessed it. / # (Actually) I know that for a fact.

 (Izvorski 1997: 228)

Izvorski proposes that this evidential is an epistemic modal with an added presupposition that the speaker has indirect evidence for the embedded proposition.

(4) a. Presupposition: The speaker has indirect evidence for p.
 b. Assertion: $\Box\, p$ in view of the speaker's knowledge state.

 (Izvorski 1997: 226)

In this analysis, the modal base is the set of worlds in which all the propositions considered evidence in w are true (Izvorski 1997: 230). The ordering source ranks the worlds of the modal base according to how many of the set of propositions believed by the speaker concerning the available indirect evidence are true in that world (e.g., propositions concerning what the speaker believes about the likelihood of the prejacent given some evidence proposition in the modal base). Crucially, the modal claim in Izvorksi's analysis is at-issue, while the evidential contribution is presupposed.

2.2 An illocutionary analysis of evidentials

Faller (2002) analyzes the direct, reportative, and conjunctural evidentials in Cuzco Quechua as illocutionary operators. She adopts Vanderveken (1990)'s approach to speech acts, analyzing the evidentials as playing a role in determining the illocutionary point, sincerity conditions, and strength of speech acts. In Vanderveken's (1990) theory, every speech act has an illocutionary force (e.g., assertion, directive, commissive) determined by six components: the illocutionary point, mode of achievement, propositional content conditions, preparatory conditions, sincerity conditions, and strength. The illocutionary point of a speech

---

[7] As discussed in Smirnova (2013), the Bulgarian perfect of evidentiality can in fact be used with direct evidence, but then it expresses mirativity.

act specifies its word-to-world relation: assertions match or describe the world, while directives attempt to change to world to match the propositional content, for instance. The sincerity condition of a speech act requires that the speaker has the mental state expressed in the performance of the speech act; if a sentence has the illocutionary force of an assertion, for instance, there is a sincerity condition that the speaker must believe the proposition to be true. Strength is a property of this mental state, playing a role in distinguishing between giving testimony and making a conjecture, for instance, because the speaker's degree of belief differs between them. For Faller, the evidentials impose sincerity conditions to do with the speaker's information source. The reportative also affects the illocutionary force of the speech act, while the direct evidential affects the 'strength' of the speech act.

To illustrate, when the direct evidential -*mi* combines with a speech act *ASSERT(p)*, the illocutionary point remains one of assertion, but the direct evidential adds a sincerity condition that the speaker must have the 'best possible grounds' for uttering *p*, usually seeing the event e_p described by *p*. Use of -*mi* also strengthens the assertion (from a default value 0 to +1).

(5) *Para-sha-n-**mi***.
rain- PROG -3-**mi**
p = 'It is raining.'
ILL=ASSERT$_s$(*p*)
SINC = {$Bel(s, p)$, EV = $See(s, e_p)$}
STRENGTH = +1   (Faller 2002: 164)

When the reportative evidential -*si* combines with a speech act *ASSERT(p)*, it alters the illocutionary point to one of presentation, rather than assertion, meaning that the speaker does not claim the propositional content to fit the world, but simply presents the propositional content to the hearer. The use of the reportative also adds a sincerity condition such that a third party asserted *p*.[8]

---

[8] Because the utterance has the illocutionary point of *presentation*, the speech act must also have a different illocutionary force than an assertion. This is because the illocutionary force of a speech act is determined by its components, and only when all the components are identical is the same type of illocutionary force expressed (Vanderveken 2001: 28). Faller therefore introduces a new type of speech act: PRESENT (Faller 2002: 199).

(6) *Para-sha-n-**si***.
rain-PROG-3-**si**
p = 'It is raining.'
ILL = PRESENT$_s(p)$
SINC = $\{\exists s_2[\text{ASSERT}(s_2, p) \wedge s_2 \notin \{h,s\}]\}$ (Faller 2002: 199)
(where s = speaker, h = hearer, s_2 = source of the report)

The illocutionary point of presentation allows the speaker to utter p based on another person's report without believing the report to be true, as in (7).

(7) *Para-sha-n-**si**, ichaqa mana crei-ni-chu.*
rain-PROG -3-**si** but not believe-1-NEG
'It is raining, but I don't believe it.' (Faller 2002: 194)

Crucially, the analysis of evidentials as illocutionary operators means that the evidentials do not contribute to the at-issue content of the clause, though they may affect the illocutionary force of the utterance.

3 Applying diagnostics in ʔayʔaǰuθəm

In this section, I first identify diagnostics for modal and nonmodal evidentials (section 3.1). These diagnostics involve testing whether the evidential can take scope relative to other at-issue content, whether the evidential contributes a modal claim that can be challenged, and the effect the evidential has on the entailments of the prejacent. I then discuss the implementation and results of the diagnostics for ʔayʔaǰuθəm (section 3.2). I find that ʔayʔaǰuθəm evidentials can embed under attitude verbs, contribute a modal claim that can be challenged, and alter the entailments of the prejacent in manner consistent with a modal claim.

3.1 Identifying diagnostics

The key to determining whether an evidential is modal or nonmodal involves determining (a) whether the at-issue contribution of an utterance with the evidential is a modal claim concerning p or the assertion/presentation of p itself, and, related to this, (b) whether the evidential operates at the propositional or illocutionary level. There are several empirical differences corresponding to these possibilities: (i) an illocutionary evidential may allow a speaker to utter p without committing even to the possibility of *p*, but with a modal evidential, the speaker must be committed at least to the possibility of *p*, (ii) modal evidentials, but not illocutionary evidentials, should be able to take scope under other semantic operators, (iii) the contribution of an illocutionary evidential cannot be challenged, since it is not at-issue (though the prejacent itself is), while the modal claim (but not the evidential presupposition) should be challengeable for a modal evidential, (iv) when using a modal evidential, the speaker does not assert *p* to be true in the actual world, whereas when using an illocutionary evidential, the speaker asserts *p* to be true of the actual world (if making an assertion rather than presenting *p*); this affects possible continuations following *p*.

The first three of these diagnostics feature frequently in previous literature; however, these have been criticized as not actually differentiating modal from nonmodal evidentials (see Korotkova (2016) and Tan Almazán (2019) for overviews and discussion). Below, I discuss the objections to each of these three diagnostics and, where possible, the refinements required to satisfy these objections. The fourth diagnostic has not typically featured in discussions of evidentiality, and so is presented as a novel additional test.

Asserting vs. presenting: The first major apparent difference between the two analyses is the possibility of uttering the proposition without asserting it, and therefore without committing even to its possibility, under an illocutionary analysis. Crosslinguistically, however, this possibility seems confined to reportative evidentials (AnderBois 2014; Smirnova 2013), rather than being available more generally for evidentials analyzed as illocutionary operators. Moreover, at least some reportative evidentials that have been analyzed as modal (AnderBois 2014; Smirnova 2013; Tan Almazán 2019) allow for this behavior. AnderBois (2014) therefore proposes that reportatives have the ability to facilitate perspective shift (e.g., Harris and Potts 2009). Perspective shift is a pragmatic phenomenon which occurs when the speaker utters a proposition from a salient viewpoint other than their own. For instance, despite the fact that appositives are typically speaker-oriented, the underlined appositive in the short narrative below from Harris and Potts (2009: 527) clearly represents Joan's viewpoint, not the narrator's.

(8) *Joan is crazy. She's hallucinating that some geniuses in Silicon Valley have invented a new brain chip that's been installed in her left temporal lobe and permits her to speak any of a number of languages she's never studied. Joan believes that her chip, <u>which was installed last month</u>, has a twelve year guarantee.*

Perspective shift can only occur when there is another salient viewpoint in the context. AnderBois's proposal is that reportatives introduce another salient perspective – that of the reporter, the one who originally asserted the proposition. Because the reportative makes this additional perspective salient, the speaker is able utter the proposition taking the perspective of the reporter. The at-issue content of the utterance is then attributed to the reporter, not the speaker. This allows the speaker to utter the proposition without believing it. Since perspective shift is compatible with modal as well as illocutionary elements, the ability to utter the proposition without believing it true does not straightforwardly rule out a modal analysis of a reportative evidential.[9]

Taking scope: The next key prediction is that illocutionary evidentials should not be able to take scope under at-issue operators since their contribution is not-at-issue, whereas modal evidentials should be able to take scope under other at-issue content. Assuming that illocutionary evidentials realize a functional head contributing illocutionary force, illocutionary evidentials should also only occur in root clause environments, limiting their syntactic distribution as well. There are several embedding environments to consider: (i) under negation, (ii) in the antecedent of conditionals, and (iii) under attitude predicates.

The negation of at-issue content should have clear interpretive effects, making this an attractive test for semantic embedding; however, epistemic modals often seem to resist embedding under negation. This is true for certain epistemic modals such as *must* in English (see e.g., Hacquard 2006), as well as epistemic modals in S'tát'imcets (Matthewson, Rullmann and Davis 2007), for example. The necessity modal in (9a) can only be interpreted as scoping over negation, for instance, and a bi-clausal structure is required for the opposite scope (9b).[10]

(9)   a.   *He must not be home.*   □ > ¬, * ¬ > □
       b.   *It's not the case that he must be home.*   * □ > ¬, ¬ > □

Therefore, if an evidential can embed semantically under negation, this is good evidence that it is modal, but if it cannot, nothing can be concluded.

---

9 This property of reportatives could be implemented (under a modal analysis) by proposing that reportatives can have an informational, rather than realistic, modal base (Kratzer 2012: 33–34); see Matthewson (2012) for a proposal to this effect. I will adopt a variation of this approach in section 5.

10 See Hacquard (2006) for arguments that epistemic modals scope high in the clause because they are speaker-oriented and associated with the speech act domain (but still contribute to the at-issue content of the clause).

Testing for embedding in the antecedent of a conditional is a similar case. This is an environment where strong epistemic modals tend to be dispreferred in English, as shown in (10a), and epistemic modals in general may be disallowed, as in St'át'imcets (Matthewson, Rullmann and Davis 2007).

(10) Context: We're going to drive by and see if it looks like Freddie is home.
 a. *If he must be home, we'll knock on the door.
 b. If he might be home, we'll knock on the door.

However, since antecedents of conditionals are not typically root clause environments (except in Austinian ('biscuit') conditionals (Krifka 2014)), if an evidential can embed syntactically and semantically in the antecedent of a conditional, this is good evidence that it is modal.

Our final test for whether evidentials can take scope under at-issue operators involves embedding under attitude predicates. There are complications to using this test to distinguish between illocutionary and modal evidentials, however. It has been argued that certain attitude predicates, in particular verbs of saying, can embed root clauses, which correspond semantically to illocutionary acts (e.g., Hooper and Thompson 1973; Heycock 2006; Krifka 2014). In these environments, illocutionary operators should be able to embed syntactically and may be able to take scope semantically within the embedded speech act. According to Krifka (2014), for instance, embedding a root clause involves attributing a speech act to the matrix subject, which allows otherwise speaker-oriented material, such as speaker-oriented adverbs, to orient towards the matrix subject. This predicts even illocutionary evidentials to be able to orient towards matrix clause subjects in embedded root clauses.

The obvious solution is to test for embedding under predicates that do not allow embedded root clause complements. Unfortunately, environments that do and do not allow root clause embedding are not well defined cross-linguistically and diagnostics for identifying embedded root clauses (such as the availability of V2 in German) are often language-specific. This means that determining environments that may or may not embed root clauses is not trivial even in well-studied languages, let alone in understudied languages. Moreover, Anand and Hacquard (2013) argue that epistemic modals can only embed under a restricted set of attitude verbs: those which provide an information state that functions as the modal base for the embedded epistemic. These attitude verbs are typically doxastics (e.g., *say, think*), argumentatives (e.g., *claim*), and semifactives (e.g., *know, realize*), though weak epistemics can also embed under emotive doxastics (e.g., *fear, hope*) and dubitatives (e.g., *doubt*). Unfortunately for our purposes, these verbs, except for emotive doxastics and dubitatives, overlap with those claimed to be able to embed root clauses in English (Hooper and Thompson 1973). This means that embedding tests are fraught for all epistemic modals, but are particularly problematic for strong epistemic modals which, at least in English, can only embed under attitude verbs also claimed to embed root clauses.

Despite these complications, I consider embedding under attitude verbs still a worthwhile test. Not all evidentials analyzed as illocutionary operators are able to orient towards a matrix subject in this environment. In Cuzco Quechua, the reportative evidential is able to embed syntactically under verbs of saying, but when embedded in these environments, remains speaker-oriented (Faller 2014). This suggests that it may not be straightforward for illocutionary evidentials to take scope under attitude verbs, even if this is theoretically possible; modal evidentials, on the other hand, should straightforwardly take scope under attitude predicates. Therefore, if it is impossible for an evidential to ever take scope under attitude predicates, this could indicate that it is an illocutionary evidential, while the ability to scope under attitude predicates could support the claim that an evidential is modal, particularly if it can take scope under an attitude predicate that is unlikely to embed a root clause. The results of tests for embedding under attitude predicates must be interpreted carefully, however, and any argument from embedding should be corroborated by additional evidence.

Challengeability: We turn now to challengeability as a test for whether an evidential contributes at-issue content. Our prediction is that the modal claim provided by a modal evidential may be challenged since it contributes to the at-issue content of the utterance, whereas only p itself can be challenged following a plain assertion embedded under an illocutionary evidential (see Matthewson, Rullmann and Davis 2007; Matthewson 2012). Note that the validity of challengeability as a test has been questioned in previous literature (e.g., Murray 2010; Korotkova 2016; Tan Almazán 2019), since the evidential contribution cannot be challenged under either analysis (Matthewson, Rullmann and Davis 2007; Matthewson 2012 also point this out). Under a modal analysis, this is because the evidential restriction takes the form of a presupposition, while under a speech act operator analysis, this is because the contribution of the evidential is generally not-at-issue. I agree with the assessment that challenging the evidential contribution cannot differentiate between the two analyses, but dispute the claim that this test cannot differentiate between the two analyses when targeting the at-issue content (see also e.g., Matthewson, Rullmann and Davis 2007; Matthewson 2012 for arguments that this test can be used to distinguish between the two analyses).

Continuations: Our final prediction concerns continuations following a proposition with an evidential. Since a modal claim does not assert the prejacent p to be true of the actual world, unlike a plain assertion of p, a continuation that relies on accepting *p* as true of the actual world should be felicitous following a plain assertion of *p* occurring with an illocutionary evidential, but not a modal claim about *p* involving a modal evidential. Test cases are discussed in the following section.

This give us three diagnostics to distinguish between modal and illocutionary analyses of evidentials: (i) it should be possible for a modal evidential to take scope under other at-issue operators, whereas an illocutionary evidential may not take scope semantically at all, or only take scope under attitude predicates embedding speech acts, (ii) a modal evidential contributes an at-issue claim that can be challenged, whereas an illocutionary evidential does not contribute at-issue content, so that only *p* itself can be challenged, and (iii) certain continuations should be impossible following a modal claim which are perfectly felicitous following a plain assertion.[11] In the next section, I discuss the implementation of these tests in ʔayʔaǰuθəm.

3.2 Implementing diagnostics

In this section, I discuss the design of tests suitable for fieldwork using the three diagnostics identified in the preceding section. Since *čɛ* and *kʷa* are strong modals, the tests are designed with this in mind. The first diagnostic is embeddability. I consider three possible embedding environments: under negation, in the antecedent of conditionals, and under attitude predicates.

Embedding under negation: Because a modal evidential contributes to the at-issue content, it may be able to embed under negation, in which case the modal claim concerning the embedded proposition *p*, rather than *p* itself, is negated. Negating a strong modal claim has a truth conditional effect, equivalent to a weak modal scoping over negation.

---

[11] In this chapter, I focus the discussion on distinguishing between modal and illocutionary evidentials since formal semantic analyses have been proposed for both types, giving rise to concrete predictions. Since the tests adopted here are largely focused on diagnosing whether the evidentials contribute at-issue content, however, they could in principle be used to distinguish between modal evidentials and any evidential without an at-issue contribution, such as an evidential that contributed only a presupposition.

(11) Context: Two detectives are discussing which suspect is the thief.
It's not the case that the gardener must have stolen it.
Logical equivalence: The gardener might not have stolen it (based on my indirect/reported evidence).
Implicature: There is a possibility that the gardener stole it.

The evidential čɛ cannot embed under negation in ʔayʔajuθəm (this is also true of the evidential clitics in St'át'imcets, see Matthewson, Rullmann and Davis 2007). When the evidential appears enclitic on negation, it is interpreted as scoping over negation (12), as in Context 1/Interpretation 1. It cannot be interpreted as scoping under negation, as in Context 2/Interpretation 2; if this were possible, following with *qəječ ʔot nonpeganmɛt kʷʊnəs hɛɬ* 'I'm still thinking about whether it was him' should be felicitous, but it is not. As expected under both a modal and a nonmodal analysis, the evidential component cannot be targeted by negation, as in Context 3/Interpretation 3.

(12) ✓ Context 1: The detective discovers the gardener has an alibi and now knows it can't have been the gardener that stole the necklace. He says: It must not have been the gardener who stole it.
X Context 2: The detective had thought the gardener stole the necklace. Then he finds out the nephew had keys to the safe where the nephew was. Now he's not so sure. He thinks: It might not have been the gardener who stole it.
X Context 3: The detective realizes that all the evidence he had was faked. He says: There's no reason to infer the gardener stole it.

xʷaʔ čɛ	hiyas	šɛ niš	ṗaṗɛm	kʷ matoɬ.
xʷaʔ=ča	hiy+as	šə=niš	ṗaṗim	kʷ=məʔ-t-uɬ.
NEG=INFER	be+3SUBJ	DET=be.here	work	DET=get-CTR-PST
# qəječ ʔot		nonpeganmɛt	kʷʊnəs	hɛɬ.
qəji=č=ʔut		nunpigan-mi-t	kʷən=as	hiɬ
still=1SG.SBJ=EXCL		think-REL-CTR	DEM=3SUBJ	be

✓ Interpretation 1: 'It must not have been the gardener that took it. # I'm still thinking about whether it was him.'
X Interpretation 2: 'It might not have been the gardener. I'm still thinking about whether it was him.' (= 'It is not the case that it must have been the gardener...').
X Interpretation 3: 'There is no evidence that it was the gardener that took it. I'm still thinking about whether it was him.' sf

čɛ also cannot follow the embedded predicate in order to scope under negation (13). Negation likely forms a biclausal construction in ʔayʔajuθəm, with negation acting as a predicate selecting for a subordinate subjunctive clause (Davis 2005); it is possible that the embedded clause does not have the full set of functional projections, so that the head hosting the evidential clitics is not projected making it impossible for the evidentials to appear within the embedded clause.

(13) * xʷaʔ   hiyas **čɛ**   šɛ niš   p̓ap̓ɛm kʷ matoɬ
        xʷaʔ   hiy+as=**ča**   šə=niš   p̓ap̓im kʷ=mə?-t-uɬ
        NEG   be+3SUBJ=INFER   DET=be.here   work=get-CTR-PST
        Intended: 'It's not the case that it must have been the gardener that took it.' sf

The evidential *k̓ʷa* is usually interpreted as scoping over negation as well, as in Context 1/Interpretation 1 in (14). Unlike the inferential clitic, however, it also seems to be compatible with a context (Context 2) where the speaker cannot be sure of the truth of the negated prejacent – which would be compatible with the interpretation of a strong modal scoping under negation (Interpretation 2). However, as we will see below in the discussion of embedding under attitude predicates, *k̓ʷa* behaves in many respects as a strong modal, yet is compatible with the speaker not believing the prejacent to be true. Since this is possible even when *k̓ʷa* is not embedded under negation, the availability of this interpretation in (14) cannot be taken as evidence that *k̓ʷa* is taking scope under negation; I will argue below that the availability of this interpretation is better explained in terms of perspective shift (AnderBois 2014). As expected for both modal and nonmodal evidentials, the evidential contribution cannot be targeted by negation (Context 3/Interpretation 3).

(14) ✓ Context 1: I heard from Freddie's daughter that Freddie didn't go to the elder's gathering this year. I'm letting you know he didn't go.
      ✓ Context 2: I heard from an unreliable source that Freddie didn't go to the elders' gathering.
      X Context 3: You ask me if I've heard whether Freddie went go to the elder's gathering and I tell you I haven't heard.
      xʷaʔ **k̓ʷa**   θahasoɬ   Freddie   kʷ q̓atθaws   kʷ ƛ̓aχƛ̓aχay.
      xʷaʔ=**k̓ʷa**   θa=as-uɬ   Freddie   kʷ=q̓atθ-aw-s   kʷ=ƛ̓aχ~ƛ̓aχay
      NEG=RPT   go=3CNJ-PST   Freddie   DET=gather-PL-3POSS   DET=PL~elder
      ✓ Interpretation 1: 'He didn't go to the elders' gathering (based on what I heard).'

✓ Interpretation 2: 'He might not have gone to the elders' gathering (based on what I heard).' (= 'It is not the case that he must have gone to the elders' gathering (based on what I heard).')
X Interpretation 3: 'I didn't hear whether he went to the elders' gathering.' sf
Consultant's comment: You just heard he didn't go.

Just as with the inferential, the reportative cannot appear following the embedded predicate in order to take scope below negation (15).

(15) *xʷaʔ   θahasoɬ **kʷa**   kʷ q̓atᶿaws   kʷ ƛ̓aχƛ̓aχay.
     xʷaʔ   θa=as-uɬ=**kʷa**   kʷ=q̓atᶿ-aw-s   kʷ=ƛ̓aχ~ƛ̓aχay
     NEG   go=3CNJ-PST=RPT   DET=gather-PL-3POSS DET=PL~elder
     Intended: 'I heard he didn't go to the elders' gathering.'   sf

The results from attempting to embed the two evidentials are therefore inconclusive. The inability to scope under negation is predicted for speech act evidentials, but also found for modal evidentials cross-linguistically. While the reportative looks as if it may be able to embed under negation in contrast to the inferential, its ability to appear in contexts where the speaker does not believe the prejacent true is a confound for interpreting this result.

Embedding in the antecedent of conditionals: Because a modal evidential contributes at-issue content, it may also be able to take scope within the antecedent of conditionals, as in (16). Embedding in this environment should not be semantically or syntactically available for illocutionary evidentials.

(16) Context: We've been meaning to visit Freddie and we're going to check if smoke is coming from his chimney so we can tell whether he's likely to be home.
If Freddie {??must/might} be home, we will drive over to his house.

The interpretation of (16) contrasts with the case where the modal scopes over the whole conditional (*It must be that if Freddie is home, we will drive over to his house*) or there is no modal (*If Freddie is home we will drive over to his house*). In both these cases, the speaker can expect to have direct evidence that Freddie is home before driving over, whereas with the modal taking scope within the antecedent of the conditional, this is not possible. If an evidential can syntactically embed in the antecedent of a conditional, context can therefore be used to check its semantic scope.

Not all epistemic modals are able to semantically take scope in the antecedents of conditionals, however (as discussed in the previous section). This means that the results of this test are only conclusive where an evidential can semantically take scope in the antecedent of a conditional. In this case, the test indicates that the evidential contributes to the at-issue content, behaving as an epistemic modal. If an evidential cannot embed in the antecedent of a conditional, nothing can be concluded.

In ʔayʔaǰuθəm, the evidential clitics are not able to take scope in the antecedent of conditionals. This is parallel to what has been reported previously for evidential clitics in Stʼátʼimcets (Matthewson, Rullmann and Davis 2007).

(17) Context: We were planning an outing, but we're going to check what it looks like outside before we leave.
ʔot čɛ səm   čɬ,   xʷaštəm   θahat.
ʔut=ča=səm   čəɬ,   xʷaʔ=štəm   θa=at
if=INFER=FUT   rain   NEG=1PL.SBJ+FUT go=1PL. SUBJ
'If it must be going to rain, we won't go.'   sf

(18) Context: We were planning an outing, but we're going to check what the weather forecast says before we leave.
ʔot kʷ'a səm   čɬ,   xʷaštəm   θahat.
ʔut=kʷ'a=səm   čəɬ,   xʷaʔ=št+əm   θa=at
if=RPT=FUT   rain   NEG=1PL.SBJ+FUT go=1PL. SUBJ
'If it's reportedly going to rain, we won't go.'   sf

I have come across an example of kʷ'a in the antecedent of a conditional in a text, as shown in (19), but it seems that the reportative is scoping out of the conditional in this case (i.e. 'It's said that if you didn't…'). Of course, this is expected for the evidential contribution which is presupposed, but the at-issue content also does not seem to be scoping within the conditional (if it did, it would mean something like: 'If based on reported evidence you must not have done that, then…'). The speaker is discussing cultural teachings around what should be done when exiting the forest, so the 'report' is most plausibly the teachings which were passed on to her, which in this case take the form of a conditional. This means the reportative is semantically scoping over the whole conditional.

(19) ʔotčxʷ kʷ'a   xʷaʔ   ʔəχtiysxʷaxʷ,   nɛ kʷ'a
ʔut=čxʷ=kʷ'a   xʷaʔ   ʔəχtiy-sxʷ=axʷ,   niʔ=kʷ'a
if=2SG. SBJ=RPT   NEG   do.like-CAUS=2SUBJ be.there=RPT

kʷʊθ qaymɪxʷanən ʔəxʷȷ̃ kʷ θičɪm.
kʷə=θ=qaymixʷanan ʔəxʷi kʷ=θičim
DET=2SG.SBJ=spirit left DET=woods
'If you didn't do that then your spirit would be left up there in the back woods.' (Watanabe 2020: 287)

Since consultants do not accept *ča* and *k̉ʷa* taking scope in the antecedent of conditionals, this test is inconclusive and cannot be used to argue for a modal analysis of the clitics.

Embedding under attitude verbs: We now turn to embedding under attitude verbs. In order to show that the evidentials are semantically embedded in these environments, it is necessary to show that they can occur where the speaker cannot felicitously make a modal claim, but the subject of the matrix clause can. One such environment is where the speaker has direct evidence that the embedded proposition is true. Since it would be infelicitous for the speaker to make a modal claim when in possession of direct evidence for the proposition, the utterance should only be felicitous where the modal claim is attributed to the matrix clause subject.

(20) Context (based on *Tom and Mittens*, Rolka and Cable 2014): Tom told his cat that it needed a bath. The cat ran out of the room and into another where it hid in a box. I saw the cat run and hide in the box and then I watched Tom figuring it out. I say:
  a. *Tom realized his cat must be hiding.*
  b. # *His cat must be hiding.*

Another such environment is where the speaker knows the embedded proposition to be false. In order to make a modal claim, the speaker should believe that the prejacent is possibly or necessarily true. If the context is such that the speaker believes the embedded proposition to be false, the utterance should only be felicitous where the modal claim is attributed to the matrix clause subject.

(21) Context: Gloria saw Daniel buying bus tickets to Vancouver, so she thinks he's planning a trip and she tells me. I happen to know that he was buying them for a friend.
  a. *Gloria told me Daniel must be going to Vancouver, but he's not.*
  b. # *Daniel must be going to Vancouver, but he's not.*

Of course, as discussed above, the results of embedding tests using attitude predicates must be treated with caution; strong epistemic modals only embed under doxastics (e.g., *say*, *think*), argumentatives (e.g., *claim*), and semifactives (e.g., *know*, *realize*) in English (Anand and Hacquard 2013), which are environments that have also been argued to embed root clauses (Hooper and Thompson 1973). While we do not know if the same pattern holds in ʔayʔajuθəm, independent diagnostics for embedded root clauses have not yet been developed. This means that if evidentials embed under attitude predicates of these types, we cannot rule out the possibility that they are appearing in root clauses, which may also allow embedding of illocutionary evidentials. This means that the test is most conclusive if it is not possible for an evidential to take scope in an embedded clause, since this would support an illocutionary analysis. If an evidential can take scope in an embedded clause, this may support a modal analysis, but is not conclusive evidence.

For testing embedding under attitude predicates in ʔayʔajuθəm, I use matrix verbs that take nominalized clausal complements. That way, if the evidentials appear within the subordinate clause complement, the morphology clearly indicates that they are in a syntactically embedded environment. To show the evidentials take scope within the embedded clause, I construct contexts where the speaker cannot felicitously make a modal claim, but the matrix clause subject can. As in English, these are environments where the speaker knows the embedded proposition to be true or false, and therefore does not need to make an inference. Both the inferential and the reportative are infelicitous if the speaker has direct evidence for the prejacent (22), for instance.

(22) a. Context: I hear rain on the roof so I think it's raining, and then I walk outside and I see rain.
čɩčɬ čɛ
čə~čɬ=ča
PROG~rain=INFER
Intended: 'It's raining.'   sf
Consultant's comment: No, 'cause you see it.

b. Context: I see Freddie in his driveway.
ʔamot čɛ   Freddie.
ʔamut=ča   Freddie
be.home=INFER   Freddie.
'Freddie must be home.'
Corrected to *oh, niʔala ʔamut* 'Oh, he's home!'

c. Context: I heard that Roger has a girlfriend, but I also have firsthand evidence because I've seen them together.
# nɛʔ=k̓ʷa   šɛ watlas   Roger
niʔ=k̓ʷa   šə=watla-s   Roger
be.there=RPT   DET=sweetheart-3POSS   Roger
Intended: I heard Roger has a girlfriend.'   sf
Consultant's comment: niʔ=k̓ʷa... you only heard it, you didn't see it.

d. Context: Freddie had gone down to Vancouver. Gloria tells me he's back home and later I see him in his driveway. Later, I tell you:
# nɛ k̓ʷa   ʔamot   Freddie.
niʔ=k̓ʷa   ʔamut   Freddie
be.there=RPT   be.home   Freddie
'Freddie's at home.'   sf
Consultant's comment: [With] k̓ʷa, it's still hearsay.

The speaker also cannot felicitously make a modal claim using the inferential clitic when the speaker knows the prejacent to be false (23).

(23) a. Context: I thought it was raining because I heard raindrops, but I go outside and it's not raining.
* čɩč̓ɬ čɛ   ʔi   xʷaʔ   čɩč̓ɬas.
čə~č̓ɬ=ča   ʔi   xʷaʔ   čə~č̓ɬ=as
PROG~rain=INFER   CONJ   NEG   PROG~rain=3CNJ
'It must be raining, but it's not raining.'   sf
Corrected to: xʷaʔak̓ʷʊt čəč̓ɬas 'Oh, it's not raining!'

b. Context: I see Freddie's car in his driveway, so I think he's home, but later I found out he's went in someone else's car on the trip and they're not back yet.
* ʔamot čɛ   Freddie   ʔi   xʷaʔ   ʔamotəs.
ʔamut=ča   Freddie   ʔiy   xʷaʔ   ʔamut=as
be.home=INFER   Freddie   CONJ   NEG   be.home=3CNJ
'Freddie must be home, but he's not home.'   sf
Consultant's comment: You're saying he's home, but then you're saying he's not.

The case of the reportative is slightly more complex. Denying the prejacent is often infelicitous, as shown in (24a,b).

(24) a. Context: There was a rumour that Freddie won the lottery, but I talked to him and found out the rumour is not true. Later we're talking about this and I say:
λúxʷʔəm kʼʷa   Freddie qəχ   tala.   xʷaʔ λúxʷʔəməs
λəxʷ-ʔəm=kʼʷa   Freddie qəχ   tala   xʷaʔ λəxʷ-ʔəm=as
win-ACT.INRT   Freddie lots   money   NEG   win-ACT.INTR=3SUBJ
'Freddie won a lot of money (I heard). He didn't win it.'   sf

b. Context: It was forecasted that it would be raining all day today, but it hasn't been raining, just a bit overcast.
čɬ kʼʷa səm   ʔi   xʷaʔ čɛ səmt.
čəɬ=kʼʷa=səm   ʔiy   xʷaʔ=ča=səm=t
rain=RPT=FUT   CNJ   NEG=INFER=FUT=EXCL
'It's going to rain but it's not going to.'   sf
Consultant's comment: It kind of contradicts.

In (25), however, where the denial is marked as surprising by the sequence of negation plus reportative and exclusive, the result is much improved.[12]

(25) Context: Same as (24a).
? λúxʷʔəm kʼʷa   Freddie qəχ   tala.   xʷaʔakʼʷut!
λəxʷ-ʔəm=kʼʷa   Freddie qəχ   tala.   xʷaʔ+ala+kʼʷa+ʔut
win-ACT.INTR   Freddie lots   money   NEG+EXCLAM+RPT+EXCL
'Freddie won a lot of money (I heard), but it turns out not!'   sf

I take this to indicate that the expression of surprise is used to signal perspective shift; the speaker utters the prejacent from the perspective of the person who originally made the 'report' before marking a shift back to her own perspective through mirativity.[13] As discussed in section 3.1, AnderBois (2014) argues that reportative evidentials facilitate perspective shift cross-linguistically because they introduce another perspective holder – the 'reporter'. He discusses similar

---

12 How the meaning of surprise arises compositionally in these cases is not well understood at this point. Note that the use of evidentials to mark mirativity is not uncommon, however (e.g., DeLancey 2001; Rett and Murray 2013). An anonymous reviewer suggests that a pragmatic account may be in order. I hope to explore this possibility in future research.

13 Another possibility, raised by an anonymous reviewer, is that the time at which the evidence was valid plays a role. However, since the context is constant in (24a) and (24b) it is not clear how timing of the validity of the evidence could explain the contrast. The modal perspective and orientation (Condoravdi 2002) of these evidentials certainly deserves attention, but a full discussion of these properties is outside the scope of this chapter.

data from a number of languages where bare denials of the proposition with the reportative are infelicitous, but the inclusion of evaluative language in the denial, often in the form of adverbials or first person attitude reports, saves the denial's felicity. AnderBois points out that perspective shift is a risky strategy (as originally discussed in Harris and Potts 2009), since the addressee may fail to follow the speaker's intended shift. Inclusion of evaluative language helps ensure that the addressee correctly interprets the intended shift.

We have seen that neither the inferential nor the reportative can be used where the speaker knows the prejacent to be true. The inferential also cannot be used when the speaker knows the prejacent to be false, and this is generally true of the reportative as well, though perspective shift can save these utterances. In order to test for semantic embedding, I therefore use contexts where the speaker knows that the embedded proposition is true or false, but the matrix clause subject does not. Since the speaker cannot use *čɛ* when the prejacent is known to be true or false, if the evidential is felicitous in the embedded environment, it must be attributed to the matrix subject. For the reportative *k̓ʷa*, only the cases where the speaker knows the embedded proposition to be true unambiguously involve semantic embedding, because of the possibility of perspective shift, but data for both cases where the speaker believes the embedded proposition to be true and cases where the speaker believes the embedded proposition to be false are included.

We find that both *čɛ* and *k̓ʷa* can be semantically embedded in these environments, both when the speaker knows the embedded proposition to be true, as in (26) and (27), and when the speaker believes the embedded proposition to be false, as in (28) and (29).

(26) Context: Tom (Tɛqaw) and Mittens storyboard (Rolka and Cable 2014) – the cat just ran out of the room and into another where it hid in a box. I saw the cat run and hide in the box, and then I watched Tɛqaw figuring it out. Now I'm describing Tɛqaw.

nopʊxʷəm   Tɛqaw   hɛs čɛ   kʷ k̓ʷaxʷa
nup-əxʷ-əm   Tiqaw   hiɬ=s=ča   kʷ=k̓ʷaxʷa
think-NCTR-PASS tiqaw   be=3POSS=INFER   DET=box
kʷayɪts   šɛ mɛmaẇs.
kʷay-ít=s   šə=mimaẇ-s
get.hidden-STAT=3POSS   DET=cat-3POSS
'Tɛqaw realized that his cat must be hiding in a box.'   sf

(27) Context: Gloria finds out that Roger has a girlfriend and she's excited to spread the news, so she tells me. I've already met his girlfriend though. Later I tell you about it.

tatawθiyəm	Gloria	sk̓ʷa kʷa	watlaʔit
tataw-θiy-əm	Gloria	s=k̓ʷa=kʷa	watla-ʔiyt
PROG~tell-CTR.1SG.OBJ-PASS	Gloria	NMLZ=RPT=CL.DEM	sweetheart-PRF

Roger.	toχʷnɛxʷołč ʔot.		qəmgusʊxʷołč
Roger.	təχʷ-n\<i>xʷ-uɬ=č=ʔut.		qəmgus-əxʷ-uɬ=č
Roger	know-NCTR\<STAT>-PST=1SG.SBJ=EXCL		meet.up-NCTR-PST=1SG.SBJ

ʔi	tawθəs.
ʔiy	taw-θ-as
CONJ	tell-CTR.1SG.OBJ-3ERG

'Gloria told me (she heard) Roger got a girlfriend. I already knew. I met up with them and he told me.' sf

(28) Context: Gloria saw Daniel buying bus tickets to Whistler and thinks he must be going on a trip there. She tells this to me, and then I talk to Daniel and find out that actually he bought them for a friend. Later, I tell you:

tatawθiyəm	Gloria	ho(s)čɛsəm	Daniel
ta~tawθiyəm	Gloria	hu=s=ča=səm	Daniel
PROG~tell-1SG.OBJ-PASS	Gloria	go=3POSS=INFER=FUT	Daniel

ʔəkʷ Whistler.	k'ʷʊnɛtasoɬ	yiyqʔamʔos
ʔə=kʷ=Whistler	k'ʷən-í-t-as-uɬ	yə~yq-ʔəm-uɬ=s
OBL=DET=Whistler	see-STAT-CTR-3ERG-PST	PROG~buy-ACT.INTR-PST=3POSS

kʷ pipa	kʷs θos	ʔəkʷ Whistler.
kʷ=pipa	kʷ=s=hu=3POSS	ʔə=kʷ=Whistler
DET=paper	DET=NMLZ=GO=3POSS	OBL=DET=Whistle

qʷaqʷaysxʷołč	Daniel	tatawθas	xʷa(s)
qʷa~qʷay-sxʷ-uɬ=č	Daniel	ta~taw-θ-as	xʷaʔ=s
PROG~talk-CTR-PST=1SG.SBJ	Daniel	PROG~tell-1SG.OBJ-3ERG	NEG=3POSS

hiyas	θo.	heɬ	šɛ patnas	yəqʔəmtasoɬ	pipa
hiy+as	θu	hiɬ	šə=patna-s	yəq-ʔəm-t-as-uɬ	pipa
be+3SUBJ	go	be	DET=partner-3POSS	buy-IND-CTR-PST	paper

kʷs θos	Whistler
kʷ=s=θu=s	Whistler
DET=NMLZ=go=3POSS	Whistler

'Gloria told me Daniel must be going to Whistler. She saw him buy tickets for going to Whistler. I talked to Daniel. He told me it's not him that's going. He bought the tickets to Whistler for his friend.' sf

(29) Context: Gloria hears Freddie won at bingo so she's excited and tells me
about it. I was actually there, so I know that Freddie didn't win.

tatawθiyəm	Gloria	sk̓ʷa kʷa	ƛ̓ʊxʷʔəm
ta~taw-θiy-əm	Gloria	s=k̓ʷa=kʷa	ƛ̓əxʷ-ʔəm
PROG~tell-1SG.OBJ-PASS	Gloria	NMLZ=REP=CL.DEM	win-ACT.INTR

Freddie	ʔəkʷ	qəχ	tala,	ʔi	xʷaʔ,	hɛɫ	Daniel
Freddie	ʔə=kʷ	qəχ	tala.	ʔiy	xʷaʔ,	hiɫ	Daniel
Freddie	OBL=DET	lots	money	CONJ	NEG	be	Daniel

ƛ̓ʊxʷʔəmoɫ.
ƛ̓əxʷ-ʔəm-uɫ.
win-ACT.INTR-PST

'Gloria told me (she heard) Freddie won a lot of money, but no! It was Daniel
who won.'   sf

In this section, we have seen evidence that both *čɛ* and *k̓ʷa* can be embedded under attitude verbs. This shows that they can take scope under other at-issue content, supporting a modal analysis where the evidentials contribute at-issue content. This evidence is not conclusive, however, since it is possible that speech act operators could also embed in these environments.

Challengeability: Our next diagnostic concerns the challengeability of the modal claim. Under a modal analysis, it should be possible to challenge the modal claim, whereas under a non-modal analysis, it should only be possible to challenge the prejacent itself. Challenging a modal claim typically involves denying one of the premises which narrow the set of possible worlds the modal is quantifying over (Faller 2002; Matthewson, Rullmann and Davis 2007). For instance, in (30), the second detective challenges the premise that only someone with keys could have gotten into the house to steal the necklace. In languages with modals of different strengths, this type of challenge may involve the alternate weaker modal. For instance in (30), the modal claim made with the strong modal is challenged with a weaker modal claim, which allows worlds where someone entered the house using a ladder into the modal base. Note that the same challenge is not felicitous in response to the plain assertion (31).

(30) a. Context: There are two detectives discussing the case of a stolen necklace. Knowing the neighbour had keys to the house, one of the detectives utters:
The neighbour had keys to the house. He must have stolen the necklace.

b. The other detective, knowing that the gardener had a ladder that would allow him to get in the window, utters:
That's not true. It might not have been him. It might have been the gardener. He had a ladder that could reach the window.

(31) a. Context: There are two detectives discussing the case of a stolen necklace. One of the detectives, having interviewed the suspect, is convinced that it was him and utters:
The neighbour stole the necklace.

b. The other detective disagrees and utters:
That's not true. # It might not have been him. It might have been the gardener.

In order to elicit modal challenges, then, it is necessary to construct a context where there are two characters making inferences concerning the same proposition, but with different propositions in the modal base of each. Matthewson, Rullmann and Davis (2007) also point out that it is important that the challenge in the target language takes a form corresponding to 'that's not true' in English to be sure that the at-issue content is being challenged, since presuppositions can also be challenged but with different responses such as 'hey, wait a minute!'.

For both *čɛ* and *k̓ʷa* in ʔayʔaǰuθəm, the modal claim can be challenged. The following examples show that both the modal claim and the prejacent are possible targets for challenge with *xʷaʔ gənʊxʷəs* 'That's not true'. When challenging the modal claim, the challenger does not assert that the prejacent is false, but rather objects to the premises used to narrow down the modal base or the reasoning from the premises. The challenger can therefore still believe there is a possibility that the prejacent is true. This is illustrated in the examples below.

In (32B), B challenges A's premise that if Freddie's lights are on, he is home (this example is taken from Matthewson, Rullmann and Davis 2007; Matthewson 2012). B uses *qʷayin*, which is a clausal adjunct marking epistemic uncertainty; it is variably translated as *probably, might be,* and *I think*. B's use of *qʷayin* indicates that B has not determined the prejacent to be false, and so is not challenging the prejacent itself, but rather the reasoning used to assert it. In contrast, the prejacent is directly challenged in (32B').

(32) Context: A and B are driving past Freddie's house and see that Freddie's lights are on...
    A: χʷawɪt   nɪkʷayus   Freddie. ʔamot čɛ.
        χʷəẇ-ít   nɪkʷayu-s Freddie   ʔamut=ča
        get.lit-STAT light-3POSS Freddie be.home=INFER
        'Freddie's lights are on. He must be home.'

    B: xʷaʔ gənʊxʷas. qʷayɪn xʷaʔ ʔamotas.   payɛ ʔot
        xʷaʔ gənəxʷ=as qʷayin xʷaʔ amut=as   paya?=ʔut
        NEG   true=3SUBJ EPST   NEG be.home=3SUBJ always=EXCL
        χʷawɪtsxʷas   nɪkʷayus.
        χʷəẇ-ít-swʷ-as   nɪkʷayu-s
        get.lit-STAT-CAUS-3ERG light-3POSS
        'That's not true. He's probably not home. He always leaves his lights on.'

    B': xʷaʔ gənʊxʷas. tawθasoɬ   χʷoχʷsəm   xʷukʷts.
        xʷaʔ gənəxʷ=a   taw-θ-as-uɬ   χʷuχʷ=səm   xʷukʷts
        NEG   true=3SUBJ tell-1SG.OBJ-3ERG-PST long.time=FUT not.exist
        'That's not true. He told me he would be gone a long time.'   sf

In (33), B challenges A's premise that the source of the report is reliable. Again, use of *qʷayin* in the challenge indicates that B is not certain that the prejacent is false, so that *xʷaʔ gənəxʷas* 'that's not true' cannot be targeting the prejacent directly, but rather the reliability of the prejacent. (33B'), in contrast, is a challenge to the prejacent itself.

(33) Context: A had a conversation with Daniel earlier. Now A is telling B what Daniel told her...
    A: tatawθiyəm   Daniel ninɪǰɛ Freddie. qʷol ḱʷa
        ta~taw-θiy-əm   Daniel niniǰa   Freddie qʷəɬ=ḱʷa
        PROG~tell-CTR.1SG.OBJ-PASS Daniel about   Freddie come=PRT
        hɛwt   sǰɛsoɬ.
        hiwt   sǰasuɬ
        get.home yesterday
        'Daniel was telling me about Freddie. He got home yesterday (he said).'

B: | xʷaʔ | gənʊxʷas. | payɛ | gaχgaχnomot | Daniel. | qʷayın
| xʷaʔ | gənəxʷ=as | payaʔ | gəχ~gaχ-nu-mut | Daniel. | qʷayin
| NEG | true=3SUBJ | always | PL~dream-NCTR-REFL | Daniel | EPST
| xʷaʔ | ʔamotas | Freddie.
| xʷaʔ | ʔamut=as | Freddie.
| NEG | be.home=3SUBJ | Freddie
'That's not true. Daniel's always fantasizing/making up stories. Freddie is probably not home.'

B': | xʷaʔ | gənʊxʷoθəs | | Daniel. | xʷaʔ | ʔamotas | | Freddie.
| xʷaʔ | gənəxʷ-uθ=as | | Daniel | xʷaʔ | ʔamut=as | | Freddie.
| NEG | true-mouth=3SUBJ | Daniel | NEG | be.home=3SUBJ | Freddie
'It's not true what Daniel said. Freddie's not home.' sf

The next few examples all involve dialogue between two detectives on a single case. In (34), detective B challenges detective A's premise that the gardener is no longer a suspect. Detective B's use of *qʷayin* indicates that the prejacent is not directly contradicted, but rather Detective A's modal claim.

(34) Context: Two detectives are discussing the case of a missing necklace. They have two suspects remaining – the nephew of the person whose necklace was stolen and the gardener. Detective A is feeling quite sure that the nephew did it, given all the evidence, but detective B still thinks it could be the gardener.

A: | hɛ čɛ | tθeyʊxʷs.
| hiɫ=ča | tθiyəxʷ-s
| be=INFER | nephew-3POSS
'It must have been the nephew.' vf

B: | xʷaʔ | gənʊxʷas. | qʷayın | xʷaʔ | hiyas. | qʷayın | hɛɫ
| xʷaʔ | gənəxʷ=as | qʷayin | xʷaʔ | hiy+as | qʷayin | hiɫ
| NEG | true=3SUBJ | EPST | NEG | be+3SUBJ | EPST | be
| šɛ niš. | p̓ap̓ɛm. | ču?otən k̓ʷa
| šə=niš | p̓ap̓im | ču?utən=k̓ʷa
| DET=be.here | work | thief=RPT
'That's not true. It likely wasn't him. It was probably the gardener. It's said he's a thief.' sf

For this dialogue, I have a second version from another speaker, in (35). This older speaker felt that *xʷaʔ gənʊxʷəs* 'That's not true' could not be used by detective B in this context because detective B is not directly contradicting detective A's claim that the nephew is the thief. Instead she preferred a response beginning with *qʷayɩn xʷaʔ* 'It might not be.' Several conversations with her have made it clear that she feels that using *xʷaʔ gənʊxʷəs* is quite confrontational. In light of this, it seems that for her *xʷaʔ gənəxʷas* is only appropriate where the challenger can challenge the truth of the prejacent itself, not just the reasoning behind the assertion. The absence of *xʷaʔ gənʊxʷəs* is somewhat problematic, however, as challenges with *xʷaʔ gənʊxʷəs* 'that's not true' unambiguously target at-issue content, while challenges without *xʷaʔ gənʊxʷəs* 'that's not true' may target other aspects of the utterance (e.g., Matthewson, Rullmann and Davis 2007). Though this casts some doubt on the conclusiveness of this data, the content of B's challenge makes it clear that B is not sure that prejacent is false and is therefore most plausibly challenging A's inference, rather than the prejacent itself. I therefore conclude, though more tentatively, that this dialogue also illustrates a challenge to a modal claim.

(35) Context: As in (34).
A: *hɛ čɛ tᶿeyʊxʷs.*
hił=**ča** tᶿiyəxʷ-s
be=INFER nephew-3POSS
'It must have been the nephew.

B: *qʷayɩn xʷaʔ. čɩm ga šɛ niš p̓ap̓ɛm?*
qʷayin xʷaʔ čəm̓=ga šə=niš p̓ap̓im
EPST NEG why/how=DPRT DET=be.here work

hoštəm qʷɛqʷaysxʷ šɛ niš p̓ap̓ɛm.
hu=štəm qʷi~qʷaysxʷ šə=niš p̓ap̓im
go=1PL.SBJ+FUT PROG~talk-CAUS DET=be.here work
'It probably wasn't him. What about the gardener? Let's talk to   vf
the gardener.'

We turn now to a parallel example involving reported evidence. In (36B), B challenges A's certainty in making the claim with the reportative in (36A). B is clearly not in possession of facts to challenge the prejacent directly, since B is still speculating about the possible identity of the thief. (36B') is a challenge to the prejacent itself.

(36) Context: Two detectives are discussing the case of a missing necklace. They have two suspects remaining – the nephew of the person whose necklace was stolen and the gardener. Detective A is convinced by a witness that the nephew did it, but detective B distrusts the witness.

A: nɛtəm   šɛ payɛs   xʷukʷts   talas.
   ni-t-əm   šə=payaʔ=s   xʷukʷt-s   tala-s.
   say-CTR-PASS DET=always=3POSS   not.any-?   money-3POSS
   hɛ k̓ʷa   šɛ t̓θeyʊxʷs.
   hi=k̓ʷa   šə=t̓θiyəxʷ-s
   be=RPT   DET=nephew
   'It's said he never has money. It's said it was the nephew.'

B: xʷaʔ   gənʊxʷəs.   qʷayın xʷaʔ   hiyas   šɛ t̓θeyʊxʷs.
   xʷaʔ   gənəxʷ=as   qʷayin xʷaʔ   hiɬ+as   šə=t̓θiyəxʷ-s
   NEG   true=3SUBJ   EPST   NEG   be+3SUBJ   DET=nephew-3POSS
   qʷayın hɛɬ   šɛ niš   p̓ap̓ɛm.   hoy k̓ʷot   nɛʔoɬ
   qʷayin hiɬ   šə=niš   p̓ap̓im   huy=k̓ʷa+ʔut   niʔ-uɬ
   EPST   be   DET=be.here   work   finish=RPT+EXCL   be.there-PST
   p̓ap̓ɛm   šin   t̓θokʷ   ʔi   gaq̓ɛtoɬ   šɛ ʔɛmɛn
   p̓ap̓im   šiṅ   t̓θuk̓ʷ   ʔiy   gəq̓-it-uɬ   šə=ʔimin
   work   DEM   day   CONJ   open-STAT-PST   DET=door
   'That's not true. It probably wasn't his nephew. It was probably the
   gardener. He was the only one working there that day and the door
   was open.'

B': xʷaʔ   gənʊxʷoθəs.
    xʷaʔ   gənəxʷuθ=as
    NEG   true-mouth=3SUBJ
    'What he said is not true.'   sf

For this dialogue, I also have a second version from the older speaker. Again, *xʷaʔ gənʊxʷəs* 'That's not true' is absent in B's challenge for this speaker. Nevertheless, B is clearly challenging the premise that the witness is reliable, rather than the prejacent itself.

(37) Context: As in (36). Note that the witness = Daniel.
      A: qʷɛqʷaysxʷoɬč   Daniel.   hɛ k̓ʷa   šɛ t̓θeyʊxʷs
          qʷɛ~qʷay-sxʷ-uɬ=č   Daniel   hi=k̓ʷa   šə=t̓θiyəxʷ-s
          PROG~talk-CAUS-PST=1SG.SBJ Daniel   be=RPT   DET=nephew
          kʷ maʔt.
          kʷ=mə?-t
          COMP=take-CTR
          'I spoke to Daniel. It was the nephew that took it (he said).'

B: | qʷayın | xʷaʔ. | qʷayın | naynayəw | Daniel. | hoštəm |
|---|---|---|---|---|---|
| qʷayin | xʷaʔ | qʷayin | nay~nayəw | Daniel | hu=štəm |
| EPST | NEG | EPST | CHAR~forget | Daniel | go=1PL.SBJ+FUT |

qʷεqʷaysxʷ   še niš   p̓ap̓εm.
qʷi~qʷay-sxʷ   šə=niš   p̓ap̓im
PROG~talk-CAUS   DET=be.here   work

'It might not be. Daniel might be mistaken. Let's go talk to the gardener.'   sf

Throughout these dialogues we have seen that there is a contrast between challenging the prejacent and challenging the modal claim. Challenging the prejacent involves denying the truth of the previous utterance. In contrast, challenging the modal claim involves denying the validity of the inference, but allows uncertainty about whether the prejacent is in fact false. Since both types of challenges are possible in response to a claim with čε and k̓ʷa, these dialogues support an analysis where čε and k̓ʷa are modals, contributing at-issue content that can be challenged.

Continuations: We now turn to the final test for diagnosing the at-issue content, examining what can felicitously follow an utterance with the evidential. Modal and illocutionary evidentials will have different effects on possible continuations since a modal claim changes the at-issue content of the utterance, whereas an illocutionary evidential does not. In what follows, I first lay out the predictions for a modal evidential, and then examine the contrasting predictions for an illocutionary evidential.

A modal claim does not assert the prejacent to be true of the actual world, unlike a plain assertion. Therefore, a continuation that relies on accepting *p* as true of the actual world should be felicitous following a plain assertion of *p*, but not a modal claim of *p*. For instance, if I have accepted the proposition that Freddie travelled to another city, and then I accept the proposition that Freddie is home now, then these two propositions together entail that Freddie has returned home. This makes a continuation that asserts Freddie's return possible without further inference, even though I didn't directly witness his return, as in (38).[14]

---

[14] It is also possible to use *must* in the continuation: *He must have come back from New Westminster*. This is expected under von Fintel and Gillies' (2010) analysis of epistemic modals which I will adopt in section 5. Basically, their approach predicts that *must* will be felicitous wherever the speaker does not have a single 'piece' of direct information that settles whether the prejacent is true. Since the continuation in (38) is not entailed by the prejacent alone, but by the prejacent in conjunction with the knowledge that Freddie had been away, the felicity conditions are satisfied.

(38) Context: Freddie was on a trip to New Westminster. He's back home now, and I visited him this morning. Now I tell you:
Freddie is home. He came back from New Westminster.

There is a contrast if I am only inferring that Freddie is now home. In this case, it is not entailed that Freddie has returned from his trip. I therefore cannot assert that this is the case; I can only infer it, as illustrated in (39).

(39) Context: Freddie was on a trip to New Westminster. This morning, I saw his car in his driveway. Now I tell you:
Freddie must be home. # He came back from New Westminster. (Ok: *He must have come back from New Westminster.*)

We expect this behaviour for modal evidentials. If a modal evidential combines with the prejacent p, p is claimed only of possible worlds, and a continuation q which is entailed by the plain prejacent in the context, is entailed only in the possible worlds where p is true. The continuation q must thefore also appear with a modal element. In contrast, a plain assertion of the prejacent p claims p to be true in the actual world and entails q in the actual world; therefore, q is predicted to not require a modal even if not directly witnessed.

Nonmodal evidentials are not expected to show a parallel contrast. If the indirect evidential is a speech act operator that is required whenever the prejacent is not known through direct evidence, the continuation *He came back from New Westminster* should require the evidential in both the context of (38) and (39). If the indirect evidential is a speech act operator that marks inference, we also do not expect a contrast. Since the evidential would not involve a modal claim, the prejacent p *Freddie is home* will be claimed to be true in the actual world in both the equivalent of (38) and the equivalent of (39). Therefore, the continuation q should be entailed in both and not require the presence of the evidential.

The hypothetical cases outlined above assume an evidential speech act operator that involves an assertion of the prejacent. This test cannot distinguish between a modal evidential and an evidential speech act operator that only involves presenting the prejacent. If the prejacent p appears with such an evidential it will not be claimed of the real world w, but only presented to the addressee. The continuation q is therefore also not entailed in the real world and therefore would likely also have to appear with the evidential, if it can be felicitously uttered at all. It is therefore necessary to conduct the continuation test in conjunction with tests that show whether the prejacent needs to be believed true in the actual world when the evidential is used.

With this background in place, we can go about implementing this test in ʔayʔajuθəm. In order to keep the contexts clear, I used short storyboards. The storyboard in Figure 1 was used as a baseline.[15] The first panel sets up the background knowledge that Freddie is in New Westminster (*kʷins pala*), the next shows Freddie at home in his driveway, and the speaker interacting with him. The final panel shows the speaker saying that Freddie is home, having returned from New Westminster. The storyboard was explained to the consultant and then the consultant was asked to judge whether a suggested utterance for the speaker in the storyboard was a good fit to the context. I then presented the two options: one where the claim that Freddie returned from New Westminster had the inferential evidential and one where the claim did not.

Figure 1: Testing continuations, baseline context.

Figure 2 sets up the context where the prejacent *p* is known through inference. The first panel is as in the previous context. The second panel differs. The speaker does not see Freddie at home, but just that his car is in front of his house. In the final panel, the speaker is saying that the Freddie is home, having returned from New Westminster – but in this case is basing the claim on Freddie's car being in the driveway. The storyboard was presented to the consultant in the same manner as the previous.

The results for this test indicate that an assertion with *čɛ* is an assertion about possible worlds, not an assertion about the real world. In both (40) and (41), for instance, the speaker does not directly witness Freddie's trip home. However, if the speaker asserts Freddie to be home, it is entailed that he has come home from his trip and the inferential need not be used to assert this second proposition

---

15 All drawings in this chapter are made by the author.

Figure 2: Testing continuations, inferential context.

(40). If, on the other hand, the speaker uses čɛ in the claim that Freddie is home, it does not follow that Freddie has come home from his trip in the real world and the following proposition must be marked with the inferential (41).

(40) Context: Freddie has been away in New Westminster. This morning I saw him in his driveway. Then I say:
ʔamot   Freddie. kʷa   qʷoi̓   χəpi   tawa   kʷins   pala.
ʔamut   Freddie kʷa   qʷəi̓   χəpəy   tawa   kʷins   pala
be.home   Freddie CL.DEM come   return from   kʷins   pala
'Freddie is home. He has returned from New Westminster.'   sf

(41) Context: Freddie has been away in New Westminster. This morning I saw his car in the driveway. Then I say:
ʔamot čɛ   Freddie. #(čɛ) kʷa   qʷoi̓   χəpi   tawa
ʔamut=ča   Freddie   ča=kʷa   qʷəi̓   χəpəy   tawa
be.home=INFER   Freddie   INFER=CL.DEM   come   return from
kʷins   pala.
kʷins   pala
kʷins   pala
'Freddie must be home. He #(must have) returned from New Westminster.'   sf

This test can also be used for the reportative. The baseline case is the same as before. The test case involves the speaker hearing from someone that Freddie is home and then passing this knowledge on to someone else. For this case, I used the storyboard in Figure 3. The first panel is as in the previous storyboards. In the second, the speaker hears from someone that Freddie is home. In the third panel, the speaker again says that Freddie is home, having come back from New Westminster, but is now basing this claim on reported evidence. As before, the consultant was asked to judge whether the speaker in the storyboard's final utterance matched the context where this final utterance had or did not have a modal evidential.

Figure 3: Testing continuations, reportative context.

The results for the reportative are parallel to those for the inferential. If the speaker claims Freddie to be home based on reported evidence, the second proposition must be marked with an inferential (42). The speaker only knows Freddie to be home in all worlds compatible with the report, but does not know him to be home in the real world, so his return also cannot be asserted of the real world. The inferential, rather than the reportative, is used in the felicitous continuation because Gloria's report did not include the information that Freddie had returned from New Westminster. If she had also provided this information, the reportative could have been used instead.

(42) Context: Freddie has been away in New Westminster. This morning Gloria told me that he is home. Then I say:

ʔamot k̓ʷa	Freddie.	#(čɛ) kʷa	qʷoɫ	χəpi	tawa	kʷins	pala.
ʔamut=k̓ʷa	Freddie	ča=kʷa	qʷəɫ	χəpəy	tawa	kʷins	pala
be.home=RPT	Freddie	INFER=CL.DEM	come	return	from	kʷins	pala

'Freddie must be home. He #(must have) returned from New Westminster.' sf

I also checked this with a second set of storyboards. In this case, the speaker has a cat that keeps climbing up to the roof. For the first storyboard, the speaker has direct evidence that the cat is on the roof and knows the cat climbed up the ladder to get there (43).

(43) Context: M has a cat that likes to climb up to the roof, using a ladder that goes up to the roof. The ladder is the only way to the roof. M goes up the ladder and sees her cat on the roof. She says:

nɛʔ	kʷ ʔiyɪtxʷ	tᶿ mɛmaẇ.	(čɛ)	θo	šɛʔ	qey	tə hayšɪn.
niʔ	kʷ=ʔiyitxʷ	tᶿ=mimaẇ	ča	θu	šə?	qəji	tə=hayšin
be.there	DET=roof	1SG.POSS=cat	INFER	go	up	again	DET=ladder

'My cat is on the roof. It went (must have gone) up the ladder again.'   sf

For the second storyboard, the speaker does not see the cat on the roof, but only hears it meowing. In this case, where the initial proposition is inferred, the inferential is also required in the second sentence in (44).

(44) Context: M has a cat that likes to climb up to the roof, using a ladder that goes up to the roof. The ladder is the only way to the roof. M hears her cat meowing from the roof. She says:

nɛ čɛ   kʷ ʔiyɪtxʷ   tᶿ mɛmaẇ.   #(čɛ)   θo   šɛ   qey
niʔ=ča   kʷ=ʔiyitxʷ   tᶿ=mimaẇ.   ča   θu   šə? qəjɪ
be.there=INFER DET=roof   1SG.POSS=cat INFER   go   up   again
tə hayšɪn.
tə=hayšin
DET=ladder
'My cat must be on the roof. It must have gone up the ladder again.'   sf

For the final version of the storyboard, the speaker finds out that her cat is on the roof from a friend. In this case, where the initial proposition is based on reported evidence, the inferential is required in the second sentence of (45).

(45) Context: M has a cat that likes to climb up to the roof, using a ladder that goes up to the roof. The ladder is the only way to the roof. M's friend tells her that her cat is on the roof. She says:

nɛ kʷa   kʷ ʔiyɪtxʷ   tᶿ mɛmaẇ.   #(čɛ)   θo   šɛʔ qey
niʔ=kʷa   kʷ=ʔiyitxʷ   tᶿ=mimaẇ.   ča   θu   šə? qəjɪ
be.there=RPT DET=roof   1SG.POSS=cat INFER   go   up   again
tə hayšɪn.
tə=hayšin
DET=ladder
'My cat is (reportedly) on the roof. It must have gone up the ladder again.'

If čɛ and k̓ʷa did not contribute a modal claim, but left the at-issue content unaltered, the second target proposition should be entailed in all of the above examples and there should be no contrast in where the evidentials are required to appear. If čɛ and k̓ʷa are modals altering the truth conditions so that the prejacent is only asserted to be true in possible worlds, the contrasts in where the evidentials are required in the above examples are expected. I therefore conclude that these results support a modal analysis of these evidentials.

3.3 Conclusion

In this section, we examined whether the inferential čɛ and reportative k̓ʷa in ʔayʔaǰuθəm are best characterized as modal or illocutionary evidentials. We saw that these evidentials can embed under attitude predicates and have an at-issue contribution that can be challenged. We also saw evidence that the presence of čɛ or k̓ʷa affects possible continuations in a way consistent with a modal analysis. While the evidence from each of these tests is subtle, taken together, the results of these tests indicate that these evidentials are best characterized as modal.

4 Evidentials in questions

In this section, I discuss čɛ and k̓ʷa in questions and address a possible counterargument to the claim that the reportative is an epistemic modal. The potential counterargument concerns cases where the reportative appears to embed questions; this behaviour is one of the reasons Faller (2002) argues the reportative in Cuzco Quechua is an illocutionary evidential. Before examining these cases, however, we set a baseline by examining more canonical uses of these evidentials in questions.

Both the inferential and the reportative can occur in questions, scoping under the question particle. In these cases, the speaker asks the addressee to answer based on inferential or reported evidence (46–48). These cases are compatible with a modal analysis – the presupposition projects, as the speaker expects the addressee to have indirect or reportative evidence, while the alternative answers are each modal claims (assuming a Hamblin 1973 semantics for questions).[16]

---

[16] The inferential also appears in conjectural questions; these are cases where the use of the inferential enclitic in a question gives rise to a non-interrogative reading roughly translatable as 'I wonder...', as in (1a). For a modal analysis of conjectural questions, see Littell, Matthewson and Peterson (2010).

(46) Context: Using the Tom and Mittens storyboard (Rolka and Cable 2014), the speaker is telling the story to a child. In the story, Tom's cat is hiding because he doesn't want a bath. The speaker knows the story and therefore knows where the cat is hiding. In order to keep the child engaged, however, the speaker addresses this question to the child.
 hɛ **čɛ**   kʷ čɛ   ʔəxʷ nɛʔs   kʷayıt?   tamat ga!
 hiɬ=**ča**   kʷ=ča   ʔə=xʷ=niʔ=s   kʷay-ít   tam-at=ga
 be=INFER DET=where OBL=PRT=be.there=3POSS hide-STAT guess-CTR=PRT
 'Where do you think the cat is hiding? Guess!'   vf
 Speaker has direct evidence.
 Addressee has inferential evidence.

(47) Context: Freddie says his dog didn't eat this morning. I ask him:
 kʷukʷtəma **ča**?
 kʷəkʷt-əm=a=**ča**
 sick-MD=Q=INFER
 'Is he sick?'   sf
 Speaker does not have indirect evidence (beyond addressee report).
 Addressee has indirect evidence.

(48) Context: Gloria just got off the phone with Freddie's daughter. I think she might have heard whether Freddie is at home.
 kʷuna **kʷa**   qʷol   hɛwt.
 kʷən=a=**kʷa**   qʷəl   hiwt
 COMP=Q=RPT   come   get.home
 'Is he home?'   vf
 Speaker does not have reported evidence
 Addressee has reported evidence.

However, the reportative can also receive another interpretation in questions, where the speaker uses the reportative when conveying the question of a third party. In these cases, the reportative embeds the speech act, rather than a proposition (49). Of the two speakers I have been able to check these with, one accepts these cases and the other rejects them.

(49) Context: Laura, who is soft-spoken, asks Freddie if he wants tea. He doesn't hear, so I pass on the question.
 ʔəθ χaƛa **kʷa**   kʷ tihaya?
 ʔəθ=χaƛ=a=**kʷa**   kʷ=tihaya?
 2SG.POSS=want=Q=RPT DET=tea
 'Do you want tea (she said)?'   vf

The ability to embed speech acts is sometimes taken to be the most convincing evidence for an illocutionary analysis of evidentials (Faller 2002). It is not clear whether a modal could take scope over a speech act, while under Faller's analysis, illocutionary evidentials always compose with speech acts. Her proposal for these cases is that the reportative combines with the speech act that has the illocutionary force of a question and changes the illocutionary force to presentation – the speaker presents someone else's question, but is not actually asking the question. While this accounts for the 'quotative' cases such as (49) quite elegantly, her proposal then faces challenges for the more canonical cases of evidentials in questions, where the evidentials scope *under* the question operator, so that the addressee is expected to answer based on indirect evidence. In order for her proposal to work for these more canonical cases, she must abandon a straightforward Hamblin-style analysis of a question as a set of its possible answers and propose that questions involve two illocutionary operators: a REQUEST that the addressee ASSERT a proposition from the set of alternative answers. She proposes that the evidential can scope either over or under the REQUEST operator, giving rise to the two readings.

While Faller's proposal is a possible analysis of questions, it is not the standard approach. As Faller herself points out, it also predicts that the inferential evidential should similarly be able to scope over the REQUEST operator, as well as under, but this does not seem to be possible. Another problematic prediction, at least for ʔayʔajuθəm, is that the reportative should be able to take scope over other types of speech acts, allowing the speaker to pass on someone else's request, for instance. This does not seem to be possible, even for the speaker who accepts the reportative scoping over questions (as in (49)).[17]

(50) Context: Gloria asks Freddie to pass the sugar. He doesn't hear so I pass on her request.
*χanaθ *k̓ʷa*   ʔə tə šukʷa.
χan-aθ=*k̓ʷa*   ʔə=tə=šukʷa.
give-CTR+1SG.OBJ=RPT OBL=DET=sugar
'Pass the sugar (she said).'   sf

---

17 The inferential also cannot appear in imperatives, even if the speaker's motivation for the request is inference (i). This is expected under a modal analysis, since modals combine with propositions, not speech acts, and a modal claim is a claim concerning a proposition, not a speech act; the compatibility of modals with questions is not a counterexample because questions are modeled as sets of propositions, so a question with a modal will be a set of propositions containing the modal.

In any case, since the quotative uses are less common than cases where the reportative scopes under the question operator (and actually impossible for some speakers) in ʔayʔajuθəm, building an analysis that works well for these uses, but complicates the more canonical cases seems misguided. Of course, adopting an illocutionary analysis would be problematic regardless, given that we have seen evidence that both the inferential and reportative contribute at-issue content.

ʔayʔajuθəm is not unique in having a reportative evidential that patterns as a modal, but has quotative uses. Tan Almazán (2019) argues that the reportative *daw* in Tagalog is an epistemic modal, but also discusses uses of the reportative parallel to (50). Tan Almazán concludes that scope in questions cannot distinguish an illocutionary from a modal analysis of evidentials. Developing an analysis of the 'quotative' cases is beyond the scope of this chapter, however, and the reader is referred to Tan Almazán (2019) for further discussion (though she also does not provide a complete analysis of these particular cases).

5 Formal analysis

We have now seen evidence that *čɛ* and *kʷa* contribute to the at-issue content of the clause and are therefore best analyzed as epistemic modals. In this section I propose a formal analysis to capture the behavior of each of these modals. Since neither is compatible with contexts where the speaker knows the proposition to be true or false based on direct evidence (leaving aside the question of perspective shift induced by the reportative momentarily), I adopt von Fintel and Gillies' (2010) approach to epistemic modals. They propose that epistemic modals are evidentials that presuppose that the speaker's direct information in the context does not settle whether *p* is true or false; the speaker's direct information is the information the speaker treats as 'direct trustworthy evidence', often, but not exclusively, known through direct observation (von Fintel and Gillies 2010: 369).

(i) Context: I see you are looking quite pale. I tell you to go to bed and rest.
   ho (*čɛ) ga   ʔaχɛθ.
   hu=čа=ga   ʔaχiθ.
   go=INFER=DPRT lie.down
   'Go lie down.'   sf

Faller's (2002) speech act analysis may also predict this behavior for the inferential. Although Faller proposes that the inferential (referred to as the 'conjectural') in Cuzco Quechua is a speech act operator, she also gives it a modal component, which could be taken to rule out uses in imperatives.

They formalize the direct information available to the speaker as a set of propositions, which they call a kernel (K). The modal base (B) of an epistemic modal is the intersection of these propositions.

(51) K is a kernel for B_K, B_K is determined by the kernel K, only if:
 i. K is a set of propositions (if $P \in K$ then $P \subseteq W$)
 ii. $B_K = \cap K$ (von Fintel and Gillies 2010: 371)

Using these tools, von Fintel and Gillies formalize the condition that the speaker does not have direct information that settles whether the prejacent is true or false. For them, the kernel directly settles whether p if there is direct information in K that entails or contradicts the prejacent.

(52) K directly settles whether P iff either $X \subseteq P$ or $X \cap P = \varnothing$ for some $X \in K$.
                                                               (von Fintel and Gillies 2010: 374)

Epistemic modals presuppose that the kernel does not settle whether p. An epistemic necessity modal such as *must* or *čε* then asserts that the modal base (i.e. the intersection of all the propositions in the kernel, which represents the direct information the speaker has in the context) entails that p is true. That is, p is true in all the worlds compatible with all the direct information available to the speaker. I introduce the kernel as a parameter of evaluation.[18]

(53) i. $[\![\text{čε } \phi]\!]^{c,w,g,K}$ is defined only if K does not directly settle $[\![\phi]\!]^{c,g}$
 ii. If defined, $[\![\text{čε } \phi]\!]^{c,w,g,K} = 1$ iff $B_K \subseteq [\![\phi]\!]^{c,g}$ (adapted from von Fintel and Gillies 2010: 372)

---

18 This is similar to Yalcin's (2007) approach to epistemic modals which involves an information state parameter for evaluation (see also Veltman 1996); in Yalcin's analysis, however, an information state is a set of worlds compatible with the speaker's (or attitude holder's) information, while I adopt von Fintel and Gillies' notion of a kernel, which is a type of information state consisting of a set of propositions. Yalcin also allows attitude predicates such as *imagine* to update the information state for the evaluation of an embedded proposition to a set of worlds compatible with the attitude holder's imaginings, rather than information known about the real world. Anand and Hacquard (2013), however, argue that only representational attitude predicates provide information states and therefore information states are always determined by the attitude holder's knowledge or beliefs (see footnote 20); this allows them to capture the distribution of epistemic modals, which they argue to only occur under embedding predicates that provide an information state. I will assume Anand and Hacquard (2013) are correct here.

This analysis allows us to capture the behavior of the ʔayʔajuθəm inferential čɛ́. It straightforwardly predicts its epistemic flavour, strong modal force, and requirement that the speaker does not have direct evidence for the prejacent. Because the modal contribution is at-issue, this analysis also captures its challengeability and effect on possible continuations.[19]

In the case of embedding under attitude predicates, the kernel must reflect the direct information available to the matrix subject, rather than the speaker; the kernel is not strictly speaker-oriented but tracks the information available to the individual by whom the modal claim is made. Formally, this can be represented by having the matrix attitude predicate provide the kernel for the embedded proposition. I sketch such an approach below.

I base my approach on Anand and Hacquard's 2013 analysis of attitude predicates. They claim that certain attitude predicates – those they call representational[20] – provide the information state for embedded epistemic modals, adopting Yalcin's (2007) proposal that epistemic modal claims are evaluated relative to an information state parameter. Adapting Anand and Hacquard's (2013) analysis of attitude predicates to incorporate kernels, we can give $nopʊx^w$ 'realize' from

---

19 Actually, the continuation facts are not completely straightforward to handle under von Fintel and Gillies' particular modal analysis. In their model, the modal base, the intersection of the speaker's direct information, entails the prejacent; they adopt this position since it is their central claim that a proposition with *must* is not weaker than a plain assertion. In order to capture the continuation facts with čɛ́, however, we need the prejacent not to be entailed. I therefore assume that čɛ́ comes with an ordering source, as in more traditional analyses (e.g., Kratzer 1991), though I abstract away from this in the representation above for simplicity. The ordering source ranks the worlds in the modal base according to how stereotypical they are. čɛ́ asserts the prejacent to be entailed only in the highest ranked of these worlds. The at-issue portion of the denotation for čɛ́ would then be as in (54), with f as the ordering source – which assigns to each world in the modal base a set of propositions representing norms A and ranks the world according to how many of these propositions are true in it – and $BEST$ identifying the best possible worlds as ranked by the ordering source (adopting the representation of the ordering source from Matthewson 2016: 531):

(i) $[\![čɛ́\ \phi]\!]^{c,w,g,K} = \lambda f_{\langle s, \langle st, t \rangle \rangle}. BEST_{f(w)}(B_K) \subseteq [\![\phi]\!]^{c,g}$
Where for a given order on worlds $\leq_A$, $\forall X \in W[BEST_A(X) = \{x \in X: \neg \exists w' \in X[w' \leq_A w]\}]$
Where for all worlds w and $z \in W$: $w \leq_A z$ iff $\{p: p \in A$ and $z \in p\} \subseteq \{p: p \in A$ and $w \in p\}$

With an ordering source added, a proposition with čɛ́ is not guaranteed to entail the prejacent in the real world, since the world does not always unfold in a sterotypical manner. This in turn means that entailments of the prejacent are not guaranteed to be true in the real world. This gives rise to the continuation patterns discussed in section 3.2. The denotation I introduce for $k̓ʷa$ in (62) likewise abstracts away from the ordering source, but I also assume there to be an ordering source for $k̓ʷa$ in order to handle the continuation facts.

20 For Anand and Hacquard (2013), following Bolinger (1968), representational attitudes describe the content of a propositionally consistent attitudinal state.

(54) (repeated from (26)) the denotation in (55). The denotation given in (55) is a simplified representation that captures only the epistemic and factive character of this predicate, not the details of meaning that would differentiate *nopʊxʷ* 'realize' from a predicate like *toχʷnɛxʷ* 'know' for instance. This denotation asserts the embedded proposition ϕ to be entailed by the intersection of the matrix subject's kernel $k_w^{\prime x}$;[21] the embedded proposition is true in all worlds compatible with all the matrix subject's direct information. The embedding predicate also updates the kernel parameter for the embedded proposition to be the kernel of the matrix subject. This means that any epistemic modal within the embedded proposition will be evaluated relative to the matrix subject's kernel.

(54) Context: Tom (Tɛqaw) and Mittens storyboard (Rolka and Cable 2014) – the cat just ran out of the room and into another where it hid in a box. I saw the cat run and hide in the box and then I watched Tɛqaw figuring it out. Now I'm describing Tɛqaw.

nopʊxʷəm   Tɛqaw   hɛs čɛ   kʷ k̓ʷaxʷa
nup-əxʷ-əm   Tiqaw   hiɫ=s=ča   kʷ=k̓ʷaxʷa
think-NCTR-PASS Tiqaw   be=3POSS=INFER   DET=box
kʷayıts   šɛ mɛmaẇs.
kʷay-ít=s   šə=mimaẇ-s
GET.HIDDEN-STAT=3POSS   DET=cat-3POSS
'Tɛqaw realized that his cat must be hiding in a box.'   sf

(55) $[\![nopʊxʷ\ \phi]\!]^{c,w,g,K} = \lambda x\ .\ \cap K_w^{\prime x} \subseteq [\![\phi]\!]^{c,g,K_w^{\prime x}}$

We can then give (54) the truth conditions in (56). The attitude predicate provides the kernel for the embedded epistemic, including the presuppositional content. The at-issue content of the modal essentially replicates the contribution of the matrix predicate, but the presupposition ensures that the matrix subject does not have direct information settling whether the prejacent is true.

(56) $[\![nopʊxʷ\ Tɛqaw\ hɛs\ čɛ\ kʷ\ k̓ʷaxʷa\ kʷayıts\ šɛ\ mɛmaẇs]\!]^{c,w,g,K_w^S}$ is defined only if:
  i. $K_w^{\prime t}$ does not directly settle whether [$\lambda w'$. his_t *cat is hiding in a box in w'*]
  ii. If defined $[\![nopʊxʷ\ Tɛqaw\ hɛs\ čɛ\ kʷ\ k̓ʷaxʷa\ kʷayıts\ šɛ\ mɛmaẇs]\!]^{c,w,g,K} = 1$ iff $\cap K_w^{\prime t} \subseteq [B_{K_w^{\prime t}} \subseteq [\lambda w'.\ his_t\ cat\ is\ hiding\ in\ a\ box\ in\ w']]$

---

21 The intersection of the kernel is equivalent to the modal base defined in (51), but I do not refer to it with B_K to avoid terminological confusion.

The kernel K for the main clause will be speaker-oriented by default. This is represented in (56) by the s index on K accompanying the matrix interpetation brackets. Since the matrix clause does not constitute a modal claim, however, the speaker's kernel is not involved in calculating the truth conditions.

We turn now to questions. In questions the kernel can be addressee–oriented. Adopting a Hamblin (1973) semantics for questions, where a question denotes its set of possible answers, the question with the epistemic modal will denote a set of modalized propositions (answers). The kernel for the modal claim of each proposition in the set of possible answers reflects the knowledge of the addressee. This captures the readings where the speaker asks a question she expects the addressee to answer based on an inference, as in (46–48). For instance, the semantics for the polar question with the inferential in (47), repeated here as (57), would be as in (58), where the modal base for each proposition in the set of possible answers is determined by the addressee's kernel.

(57) Context: Freddie says his dog didn't eat this morning. I ask him:
 kʷukʷtəma č̓a?
 kʷəkʷt-əm=a=č̓a
 sick-MD=Q=INFER
 'Is he sick?' sf
 Speaker does not have indirect evidence (beyond addressee report).
 Addressee has indirect evidence.

(58) $\{[B_{K_w^a} \subseteq is.sick(he_1)], [B_{K_w^a} \subseteq \neg[is.sick(he_1)]]\}$
 Where each proposition in the set of answers is defined iff $B_{K_w^a}$ does not settle whether the prejacent is true.

In order to capture the shift in the orientation of the kernel formally, we need a shift operator for questions. I adapt (59) from McCready (2007) who proposes a similar operator to shift the judge parameter from the speaker to addressee in questions involving predicates of personal taste. In (59), I represent the kernel as indexed to the speaker by default, and then shifted by the operator to be indexed to the addressee.

(59) $Sh(\llbracket \phi \rrbracket^{c,w,g,K_w^s}) = \llbracket \phi \rrbracket^{c,w,g,K_w^a}$
 where s is the speaker and a is the addressee in the utterance context.

McCready proposes that this shift operator accompanies the question operator, but is independent of it. The shift operator applies prior to the question operator. Applying the shift operator in the analysis of (57), we get (60) (using *pro* to represent the null third person subject). The result is that the addressee is presupposed not to have direct information settling whether the dog is sick, and in answering, the addressee is expected to make an epistemic modal claim.

(60) $Q(Sh([\![k^wuk^wtəm\ pro_1]\!]^{c,w,g,K_w^S})) = Q([\![k^wuk^wtəm\ pro_1]\!]^{c,w,g,K_w^a}) =$
$\{[B_{K_w^a} \subseteq is.sick(he_1)], [B_{K_w^a} \subseteq \neg[is.sick(he_1)]\}$
Where each proposition in the set of answers is defined iff $B_{K_w^a}$ does not settle whether the prejacent is true.

Before leaving the discussion of čɛ̣, I would like to offer further motivation for treating the felicity condition as a presupposition. We have a developed an analysis where the felicity condition associated with čɛ̣ projects in both embedding environments and questions, though the anchoring of the modal base changes. We have not seen negative data showing that the felicity condition must be met in these environments. (61) shows that the felicity condition does in fact project in questions and causes infelicity if not met. In (61), the addressee should have direct evidence that settles whether the possible answers are true or false, since it is a question about the addressee's personal state; the use of the inferential is therefore infelicitous.

(61) # q̇aq̇ahačxʷ čɛ̣?
q̇aq̇a=a=čxʷ=čạ
hungry=Q=INFER
'Are you hungry?' sf

The conjectural question reading (see footnote 16) cannot rescue (61) since it would be pragmatically odd for the speaker to be speculating about the addressee's hunger, when the addressee, the authoritative source of information on the matter, is present.

Up to this point, the discussion has centered on the inferential. We turn now to the modifications required to capture the contribution of the reportative in this framework. Matthewson (2010) builds on von Fintel and Gillies' 2010 proposal to analyze the reportative *ku7* in St'át'imcets. She proposes that *ku7* has a two-fold presupposition: (i)) that the speaker does not have direct sensory evidence for the prejacent ϕ, and (ii) the speaker's kernel contains a report of ϕ.[22]

---

[22] An anonymous reviewer points out that this requirement is very strong, since it places a restriction on the form of the reported evidence. While it may be possible to somewhat weaken the requirement, it is not sufficient for the reported evidence to give rise to an inference that the prejacent is true, as shown in (i).

(62) $[\![\acute{k}^wa\ \phi]\!]^{c,w,g,K}$ is defined only if:
   i. K contains a proposition of the form 'someone said ϕ'.
   ii. K_{SENS} does not directly settle ϕ.
   iii. If defined, $[\![\acute{k}^wa\ \phi]\!]^{c,w,g,K} = 1$ iff $B_k \subseteq [\![\phi]\!]^{c,g}$

(adapted from Matthewson 2010)[23]

Notice that Matthewson's approach imposes structure on K so that direct sensory evidence K_{SENS} can be referenced separately from direct information in general K. This is because the S'tát'imcets reportative can be used even where the proposition is general knowledge if the speaker does not have direct sensory evidence for p; this is different than for epistemic modals like *must* which cannot be used for general knowledge even if not experienced directly (e.g., # *Antarctica must be cold*.). Since general knowledge would typically count as direct information for epistemic modals, Matthewson partitions the kernel so that the presupposition that the kernel does not settle whether p only involves direct sensory evidence for the reportative.

The same facts are true of ʔayʔaǰuθəm. $\acute{k}^wa$ is compatible with knowledge that has not been directly experienced, but is general knowledge learnt from a teacher or textbook – one of my consultants even judges it to be obligatory in this context.

(i) Context: Gloria tells me in the morning that Daniel is on his way to Tla'amin. Later, in the afternoon, I tell you Daniel is coming: $q^woq^wol\ \acute{k}^wa\ Daniel\ nɛʔɛtəm\ Gloria$. 'Gloria said Daniel is coming.' You ask me when Daniel will be here. Gloria didn't tell me when he would arrive, but I guess based on when she told me he left:

#hɛ $\acute{k}^w$a səm	tiṅ	nanat	q^{w}ols	təs.
hiɬ=k̓^{w}a=səm	tiṅ	nanat	q^{w}əɬ=s	təs
COP=RPT=FUT	DEM	evening	come=3POSS	arrive

'He'll arrive tonight.' sf

It may be that the report can differ in content from the prejacent so long as it entails the prejacent. This requires further investigation.

23 Matthewson (2015) suggests another possible analysis for reportative evidentials within von Fintel and Gillies' framework; she proposes that the reportative presupposes only that the kernel contains a proposition of the form 'someone said ϕ', as in (62i), while the indirect evidence requirement (62ii) arises via implicature. I adopt her earlier version since it is more parallel with the denotation for the inferential and the two evidentials behave similarly with respect to their indirect evidence requirement. Further research is needed to see whether indirect evidence requirement for the reportative could be reduced to implicature.

(63) a. Context: I've learnt that it's cold in the Antarctic but I've never been there. Now I'm passing on this knowledge to a child.
čımčıṁmot k̓ʷa   gıǰɛ.
čəmčəṁ-mut=k̓ʷa   gəja
CHAR~cold-INT=RPT   land
'It is a cold land.'   vf

b. Context: I learnt about the Titanic, but I wasn't alive yet when it sank.
θayɛʔmoł k̓ʷa   kʷ tihmot   tinpot   sχʷoχʷoł.
θay-əm-ʔuł=k̓ʷa kʷ=tih-mut tinput   s=χʷuχʷuł
sink-MD-PST=RPT DET=big-INT steam.boat NMLZ=long.time
'The big steamboat sank a long time ago.'   vf

To account for the ʔayʔajuθəm reportative, I therefore adopt the partition of the kernel proposed in Matthewson (2010), allowing direct sensory evidence to be referenced apart from direct information in general.

The semantics for k̓ʷa proposed in (63) does not straightforwardly predict the ability of the speaker to utter p without believing p to be true. Recall that I attributed this possibility to perspective shift, following AnderBois (2014). Within von Fintel and Gillies' framework, this can be implemented by allowing the kernel for the at-issue content to be that of the reporter, rather than the speaker. The presupposed content remains anchored to the speaker. So, for example, (64) (repeated from (25)) signals that the speaker has reported evidence for the prejacent and does not have direct information that settles the prejacent. The claim that Freddie won is attributed to the reporter.

(64) Context: There was a rumour that Freddie won the lottery, but I talked to him and found out the rumour is not true. Later we're talking about this and I say:
ʔƛ̓uxʷʔəm k̓ʷa Freddie qəχ tala. xʷaʔak̓ʷʊt!
ƛ̓əxʷ-ʔəm=k̓ʷa Freddie qəχ tala. xʷaʔ+ala+k̓ʷa+ʔut
win-ACT.INTR Freddie lots money NEG+EXCLAM+RPT+EXCL
'Freddie won a lot of money (I heard), but it turns out not!'   sf

Formally, the perspective shift of (64) could be achieved with a perspective shift operator. The *P-Sh* operator shifts the anchoring of the kernel for the at-issue content from the speaker to the salient individual who made the report.

(65) $P\text{-}Sh(\llbracket \acute{k}^wa\ \phi \rrbracket^{c,w,g,K_w^S})$ is defined only if:
  i. contains a proposition of the form ɸ.
  ii. If defined, $P\text{-}Sh(\llbracket \acute{k}^wa\ \phi \rrbracket^{c,w,g,K_w^S}) = 1$ iff $B_{K_w^i} \subseteq \llbracket \phi \rrbracket^{c,g}$

In (65), I have not included the reportative's presupposition that the speaker's kernel does not contain direct information settling whether the prejacent is true (as in (62ii)). This is because I have not yet directly investigated whether this presupposition survives in the perspective shift cases. It seems likely that the speaker could have direct evidence settling that the prejacent is not true (but the cases we have seen, such as (64), involved indirect evidence). If this is the case, there are a few possible solutions. One is to treat this requirement as a cancellable implicature, as in Matthewson (2015) (see footnote 23). Another option is to modify the requirement so that it only mandates that the speaker's kernel does not settle whether the prejacent is true (but allows it to be settled as false). Of course, this depends on whether the converse is possible – whether the speaker can have direct evidence settling that the proposition is true – in perspective shift cases. I leave this for future research.

Of course, representing perspective shift with the *P-Sh* operator does not add much. To be descriptively adequate we would need to capture the conditions governing where the *P-Sh* operator can be used, while to be explanatory, we would have to be able to derive these in a principled way. This will have to wait for future work. For now, I can only reiterate that in order for perspective shift to felicitously occur, particularly where the speaker does not believe the prejacent to be true, there must be contextual and linguistic cues, typically some sort of evaluative language, that such a shift has taken place (as pointed out in AnderBois 2014). This ensures that the addressee understands that the shift has occurred. The reason that perspective shift is possible with the reportative, but not other evidentials, is because the reportative itself introduces another perspective holder – the source of the report – meaning that the reportative inherently facilitates perspective shift (AnderBois 2014). Where perspective shift occurs, the approach proposed here essentially means allowing the reportative to have an informational modal base, as suggested for the German reportative *sollen* in Kratzer (2012) (see also discussion in Matthewson 2012). The availability of an informational modal base is pragmatically restricted, however, as it is predicted to be found only in contexts where perspective shift is possible.[24]

---

[24] Another possibility, raised by an anonymous reviewer, is that the speaker's kernel for the reportative consists of a set of propositions uttered by the reporter. That is, the kernel for the reportatave is always a potentially unrealistic modal base consisting of the reports received from some salient individual. My hesitation with this approach is that it predicts any proposition that

6 Conclusion

In this chapter, I have argued that the inferential clitic čɛ and the reportative clitic k̓ʷa in ʔayʔajuθəm are epistemic modals. In order to establish their modality, I identified and implemented three diagnostics to probe whether these evidentials contribute to the at-issue content of the clause: (i) embeddability, (ii) challengeability, and (iii) the status of continuations entailed by the prejacent. The first two of these diagnostics appear frequently in previous literature and were discussed critically in terms of how they are applied and what they show; the third was introduced as a novel test. The results of these three tests indicated that both the inferential and the reportative contribute to the at-issue content of the clause and are best analyzed as epistemic modals. The reportative shows certain unexpected behaviours for this analysis, such as allowing the speaker to utter the prejacent without believing it to be true. I proposed that these facts are best understood in terms of perspective shift (AnderBois 2014). Finally, I adopted a formal analysis from von Fintel and Gillies (2010) and Matthewson (2010), and suggested how perspective shift might be implemented using this approach.

The fact that these ʔayʔajuθəm evidentials behave as epistemic modals provides further evidence for a tight link between evidentiality and epistemic modality (contra De Haan 1999; Aikhenvald 2004). Evidentials from a wide range of languages have now been argued to encode epistemic modality, including St'át'imcets (Matthewson, Rullmann and Davis 2007), Gitksan (Peterson 2010), Tagalog (Tan Almazán 2019), Bulgarian (Izvorski 1997), Tibetan (Garrett 2001), among others, though in many of these analyses modal evidentials are argued to co-exist with nonmodal evidentials, even within the same language. In this chapter, I argued that certain behaviours used to argue for a nonmodal analysis of evidentials do not in fact distinguish between modal and nonmodal evidentials (in part following AnderBois 2014; Tan Almazán 2019), while other tests that have been criticized in previous literature can in fact distinguish between the two types of evidentials if applied carefully. It remains an interesting question to what extent epistemic modality and evidentiality overlap and whether these should actually be considered distinct categories (Matthewson 2012; von Fintel and Gillies 2010; Kratzer 2012).

---

the speaker has heard from a third party to be felicitous with k̓ʷa, provided the speaker does not have direct information that settles whether the proposition is true. It does not predict the infelicity that arises in cases like (24). This approach may be rescued with additional pragmatic factors, but then it is not so clear how this approach differs from an analysis in terms of perspective shift, at least as sketched here, and whether the two approaches make different predictions.

References

Aikhenvald, Alexandra. 2004. *Evidentiality*. Oxford: Oxford University Press.
Aikhenvald, Alexandra. 2007. Information source and evidentiality: What can we conclude? *Rivista di Linguistica* 19. 209–227.
Anand, Pranav & Valentine Hacquard. 2013. Epistemics and attitudes. *Semantics and Pragmantics* 6. 1–59.
AnderBois, Scott. 2014. On the exceptional status of reportative evidentials. In Todd Snider, Sarah D'Antonio & Mia Weigand (eds.), *Proceedings of Semantics and Linguistic Theory (SALT) 24*, 234–254. Washington, DC: Linguistic Society of America.
Bochnak, Ryan & Lisa Matthewson. 2015. *Methodologies in semantic fieldwork*. Oxford: Oxford University Press.
Bolinger, Dwight. 1968. Post-posed main phrases: An English rule for the Romance subjunctive. *Canadian Journal of Linguistics* 14. 3–30.
Brugman, Claudia M. & Monica Macaulay. 2015. Characterizing evidentiality. *Linguistic Typology* 19 (2). 201–237.
Condoravdi, Cleo. 2002. Temporal interpretation of modals: Modals for the present and the past. In David Beaver, Luis Casillas Martinez, Brady Clark & Stefan Kaufmann (eds.), *The construction of meaning*, 59–88. Stanford: CSLI Publications.
Davis, Henry. 2005. On the syntax and semantics of negation in Salish. *International Journal of American Linguistics* 71. 1–55.
De Haan, Ferdinand. 1999. Evidentiality and epistemic modality: Setting boundaries. *Southwest Journal of Linguistics* 18 (1). 83–101.
DeLancey, Scott. 2001. The mirative and evidentiality. *Journal of Pragmatics* 33. 369–382.
Faller, Martina. 2002. *Semantics and pragmatics of evidentials in Cuzco Quechua*. Stanford, CA: Stanford University dissertation.
Faller, Martina. 2014. Do speech act evidentials embed after all? Paper presented at the Workshop on the Semantics of Embedding and the Syntax of the Left Periphery, University of Oxford, 2 September. https://www.academia.edu/8202259/Do_speech_act_evidentials_embed_after_all (accessed 28 February 2022).
Garrett, Edward. 2001. *Evidentiality and assertion in Tibetan*. Los Angeles, CA: University of California, Los Angeles dissertation.
Gillon, Carrie. 2006. *The semantics of determiners: Domain restriction in Sk̲wx̲wú7mesh*. Vancouver, BC: University of British Columbia dissertation.
Grice, H. Paul. 1989. *Studies in the ways of words*. Cambridge, MA: Harvard University Press.
Hacquard, Valentine. 2006. *Aspects of modality*. Cambridge, MA: Massachusetts Institute of Technology dissertation.
Hamblin, Charles Leonard. 1973. Questions in Montague grammar. *Foundations of Language* 10. 41–53.
Harris, Jesse A. & Christopher Potts. 2009. Perspective-shifting with appositives and expressives. *Linguistics and Philosophy* 32. 523–552.
Heycock, Caroline. 2006. Embedded root phenomena. In Martin Everaert & Henk van Riemsdijk (eds.), *The Blackwell companion to syntax, Vol. II*, 174–209. Oxford: Blackwell.
Hooper, Joan B. & Sandra A. Thompson. 1973. On the applicability of root transformations. *Linguistic Inquiry* 4. 465–497.

Huijsmans, Marianne, D.K.E. Reisinger, Roger Lo & Kaining Xu. 2018. A preliminary look at determiners in ʔayʔaju̓θəm. In Lisa Matthewson, Erin Guntly, Marianne Huijsmans & Michael Rochemont (eds.), *Wa7 xweysás i nqwal'utteníha i ucwalmícwa: He loves the people's languages. Essays in honour of Henry Davis*, 329–340. Vancouver, BC: UBCOPL 6.

Izvorski, Roumyana. 1997. The present perfect as an epistemic modal. In Aaron Lawson (ed.), *Proceedings from Semantics and Linguistic Theory VII*, 222–239. Ithaca, NY: Cornell University.

Korotkova, Natalia. 2016. *Heterogeneity and uniformity in the evidential domain*. Los Angeles, CA: University of California, Los Angeles dissertation.

Kratzer, Angelika. 1991. Modality. In Arnim von Stechow & Dieter Wunderlich (eds.), *Semantics: An international handbook of contemporary research*, 639–650. Berlin: de Gruyter.

Kratzer, Angelika. 2012. *Modals and conditionals*. Oxford & New York: Oxford University Press.

Krifka, Manfred. 2014. Embedding illocutionary acts. In Tom Roeper & Margaret Speas (eds.), *Recursion: Complexity in cognition*, 59–87. Springer.

Littell, Patrick, Lisa Matthewson & Tyler Peterson. 2010. On the semantics of conjectural questions. In Tyler Peterson & Uli Sauerland (eds.), *Evidence from evidentials*, 89–104. Vancouver: UBCWPL.

Matthewson, Lisa. 1998. *Determiner systems and quantificational strategies: Evidence from Salish*. The Hague: Holland Academic Graphics.

Matthewson, Lisa. 2004. On the methodology of semantic fieldwork. *International Journal of American Linguistics* 70. 369–415.

Matthewson, Lisa. 2005. Presuppositions and cross-linguistic variation. In Christopher Davis, Amy Rose Deal & Youri Zabbal (eds.), *Proceedings of the 36th Annual Meeting of the North East Linguistics Society*, 63–76. Amherst: GLSA.

Matthewson, Lisa. 2010. Evidential restrictions on epistemic modals. Presentation given at the Workshop on Epistemic Indefinites, University of Göttingen, 11 June. http://www.engl-ling.unigoettingen.de/epistemic/Program_files/Matthewson%20 Goettingen.pdf (accessed 23 May 2020).

Matthewson, Lisa. 2012. Evidence about evidentials: Where fieldwork meets theory. In B. Stolterfoht & S. J. K. Featherston (eds.), *Empirical approaches to linguistic theory: Studies in meaning and structure*, 85–114. Berlin: de Gruyter.

Matthewson, Lisa. 2015. Evidential restrictions on epistemic modals. In Luis Alonso-Ovalle & Paula Menéndez-Benito (eds.), *Epistemic indefinites: Exploring modality beyond the verbal domain*, 141–160. Oxford: Oxford University Press.

Matthewson, Lisa. 2016. Modality. In Maria Aloni & Paul Dekker (eds.), *The Cambridge handbook of formal semantics*, 525–559. Cambridge: Cambridge University Press.

Matthewson, Lisa, Hotze Rullmann & Henry Davis. 2007. Evidentials as epistemic modals: Evidence from St'át'imcets. In Jeroen Van Craenenbroeck (ed.), *Linguistic variation yearbook 2007*, 201–254. Amsterdam: John Benjamins.

McCready, Eric. 2007. Context shift in questions and elsewhere. In Louise McNally & Estela Puig-Waldmüller (eds.), *Proceedings of Sinn und Bedeutung 11*, 433–447. https://ojs.ub.unikonstanz.de/sub/index.php/sub/article/view/656 (accessed 9 May 9 2022).

Murray, Sarah. 2010. *Evidentiality and the structure of speech acts*. New Brunswick, NJ: Rutgers University dissertation.

Peterson, Tyler. 2010. *Epistemic modality and evidentiality in Gitksan at the semantics-pragmatics interface*. Vancouver, BC: University of British Columbia dissertation.
Reisinger, Daniel. 2018. Modality in Comox-Sliammon. In Marianne Huijsmans, Roger Lo, Daniel Reisinger & Oksana Tkachman (eds.), *Papers for the Fifty-Third International Conference on Salish and Neighbouring Languages*, 197–227. Vancouver: UBCWPL.
Rett, Jessica & Sarah E. Murray. 2013. A semantic account of mirative evidentials. In Todd Snider (ed.), *Semantics and Linguistic Theory (SALT)*, 23 . 453–472. Ithaca, NY: CLC Publications.
Rolka, Matthew & Seth Cable. 2014. Tom and Mittens. Totem Field Storyboards. http://www.totemfieldstoryboards.org (accessed 27 April 2020).
Smirnova, Anastasia. 2013. Evidentiality in Bulgarian: Temporality, epistemic modality, and information source. *Journal of Semantics* 30. 479–532.
Tan Almazán, Jennifer. 2019. *Evidentiality in Tagalog*. Madrid: Universidad Autónoma de Madrid dissertation.
Vanderveken, Daniel. 1990. *Meaning and speech acts*. Cambridge: Cambridge University Press.
Vanderveken, Daniel. 2001. Universal grammar and speech act theory. In Daniel Vanderveken & Susumu Kubo (eds.), *Essays in Speech Act Theory*, 25–62. Amsterdam: John Benjamins.
Veltman, Frank. 1996. Defaults in update semantics. *Journal of Philosophical Logic* 25. 221–261.
von Fintel, Kai & Anthony S. Gillies. 2010. Must . . . stay . . . strong! *Natural Language Semantics* 18 (4). 351–383.
Watanabe, Honoré. 2003. *A morphological description of Sliammon, Mainland Comox Salish, with a sketch of syntax*. ELPR Publications Series AZ-040. Osaka: Osaka Gakuin University.
Watanabe, Honoré. 2020. A Sliammon text: "When coming out of the woods", as told by Mary George. *Northern Language Studies* 10. 275–294.
Willett, Thomas. 1998. A cross-linguistic survey of the grammaticalization of evidentiality. *Studies in Language* 12. 51–97.
Yalcin, Seth. 2007. Epistemic modals. *Mind* 116. 983–1026.

Pablo Fuentes
10 Parameters for the production of discourse contexts: Eliciting the semantics of obligations and desires in Mapudungun

Abstract: Mapudungun is an endangered Araucanian language that possesses a very productive frustrative suffix (*-fu-*). As with other frustratives across languages, *-fu-* is used to express the non-realization of an expected outcome or state, as well as counterfactuality. When combined with modals, the suffix brings about various semantic shifts, such as (i) strong to weak necessity, (ii) attainable to unattainable desires, and (iii) actual to counterfactual desires and obligations. The attested range of meanings strongly suggests that Mapudungun behaves like so-called transparent OUGHT/WISH languages. The focus of this chapter is on overcoming the methodological challenges posed to the researcher when eliciting primary data related to these phenomena. More constructively, I provide a basic guideline for producing controlled scenarios that can be used as the basic content of appropriate discourse contexts. I show that the task can be greatly simplified by mapping the modal territory with the following circumstantial parameters: achieved/unachieved, compulsory/advisory, attainable/unattainable, and actual/counterfactual.

1 Introduction

Mapudungun (ISO 639-2 code *arn*) is a language isolate from the Araucanian family. Although valuable studies written in Spanish date from colonial times, an exhaustive monography accessible for the global scientific community has only

---

Acknowledgments: I would like to thank two anonymous reviewers and the editors, especially Jozina Vander Klok, for their careful readings and insightful comments. I thank my native speaker consultants, Héctor Mariano and Renan Vita, for their collaboration on the collection and discussion of the Mapudungun data presented in this chapter. I am also greatly indebted to sisters Sonia and Mónica Vita Manquepi, and to all members of the Vita Manquepi family, for an endearing and laborious journey to the Pewenche summerland.

Pablo Fuentes, Universidad Católica de la Santísima Concepción, Departamento de Ciencias del Lenguaje y Literatura, Alonso De Ribera 2850, Concepción, Chile, e-mail: pablo.fuentes@ucsc.cl

recently been made available (Smeets 2008). Formal studies within semantics and syntax are still incipient (but see Fasola 2015), and modality is a topic that remains relatively understudied (but see Golluscio 2000 for a pragmatic-driven approach).

Mapudungun possesses a verbal suffix (-*fu*-) that behaves in similar ways to frustrative particles in several unrelated languages (Carol and Salanova 2021 for Chorote and Mebêngôkre, Copley 2005 for Tohono O'odham, Davis and Matthewson in press for St'át'imcets, Kroeger 2017 for Kimaragang, Sparing-Chávez 2003 for Amahuaca). As with other frustratives across languages, -*fu*- is used to express the non-realization of an expected outcome or state, as well as counterfactuality. When combined with modals, the suffix effects various semantic shifts, such as (i) strong to weak necessity, (ii) attainable to unattainable desires, and (iii) actual to counterfactual desires and obligations. As shown elsewhere (Fuentes 2020, to appear), the attested range of meanings strongly suggests that Mapudungun behaves like so-called transparent OUGHT/WISH languages (von Fintel and Iatridou 2008, *under submission*).[1] The attested semantic effects give rise to the empirical question as to whether other frustrative languages are also OUGHT/WISH transparent. They also pose a challenge to existing and prospective analyses of -*fu*-, which should be able to account for both its core frustrative readings and its semantic effects in both conditional and modal environments.

The focus of this chapter is on a preliminary task presented to researchers interested in a linguistic survey of this type: the production of discourse contexts (DCs hereafter). In line with standard procedures in semantic fieldwork, a significant part of the task consists in coming up with the precise circumstances under which different strings of language are rendered felicitous and/or true. For instance, see Matthewson (2004) and Matthewson and Bochnak (2015) for technical guidance on elicitation techniques; Cover (2015) for a more specific approach to tense, aspect and modality; and Vander Klok (2014, this volume) for a modal questionnaire for cross-linguistic use. Although the range of circumstances at the Mapudungun frustrative-modal crossroad vary considerably, I show that the mentioned task can be completed with a rather minimal set of circumstantial parameters: achieved/unachieved, compulsory/advisory, attainable/unattainable, and actual/counterfactual. The goal is that by managing a controlled variety of scenarios, the researcher can prepare a basic semantic toolkit and explore this fascinating territory with somewhat greater visibility.

---

1 Throughout the chapter, italics are used for language-specific terms and small capitals for cross-linguistic predicates (although I will on occasions use the small caps to refer, rather, to the statement containing the predicate). Thus, *want* and *querer* are English and Spanish lexical variants for WANT (or the statement expressing the desire).

The paper is organized as follows: in section 2, after briefly introducing the Mapudungun modal and tense system (section 2.1), I describe the frustrative-modals interactions (section 2.2). My aim is to show that frustrative -*fu*- plays the relevant role of so-called X-morphology in Mapudungun's transparent OUGHT/WISH predications. In section 3, I present and discuss the four parameters of my methodological guideline: achieved/unachieved, compulsory/advisory, attainable/unattainable, actual/counterfactual. Section 4 concludes.

Lastly, I emphasize that the scope of the chapter is mostly on the practical side. My purpose is to present Mapudungun transparency as a case study on the frustrative-modal interactions so as to provide a general guideline for the production of DCs in future investigations in this field. Taking a DC to be a representational device used as a stimulus in the relevant elicitation tasks, I will elaborate on the *production* of such inputs *for* the translation and judgments tasks (rather than on the implementation and interpretation of these tasks, which I will leave fairly underspecified in the examples throughout). The focus, then, will be on the craft rather than on the function.

2 Mapping the territory

Recently, Cover and Tonhauser (2015) presented a thoughtful discussion about the interplay between semantic theory and fieldwork research. The authors convincingly argue that the influence of these two ends is bidirectional: semantic theory can guide fieldwork (resulting in a more comprehensive description of the semantic properties under investigation), and theoretically informed fieldwork can ultimately improve our theories and understanding of language variation and universals. In my own one-way journey from theory to fieldwork, one of the theories that shaped a significant part of my research plan on Mapudungun was that described in the seminal paper on transparent OUGHT by von Fintel and Iatridou (2008). According to the authors, an OUGHT transparent language is one that uses X-morphology to turn a strong necessity statement into a weak necessity one (where X-morphology, in the authors' most recent terminology, is the morphology that occurs in what is more traditionally referred to as *counterfactual* or *subjunctive conditionals*; see von Fintel and Iatridou *under submission*).[2] Interestingly, the basics of the theory were, by 2018, being integrated into a much wider

---

[2] Crucially, X-marked conditionals include constructions that (despite being thus marked) do not give rise to counterfactual inferences. So-called 'future less vivid' conditionals and Anderson-case counterfactuals are examples.

picture, which eventually took shape in the authors' most recent *Prolegomena to a theory of X-marking* (von Fintel and Iatridou under submission), a proposal that still remains fairly programmatic.

In presenting an overview of how *-fu-* plays the role commonly attributed to X-morphology in this section, I will also highlight some of the questions that arise when analysing a frustrative language under the mentioned theoretical framework. This will clear the ground for the more practical task of the chapter, which is to present a basic toolkit for the production of the relevant DCs in section 3.

2.1 The Mapudungun frustrative-modal crossroad

Let us start by identifying the basic grammatical ingredients relevant to describing the frustrative-modals interactions in a language like Mapudungun—starting with tense. As with other Amerindian languages, Mapudungun exhibits no overt marking that encodes past or present temporal reference (1a). Future interpretations, however, are necessarily conveyed by the verbal suffix *-a-* (1b). In embedded clauses, *-a-* renders future-to-the-past (1c) and future-to-the-present (1d) readings. As shown in Fuentes (2020), these readings suggest that *-a-* constitutes an aspectual prospective marker that combines with a non-future tense, in the way it has been described for some WOLL predicates in the Amerindian sphere (see Matthewson 2006 for an original approach to St'át'imcets).[3,4]

---

[3] The Mapudungun data discussed in this chapter stem from my personal fieldwork in Chile at different locations and periods over the last three years. My main consultant was Héctor Mariano (HM), a native speaker of a dialect known as Moluche, the most widely used among Mapudungun speakers. My second consultant, Renan Vita (RV), speaks the more confined dialect of the Pewenche people, commonly referred to as Chedungun by its speakers. Although differences between the dialects are undeniable, they are mostly phonetic in kind, and a shared morphosemantic skeleton allows mutual intelligibility. For reasons of space, and given the fact that Moluche represents a more widespread and standardized dialect, I present data as uttered or judged by HM but verified in two dedicated sessions by RV. I omit numerous variances of the Chedungun dialect that are irrelevant for the morphosemantic properties under discussion here. The few relevant discrepancies between the two consultants are noted. It should also be said that, for reasons of space, the data displayed in this section is presented in a rather raw state, without the original DCs (some of which will be properly examined in the next section).

[4] I follow the Leipzig Glossing Rules. The following abbreviations are used: 1/2/3: first, second and third person, COND conditional; FRUST frustrative; IND indicative; INST instrumental; NEG negation; NMLZ nominalizer; POSS possessive; PROSP prospective; REFL reflexive; S singular; ST stative; SUBJ subjunctive.

(1) a. *María amu-y   Pitril.*
       María   go-IND.3S   Pitril
       'María is going/went to Pitril.' / * 'María will go to Pitril.'

   b. *María amu-a-y   Pitril.*
      María   go-PROSP-IND.3S Pitril
      'María will go to Pitril.' / * 'María is going / went to Pitril.'

   c. *María troki-w-fu-y   ñi   aku-**a**-el*
      María opine-REFL-FRUST-IND.3S   POSS.3   arrive-PROSP-NMLZ
      miércoles   mew.
      Wednesday   INST
      'María thought she was going to arrive (last) Wednesday.'

   d. *María troki-w-küle-y   ñi   aku-**a**-el*
      María opine-REFL-ST-IND.3S   POSS.3   arrive-PROSP-NMLZ
      fiernes   mew.
      Friday   INST
      'María thinks she will arrive (tomorrow) Friday.'

As for the frustative suffix *-fu-*, it can mark either dynamic or stative predicates. With dynamic predicates, an unachieved-goal reading is commonly obtained (2a-2b). With statives, the reading tends to be non-continuation (2c) (see Copley 2005 and Copley and Harley 2014 on these readings in Tohono O'odham).

(2) a. *María amu-**fu**-y   Pitril.*
       María   go-FRUST-IND.3S   Pitril
       'María was going to Pitril' (but she had to come back).

   b. *María amu-**fu**-y   Pitril.*
      María   go-FRUST-IND.3S   Pitril
      'María went to Pitril in vain' (the chief wasn't there).

   c. *Juan nie-**fu**-y   epu   kawellu.*
      Juan have-FRUST-IND.3S   two   horse
      'Juan had two horses' (but not anymore).

   d. *Juan nie-**fu**-y   kiñe kawellu.*
      Juan have-FRUST-IND.3S   a   horse
      'Juan has a horse' (but is useless for our purpose of ploughing the field).

Observe that with both dynamic and stative predicates, the frustrated event/ state can but need not be the one described in the sentence. In (2b), the event that failed realization was not that described in the unmarked sentence (going to Pitril), but one teleologically linked to it (meeting with the chief). Example (2d), in turn, shows that *-fu-* clauses can render present temporal interpretations, in which case the denoted state can hold true of the actual world (while the non-realization is linked to a contextually salient goal).

As with other frustratives (see in particular Kroeger 2017 on Kimaragang), *-fu-* also occurs in the consequent of a counterfactual conditional:

(3)   *nie-fu-li*   *plata,*   *mapu*   *ngilla-ya-**fu**-n.*
     have-FRUST-COND.1S   money   land   buy-PROSP-FRUST-IND.1S
     'If I had money, I would buy land.'

While *-fu-* is systematically attested in the consequent of the Mapudungun counterfactual conditional, its occurrence in the antecedent is subject to unsystematic variation. From a pure empirical point of view, data do not seem conclusive in this respect (see Fasola 2015 for a similar conclusion). It should be emphasized, though, that the occurrence of the suffix in the consequent of the counterfactual construction is reported by all authors, with no exception. In this paper, I work under the assumption that it is this latter occurrence that makes the relevant semantic contribution to the sentence.

As for Mapudungun modal clauses, I will focus on the expression of obligations and desires (and, more specifically, on deontic necessity and a subclass of bouletic statements). Regarding the former, as with many other languages (see Bhatt 1997 and references therein), Mapudungun expresses obligation by means of an existential predicate (4a). As shown below, the predicate takes a non-finite nominalized complement, which is marked with the prospective suffix *-a-*. The same type of complement occurs in bouletic clauses with the attitude verb *pi-*, which expresses WANT (4b). Alternatively, a synonymous bouletic construction can be built with the indeclinable unit *küpá* preceding a finite form (4c).

(4) a.   Mapudungun deontic HAVE TO
        María **müle-y**   *ñi*   *amu-a-el*   *Pitril.*
        María   be-IND.3S   POSS.3   go-PROSP-NMLZ   Pitril
        'María must go to Pitril.'

    b.   Mapudungun WANT (attitude verb)
        María **pi-y**   *ñi*   *amu-a-el*   *Pitril.*
        María   want-IND.3S   POSS.3   go-PROSP-NMLZ   Pitril
        'María wants to go to Pitril.'

c. Mapudungun WANT (preverbal unit)
   *María **küpá** amu-y   Pitril.*
   María want   go-IND.3S Pitril
   'María wants to go to Pitril.'

All the facts above were gathered by the author in recent fieldwork, and they are also easily traceable in the literature (see Smeets 2008 for a wide range of data and Golluscio 2000 for a pragmatic characterization of *-fu-*). It should be said that none of the mentioned authors glosses *-fu-* as a frustrative, although Smeets' informal characterization categorizes the suffix as an *impeditive* (Smeets 2008: 230–235).

2.2 Frustrative-modal interactions

Let us now enter the underdescribed region where the frustrative meets modality. What are the effects of *-fu-* in Mapudungun modal clauses? The first and most predictable reading that is attested renders something very close to the unachieved-goal interpretation in (2a). As shown below, this runs across both domains: obligations and desires. Note that when a Mapudungun speaker intends to express that an obligation was satisfied, the *-a-el* ending of the strong necessity construction in (4a) is replaced with an alternative non-finite suffix (*-(ü)n*), as shown in (5a). On the other hand, when the speaker intends to express that the obligation was not satisfied, the frustrative surfaces in the main existential predicate (5b). As for desires, while the constructions in (4b) and (4c) are acceptable for past fulfilled desires (given the absence of tense markers for past and present interpretations), the frustrative occurs when the denoted desire was unfulfilled. It does so in two distinct ways: marking the attitude verb *pi-* (5c) and the finite clause following *küpá* (5d).

(5) a. *María müle-y   ñi   amu-n   Pitril.*
       María be-IND.3S POSS.3 go-NMLZ Pitril
       'María had to go to Pitril' (*but she did not go).

   b. *María müle-**fu**-y   ñi   amu-a-el   Pitril.*
      María be-FRUST-IND.3S POSS.3 go-PROSP-NMLZ Pitril
      'María had to go to Pitril' (but she did not go).

   c. *María pi-**fu**-y   ñi   amu-a-el   Pitril.*
      María want-FRUST-IND.3S POSS.3 go-PROSP-NMLZ Pitril
      'María wanted to go to Pitril' (but couldn't go).

d. *María küpá amu-**fu**-y Pitril.*
María want go-FRUST-IND.3S Pitril
'María wanted to go to Pitril' (but couldn't go).

This set of examples provides the first of our circumstantial parameters: achieved/unachieved. The parameter resonates with the already observable contrast between a core frustrative clause such as (2a) and its unmarked counterpart in (1a) (when interpreted for the past). This similarity needs, of course, be scrutinized at a more analytical level. For now, let us stick this circumstantial parameter as a first mark in the ground and move on to a present temporal perspective, where a less predictable landscape is revealed.

As already anticipated, results related to Mapudungun deontic domain demonstrated that *-fu-* effects a semantic change from strong to weak necessity. Broadly speaking, a typical scenario in which weak necessity is expressed is when a salient normative ideal competes with another standard. To illustrate, while non-trespassing private property is obligatory by law ('You mustn't trespass on your neighbour property, *no matter what*'), being kind to one's neighbour is only advisory ('You should be kind to your neighbours, although *you might prefer* to keep distance and mind your own business'). In a similar vein, while going to school is obligatory by law, checking with the doctor is only advisable in virtue of an ideal such as taking care of one's health. One and the same type of action can also be subject to obligatory or advisory consideration, depending on the surrounding circumstances, as the following pair shows:

(6) a. *Pedro müle-y ñi amu-a-el kolekio mew.*
Pedro be-IND.3S POSS.3 go-PROSP-NMLZ school INST
'Pedro must go to school' (since school is obligatory by law).

b. *Pedro müle-**fu**-y ñi amu-a-el kolekio mew.*
Pedro be-FRUST-IND.3S POSS.3 go-PROSP-NMLZ school INST
'Pedro should go to school' (school is not obligatory by law, but advisable).

This provides our second parameter: compulsory/advisory. As we shall presently see, the parameter is not exhaustive and can be blurred by codes of politeness (among other things). Interestingly, the compulsory/advisory pair is not mirrored in the bouletic domain. The results suggest that, for a present temporal perspective, the attainable/unattainable contrast stands as a better representation of the circumstances surrounding the subject. I illustrate with *küpá* 'want' below, but the pattern has also been verified for *pi-* 'want'. While (7a) and (7b) are perfectly attainable desires, (7c) is unlikely to be satisfied and (7d) is counterfactually impeded.

(7) a. *María küpá amu-y trawün mew.*
María want go-IND.3S meeting INST
'María wants to go to the meeting' (she is getting dressed).

b. *María küpá nie-y kiñe lamngen.*
María want have-IND.3S a sister
'María wants to have a sister' (her parents are also keen on the idea).

c. *María küpá amu-**fu**-y trawün mew.*
María want go-FRUST-IND.3S meeting INST
'María wishes she would go to the meeting' (but she has a night shift).

d. *María küpá nie-**fu**-y kiñe lamngen.*
María want have-FRUST-IND.3S a sister
'María wishes she had a sister' (she is the only daughter of her late parents).

The mismatch between these two pairs of parameters (compulsory/advisory and attainable/unattainable) gives rise to some questions. Does the variance merely reflect a difference in the lexical meaning of the modal predicates? Or is there a detectable difference in the semantic contribution of the frustrative to the advisory/unattainable statements?

The fourth and final parameter is related to the actual/counterfactual ingredients of the denoted obligations and desires. Since *-fu-* typically appears in the consequent of Mapudungun counterfactual conditionals (3), the counterfactual status of the obligation in (8a)[5] and the desire in (8b) is somewhat expected.[6]

(8) a. *nie-fu-le kechu tripantu,*
have-FRUST-COND.3S five years
*Pedro müle-**fu**-y ñi amu-a-el kolekio mew.*
Pedro be-FRUST-IND.3S POSS.3 go-PROSP-NMLZ School INST
'If he were 5 years old, Pedro would have to go to school.'

---

5 Although *-a-* systematically precedes *-fu-* in counterfactual consequents (see (3)), HM tends to omit the suffix in the main predicate of both counterfactual obligations and desires' consequents (while RV marks *-a-* for the latter, see (8b)). I have observed HM's omission in written text by other speakers. I have no explanation for these omissions. It should be noted that *-a-* occurs in the complement of necessity statements, but this both in conditional and non-conditional environments.

6 A different issue is whether the counterfactual yield (tout court) can be accounted for by a defined semantics of the frustrative. See Kroeger (2017: 22-23) and Fuentes (*to appear*) for discussion in Kimaragang and Mapudungun, respectively.

b. *müle-fu-le   wariya   mew,*
   live-FRUST-COND.3S   city   INST
   *Pedro küpá   müle-(a)-**fu**-y   mawida   mew.*
   Pedro   want   live-PROSP-FRUST-IND.3S   mountain   INST
   'If he lived in the city, Pedro would want to live in the mountains.'

The data sketched above suggest that Mapudungun effects transparency in both the deontic and bouletic domains. As already mentioned, a transparent OUGHT/WISH language is one that uses X-morphology (to recall: the morphology that occurs in what is traditionally known as counterfactual or subjunctive conditionals) to effect two semantic shifts: (i) HAVE TO to OUGHT and (ii) WANT to WISH. We have identified the relevant circumstances invoked by these minimal pairs by means of two parameters: compulsory/advisory and attainable/unattainable. Additionally, as reported for other transparent OUGHT/WISH languages, the following ambiguities obtain: (i) between OUGHT and WOULD HAVE TO, and (ii) between WISH and WOULD WANT. The ambiguities are predictable since the contribution of the X-morphology in the latter elements of each pair (WOULD HAVE TO and WOULD WANT) is the expected one. The relevant split, then, is observed across both domains and can be captured with a single parameter: actual/counterfactual.

Finally, it should be noted that in contrast to other transparent languages, and in virtue of the fact that Mapudungun does not possess a past marker, the constructions at issue are also rendered ambiguous with respect to unachieved obligations and desires. I have pinned down this contrast with the circumstantial parameter achieved/unachieved. The following summarizes the proposed parameters.

(9) Circumstantial parameters
 a. Achieved/unachieved parameter
    Mapudungun HAD TO
    Mapudungun HAD TO + FRUSTRATIVE (= HAD TO (BUT . . .))
    Mapudungun WANTED
    Mapudungun WANTED + FRUSTRATIVE (= WANTED (BUT . . .))

 b. Compulsory/advisory parameter
    Mapudungun HAVE TO
    Mapudungun HAVE TO + FRUSTRATIVE (= OUGHT)

 c. Attainable/unattainable parameter
    Mapudungun WANT
    Mapudungun WANT + FRUSTRATIVE (= WISH)

d. Actual/counterfactual parameter
    Mapudungun HAVE TO
    Mapudungun HAVE TO + FRUSTRATIVE (= WOULD HAVE TO)
    Mapudungun WANT
    Mapudungun WANT + FRUSTRATIVE (= WOULD WANT)

The guideline offered in the next section is meant to aid the fieldworker in producing the DCs that would verify the semantic variants laid out above. This excludes the methodological issue of how to produce DCs that empirically demonstrate the frustrative properties of the relevant X-morpheme; independent dedicated research is needed for that purpose.[7] Needless to say, once these two empirical surveys are completed, the task remains to integrate the dataset into an (existing or novel) semantic analysis, so as to theoretically account for each of the attested meanings in a unifying comprehensive way.

3 Guidelines for producing discourse contexts for the semantics of obligations and desires

3.1 Preparing the ground

I first would like to address a preliminary question that commonly arises for the fieldworker when considering the use of DCs as a methodological tool: how idiosyncratic and descriptive should a discourse context be? In answering this question, I will also highlight some aspects of the specific situations that involves obligations and desires. Since the following methodological precepts are subject to various contingent factors (time disposed for fieldwork, familiarity with the consultants, etc.), I will only provide a tentative and adjustable guideline.

First, the issue of idiosyncrasy. My own experience is that building DCs that evoke familiar scenes to the consultants is worth the effort. More concretely for the elicitation of deontic and bouletic expressions, I would recommend that the fieldworker elaborates a list of what her consultants usually do (either willingly or

---

[7] This needs not be a preliminary task. In effect, for several practical reasons, I conducted these two empirical surveys at different fieldwork periods: while deontic and bouletic transparency were tested on a par in my first fieldtrip in Chile in May–June 2018, the fieldwork research on the frustrative properties of *-fu-* was only conducted at a later stage (November 2019–March 2020). See Fuentes (*to appear*) for a modal analysis of *-fu-* that integrates the overall results.

forcefully).[8] I find this seemingly trivial task very useful. An enriched and varied pool not only can make the process of creating single-target DCs more fluent, but also put at the linguist's disposal a variety of episodic turns for building overarching storylines, as recommended by Louie (2015).

As for the question of how descriptive a DC should be, a common practice among semanticists is to be brief. Although it is certainly the case that larger descriptions are on occasions necessary (either for eliciting subtle semantic data or making the proffered situation clear), it is recommendable to disfavour DCs that demand too many specifications. For the beginner fieldworker, this may seem to contravene the intuition that briefer DCs may lead to undesirable under-specifications. However, I think that it is important to highlight the fact that under-specifications are not per se undesirable. *On occasions*, and especially when dealing with deontic necessity, briefer underspecified DCs *can* be more effective than larger ones.

Let me use a fictitious example to illustrate the point. Assume a fieldworker intending to test the strong necessity utterance equivalent to 'Juan has to help María'. To this end, she elaborates a very simple DC: *Juan has promised María to help her with the orchard on Sunday. The day has arrived*. Despite its simplicity, this DC does just fine for the purpose at hand. Now let us assume that the researcher feels that the DC is too simple, that the situation should be described more vividly, so as to make the consultant aware of the fact that Juan feels that it is his inescapable duty to help María. To this end, the fieldworker adds the following text: *Even though his son has asked him to go fishing that morning, Juan feels the strong obligation to comply with the promise made*.

Now, what is the effect of this more descriptive DC? Has the fieldworker really refined her tool by making the situation more vivid? Not necessarily so, I think. For notice the gap that it has just been opened: the consultant might now have a dissenting opinion on whether Juan is really under the stringent obligation to help María ('what if Juan's son really wants to go fishing?'; 'what if it is not the first time that Juan denies to his son going fishing on a Sunday?'; 'but Juan can certainly call María and explain, right?').

I do not, of course, intend to suggest that the consultant is wrong in thinking this way. My methodological point is that by making a perfectly fine context more vivid, the fieldworker may open the space for a dissenting opinion precisely at

---

8 An unorganised sample can look like this: *possession of land, daily transport, health care, herding and animal care, seeking employment, participating in traditional ceremonies, school attendance, music festivals, traditional healing, mate drinking, recollection of seeds, preparation of food, speaking the language of one's ancestors, going fishing, drinking wine, conflicts with local authorities, sending local goods to relatives in the city*, etc.

the point where an unquestionable assumption is needed.[9] This takes me to a more practical point, one that I think it should not be overlooked by beginner fieldworkers: that the domains of human obligations and desires are highly opinionable. For the task at issue, this can bring along all sorts of distracting factors, some of which may lead to the undesired situation in which the consultant ultimately disagrees with the fieldworker with respect to the nature of the presumed scenario.

Fortunately, a straightforward strategy to avoid opening a disagreement gap is to avoid too descriptive (and relativizable) scenarios and target simpler (and more rigid) ones.[10] An intuitive distinction that may be useful in this respect is that between stringent duties (obligations one must comply with *no matter what*) and supererogatory ones (acts that go beyond what is required). Thus, while one must pay one's taxes (by law), it is supererogatory that one gives money to social causes. The former type of duty is less relativizable than the latter, and hence leaves no space for the emergence of dissenting factors. In general, law-like scenarios lead naturally to good examples of the stringent type. For the sake of variance, though, it is up to the creative skills of the fieldworker to craft ordinary life circumstances into a convincing plot that depicts a strict obligation. If of any help, I tend to class as stringent duty circumstances different sorts of hierarchical practices (following orders, compliance with procedures, fulfilling requirements, etc.) and to some extent interpersonal commitments, such as reciprocity and promises (when *not* relativized by secondary considerations, such as making Juan's son happy). For the more relativizable side of things, I include moral virtues, behavioural precepts, good manners, and some cultural ideals. Doing fieldwork with Mapudungun speakers, these include, e.g., attending family meetings, showing respect to the elderly, and speaking the language of one's ancestors. These can be very useful as the prime content of DCs targeting weak necessity statements.

In the case of desires, I think it is recommendable to work with situations that involve desires (and intentions more generally) that are satisfiable by a single action (taking the bus to go the market, stacking hay to feed the herd), rather than multiply-realizable ideals (the desire to build a just society, to live a more significant life, to transcend, etc.). Ideals such as these are all cherished, but not too

---

9 It should be clear that I am only pointing to a possibility of what might happen, and that the fieldworker may actually succeed in depicting a strong necessity scenario by enlarging the original DC. This is especially likely if she does this *with* the consultant, as recommended by Cover (2015: 248–253). My own experience is that these instances of collaborative work, when they occur, turn out to be the most productive.
10 This applies only for eliciting strong necessity statements. Evidently, a somewhat more relativizable type of scenario is needed for eliciting weak necessity utterances.

practical for eliciting data. It is recommendable to prioritize simple core examples rather than uncommon or borderline cases, at least for a first recollection of data.

Lastly, I would like to clarify that each of the DCs displayed in what follows were originally presented in Spanish. The language choice relied mainly on a practical reason: my level of fluency in the object language made it a more natural option to present the DCs in the contact language. This choice was made easier by the widespread bilingualism in virtually all Mapuche communities. This is reflected by my main two consultants, who are both fluent native speakers of Spanish and Mapudungun. Although translating a number of predetermined felicitous DCs into the object language is an option, the fact that the semantic space under investigation presents a rather large chain of ambiguities demands having full control of the ingredients used for the aimed representation. Thus far, I have not detected any practical or theoretical inconvenience related to the language choice, and I agree with AnderBois and Henderson (2015) that there is no a priori reason to prefer either the object or the contact language for the purpose at issue.

3.2 Parameters for eliciting the frustrative-modal interactions

3.2.1 Achieved/unachieved parameter

An essential aspect of the first parameter, achieved/unachieved, is that it evokes circumstances that are located in the past. Within that temporal frame, the split relates to the (in)capacity of the agent to fulfil the ascribed obligation/desire. The task ahead is, then, relatively simple: to create a non-relativizable scenario in which an agent was under an obligation/had a desire (let us refer to this as the neutral DC), to then split the described circumstances into two minimal pairs: one in which the obligation/desire was satisfied (+ achieved) and one in which it was not (+ unachieved). S refers to the target sentence. As shown in (10) below, the split can be effected by one simple sentence. Among types of rigid, non-relativizable duties, I illustrate here with a social commitment: attending a medical appointment. As for desires, going to a meeting is appropriate.

(10) a. Obligation
Neutral DC: *You had an appointment with the doctor very early this morning.*
+ achieved: *You were there on time.*
+ unachieved: *But you overslept.*
S: I had to go to the doctor this morning.

b. Desire
Neutral DC: *There was a friendly meeting in town last Saturday and you wanted to go.*
+ achieved: *You picked up María and were there from noon till midnight.*
+ unachieved: *Unfortunately, you had work to do.*
S: I wanted to go to town.

The DCs can be completed with a simple sentence such as 'You later tell a friend about it', so as to clear the ground for the eliciting question ('How would you say to him 'S'?', 'Is it okay in this context to say to him 'S'?', etc.). Examples (11a) and (11b) were the elicitations obtained for achieved and unachieved obligations, and examples (12a) and (12b) for achieved and unachieved desires. As hypothesized, *-fu-* surfaces in the (b) examples, but not in (a).

(11) a. *iñché müle-y ñi amu-n lawentuchefe mew*
I be-IND.3S POSS.1S go-NMLZ medicine.man INST
tüfachi liwen.
this morning
'I had to go to the doctor this morning' (and I did).

b. *iñché müle-**fu**-y ñi amu-a-el*
I be-**FRUST**-IND.3S POSS.1S go-PROSP-NMLZ
lawentuchefe mew tüfachi liwen.
medicine.man INST this morning
'I had to go to the doctor this morning' (but I overslept).

(12) a. *iñché küpá amu-n wariya mew.*
I want go-IND.1S town INST
'I wanted to go to town' (and I did).

b. *iñché küpá amu-**fu**-n wariya mew.*
I want go-**FRUST**-IND.1S town INST
'I wanted to go to town' (but I couldn't).

I should say that in the case of achieved desires (12a) my main consultant has shown signs of hesitation. This seems to derive from the fact that an utterance of the form 'I wanted to go to town (and I did)', when true and felicitous, pragmatically competes with the more natural 'I went to town'. It seems that in absence of any further information, 'I went to town' conversationally implicates that the speaker did it voluntarily, and hence that she wanted to go. There was one occasion in which HM, after judging S acceptable, manifestly commented (in Spanish): "Or just 'I went to town'".

Note that working with this contrasting pair excludes cases in which the obligation/desire was not fulfilled because the agent was not interested in doing so (since *(un)achieved* seems to entail the intention to achieve). Such cases are of course perfectly conceivable, although they are more difficult to depict for desires than for obligations (where not complying with a duty due to lack of interest is actually a familiar scene). I have tested those scenarios to verify if they involved a morphological variance, but the frustrative component seems to suffice. This, of course, might not be the case for other (frustrative and non-frustrative) languages. As an experienced fieldworker puts it, be prepared for surprises (Bohnmeyer 2015: 38).

Note also that the adversative clause that identifies what impedes the satisfaction of the desire ('Unfortunately, you had work to do') may be translatable into a strong necessity statement ('You had to work'), which can be incorporated in the eliciting question, so as to test an unachieved desire/achieved obligation conjunction (equivalent to 'I wanted to go to the meeting, but I had to work'). The natural opposition between desires and duties can be used productively to either test two utterances at once or confirm previous results.

3.2.2 Compulsory/advisory parameter

In contrast to the achieve/unachieved parameter, the compulsory/advisory pair is circumscribed to only one of the two domains under examination (namely, deontic necessity).

To recall, the tested hypothesis was that Mapudungun X-morphology effects the semantic change from strong to weak necessity. With that purpose in mind, the preliminary task consisted in creating DCs that tell apart the circumstances that make an action/state of affairs compulsory (and hence non-negotiable) and those that make it (only) advisable. For the sake of cohesiveness, I have preferred to use one and the same (type of) action on both sides of the split. Thus, the relevant action had to be adjustable enough so as to be subject to both normative constraints and individual opinions. As an example, take attendance to primary school: while there are locations/times in which attendance to school is/was mandatory by law, one can at least conceive of locations/times in which it is/was not. This suffices to integrate this course of action as part of a basic plot in a neutral DC. As with the DCs in the previous section, the relevant split can be effected by a brief addendum, which should describe the contrasting normative and advisory circumstances.

(13) Neutral DC. *Pedro is five years old. His parents are not sure whether to send him to school or not.*
+ compulsory: *School is obligatory by law since age five.*
S: Pedro must go to school
+ advisory: *School is not obligatory by law, but you think is advisable that he attends.*
S': Pedro should go to school

While the former of these combinations targets a strong necessity utterance (S), the latter targets a weak necessity one (S'). The elicitation of S' confirmed the occurrence of the frustrative suffix *-fu-*, as the following shows:

(14) a. *Pedro   müle-y   ñi   amu-a-el   kolekio mew.*
         Pedro   be-IND.3S   POSS.3 go-PROSP-NMLZ   school   INST
         'Pedro must go to school.'

   b. *Pedro   müle-**fu**-y   ñi   amu-a-el   kolekio mew.*
         Pedro   be-**FRUST**-IND.3S POSS.3 go-PROSP-NMLZ   school   INST
         'Pedro should go to school.'

It should be noted that despite the occurrence of *-fu-*, the advisory reading in (14b) is not intuitively linked to the unachieved-goal meaning that the suffix conveys in non-modal clauses (see (2) above). This is reflected by the fact that the circumstances depicted in the DC above do not contain a 'something going wrong' element (at least not in the most obvious sense). Moreover, S' leaves open whether the promoted course of action will be brought into existence or not. Taken together with the fact that there is no detectable link to the core non-continuation reading, the indication seems to be that the contribution of *-fu-* to weak necessity is associated to X-marking rather than to the meanings attested in non-conditional and non-modal environments. It is of course a more analytical task to determine whether this difference in the semantic yields of *-fu-* can be accounted for by a unifying account of the frustrative. See Fuentes (*to appear*) for a modal analysis of *-fu-*.

Note also that the advisory element in the required DC can be brought about by explicitly hypothesizing a situation in which a depicted character asks the consultant for advice, as in (15a) below. The fieldworker should bear in mind that (for the task at hand) what is advised must not be of the compulsory type (as in the ineffective scenario in (15b)):

(15) a. *María knocks on your door for advice. School is not obligatory by law, and she wonders whether it would be better if Pedro attends school or helps with the work at home. You think it would be better that he attends school.*

b. [Ineffective] *María knocks on your door for advice. School **is** obligatory by law, but she wonders whether it would be better that Pedro helps her with the work at home. You think it would be better that he attends school.*

The reason why the DC in (15b) is ineffective for the purpose of eliciting a weak necessity statement is that it leaves enough space for the consultant to go both ways (that is to say, to judge acceptable either a strong or a weak necessity construction), making the elicitation task pointless. Note that even if the advisory element is explicitly spelled out ('knocks on your door for advice'; 'You think it would be better ...'), introducing a stringent type of duty in the discourse context ('school is obligatory by law') can easily distract the consultant, who at the time the weak necessity statement S' is judged or prompted, can (faultlessly) think 'But he really *must* go to school'. This may lead her to utter S instead of S', and consequently create the impression that the language does not have a marked statement to express weak necessity (when what really happened is that the fieldworker forced a stringent interpretation of the situation). This relatively minor methodological point raises the question as to whether a weak utterance such as 'Pedro should go to school', *in a compulsory context such as* (15b), constitutes a felicitous sincere advice. I will not discuss this issue here, but this may raise some questions at a more pragmatic level.

All in all, the practical point should be clear: to elicit a weak necessity construction by a DC that involves the speech act of advising, the fieldworker needs to ensure that the content of the advice is *weak* (negotiable) as opposed to *strong* (unnegotiable). On the other hand, when testing strong necessity utterances, the fieldworker should be aware of the fact that, more often than not, human agents might find ourselves in situations where we *suggest* (advice) to do something which is rather compulsory (because of politeness, pretense, or what have you). Testing with different DCs, at different occasions, and verifying intra-speaker reproducibility is crucial.

It is important to point out that there is a way to identify weak necessity predicates cross-linguistically that has become common practice among semanticists. The procedure is exemplified in von Fintel and Iatridou (2008: 120) and is based in the following contrast:

(16) a. *You ought to do the dishes but you don't have to.*
b. *#You have to do the dishes but you don't have to.*

The contrast suggests that a weak necessity statement can be conjoined with the negation of a strong necessity (scoping over the same prejacent) without contradiction. This is somewhat implicit in the description of the scenario in (15a), given that the relevant obligation (attending to school) is clearly described as non-compulsory ('school is not obligatory by law'). Crucially, under the provided DC, attendance to school is naturally advised by the speaker by marking the strong necessity construction with -*fu*-, as (14b) shows. Despite these results, though, my own experience with the test referred above has not run smoothly: the responses from my consultant to the Mapudungun equivalent of (16a) have ranged from hesitating acceptance to plain rejection.

Until now, I have not been able to determine what is the source of these different responses. Perhaps the fact that the same existential verb (*müley*) is used in both conjuncts (one inflected with -*fu*-, the other with negation) creates the illusion of a contradiction.[11] This illusion would not arise in English, given the lexical specificity in the pair *ought/don't have to*. I suspect that this may also explain why *some* Spanish speakers also hesitate when asked to considered (16a) built with the pairs *tendría/no tiene que*. Be this as it may, the point to be highlighted here is merely practical: that the in-the-field implementation of the test might not run as smooth as in the semanticist's armchair, especially when investigating transparent languages that do not show the lexical specificity to express weak necessity as English does.

A more substantial point is related to the conceptual reliability of the test. To my mind, that weak necessity statements *can* be conjoined with the negation of its strong necessity counterpart does not mean that they always do. In effect, I have found contexts in which the 'OUGHT but don't HAVE TO' assertion comes very close to a contradiction—even in English. An interesting feature of these contexts is that the weak necessity predication (exemplified with *should* below) is used to promote a strong normative standard that is already in force.

Consider the following situation. In a certain state, post-graduate students pay a regular tariff for public transport. This has raised some debate among the state representatives, who are now debating on whether the regulations should be changed or sustained. Representatives of the two disputing parties will have the chance to defend their views by replying to the question(s): Why should/shouldn't post-graduate students pay for public transport? Consider now the opening speech of a defender of the current regulations:

---

11 The same unacceptability of this test was found in Javanese (Austronesian), which interestingly also uses the same modal expression in both conjuncts (one suffixed with –*ne*, the other modified by negation) (Jozina Vander Klok, pers. comm.).

(17) *Postgraduate students should pay a regular tariff for public transport, (#but they don't have to).*

The addition of the second conjunct in (17) is contradictory because in the actual state of affairs students *do* have to pay for a regular tariff—and that is exactly what the representative wants to defend. As far as I can see, nothing prevents the representative from using *should* when promoting the prevailing regulation.

Admittedly, I am not sure what the implications of this example are. But I suspect that one issue that might deserve further scrutiny is that weak necessity predications seem more firmly linked to the promotional element than to the release from strong obligation. In effect, what the example shows is that *should* serves to promote a strong obligation that is already in force.

Finally, I should say that on occasions I have found myself breaking my self-imposed keep-it-brief policy. This has occurred when the utility of the DC goes beyond data collection – say, when used for *both* data collection *and* explanatory purposes in written production. The following is an example.

(18) *Pedro has just turned five and he will start attending school next month. There are two options: a Chilean-oriented school (closer to home) where everything is taught exclusively in Spanish; and a Mapuche-oriented school (15 kilometres from town) where most of the classes are imparted in Mapudungun. His mother, Victoria, asks for your advice. Although you understand the practical issue of the distance from home, your own opinion is that Pedro's learning the language of his ancestors is more important.*

The reason why I used this DC (despite its being considerably larger and perhaps more unpractical than the previous ones) is that it contraposes two competing ideals: being close to home and speaking the language of one's ancestors. Weak necessity statements are commonly attested in this type of competing background. As it has been described in the literature (see Rubinstein 2014 for an illuminating characterization), the promotion of competing ideals seems to be a key pragmatic element in the expression of weak necessity. The DC in (18) can be used to illustrate the point to an unfamiliar reader. This highlights a somewhat understated fact about DCs, namely, that they can be used distinctively for two complementary tasks: one circumscribed to data collection, the other extended also to explanatory purposes in written production.

3.2.3 Attainable/unattainable parameter

We now turn to our third parameter, which deals with the circumstantial arrangements that make an ascribable desire either attainable or unattainable. This split has been recognized as an important aspect of the denotation of bouletic constructions (see Heim 1992 and von Fintel 1999 for early formal approaches). More recently, the distinction has received a new spate of attention in light of new insights on the semantics of desires, which has come to be understood as an integral part of a more general theory of X-marking (von Fintel and Iatridou *under submission*).

Although borderline cases have proved difficult to tame, one widely shared assumption among semanticists is that while WANT typically expresses a desire for something attainable, WISH tends to ramble through the more intricate space of what is unattainable. Before we turn into the issue of how the circumstantial backgrounds on both sides of this split can be depicted, consider the wide range of intended meanings available only for a present temporal perspective in English:

(19) a. *Pedro wants to go to the party (he is getting dressed).*
 b. *Pedro wishes he had a brother (he is the only son of his late parents).*
 c. *Pedro wishes he had had a brother (back in primary school).*
 d. *Pedro wishes María would come to the party tonight (but she has a night shift).*

This list is not exhaustive, but I will focus on these core cases to identify some essential circumstantial ingredients and comment briefly on some terminological choices.

Four initial observations are in place. First: all the desires illustrated above are current desires. This includes (19c), which is not a desire that Pedro had back in primary school (on the contrary, (19c) leaves open the possibility that Pedro did not want a brother when he was in primary school). Second, despite the fact that the term *counterfactual wishes* was used in the previous literature to refer to (19b-d), the desires above are all actual.[12] The term *counterfactual wishes*, in turn, is more properly used when referring to the type of desires examined in the next section. Third, only (19a) expresses a desire for something attainable. As for the complements in (19b-d), each of them denotes a situation that is, in one way or another, out of reach. Fourth and finally, while the unattainability of (19b-c) is hopelessly counterfactual, that of (19d) is only circumstantial. In effect, the

---

[12] von Fintel and Iatridou (*under submission*) express their preference for the term *unattainable desires*.

content of the desire in the former pair (Pedro having a brother) runs counter to present facts in (19b) (Pedro does not have a brother at the time of utterance) and counter to past facts in (19c) (Pedro did not have a brother back in primary school). On the other hand, (19d) expresses a desire for a future situation that is unlikely to occur, but not irremediably out of reach. Iatridou (2000) illustrates this latter reading with similar examples ('I wish he would leave tomorrow') and characterizes the construction as the *wish* equivalent of a *future less vivid* conditional. Accordingly, I will refer to this type of expressions as future less vivid wishes.

Now, the unlikelihood that is conveyed by future less vivid wishes, along with the fact that the desired situation is located in the future of the speech time, makes this a difficult case to pin down. As the future has not materialized into facts yet, (19d) does not seem to express a desire for something strictly counterfactual.[13] What Pedro desires in (19d) is very unlikely to happen, but nothing impedes the circumstances from unexpectedly changing for the good and María going to the party in the end. So perhaps the unattainability of the desire is only circumstantial. This way of describing things would make a first split between attainable (19a) and unattainable (19b-d) desires; and a second split between counterfactually unattainable (19b-c) and circumstantially unattainable (19d = future less vivid) desires.

The classification above may not convince the more advanced semanticist out there, who might want to depict the bouletic landscape differently. The purpose here is practical, and the terminological choice should remain open to revisions at a higher analytical level. With these caveats in mind, let me recast the four possible scenarios in which WANT (20a) and WISH (20b-d) statements may be uttered:

(20) a. Scenarios in which the subject desires something attainable (S: 'Pedro wants to go to the party').

   b. Scenarios in which the subject desires something counterfactually unattainable with respect to a present state of affairs (S: 'Pedro wishes he had a brother').

---

[13] Although Iatridou (2000) treats future less vivid conditionals as future counterfactuals, in her most recent collaborative work future less vivid are characterized as X-marked conditionals that do not convey counterfactuality (von Fintel and Iatridou *under submission*). It is an interesting question how this translates into the *unattainability* of future less vivid wishes. As far as I can see, the authors do conceive of future less vivid wishes as unattainable (yet not counterfactual). Any errors or oversights are my own.

c. Scenarios in which the subject desires something counterfactually unattainable with respect to a past state of affairs (S: 'Pedro wishes he had had a brother').

d. Scenarios in which the subject desires something circumstantially unattainable (S: 'Pedro wishes María would come to the party').

Once these basic scenarios are distinguished, the production of the DCs should follow suit. A very simple strategy that I have used involves a secondary character having either wrong beliefs or incomplete knowledge about the main situation. Basically, by using the simple schema 'subject is (not) doing x to attain y', one can introduce the question 'why the subject is (not) doing x?', which in turn naturally elicits the target response 'subject wants/wishes y'. This is in line with my previous suggestion of depicting 'single-action satisfaction' instead of 'multiply realizable ideals'. Below I present some brief samples for WANT (21a) and WISH, both counterfactually (21b) and circumstantially unattainable (21c).

(21) a. *Juan wonders what Mary is doing at the bus stop. You tell him that she is waiting for the bus to Pitril. He asks why.*
S: 'Mary wants to go to the cemetery.'

b. *Today is the day for animal vaccination and people are taking their animals to the village's corral. María asks why aren't you going. She seems to believe that you have a horse. You don't.*
S: 'I wish I had a horse.'

c. *You are waiting for the bus that takes you to the festival this afternoon. Your friend Juan shows up and tells you that María isn't going. Apparently, she has work to do. This makes you sad. Juan asks what's wrong.*
S: 'I wish María would go to the festival.'

One of my working hypotheses during my first fieldtrip to the Andes in 2018 was that Mapudungun effected the semantic shift from WANT to WISH by means of its X-morphology. The main results of my survey confirmed this, each elicited using the DCs in (21):

(22) a. María   küpá   amu-y   eltuwe   mew.
       María   want   go-IND.3S   cemetery   INST
       'María wants to go to the cemetery.'

b. iñché küpá nie-**fu**-n kiñe kawellu.
   I   want go-**FRUST**-IND.1S a horse
   'I wish I had a horse.'

c. iñché pi-**fu**-n   María ñi   amu-a-el
   I   want-FRUST-IND.1S María POSS.3 go-PROSP-NMLZ
   festival mew.
   festival INST
   'I wish María would go to the festival.'

I would like to draw the attention to only one of the many questions that arise once the collection of the relevant data is relatively completed: what is the difference in meaning between the unattainable desire statements (marked with -*fu*-) and the unachieved desire ones (also thus marked)? A rather obvious answer to this question is that the attested meanings differ in their temporal yield (the former denote current desires, the latter past desires). The question gains considerable depth, though, once we change the focus of attention to the semantic contribution of the frustrative to each of these readings. For one, here is a possibility: far from being reducible to purely temporal terms, the difference in meaning may also involve a difference in what the frustrative conveys in each of these utterances. The thought is that while the frustrative's contribution to unachieved desires is inherently linked to its core meaning in non-conditional environments, its contribution to unattainable desires is associated to what the suffix conveys in X-marked conditionals. Another way of putting this is to say that while Mapudungun unattainable desires constitute a genuine case of X-marking, unachieved desires do not. Needless to say, this pattern of thought can also extend to unachieved obligations and weak necessity. Many questions arise at this point. See Fuentes (*to appear*) for discussion.

Lastly, a note of caution about politeness should be added. It is a well-known fact that social codes across cultures consider appropriate to express a rather firm desire ('I want to leave now') in counterfactual guise ('I would really like to leave now'). Something along these lines also occurs when presenting a strong obligation ('You must listen to what she says') disguised as a weak necessity ('You should listen to what she says'), or a weak necessity ('you should check with your doctor') as a likely desire ('You might want to check with your doctor'). These are all conversions that deserve research in their own right. Once I decided to explore the more explicit (non-polite) skeleton of modal statements, though, I became aware of an understated problem. Asking consultants 'How would you say S in such-and-such situation?' may give the impression that the researcher is asking for codes of etiquette. This is most likely to occur when S expresses a desire. Fortunately, this can be avoided if the DC that precedes the eliciting question is deprived of thick social hierarchies, ceremonial ingredients, or any circumstantial element that the fieldworker thinks may influence the consultant's response in this respect. Openly telling the consultant that the survey is not about codes of etiquette is also an option. A reported advantage of one-on-one fieldwork (as opposed to large-scale experiments) is that potential misunderstanding about the task at hand can be more easily detected and mitigated (Bochnak and Matthewson 2015: 5).

3.2.4 Actual/counterfactual parameter

Finally, the fourth parameter relates to a more fundamental split – one that brings into consideration what can be properly referred to as counterfactual obligations and desires. That is, obligations and desires that are ascribed to the subject only under an assumption that is, by implicature, false.

A note of warning is immediately necessary: the counterfactual obligations and desires referred to when presenting this type of DCs are obligations and desires counter to the facts previously stipulated in the DC. This adds a certain peculiarity to the task of building the appropriate DCs, since the fieldworker will need to orchestrate a double assumption. Typically, the consultant will be asked to assume a first scenario in which someone assumes a second scenario in which an agent cannot escape having an obligation/desire. Let us consider first an example without any explicit reference to obligations or desires, so we can extract a basic template as a starter:

(23) *Let's say that you live in an Andean valley where the only fishing available is by small streams and a couple of rivers. Although your son Pedro is frequently invited, he doesn't seem interested. You think that if you both lived by the sea, he would go fishing.*

Even though the above is not a DC that targets a counterfactual obligation/desire statement (at least not explicitly), let us filter out the decorative elements so as to identify its essential ingredients. Very schematically, the consultant is invited to make a double assumption: (i) that P and not-Q (you live in an Andean valley and Pedro does not go fishing), and (ii) that she thinks (in that situation) that if R, then Q (if you lived by the sea, Pedro would go fishing). Let us refer to the scenario in (i) as the ground-scenario and the scenario in (ii) as the counter-scenario. As already mentioned, the counter-scenario is a counterfactual scenario with respect to the facts in the ground-scenario. Thus, we have a template of the following form:

(24) Fieldworker asks the consultant to assume that:
  (i) P and not-Q (ground-scenario)
  (ii) if R, then Q (counter-scenario)

A DC thus designed can target utterances of the type 'if R, then Q', where R contradicts P.[14] From here, what we want is to create DCs in which Q conveys deontic and bouletic meanings. Let us first focus on counterfactual obligations. Here is a simple strategy: since a significant number of obligations are triggered by local/regional standards (laws, social rules, conventions, etc.), a simple procedure one may adopt is to introduce a new location (and hence a new normative standard) in the counter-scenario R. Consider the following DC, which targets a present counterfactual:

(25) *Let's say that you and your son Pedro live in an Andean valley. Pedro goes fishing regularly. Fortunately, he does not have to buy a fishing license in this region. But you know that if you lived in a coastal region of the country, Pedro would have to buy a fishing licence.*

The plot is very close to that of (23), except that Q conveys deontic necessity. The template can be minimally changed in order to create the DC for past and future counterfactuals.[15]

Note that I have illustrated with a DC that locates us in a non-obligational ground-scenario (P and not-Q) to then make our journey to an obligational counter-scenario (if R, Q). The latter counter-scenario could also involve a weak necessity. That is to say, the consultant may be invited to consider a counter-scenario which involves a necessity of the non-compulsory type. To see the point more sharply, replace 'Pedro would have to buy a fishing licence' (in 25) with 'Pedro would have to buy a good fishing wader' (say, for the sake of comfort). This will result in a counterfactual weak necessity: in the counter-scenario R, it is advisable that Pedro buys a good fishing wader. Arguably, for the sake of cohesiveness, one would also need to change not-Q in the ground-scenario (e.g., Pedro does not need fishing waders because the water is shallow in the valley).

---

14 It is worth reminding that conditionals that convey counterfactual meaning can vary in their temporal interpretations. This is well described in the literature; see in particular Iatridou 2000 as a starting point. Space prevents me from a more detailed consideration of all temporal variants.

15 In my personal experience, though, not all DCs initially designed for eliciting present counterfactuals convert naturally to past and future less vivid counterfactuals. This is where the creativity (and patience) of the researcher is put to work.

Note also that since transparent OUGHT languages express weak necessity by means of X-marking, the elicited utterance is likely to have the same morphological dressing as its strong (counterfactual) counterpart. This has an interesting bearing: if the researcher leaves unspecified in the DC whether the provision of waders is either advisable or obligatory, the difference in strength may not come to the surface. In other words, an elicited utterance of the form 'if p, would have to q' may leave it open as to whether the consultant takes it as advisable or rather compulsory to q (in p-worlds).

A similar procedure can be implemented for building DCs targeting counterfactual desires, although in this case the background circumstances that comprise the ground-scenario P and the counter-scenario R influence the subject's preferences with respect to Q. Again, the invitation is first to assume a scenario P in which there is a preference for not-Q, to then consider a counter-scenario R in which Q is desired:

(26) *Pedro and his mother moved to the city a year ago. She tells you that her son Pedro has not adapted very well to the changes and that he does not want to go to school anymore. You think that the reason is that city schools lack green areas. If Pedro lived in the mountains, he would want to go to school.*

The DC above fits a similar template and does not seem to introduce any intricacy to the task. However, I should say that things are slightly more complicated when it comes to counterfactual desires. When resolving a judgment task with the DC above, one of my consultants (RV) expressed his preference for (the target language equivalent to) 'he would go to school' rather than 'he would want to go to school' (hence, omitting the bouletic predicate). In a second task, after openly explaining to RV that I was after the expression of the 'wanting' rather than the 'doing', he accepted S, but not without some hesitation. My other regular consultant (HM), instead, accepted the utterances from the beginning, but he had shown similar signs of hesitation when eliciting achieved desires ('he wanted to go and went', see comments on example (12)). This strongly suggests to me that the hesitation is related to one and the same aspect: given that preferences (wanting to go) commonly result in behaviour (going), there seems to be a natural pragmatic tendency to report the former by the latter. From a methodological point of view, at least, it might take some effort to elicit the ascription of a desire rather than its consequent action.

All in all, I have elaborated other DCs that outperform (26) (for the purpose of eliciting counterfactual desires). The trick consisted in iterating a stative predicate in the antecedent and the consequent. The following DC has proved infallible:

(27) Pedro lives in the mountains and wants to live in the city. But you think that if Pedro lived in the city, he would want to live in the mountains.
S: 'If he lived in the city, Pedro would want to live in the mountains.'

müle-fu-le		wariya	mew,
live-FRUST-COND.3S		city	INST
Pedro	küpá	müle-(a)-***fu***-y	mawida mew.
Pedro	want	live-PROSP-**FRUST**-IND.3S	mountain INST

Not surprisingly, counterfactual meanings demand of the fieldworker a more meditated and careful procedure. The eliciting sessions can be especially demanding and the metalinguistic discussion not always intuitive, especially if paraphrasing strategies are involved. Without doubt, this is where the linguist and consultant's co-working capacities are put to the test. With respect to conditionals more generally, Louie (2015) has claimed that "certain types of felicity judgments only arise in contexts with complex narrative structures" (Louie 2015: 68). Mostly for practical reasons, I have not implemented storylines in my own fieldwork yet, but I would certainly recommend it if the fieldworker experiences the kind of difficulties described by Louie with respect to conditionals (2015: 62–64). (See also the discussion on the use of storylines in Ferreira and Müller, this volume, and of storyboards in Kolagar and Vander Klok, this volume.)

4 Conclusion

This chapter has provided a basic guideline for producing a controlled variety of DCs whereby a researcher can explore the varied semantic landscape where frustratives meet modals. Taking Mapudungun as a case study, I have shown that the task can be organised with a rather small set of circumstantial parameters. While non-exhaustive, the proposed parameters can serve as a first approximation to a semantic region that calls for in-depth collaborative research.

References

Bhatt, Rajesh. 1997. Obligation and possession. In Heidi Harley (ed.), *MIT Working Papers in Linguistics* 32. 21–40.

Bochnak, M. Ryan & Lisa Matthewson (eds.). 2015. *Methodologies in semantic fieldwork*. Oxford: Oxford University Press.

Bohnemeyer, Jürgen. 2015. A practical epistemology for semantic elicitation in the field and elsewhere. In M. Ryan Bochnak & Lisa Matthewson (eds.), *Methodologies in semantic fieldwork*, 13–46. Oxford: Oxford University Press.

Carol, Javier Jerónimo & Andrés Pablo Salanova. 2021. Frustratives and aspect. In *Proceedings of Semantics of Under-Represented Languages of the Americas* 11. UMASS Amherst: GLSA.

Copley, Bridget. 2005. When the actual world isn't inertial: Tohono O'odham *cem*. In Michael Becker & Andrew McKenzie (eds.), *Proceedings of the 3rd Conference on the Semantics of Underrepresented Languages in the Americas*. Vol. 33, 1–18. Amherst, Mass: University of Massachusetts Occasional Papers.

Copley, Bridget & Heidi Harley. 2014. Eliminating causative entailments with the force-theoretic framework: The case of the Tohono O'odham frustrative *cem*. In Bridget Copley & Fabienne Martin (eds.), *Causation in grammatical structures,* 120–151. (Oxford Studies in Theoretical Linguistics 52). Oxford: Oxford University Press.

Cover, Rebecca T. 2015. Semantic fieldwork on TAM. In M. Ryan Bochnak & Lisa Matthewson (eds.), *Methodologies in semantic fieldwork*, 233–268. Oxford: Oxford University Press.

Cover, Rebecca T. & Judith Tonhauser. 2015. Theories of meaning in the field: Temporal and aspectual reference. In M. Ryan Bochnak & Lisa Matthewson (eds.), *Methodologies in semantic fieldwork*, 306–349. Oxford: Oxford University Press.

Davis, Henry & Lisa Matthewson. In press. St'át'imcets frustratives as not-at-issue modals. *Linguistics: An Inter-Disciplinary Journal of the Language Sciences*.

Fasola, Carlos. 2015. *Topics in the syntax of Mapudungun subordinate clauses*. New Jersey: Rutgers University dissertation.

von Fintel, Kai. 1999. NPI-licensing, Strawson-entailment, and context-dependency. *Journal of Semantics* 16. 97–148.

von Fintel, Kai & Sabine Iatridou. 2008. How to say *ought* in foreign: The composition of weak necessity modals. In Jacqueline Guéron & Jacqueline Lecarme (eds.), *Time and modality*, 115–141. Dordrecht: Springer.

von Fintel, Kai & Sabine Iatridou. Under submission. Prolegomena to a theory of X-marking. *Linguistics and Philosophy*.

Fuentes, Pablo. 2020. Mapudungun expressions of desire. *International Journal of American Linguistics* 86 (2). 165–199.

Fuentes, Pablo. To appear. Mapudungun frustrative *-fu-*: A modal analysis. *Canadian Journal of Linguistics*.

Golluscio, Lucía. 2000. Rupturing implicature in the Mapudungun verbal system: The suffix *-Fi*. *Journal of Pragmatics* 32. 230–263.

Heim, Irene. 1992. Presupposition projection and the semantics of attitude verbs. *Journal of Semantics* 9. 183–221.

Iatridou, Sabine. 2000. The grammatical ingredients of counterfactuality. *Linguistic Inquiry* 31 (2). 231–270.

Kroeger, Paul. 2017. Frustration, culmination, and inertia in Kimaragang grammar. *Glossa: A Journal of General Linguistics* 56 (1). 1–29.

Louie, Meagan. 2015. The problem with no-nonsense elicitation plans (for semantic fieldwork). In M. Ryan Bochnak & Lisa Matthewson (eds.), *Methodologies in semantic fieldwork*, 47–72. Oxford: Oxford University Press.

Matthewson, Lisa. 2004. On the methodology of semantic fieldwork. *International Journal of American Linguistics* 70 (4). 369–415.

Matthewson, Lisa. 2006. Temporal semantics in a superficially tenseless language. *Linguistics and Philosophy* 29 (6). 673–713.
Rubinstein, Aynat. 2014. On necessity and comparison. *Pacific Philosophical Quarterly* 95 (4). 512–554.
Smeets, Ineke. 2008. *A grammar of Mapuche*. Berlin: Mouton de Gruyter.
Sparing-Chávez, Margarethe. 2003. I want to but I can't: The frustrative in Amahuaca. Paper presented at the July 2002 Functional Grammar Conference in Amsterdam, Netherlands. Published as SIL electronic working paper 2003-002.
Vander Klok, Jozina. 2014. Questionnaire on modality for cross-linguistic use. URL http://www.eva.mpg.de/lingua/tools-at-lingboard/questionnaires.php

Subject index

Ability (modal) 55, 56, 59, 73–74, 98, 171, 175–179, 210, 260, 262, 270–272, 285, 288, 324, 350
Acquisition 5, 7, 144, 191–197, 210, 219–220, 222–223
Annotation 53, 142, 143, 159, 162, 165, 170, 173
Aspect(ual) 55–56, 99–100, 109, 142, 147, 149, 163, 171–172, 175, 182, 196, 198, 211–217, 295–296, 310–311, 317, 321–322, 325–330, 392, 394
Atayal 2, 7, 8, 56, 79, 122, 257–291

Bouletic 16, 22, 28–30, 55, 63, 97, 98, 102–110, 127, 143, 149, 243, 259, 263, 266, 269, 270, 279, 396, 398, 400, 401, 411, 412, 416, 417
Brazilian Portuguese 2–3, 5, 19, 22, 116, 241, 242, 244–247, 250

Chinese 1, 3, 264, 265
Circumstantial 55–59, 64, 71, 74, 76, 79, 97, 98, 101, 102, 106–109, 121, 127, 146–149, 171–178, 182, 184, 242, 243, 259–263, 266, 269, 271–277, 279, 285, 288–291, 391, 392, 398, 400, 411, 412, 415, 418
Clitic 8, 171, 337–338, 340–341, 352–353, 355–356
Consulting 7, 141, 305
Contact language 15–22, 28, 31–33, 38, 49, 52, 69, 75, 116, 239–241, 244, 250, 265, 299, 404
Corpora 5, 100, 111, 141–144, 184–185, 277, 299
Corpus-based study 142–143, 148, 179
Counterfactual(ity) 57, 104–109, 146, 152–153, 160, 165, 169, 260, 316–330, 391–393, 396, 398–400, 411–418
Creole (language) 8, 122, 295–301, 311, 329, 331
Cross-linguistic 3–6, 9, 47–49, 51, 55, 57, 69, 80, 95, 97, 100, 106, 108–109, 112, 121, 192, 197, 223, 349, 354, 359, 408
Cuzco Quechua 343, 344, 374, 377

Deontic 2–3, 8, 41, 55–60, 64, 71, 74, 75, 77, 79–105, 111, 116–121, 127, 128, 143–147, 149, 150, 171–178, 182, 205, 206, 211–218, 237, 238, 243, 250–253, 259–263, 266, 269, 271, 279, 285–288, 300, 305, 306, 396, 398, 400–402, 406, 416
Desire 9, 28, 30, 55, 97–98, 107–108, 257, 258, 391–392, 396–401, 403–406, 411–415, 417
Discourse context (DC) 3, 6, 9, 49–56, 68, 75, 95–96, 101–121, 127–128, 149, 178, 257–258, 279–283, 391–392, 401–406, 408, 410, 413, 415–418

Elicitation 6, 8, 9, 15–28, 37–44, 50–56, 69–74, 115–122, 237, 239, 240, 244–246, 250, 252–253, 257–259, 264–266, 278, 288, 290–291, 392–393, 405–408
Embedded clause 150–154, 340, 353, 357, 394
English 1, 2, 6, 7, 31, 33, 44, 47, 52, 55, 56, 60, 69, 79, 96–99, 100, 101, 107–111, 116, 127, 128, 141–161, 170–174, 179, 180–185, 192–205, 209–223, 228, 240, 246, 250, 260, 265, 300, 342, 348–350, 357, 363, 392, 409, 411
Epistemic 2–3, 8–9, 55–59, 64–65, 73–74, 79–80, 97–113, 118–121, 143–153, 170–174, 197–221, 237–238, 242–243, 250–251, 257–258, 263, 265, 272, 274–278, 337–338, 341–344, 348–350, 354–355, 357, 363, 368, 374, 377–380, 386
Evidential(ity) 8–9, 55, 98, 102, 267–268, 337–338, 340–357, 359–360, 362, 368–369, 372, 374, 376, 377, 386
Existential 55, 67, 96, 174, 259, 266, 279, 282, 285, 287, 289, 291, 396–397, 409
Experiment 6, 9, 20, 32–33, 36, 185, 193, 197–209, 215–221, 245

Felicity judgment (task) 115, 117, 121, 128, 240, 250, 258, 291, 418
Fieldwork 4–9, 15–33, 39–40, 47–56, 69–70, 95–96, 115, 127, 173, 184–185, 191–197, 201–211, 222–223, 237, 239–240, 245, 252, 257–258, 295–296, 299–301, 307, 337–338, 351, 392–394, 401–403
Formal semantics 30, 96, 145–155, 342
Free Indirect Discourse (FID) 154–155
Frustrative 9, 107, 324, 391–394, 396–401, 404, 406–407, 418

Gitksan 1, 2, 56, 100, 122, 147, 148, 244, 343, 386

Indigenous 16, 21, 24, 32–33, 240, 261
Irrealis (mood/context) 8, 100, 171, 173–175, 178, 182, 247, 295, 316–317, 319–321, 324–331

Japanese 1, 27, 143, 261
Javanese 2, 4, 6, 52–53, 79, 95, 107, 109, 111–113, 115, 117–122, 127, 133, 260

Karitiana 6, 7, 16–41

Lexically encoded / specified 95, 97, 147, 171, 173, 266
Likert rating (task) 115, 117, 120–121
Luganda 1, 112, 116
Logoori 1, 104, 105, 108, 112, 113, 115
Lung'Ie 7, 8, 100, 295–301, 305–311, 314–319, 320–332

Mazanderani. See Tabari
Mazani. See Tabari
Modal development 7, 191, 192, 195, 196, 198, 219, 223
Modal flavour 2–4, 8, 48, 55, 67, 71, 79, 96–111, 114, 119–121, 142–152, 171–173, 177, 179–183, 197, 210, 219, 222
Modal strength 3–6, 55, 59, 78, 80, 95–97, 100–101, 106–109, 114, 119, 247, 250, 252, 257–260, 262, 265, 268–270, 272, 276–277, 279, 281–283, 285, 287, 289–291, 344–345, 362, 417

Modal-temporal interactions 6, 57, 102, 106, 109, 141–142, 146–148, 156, 170, 182–183
Modal verb 41, 63, 67, 71, 74–76, 105, 148, 158, 197, 199, 203, 211, 215, 222, 245
Mood 5, 8, 9, 65–67, 75, 77, 100, 171, 203, 262, 295–296, 310–331
Morpheme 8, 26, 151, 152, 200, 202, 215, 237–239, 241, 263, 310, 328, 330, 331, 338, 340, 341, 401
Mapudungun 7, 9, 391–400, 403, 404, 406, 409, 410, 413, 414, 418

Narrative 24–26, 41, 48–49, 50–54, 57, 142, 154–157, 159–162, 170, 172, 178, 198, 201, 221, 239, 257–259, 263–265, 281, 284, 300–309, 312, 313, 347, 418
Negation 30, 56, 66, 150, 196, 205–210, 244, 272, 275, 288, 305, 310, 317, 328, 348, 351, 352–354, 359, 409
Nez Perce 122, 205, 244, 277
Non-epistemic. See root (modality)

Obligation 2, 3, 9, 55–56, 73, 78, 98, 108, 145, 175, 178, 206, 217, 250–251, 317, 324, 391–392, 396–406, 409–416
Online form 6, 16, 17, 39, 40, 44

Paresi 1–3, 112, 113, 115, 116, 330
Participant-external 98, 102, 105–106, 127, 129
Participant-internal 98, 102, 105–108, 127, 129
Particle 3, 126, 131, 133, 210, 268, 311, 320, 322, 338, 374, 392
Permission 3, 55–56, 59, 74–75, 98, 105, 113–114, 134, 150, 174–182, 206, 250–251, 266, 269–271, 324
Picture 27–29, 48, 49, 52–57, 68, 69, 113, 122, 178, 201, 206, 210–213, 216–218, 222, 257
Production 9, 116, 196–197, 199, 201–202, 204, 209, 212, 218, 222, 239, 304–306, 311, 391–394, 410, 413

Questionnaire 5, 6, 9, 15–18, 33, 35, 38–40, 43–44, 69, 80, 95–96, 99–122, 203, 237, 239, 250, 392

Realis (mood/context) 316, 319–321, 325, 327–331
Root (modality) 4, 55, 57, 59, 63–80, 98, 102, 105–106, 117–121, 127, 129, 144, 149–151, 159, 197, 203, 206, 208, 211–212, 215–217, 242–243, 269, 279

Semi-forced choice (task) 117–121, 128
Spanish 2, 66, 192, 238, 391, 392, 404, 406, 409, 410
St'át'imcets 2, 7, 33, 56, 100, 141–142, 147–148, 170–173, 178–184, 244, 260, 283, 342, 349, 352, 355, 382, 386
Storyboard 5, 6, 8, 9, 15–18, 22, 24–33, 38, 44, 47–57, 63, 68–70, 80, 107, 109–110, 121, 178, 201–202, 217, 263–264, 295, 300, 302, 305–306, 308, 311, 370–372
Strength. See modal strength
Strong possibility 55, 97, 109
Suffix 4, 9, 118, 237, 238, 246–248, 252, 391–399, 407, 409, 414

Tabari 6, 7, 47–49, 51, 57, 62–80
Teleological 55, 59, 64, 74, 79, 97, 98, 101–104, 108, 118, 127, 143, 149, 197, 198, 199, 202, 206–210, 259, 263, 266–269, 279
Temporality 4, 55, 99, 102, 127
Temporal orientation (TO) 7, 55, 56, 99, 100, 109, 127, 128, 141, 144, 145, 170–173, 183, 203, 314
Temporal perspective (TP) 7, 55–57, 99, 100, 109, 127, 128, 141, 145, 150, 161, 170–173, 179, 398, 411

Tense 4, 16, 19, 20, 28, 33–35, 39, 40, 43, 55, 56, 65, 66, 99, 100, 106, 109, 116, 142, 147, 148, 150–157, 160, 161, 170, 171, 176, 196, 203, 295, 296, 310–319, 322–330, 392–394, 397
Traditional stories 8, 9, 295, 302, 306–309, 311–313, 315, 319, 330–331
Training session 6, 15–19, 25, 32–37, 43, 44
Transcription 117, 257–258, 278, 285, 307–308
Translation 4–5, 15–18, 26–31, 38, 39, 44, 53, 54, 69, 115–117, 121, 127, 144, 179, 180, 201, 208, 239, 240, 245–248, 250, 257–259, 263, 265, 269, 273, 279–285, 289, 290, 296, 308, 309, 393
Truth-value judgment (task) 15–21, 26–30, 31, 33, 35, 38–40, 44, 50, 128, 196, 208–210, 218, 223, 239, 263
Typology 3–5, 98, 106, 114, 115, 121, 192, 299, 308

Universal 30, 55, 67, 96, 171, 259, 276, 285, 287, 289

Variable (force) 3, 144, 178, 195, 197, 199, 200, 203, 210, 215, 217, 221, 223, 258

Washo 1, 122
Weak necessity 1, 4, 55, 57, 59, 61, 64–67, 74, 76–80, 97, 101–108, 113, 118–120, 127, 129–135, 173–174, 180, 391–393, 398, 403, 406–417

ʔayʔaɟuθəm 7, 8, 337–342, 346, 351–357, 370, 374, 376–379, 383–386

www.ingramcontent.com/pod-product-compliance
Lightning Source LLC
Chambersburg PA
CBHW061925220426
43662CB00012B/1810